—————————— THOMAS D'ARCY McGEE ——————————

# THOMAS
# D'ARCY
# McGEE

## VOLUME II

## The Extreme Moderate
## 1857–1868

DAVID A. WILSON

McGill-Queen's University Press
Montreal & Kingston · London · Ithaca

© David A. Wilson 2011

ISBN 978-0-7735-3903-7 (cloth)
ISBN 978-0-7735-4296-9 (paper)
ISBN 978-0-7735-8618-5 (ePDF)
ISBN 978-0-7735-8645-1 (ePUB)

Legal deposit third quarter 2011
Bibliothèque nationale du Québec

First paperback edition 2013

Printed in Canada on acid-free paper that is 100% ancient forest free (100% post-consumer recycled), processed chlorine free

This book was first published with the help of a grant from the Canadian Federation for the Humanities and Social Sciences, through the Awards to Scholarly Publications Program, using funds provided by the Social Sciences and Humanities Research Council of Canada.

McGill-Queen's University Press acknowledges the support of the Canada Council for the Arts for our publishing program. We also acknowledge the financial support of the Government of Canada through the Canada Book Fund for our publishing activities.

Cover image: Oil painting of D'Arcy McGee, 1868, by Frederic Marlett Bell-Smith. The plaque on the Bell-Smith painting reads: "Presented to the Honorable Thos D'arcy McGee M.P. by friends in Montreal and Ottawa on his 43rd birthday. April 13th 1868. Unhappily frustrated in the fulfillment of this intention by his Cruel Assassination at Ottawa on the 7th of April 1868. His friends now present it with their deepest sympathy to his bereaved Widow and Children." Euphrasia Quinn, McGee's older daughter, took the portrait with her when she moved from Montreal to California, and it was passed down to D'Arcy Quinn, Thomas D'Arcy McGee's great-great grandson. (Copyright and courtesy of D'Arcy Quinn; photograph by Ellen Fransdonk-Gilhuys.)

Frontispiece: Thomas D'Arcy McGee, 1863 (Notman Photographic Archives, McCord Museum, Montreal)

*Library and Archives Canada Cataloguing in Publication*

Wilson, David A., 1950-
Thomas D'Arcy McGee / David A. Wilson.

Includes bibliographical references and index.
Contents: v. 1. Passion, reason and politics, 1825–1857 – v. 2. The extreme moderate, 1857–1868.
ISBN 978-0-7735-3357-8 (v. 1). – ISBN 978-0-7735-3903-7 (v. 2)

1. McGee, Thomas d'Arcy, 1825–1868.   2. Politicians – Canada – Biography.
3. Canada – Politics and government – 1841–1867.   I. Title.

FC471.M25W54 2008       971.04092       C2007-906359-4

Set in 12/15 Bembo Pro with Cochin
Book design & typesetting by Garet Markvoort, zijn digital

TO ZSUZSA BALOGH

*Szeretlek*

# Contents

PART THREE: FENIANISM

PART FOUR: ASSASSINATION

# Illustrations

# Acknowledgments

In the course of his brief and brilliant life, Thomas D'Arcy McGee produced a dozen books, around three hundred poems, and countless public lectures, private letters, and newspaper articles. Many of these sources are available in microfilm or have been digitally reproduced, but many others are scattered throughout archives in Canada, the United States, Ireland, and Britain. This meant that my research on McGee was driven more by archival location than by a sequential investigation of his life. One result was that I was constantly being bounced between different phases of his career. In the same week, I might be reading his revolutionary republican pronouncements from 1848–49, his ultra-Catholic writings during the mid-1850s, and his monarchist speeches in the mid-1860s – a sometimes unhinging experience, but no less interesting for that. Another result was that my research notes were constantly in danger of spinning out of control and meandering all over the map.

And so I owe a special debt of gratitude to Dana Kleniewski, who took on the task of going through all those notes and restructuring them in chronological order; as a result of her work, the challenge of refining the raw material of research into the finished product of writing was made much easier. Thanks also go to Chelsea Jeffery, who searched the debates in the Canadian legislative assembly for McGee's speeches and the reactions they elicited. As I began writing the book, numerous unanticipated questions arose, which necessitated further research. In this respect, I am particularly grateful to Leigh-Ann Coffey for the thorough, thoughtful, and reliable way in which she responded to my repeated requests for information about McGee in a wide variety of

British North American newspapers. Her work in tracking down and preparing the illustrations was also a great help for a technologically challenged historian such as myself.

Chelsea and Leigh-Ann are both graduates of the Celtic Studies Program at the University of Toronto, and I extend my thanks to the Celtic Studies students in general, whose enthusiasm and engagement with Irish Canadian history has been a real morale booster. The Celtic Studies Program has been described as a gem of the University of Toronto, and with good reason. My colleagues were enthusiastic about the project right from the start and have provided a lively and stimulating environment for research and writing. Without the collective support of Ann Dooley, Máirín Nic Dhiarmada, Jean Talman, Mark McGowan, and Jo Godfrey, this book would never have got off the ground.

If the art of writing consists, as Mary Heaton Vorse put it, in applying the seat of the pants to the seat of the chair, the art of research is necessarily a collective endeavour, dependent upon institutional support and the active participation of archivists and librarians. A research grant from the Social Sciences and Humanities Research Council of Canada enabled me to travel widely in pursuit of McGee-related material. During those travels, I was fortunate to have some excellent guides: Nancy Marrelli and Vincent Ouellette of the Concordia University Archives in Montreal; Fernando Montserrat of Montreal's Fraser-Hickson Library; the archivists at Library and Archives Canada in Ottawa; and the staff at the Archdiocesan and Diocesan Archives in Hamilton, Kingston, and London, Ontario. In the United States, thanks go to William Cobert of the American Irish Historical Society in New York, to the New York Public Library, and to the archivists in the climate-controlled and ultramodern Columbia University Archives.

Across the Atlantic, I thank the keepers of the Bodleian Library at Oxford University (who make you sign a declaration before entering the archives that you will not burn down the building) and The National Archives at Kew (where such conditions apparently do not apply). In Ireland, the archivists in the National Library, the National Archives, and the Dublin Diocesan Archives helped me locate manuscript sources, as did the archivists in the Public Record Office of Northern Ireland in Belfast.

At home in Toronto, my research was facilitated by the staff of the Archives of the Roman Catholic Archdiocese, Archives Ontario, the United Church Archives, and the Thomas Fisher Rare Book Library. Jane Lynch and her colleagues in the Inter-Library Loan Department at Robarts Library have been as helpful as ever, and the librarians in the Media Commons Room deserve special thanks for their assistance in the midst of the disruptions and distractions arising from building renovations.

Taken together, the research and writing of both volumes of this biography have stretched out over the best part of a decade. McGee has been an endlessly fascinating companion, and I have received much support along the way. Peter Toner, whose knowledge of Irish Canadian nationalism is unsurpassed and whose scholarly generosity is unmatched, shared his insights about Irish Canadian identities, McGee's relationship with the Fenians, and the murder trial of Patrick James Whelan. In the course of our debates and discussions, we gradually modified each other's views and wound up in substantial agreement on most issues – much to our mutual consternation. Brandon Corcoran, my research assistant for a forthcoming book on the Fenians in Canada, supplied me with invaluable information about the intelligence reports that McGee and his fellow cabinet ministers were receiving on revolutionary activities on both sides of the Canadian-American border. Kyla Madden, another graduate of the Celtic Studies Program, subsequently a prize-winning author and now an editor at McGill-Queen's University Press, took time out of her busy schedule to read the first half of the manuscript. Her analytical insights, specific comments, and suggestions for further readings were very helpful, and this book is the better for them.

More generally, I thank the numerous scholars in Irish, British, Canadian, and American history who have provided encouragement during the McGee years – historians such as Don Akenson, Cecil Houston, Kevin James, Willie Jenkins, Simon Jolivet, Brian Lambkin, Bob Malcolmson, Ged Martin, Kerby Miller, Wilf Neidhardt, and Seamus Smyth. Thanks also go to Anthony Daly (yet another Celtic Studies graduate) for allowing me to quote from his family memoir; to Sean Conway, for his insight and enthusiasm; and to Doug Lucas, formerly of the Ontario Centre of Forensic Sciences, for taking me through the forensic issues concerning the gun that may or may not have been used to kill McGee.

It has also been a pleasure to meet members of the McGee clan. In Canada, Sheilagh D'Arcy McGee (descended from McGee's half-brother, John Joseph) related family stories about McGee's personality. During the launch of the first volume, I travelled around Ireland with D'Arcy Quinn, who has inherited much of his great-great-grandfather's charm, wit, and energy. At one event, organized in Donegal by the inestimable Hazel and Charles McIntyre, with John Hume as the speaker, the great-great-grandson of D'Arcy McGee met the great-great-granddaughter of Michael Starrs, one of the men arrested in 1868 under suspicion (falsely, as it turned out) of involvement in McGee's assassination. They shook hands in the company of several great-great-grandchildren of the man who had helped McGee escape from Ireland after the rising of 1848 – pockets of personal memories carried over from a vast story with a cast of thousands.

In bringing this story to the printed page, special thanks go to the staff of McGill-Queen's University Press, whose commitment to the highest publishing standards is a model for the industry. Don Akenson, Mary-Lynne Ascough, Philip Cercone, Jacqui Davis, Joan Harcourt, Kyla Madden, Joan McGilvray, and Roy Ward are not only consummate professionals; they are also great fun to work with. I could not have had a better copyeditor than Carlotta Lemieux, and I thank Gillian Griffith for her help with the index.

Finally, a special thank-you to Zsuzsa Balogh, who has been with this book every step of the way; the dedication says it all, in a language that she knows.

THOMAS D'ARCY McGEE

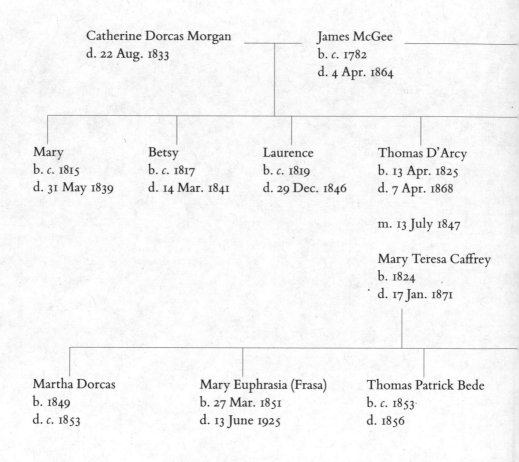

McGEE FAMILY TREE

Catherine Dorcas Morgan
d. 22 Aug. 1833

James McGee
b. *c.* 1782
d. 4 Apr. 1864

Mary
b. *c.* 1815
d. 31 May 1839

Betsy
b. *c.* 1817
d. 14 Mar. 1841

Laurence
b. *c.* 1819
d. 29 Dec. 1846

Thomas D'Arcy
b. 13 Apr. 1825
d. 7 Apr. 1868

m. 13 July 1847

Mary Teresa Caffrey
b. 1824
d. 17 Jan. 1871

Martha Dorcas
b. 1849
d. *c.* 1853

Mary Euphrasia (Frasa)
b. 27 Mar. 1851
d. 13 June 1925

Thomas Patrick Bede
b. *c.* 1853
d. 1856

Margaret Dea
m. 2 Mar. 1840

Dorcas
b. Dec. 1826
d. 27 Feb. 1887

Rose
b. 1827

Anna Maria
b. *c.* 1828–1829
d. 14 July 1868

James
b. 1830
d. 21 Feb. 1890

John Joseph
b. 6 Aug. 1840
d. 10 Apr. 1927

Rose
b. 1855
d. 1856

Agnes Clara (Peggy)
b. 6 Aug. 1857
d. 6 Jan. 1941

# Introduction

In the spring of 1861, Thomas D'Arcy McGee addressed his constituents in Montreal about the lessons he had learned since arriving in Canada four years earlier. "There is nothing to be more dreaded in this country," he said, "than feuds arising from exaggerated feelings of religion and nationality." The central task facing Canadians was to "rub down all sharp angles, and to remove all those asperities which divide our people on questions of origin and religious profession." All this could be done consistently with "the charity of the Gospel" and the "right use of human reason"; anyone who thought otherwise was a blockhead and a bigot. Although there were "in all origins men good, bad, and indifferent," McGee continued, he had learned over the years that "in all classes the good predominate."

Should the blockheads and bigots prevail, though, Canadians would find themselves staring into the abyss: "If we will carefully convey across the Atlantic half-extinguished embers of strife in order that we may by them light up the flames of our inflammable forests – if each neighbour will try not only to nurse up old animosities, but to invent new grounds of hostility to his neighbour – then, gentlemen, we shall return to what Hobbes considered the state of Nature – I mean a state of war."

McGee would spend his entire Canadian career trying to avoid this Hobbesian nightmare – to find common ground among diverse groups; to base actions on the teachings of the gospel, on kindly feelings and right reason; to make fair-minded accommodations and compromises in the light of circumstances and potential consequences. "In society we must sacrifice something, as we do when we go through a crowd," he told his audience, "we must sometimes make way for men like ourselves, though we could prove by the most faultless syllogism our right to push them from the path."[1]

There had been a time, though, when McGee himself had been seduced by faultless syllogisms – twice, in fact: first as a republican revolutionary during the terrible years of the Great Famine, and second as an ultramontane Irish Catholic in the dark days of American nativism. Oppressed nations had the right to fight for their freedom; Ireland was an oppressed nation; therefore Ireland had a right to fight for its freedom. There was only One True Religion; that religion was Roman Catholic; therefore Protestants were heretics, with whom reconciliation was neither possible nor desirable. Using such logic, McGee had been a republican revolutionary in 1848–49, and an ultraconservative Catholic during the early 1850s.

Hard-bought experience had tempered these views. McGee still believed – and continued to believe, right up to his death – that Ireland had the right to fight for its freedom and that Catholicism was the One True Faith. But any attempt to assert the abstract right of national revolution would only sacrifice living people to an impossible ideal, given the power imbalance between Ireland and Britain. And there was no contradiction between being a devout Catholic and respecting Protestants in a spirit of mutual forbearance and goodwill. There was a middle way, in which firm convictions coexisted with generosity of spirit, in which people realized the wisdom of Edmund Burke's dictum that the possible best is the absolute best, and in which the principles of moderation prevailed.

The story seems to be that of a man with strong passions and a powerful mind, driven to extremes by conditions of Irish famine and American nativism, but brought back to the centre through reason, reflection and experience. It is a story that McGee accepted himself and was shared by his contemporaries. "Sometimes, very rarely, there may be discerned a painful struggle between his fervid imaginations and his generally correct judgment," remarked one journalist in 1864.[2] Looking back on McGee's life, his friend and admirer Archbishop Thomas Connolly spoke of the conflict between his emotions and his "gigantic intellect," about the transformation of the "hot-headed youth in Ireland" into the "profound thinker, the philosopher, the accomplished statesman, in Canada."[3]

Yet the dynamic between passion and reason operated at a deeper level in McGee's Canadian career. Just as he came to embrace Burke's emphasis on compromise within a liberal-conservative consensus, McGee also inherited Burke's uncompromising attitude to all forms of religious and nationalist extremism; in this sense, McGee stood in the same relationship to the Fenians as Burke did to the Jacobins. During his first years in Canada, McGee identified the Orange Order as the main transmitter of old quarrels into the new environment; by the early 1860s, however, he increasingly felt that a much greater threat emanated from the Fenian Brotherhood and its network of secret societies across the country.

McGee was acutely aware of the ways in which Orangeism and Fenianism could feed off each other, since he himself had experienced the politics of reaction. He was acutely aware of the appeal of the absolute, since he had felt that appeal. And he was acutely aware of what it meant to be a Fenian, since he had once been a Fenian in all but name.[4] In Canada, he never ceased to have extreme tendencies; the difference was that these tendencies were now pressed into the service of moderation, as he attacked the Fenians with an intensity and passion that few of his co-religionists could reach or rival. In the process, he found himself engaging in the very politics of reaction whose consequences in other contexts he feared so much.

Hence the paradox in the title: in Canada, McGee became an extreme moderate. There was much more to him than that, of course, and no one can be reduced to a two-word label. Still, McGee's personal life remains elusive. Although he produced thousands of pages of speeches, addresses, articles, books, and poems dealing with public affairs, hardly any private correspondence remains – a few letters he wrote in his youth to his Aunt Bella Morgan and a handful written in later life to his daughters. The letters to Aunt Bella are sharp-witted, enthusiastic, and slightly self-deprecating; those written to his daughters are warm-hearted and tender. His relationship with Mary, his wife, can only be guessed at – though the fact that he was away from home so often, and that he became a binge drinker, suggests that the relation-

ship was distant as well as close, tempestuous as well as loving; in one
of the few surviving letters written by Mary, she was being driven to
despair by his alcoholism.[5] Beyond this, it is impossible to go; this book
is, perforce, a political rather than personal biography.

But it is possible to get a sense of his public personality. Here, the
sources are abundant. The cumulative image is of a physically un-
prepossessing, somewhat dishevelled, and slightly weary-looking man,
with a keen sense of humour, immense charm, and enormous energy.
As befitted someone who believed that generosity of spirit was one of
the greatest virtues, he was an extraordinarily generous man, donat-
ing money to a variety of Catholic charities, and giving fundraising
lectures in support of such causes as Montreal's "School for Female
Deaf Mutes."[6]

In November 1867, five months before his assassination at the age
of forty-two, the *Montreal Gazette* provided its readers with a pen
portrait: "Not handsome by any means, but gifted with those notice-
able eyes with which every man with an intellect above the average
is dowered, his face sallow and wrinkled, his hair liberally sprinkled
with gray, limping in his walk, leaning on a cane and a friendly arm,
worn and evidently shattered in body, it is hard to conceive of him as
the orator of the Dominion, its best thinker and most graceful writer.
His manners are social and fascinating. In conversation he is brilliant,
easy, and graceful; elegant and fluent as to his language, and betraying
his scholarship by his every word and allusion."[7] One contemporary
remembered him talking politics all through the night, thumping the
table, telling stories, and reciting poems, a man with "an exceptionally
animated personality."[8] Another recalled his visits to McGee's Montreal house: "They were delightful evenings, and McGee's vivacity and
witty sayings and anecdotes kept us amused and laughing during the
whole Evening."[9]

You always knew where McGee was in the room; that was where
people were laughing. The same applied to his speeches; they were,
wrote Fennings Taylor, "garnished with so many merry jests, and
sometimes overlaid with such rancorous levity, that their more valuable parts were hidden from ordinary eyes, and inappreciable to ordinary minds … The truth is, that Mr. McGee always seemed to be, in

spite of himself, either mischievous or playful."[10] Yet none of his biographers has managed to convey his sense of humour, sometimes leaving an erroneous impression of McGee as a serious moral prig. The problem is that his wit was dry, ironic, satirical, and situational and was embedded deep in his writings and speeches; so in order to appreciate it fully, one needs a detailed knowledge of the context. But by the time the context is described in detail and the joke explained, it is no longer funny. There is only one answer: Anyone who wants to appreciate his sense of humour fully must bypass the biography and proceed directly to his speeches and writings.

There was, in truth, a priggish side to McGee, although it was continually at odds with the warmth and conviviality of his personality. It manifested itself in various ways – his youthful self-righteousness about the "disgraceful conduct" of people who took the temperance pledge but slipped back into drinking; his tendency towards political pontification, which drew the criticism that he treated Irish Canadians as moral and intellectual infants in need of his paternal guidance; his strict adherence to Catholic moral teachings on such subjects as divorce, gender relations, and sexual propriety; and his efforts to recreate the Irish in the image of middle-class respectability.[11] He despised the "stage Oirish" Paddy caricature, especially when the Irish themselves laughed at the image.[12] Mary Ann Sadlier recalled that on one occasion in Montreal, when the audience was enjoying a stereotypical Irish song, "McGee jumped to his feet, and burning with indignation, lashed the committee for permitting such a vile outrage on an ancient and honorable race."[13] Yet this same man, having slipped back into drinking and relaxing in company, could recite a risqué ditty in an exaggerated Irish brogue about the birth of Moses and the father of the child; the human side kept breaking through.[14]

When it came to politics, McGee interacted with some equally powerful personalities. Among them was George Brown – first as an ally, later as an adversary – editor of the most influential English-language newspaper in Canada, the Toronto *Globe*, and described by one historian as "a 24 carat gold plated bastard, a bully but fortunately with his own self-destruct button."[15] Combative, quick-tempered, and arrogant, Brown turned out to be more flexible than he appeared, but less flexible than McGee hoped. He was, McGee concluded, both brilliant and narrow: "Take him off one or two hack topics, and he is an extremely ill-informed man."[16] Other central figures were John A. Macdonald and George-Étienne Cartier, first as adversaries, later as allies. Sharing with McGee a sharp sense of humour and a strong taste for whisky, Macdonald was the consummate politician – shrewd, affable, ambitious, calculating, devious, industrious, a master of patronage who never forgot friends and enemies, and who worked on ways of turning enemies into friends, as he did with McGee. Equally adept at operating the machinery of patronage was Cartier, the French Canadian anglophile, a snappy dresser who fancied himself as a ladies' man, a singer and raconteur who deployed the political weapons of charm or intimidation as the occasion demanded; he and McGee never fully trusted each other.

As he worked with or against such men, McGee grappled with the central political issues of his day – the place of the Orange Order in Canadian society, the separate school controversy, the debates over representation by population and Confederation, and the growing external and internal power of Fenianism. These issues are not studied much now, with the shift in the academy away from political history; topics such as separate schools and representation by population have long been out of fashion, and they tend to evoke a weary roll of the eyes and a dull throbbing around the temples. Yet they are fundamental to the question of minority rights and of what it meant to be Canadian. At stake was the character of the country. The process of bargaining, brokerage, accommodation, and compromise in which McGee participated was essential to the construction of Canada.

Take, for example, the bill for the improvement of the separate school system in Canada West, present-day Ontario. Its significance lay not so much in the specific provisions, important as they were, as in the deeper questions it raised. Should children of different faiths be educated together or apart? Would separate schools perpetuate religious divisions, or would they reduce them by removing a divisive issue from politics? Would separate education undermine or strengthen Canadian unity? Should an issue that applied only to Canada West be decided only by representatives from Canada West?

Many of these issues have echoed through to modern multicultural Canada; questions from the mid-nineteenth century about minority education, collective and individual rights, core values and ethnoreligious politics have assumed a new relevance. McGee's career serves both as an entry point into these issues and an exploration of the ways in which one of the most intellectually gifted men of the times responded to them. Like many recent ethnic politicians, he supported separate education, demanded ethnoreligious parity, and insisted that racial origin should be omitted from crime statistics. At the same time, and unlike some recent ethnic politicians, he believed that ethnoreligious groups must leave their old quarrels behind them and work together in building a country that synthesized their best characteristics.

Some of his other observations also have contemporary resonance – such as his comments on the incivility of parliamentary debate (MPs attacked one another with "a harshness and severity which would not be tolerated in private life") or on the difficulty of governing such a diverse country as Canada ("there is probably no country in the world in which so many various and opposite balancing interests are combined together, and in which the problem of constitutional government has more serious difficulties in its way").[17]

The difficulty of governing Canada was reflected and reinforced by the kaleidoscopic character of its politics. The boundaries between parties kept shifting, with personal and political alliances forming and dissolving around different issues, and the pull of patronage exerting its own powerful influence. Inescapably, McGee was part of this world and played the game by its unofficial rules. He began his political career in Canada as an independent, then aligned himself with George Brown's Reform Party, became a cabinet minister in John Sandfield Macdonald's Reform administration, returned to his independent status, switched parties, became a cabinet minister in John A. Macdonald's Liberal-Conservative government, and wound up in the Reform-Liberal-Conservative coalition that engineered Confederation. When one adds to this his previous career pattern – he had in turn been a constitutional nationalist, a revolutionary republican, and a conservative ultramontane writer in Ireland and the United States – it seems he was congenitally incapable of walking a straight line.

Yet the most striking thing about McGee is his consistency. His nationalist program for Canada was remarkably similar, in broad outlines, to his early nationalist program for Ireland, and it remained the yardstick against which most of his political actions should be measured. A major reason for his transition from the Reformers to the Liberal-Conservatives was his conviction that the Reformers were turning their backs on his vision. While the ends remained constant, the means varied according to circumstances; for a politician in the Burkean mould, it could hardly have been otherwise.

In Ireland, McGee's nationalism had come first; his attitude to everything else, including famine relief and social change, was governed by the degree to which it would advance or impede that cause. In Canada, a similar pattern was at work, and the means were not always pretty. When McGee viewed the Orange Order as an obstacle to his new nationality, he was unequivocal in his denunciations; when he came to believe that liberal Orangemen – the "right kind," as he put it – could strengthen Confederation, he was more than willing to work with them. If condemning patronage while in opposition would help the cause, he would condemn patronage; if using patronage while in power would help the cause, he would use patronage. If the victory of an unscrupulous and anti-Catholic politician such as Charles Fisher would help break resistance to Confederation in New Brunswick, McGee would welcome his victory, even if he had to hold his nose. McGee is often seen as a visionary, and with good reason; but he also knew how to play political hardball. His mentor in Ireland, Charles Gavan Duffy, later recalled that McGee resembled the Irish journalist, writer, and politician Thomas Davis "in everything but in the moral qualities, where Davis was unapproachable."[18] In the pages that follow, the reader will find numerous examples of McGee cutting moral corners to attain his political objectives.

Reviewing the first volume of this biography, Victor Rabinovitch identified four "unanswered questions" that awaited the analysis of McGee's Canadian career: "Was McGee merely Confederation's poet (to use Richard Gwyn's term), albeit a forceful one, or was he a genuine political force? Was he the effective godfather of the alliance that carried the Maritime colonies into union with Canada? Was he the author of the special treatment for Catholics within Canada's constitution – promoting the accommodation of minorities that is the essence of contemporary multiculturalism? And, finally, who were the individuals who carried out the assassination of D'Arcy McGee in 1868 and what did they hope to achieve?"[19]

They are good questions, which are addressed in the pages that follow. But some preliminary answers are in order. McGee was *both* Confederation's poet and a "genuine political force." He expressed the case for Confederation in memorable, poetic language that none of his political contemporaries could match. But he also commanded significant political support, with the backing not only of a wide (but diminishing) section of Irish Catholic voters but also of a large (and growing) number of Protestant voters.

The trouble with the "McGee as poet" image is that poets are often assumed to be impractical dreamers who are beyond the day-to-day tasks of practical organization; in his own lifetime, this accusation was sometimes levelled at McGee. But we need to remember that he was also a skilful political organizer, a pragmatist who thought in terms of the art of the possible, and a man who paid close attention to details. It is significant, in this respect, that one of his greatest achievements as minister of agriculture, immigration, and statistics was to rationalize the gathering of statistical data and prepare the ground for the census of 1871, described by Bruce Curtis as "one of the world's most sophisticated attempts at enumeration and analysis."[20] It is equally significant that this achievement has been completely ignored by his historians.

Was he the Godfather of the alliance that carried the Maritimes into Confederation? Yes, as long as we remember that Nova Scotia and New Brunswick joined with Canada for complex economic, political, and strategic reasons, that McGee played a secondary and often marginal role in the negotiations between Canada and the Maritimes, and that Confederation would have gone ahead without him. No other Canadian politician knew the Maritimes better than McGee, who had visited the region three times before Confederation became a practical political possibility. When Confederation did enter the picture, McGee organized the Canadian goodwill tour of the Maritimes before the Charlottetown Conference and invited Maritime politicians and jour-

nalists on a reciprocal tour of Canada. "The British North American
Provinces," he said in 1863, "were now standing back to back instead of
looking each other full in the face."[21] McGee did not magically convert
skeptical Maritimers into fervent unionists, and many of those who
admired his oratory rejected his arguments; but no Canadian politician
did more than McGee to make the British North American colonies
in the Maritimes and Canada look towards each other. It is appropriate, in this respect, that McGee's final speech in the House of Commons stressed the importance of goodwill and the "mellowing effects
of time" in reducing Nova Scotian opposition to Confederation.[22]

Was McGee the author of special treatment for Catholics within
Canada's constitution? He was not the only author, but he was certainly
a principal one. It was not McGee but the Conservative MP Richard
Scott who took the parliamentary lead in securing the improved separate school legislation in Canada West that subsequently became incorporated into the British North America Act. It was, however, McGee
who pushed hardest to ensure that these improvements would be en-
shrined in the constitution. The only time that he became visible and
audible during the Quebec Conference was when the question of education came up; thanks to his amendment, which was carried without
controversy, the existing school systems in Canada West and Canada
East were carried over into Confederation.

"So far as I know," he later said, "this is the first Constitution ever
given to a mixed people, in which the conscientious rights of the minority, are made a subject of formal guarantee. I shall never cease to
remember with pleasure that I was the first proposer of that guarantee
in the Quebec Conference; a guarantee by which we have carried the
principle of equal and reciprocal toleration a step farther in Canada,
than it has yet been carried, in any other free government – American
or European."[23] There is no doubt that his primary concern had been
to protect Catholic education in a largely Protestant state. But in doing
so, he also recognized the wider implications of the specific struggle;
all religious groups, he came to believe, whether Christian or otherwise, were entitled to the maximum of freedom in the exercise of their
beliefs, provided that they rendered a minimum of obedience to the

civil power.[24] In this sense, McGee did indeed help to open the door for modern multiculturalism.

And finally, who carried out the assassination of McGee in 1868, and what did they hope to achieve? There has been, and doubtless always will be, considerable debate over whether the man who was found guilty of the murder, Patrick James Whelan, actually committed the crime. After considering the circumstantial and forensic evidence, the course of the trial, and Whelan's own words two days before his execution, my own conclusion is that if Whelan did not shoot McGee himself, he was part of a hit squad that did. Whelan was a Fenian in the generic sense of the term, but McGee's assassination was not an authorized operation ordered from Fenian headquarters in New York City. Instead, it stemmed from internal Canadian Fenian anger – to put it mildly – at McGee's relentless attacks on Irish revolutionary nationalism.

McGee had repeatedly condemned Fenianism as an irreligious, illegal, immoral, dangerous, conspiratorial, and counterproductive movement that was setting back the cause of reform in Ireland, and damaging the position of Irish Catholics in Canada. From the perspective of the Fenians in Canada and elsewhere, he had become the archetypal traitor – the former revolutionary who had sacrificed his principles on the altar of ambition, who was betraying Ireland for power and prestige in Canada. In the mid-1860s, McGee became *the* Fenian hate-figure. He received so many death threats that he pasted them into a scrapbook; police were posted outside his Montreal home, and he frequently needed bodyguards during his public appearances. For his killer or killers, McGee's assassination was an act of revenge, a just punishment for a traitor, and a warning to anyone else who wanted to follow in his footsteps.

It was also, in a sense that they could never imagine or understand, a tribute to the tenacity and courage with which McGee defended his broad-minded, inclusive nationalism against its narrower and meaner forms.

## CHAPTER ONE

# A New Northern Nationality
## May – November 1857

It had been a long road north, with successes and failures, unexpected turns, friends becoming enemies, and enemies becoming friends. When D'Arcy McGee first left Ireland for North America in 1842, seventeen years old and brimful of Irish nationalism, he could never have imagined that he would eventually settle in Montreal and become a Father of Canadian Confederation, praised by British imperial politicians as an exemplary loyalist, and pilloried by Irish republicans as an apostate and traitor.

That some kind of prominent career lay ahead was clear; his remarkable talents, driving energy, and enormous potential attracted attention right from the start. As an earnest devotee of Father Theobald Mathew's temperance campaign and an enthusiastic admirer of Daniel O'Connell's campaign for an Irish parliament, the teenaged McGee had deeply impressed his contemporaries with his burning intelligence and brilliant oratory. Within weeks of arriving in the United States, he landed a job with the *Boston Pilot*, the major Irish Catholic newspaper in the country; two years later, at the age of nineteen, he became its editor. Returning to Ireland in 1845, he was appointed parliamentary correspondent of the Dublin *Freeman's Journal* and quickly gravitated to the Young Ireland movement grouped around Thomas Davis, Charles Gavan Duffy, and the *Nation* newspaper. By the time he was twenty-two, McGee had published three books, become secretary of the Irish Confederation, Young Ireland's political party, and established a reputation as one of the finest speakers, writers, and poets in the country.

McGee had been in the moderate wing of Young Ireland, believing that education, class cooperation, religious harmony, and constitutional methods could secure Irish legislative autonomy within the British Empire, and arguing that cultural and economic independence were essential to the moral and material well-being of his country. But a growing sense of anger about the famine, along with the hope offered by the European revolutions of 1848, propelled him into radical republicanism. That summer, he was on the five-man revolutionary council that launched an unsuccessful Irish rising, and he attempted to rally supporters in Scotland and Sligo to the cause. Escaping to the United States and declaring himself a traitor to the British government, he started up his own newspaper and carried on the struggle – defending Young Ireland from its detractors, trying to revive revolutionary morale in Ireland, and calling for an Irish-assisted revolution in Canada.

His future, at this stage of his career, appeared easy to predict; he would either remain on the radical edge of Irish American nationalism or return to his earlier constitutional nationalist position. After a brief but intense period of republicanism, it seemed that he was indeed settling back into moderate moral-force nationalism along the lines of his mentor Charles Gavan Duffy. But then something extraordinary happened. Apparently out of the blue, McGee in 1851 converted to ultramontane Catholicism, embracing the belief that only members of the One True Faith would be saved, that all legitimate authority emanated from Rome, and that religion had primacy over politics. In part, his conversion was the product of a mounting disgust with American individualism and materialism. More generally, it stemmed from his conviction that transatlantic Protestants were conducting an undeclared but very real war against Catholics in general and Celts in particular. From this perspective, anti-Catholic legislation in Britain, the Orange Order in Ireland, and nativism in America were all different manifestations of the same persecuting Protestant spirit. Neutrality was impossible; all good Catholics must follow the teachings of Rome and fearlessly assert their rights in the teeth of Protestant calumnies and conspiracies.

Initially, this position only intensified McGee's anglophobia. Britain, after all, was the epicentre of anti-Catholicism, and Canada was the bastion of North American Orangeism. Before long, however, subtle changes in his outlook started to appear. Irish Catholics in urban America, he believed, experienced discrimination, exploitation, and moral degradation; they were trapped in squalor, their children were exposed to every kind of vice, their religion was being pilloried, and their priests were being assaulted on the streets. But in Canada, things began to look different. The French fact meant that Canadian Catholics had greater political power, a more secure social position, and better educational rights than their American counterparts. Even the Orange Order was less dangerous than it seemed; only about one-fifth of Canadian Protestants were members, and many of them got on reasonably well with their Catholic neighbours. Irish Catholics, McGee concluded, were actually better off in Britain's North American empire than they were in the American republic.

If this was the case, then it made sense to encourage Irish Catholic migration to Canada – to get the immigrants out of American slums and into self-sustaining rural communities where they could practise their faith and protect themselves from Protestantism. In 1856 McGee participated in the Buffalo Convention, which was intended to establish Catholic "colonies" in Canada or the American West. For many members of the Catholic Church in the United States, including New York's Archbishop John Hughes, this was a hopelessly wrongheaded scheme. McGee was criticized for exaggerating the misery of Irish immigrants, for running away from American nativism, and for underestimating the power of Orange bigotry in Canada. Other voices joined in the chorus. Irish republicans denounced him as being anti-Irish, American Democrats condemned him as being anti-American, and Irish American nationalists attacked him as being both anti-Irish and anti-American. By the mid-1850s, McGee had become an isolated figure in American political and religious life and had alienated so many people that his newspaper, the *American Celt*, began to flounder.

As his American career fell apart, McGee's Irish Catholic Canadian admirers came to the rescue. In July 1856, he had privately signalled his intention to move north; in the autumn, some of Montreal's leading Irish Catholics invited him to start up a newspaper in the city. It was agreed that he would run for office in the next election and represent Irish Catholic interests in the Canadian parliament. In this way, he could move from the American margin to the Canadian mainstream, place himself on a more secure financial footing, and realize his political ambitions.[1]

McGee also had strong personal reasons for moving to Montreal. In the summer of 1856, he and his wife Mary had three children – the five-year-old Mary Euphrasia, or "Frasa"; Thomas Patrick Bede, who was around three years old; and the one-year-old Rose. As McGee told Bishop Armand de Charbonnel in Toronto, he wanted to ensure that they would be educated in Catholic schools and raised in a Catholic environment – something that he believed could be accomplished only in Canada.[2]

Two of his children never made it to Montreal; towards the end of 1856, Thomas Patrick and Rose died of scarlet fever. It was the latest in a long line of tragedies. In his youth, he had lost his mother, two sisters, and a brother; during the early 1850s, he and Mary had buried their first daughter, Martha Dorcas. McGee sought to console himself and his wife in his poetry, writing that their "three white-robed Innocents" had been saved from the sorrow and strife of the world and were contentedly waiting to be reunited with them at "Heaven's high gate."[3] Partly because of the shock and partly because she was pregnant again, Mary stayed in New York with her mother when McGee left for Montreal in May 1857. Three months later, Mary gave birth to a daughter, Agnes Clara, or Peggy; shortly afterwards, Mary, her mother, Frasa, and Peggy journeyed north and joined McGee in Montreal.

───

And so in the spring of 1857, at the age of thirty-two, Thomas D'Arcy McGee was reborn as a Canadian. When he arrived, the country was experiencing a severe but temporary economic recession, in contrast to robust growth earlier in the decade. During the 1850s, Canada was transforming itself from a frontier colony into a recognizably modern commercial society. Having survived the shock of Britain's transition to free trade, the economy benefited from high prices for grain and lumber and from the Reciprocity Treaty with the United States, which Lord Elgin, the governor general, had proverbially floated in on a sea of champagne in 1854. Railways were revolutionizing communications and promoting trade; around two thousand miles of track would be laid down during the decade. The scandal-ridden Grand Trunk Railway connected Montreal and Toronto, with lines going to Portland in the east and to the major Canadian and American towns in the west. Most of the population still worked in agriculture, but the best land had been taken, and the industrial sector was becoming increasingly important. Toronto grew from nearly 31,000 in 1851 to almost 45,000 in 1861, while Montreal went from 58,000 to more than 90,000 over the same period. In Canada as a whole, the population rose from just over 1.8 million in 1851 to 2.5 million at the end of the decade.[4]

The fastest growth occurred in Canada West (present-day Ontario, also known as Upper Canada) and was driven largely by immigration. In the 1850s, more than one-third of Canada West's population had been born in the British and Irish Isles. Within this movement of people, the Irish were the largest group; from the 1820s to the 1840s, they outnumbered immigrants from England, Wales, and Scotland combined. By the mid-1850s, with the shortage of good land and with new opportunities opening up in Australia and the United States, Irish immigration to Canada plummeted, never to recover. But the Irish remained the largest non-French ethnic group in Canada right up to the 1870s, comprising one-quarter of the English-speaking population. Most had arrived before the famine, and around two-thirds were Protestant. Cities such as Quebec, Montreal, and Toronto had large numbers of Irish Catholics, but most people of Irish ethnicity, Protestant and Catholic alike, lived in the countryside.[5]

Although the rising population reflected and reinforced economic expansion, it also exacerbated political tensions. Demographic growth was placing new strains on the union of the Canadas, which had been imposed in 1841 when Canada East (present-day Quebec, also known as Lower Canada) was amalgamated with Canada West to form the Province of Canada. Despite, or rather because of, the fact that French Canadians formed the majority of the population in 1841, Canada West was given the same number of seats as the numerically larger Canada East. The overrepresentation of Canada West and the concomitant underrepresentation of Canada East was designed to ensure that French Catholics could never become a political majority in the colony. The idea was to safeguard the "British" character of Canada and to create conditions in which French Canadians would eventually become assimilated into the English-speaking Protestant way of life.

Instead, French Canadian middle-class leaders turned the new arrangement to their own advantage, linked up with Reformers in Canada West to secure responsible government, and used their political power to protect French Catholic interests. In the process, the Canadian union emerged into a quasi-federal state, with joint English and French administrations. By voting largely en bloc and by forming a tactical alliance during the 1850s with centrist Conservatives in Canada West, French Canadians became an indispensable part of government. As such, they were able to influence legislation in English-speaking Canada, most notably in the contentious area of education, with the establishment of separate schools for the Catholic minority in the Protestant west.[6]

For many English-speaking Protestants, separate school legislation was an "entering wedge" of Catholicism; there was much talk, borrowed from religious controversies in Britain, about "papal aggression" in Canada.[7] This was happening at the very time that the English-speaking population was outstripping the French. As the demographic scales tipped in Canada West's favour, English speakers increasingly complained that they were being dominated by the French Canadian minority. When English-speaking Canadians had been the minority, equal representation between Canada East and Canada West had seemed satisfactory; now that the boot was on the other foot, it became a clear-cut case of discrimination. Not only that, but just over 6 per cent of Canada West's population in 1851 – some 60,000 people – were Irish-born Catholics; the ethnic group was of course significantly larger.[8] In and of themselves, the Irish Catholics may have seemed like a harmless minority in Canada West. When viewed in conjunction with French Canadian power, however, they could easily appear as the spearhead of a generalized Catholic assault on Protestantism.

In these circumstances, pressure built in English-speaking Canada to replace sectional equality with representation by population. This would have turned Canada from a quasi-federal state into a legislative union, with a permanent and expanding English-speaking Protestant majority – which French Canadians and most Irish Catholics could never accept. Against the background of demographic expansion and ethnoreligious conflict during the 1850s, the potential for a constitutional crisis was increasing. "The irony of the union," J.M.S. Careless observed, was that "while railways, commercial prosperity and rapid economic growth were bringing its two Canadian communities ever more closely together, powerful cultural and social forces were rising to drive them angrily apart."[9]

―――

As he responded to the unifying and divisive factors in Canadian life, and as he developed his vision of Canada's future, McGee drew deeply on his Irish and American experiences, selecting and adapting his earlier ideas to meet new circumstances.[10] The political, economic, and cultural nationalism that he had articulated in Ireland assumed Canadian form, just as his earlier ideas about the relationship between ethnic identity and national unity were resurrected in a Canadian context. Similarly, the insistence on Catholic education that had characterized his ultramontane years in America was carried forward into Canada. McGee also began to explore the opportunities for a new federal arrangement that would encompass all the British colonies in North America and take over the Hudson's Bay Company's territories in the West. These elements were combined in a new synthesis that was intended to create "a new northern nationality" – a phrase that was in common usage during mid-nineteenth-century Canada but which McGee made his own.[11]

The best political arrangement for Canada, and by extension British North America, in McGee's view, was to combine the maximum degree of legislative autonomy with membership in the British Empire. What the moderate Young Irelanders had failed to accomplish in Ireland now appeared attainable in Canada. There was, after all, a stronger British North American base on which to build; the colonies already enjoyed a degree of independence that Irish nationalists could only dream about. The task ahead was to widen the area of autonomy until Britain and Canada became equal partners under the Crown – the same goal that he had set for Ireland a decade earlier.

What might this look like in practice? For one thing, it meant that Canada would take more responsibility for its own defence by strengthening its militia rather than relying exclusively on British military power – something that McGee had previously wanted for Ireland.[12] For another, it meant giving Canada some control over its foreign policy, with Canadian emigration agents doubling as diplomats in European ports and a Canadian representative in Washington handling Canadian-American relations.[13] At the same time, McGee wanted to preserve and promote the prerogatives of the Crown in British North America – a return to his Young Ireland position in the prerevolutionary days of 1847, when he had extolled the "golden link of the crown" that connected Britain and Ireland.[14] His views on the "golden link" had changed under the pressure of the famine, the repression of the rising of 1848, and the religious hostilities of the early 1850s, when McGee had come to see the Crown as a central symbol of British oppression. But now, in Canada, McGee reverted to his earlier monarchism.

In Ireland, McGee had reached his "golden link" argument through history, rooted in his view that in 1541 Henry VIII had formed a "compact" with the Celtic and Norman chiefs of Ireland. In Canada, he came to the same position through geography or, more accurately, through his reading of geopolitical realities. Canada's proximity to the United States, he believed, had deterred Britain from pursuing coercive colonial policies, since such policies would have driven Canadians into the open arms of America; in this sense, the United States functioned as the guarantor of responsible government.[15] On the other hand, Canada's connection with Britain had deterred the United States from annexationism, since such a policy would have provoked an Anglo-American war; in this sense, Britain was the guarantor of Canada's continuing existence.

The imperial connection, then, provided the gravitational pull that prevented Canada from being drawn into the United States. But Britain was three thousand miles away across the Atlantic, while the rising American empire dominated the continent and constituted the greatest long-range threat to Canada.[16] One way to counter this threat, he suggested, was to invite a member of the Royal Family – the Prince of Wales, perhaps, or one of his brothers – to found a British North

American branch of the monarchy and sit on a Canadian throne. "For our part," he wrote, "as a safeguard against assimilation, absorption and subjection to and by Americanism – and as a guarantee, focus, and standard of Canadian nationality – we should gladly greet the settlement of such a permanent responsible ruler to these shores."[17] "We have forgotten neither the wrongs of Ireland, nor the just demands of democracy in advocating such a provision against the disunion and denationalization of Canada," he added, anticipating the furrowed brows of his Irish readers; "we have regarded the future with the anxious gaze of a Canadian patriot, and by that light, from this point, we have seen a constitutional crown among the not undesireable [sic] possibilities of the future."[18]

<hr />

A similar adaptation of his Young Ireland ideas to Canadian circumstances informed McGee's views about the economic basis of the new nationality. In Ireland, he had grappled with Britain's economic hegemony and had launched a "buy Irish" campaign to promote domestic manufactures. In Canada, he responded to American economic dominance with a policy of selective protectionism. If this contradicted laissez-faire orthodoxies, so be it. The "higher law of self-preservation," he wrote in 1857, overrode theories about "allowing trade to choose its own channels." This was, of course, a view that came easily to anyone who had experienced British policies during the famine, when the government's adherence to laissez-faire doctrine had made a terrible situation even worse.[19] In Canada, McGee argued, selective protectionism would encourage domestic industry, create a common sense of purpose, and foster a distinct sense of identity. Tariffs should be imposed only on goods that Canadians could produce as cheaply as Americans; in this way, both producers and consumers would benefit. "The effect of a judicious system," he wrote, "would be, *not to make them dear, but to make them here*."[20]

Under this partial protectionist umbrella, an interdependent British North American economic system could be established. "To create a domestic trade, between different classes of the same community, has been the first object of all national legislation," he wrote. "Diversity of pursuits and diffusion of wealth are the inevitable consequences of a well-balanced system, combining both artificial and agricultural employments."[21] Canadian wheat would supply Newfoundland, while the Maritime fishery would find markets in the west; an expanding fishery would increase the demand for Canadian shipbuilding, and Nova Scotia's coal would provide the energy for industrial expansion. All this would be underpinned by a uniform British North American banking system, a common currency, and a coherent set of laws.[22]

As with Ireland, McGee believed that railway development was essential for economic integration and national unity. "Four dislocated Provinces are not 'a country,' nor four estranged rural multitudes 'a people,'" he had written of his native country in 1850. "A thorough system of internal railways ... will do much to unite Ireland."[23] He now applied the same logic to British North America. Railways would connect the Atlantic with the west, transforming dislocated provinces into a country, and turning estranged communities into a people.[24] Seven years earlier, as an Irish American nationalist, McGee had vehemently attacked plans for an east-west Canadian railway system; now, as an Irish Canadian loyalist, he became one of its strongest proponents.[25]

Just as railways were strengthening connections by land, the new transatlantic telegraph promised to revolutionize communications by sea. Although the first attempt to lay a cable between Ireland and Newfoundland in 1857 ended in failure, McGee had no doubt about the project's potential. By facilitating the regular communication of "true intelligence" among different countries, the transatlantic telegraph would promote international peace, progress, and economic stability. And by establishing closer links between Britain and Canada, it would reinforce the east-west nexus that was needed to counterbalance the continental power of the United States. The Atlantic, he wrote, was becoming the new Mediterranean, the middle sea of the earth, and British North America was ideally placed to benefit.[26]

---

While selective protectionism, economic integration, and railway development would establish the material foundations for national unity, literature would supply the country with its spirit. "Literature is the vital atmosphere of nationality," McGee wrote in 1857. "Without that all-pervading, indefinite, exquisite element, national life – public life – must perish and rot. No literature – no national life, – this is an irreversible law." In taking this position, McGee was projecting Young Ireland's cultural nationalism onto Canada; his views came straight out of Thomas Davis's *Spirit of the Nation*, James Duffy's Library of Ireland series, and the entire range of Young Ireland's literary endeavours, in which McGee had played such a prominent role. Davis had aimed to create a popular literature that spoke to the condition of the people and would be "racy of the soil"; McGee now called for the same effort in Canada: "Come! let us construct a national literature for Canada, neither British nor French, nor Yankeeish, but the offspring and heir of the soil, borrowing lessons from all lands, but asserting its title throughout all!"[27]

Rapidly emerging as one of English-speaking Canada's earliest and most eloquent cultural nationalists, McGee, like those who followed him, attempted to counter the Americanization of Canadian life. The dominance of American publishers in the Canadian market was a particular source of concern; any people who lacked the means to tell their own stories, he wrote, would "soon disappear from the face of the earth, or become merged in some more numerous or more powerful neighbor."[28] It was thus essential to protect the Canadian publishing industry from American competition; the result would be "a Grand Trunk of thought, which will be as a backbone to the system we desire to inaugurate."[29]

One of the recurring arguments against cultural protectionism has been that it shelters the mediocre – a view that McGee categorically rejected. Canadian talent and creativity was waiting to be tapped, and the country itself provided a rich source of material. "On the round Canadian cedars," ran one of his poems, "Legends high await but readers."[30] A distinctly Canadian literature would draw inspiration from the "gorgeous coloring and the gloomy grandeur of the forest ..., the grave mysticism of the Red man, and the wild vivacity of the hunter of western prairies." "Its lyrics," McGee wrote, "must possess the ringing cadence of the waterfall, and its epics be as solemn and beautiful as our great rivers."[31] The Canadian identity was inseparable from the romanticized northern wilderness and its inhabitants.

Not content to prescribe for others, McGee made his own contributions to an emergent Canadian literature. During his visit to Montreal in October 1856, he wrote "Our Ladye of the Snow!" – a poem based on a French Canadian story about a lost traveller who was guided to safety by the Virgin Mary.[32] Over the next two years, he wrote several more poems on Canadian themes; they were eventually published in December 1858 in his *Canadian Ballads and Occasional Verses*. Written primarily for "the younger generation of Canadians," the book attempted to show that aspiring Canadian poets could find "many worthy themes ... without quitting their own country."[33]

Among its themes, the European discovery and exploration of North America loomed large. Sebastian Cabot, Jacques Cartier, and La Salle were presented as heroic figures who brought civilization to the wilderness and Catholicism to its inhabitants. But McGee's view of the indigenous people was respectful rather than dismissive, and his admiration for their "grave mysticism" was apparent in his "Arctic Indian's Faith":

> We worship the spirit that walks unseen
> Through our land of ice and snow:
> We know not His face, we know not His place,
> But His presence and power we know.[34]

Once the native people learned that the presence and power emanated from God, they would move through their mysticism towards Christianity. By modern standards, it was yet another version of the romantic and patronizing myth of the Noble Savage; by the standards of the time, however, McGee was sufficiently progressive to place the "aboriginal tribes" at the heart of Canadian history and to insist that they were an integral part of the country's identity.

McGee's poetry also embraced the subject of ethnoreligious reconciliation. Among his Canadian ballads, he included "Apostrophe to the Boyne," which he had composed several years earlier but seemed particularly relevant to a community in which Orange and Green tensions continued to simmer. Its hope that peace, justice, and harmony would ultimately prevail over "the bitterness of strife" struck the same chord as "An International Song," with its view that Canadians should show equal respect for the patriotic bravery of Wolfe and Montcalm – and for the Irish American hero Richard Montgomery, who was killed during the American siege of Quebec City in 1775. Orange and Green, French and English, settler and native could all unite on the basis of a common Canadian heritage; the Young Ireland influence is clear.

Yet no matter how much he believed in the poetic potential of the country, there are indications that McGee struggled to find his Canadian muse. He twice apologized in the preface of *Canadian Ballads* for the inadequacy of his efforts, and it seems that more than false modesty was at work.[35] Out of forty-one poems in the collection, only fifteen dealt with Canadian themes, and two of those had at best a marginal connection with the country.[36] The rest were counted as "Occasional Verses" and had a significant "Celtic" component. "You can hardly imagine, the interest I now take in this Country, and all that belongs to it," he later told Mary Ann Sadlier. "But it does not, and never can supply, the field for mental labor, and affectionate inspiration, which Ireland would have been."[37] In his heart, McGee remained more Irish than Canadian.

If McGee's Canadian political, economic, and cultural nationalism had Young Ireland roots, his approach to the relationship between ethnic identity and Canadian nationality drew on his Irish and American writings during the 1840s. His first sustained attempt to reconcile ethnicity with national unity occurred during the winter of 1846–47, when he argued that the Irish character stemmed from the combination of different "races," blending the influence of Danes, Saxons, Normans, Scots, Germans, and Celts.[38] McGee returned to the subject during his post-revolutionary exile in the United States after he was criticized for injecting foreign issues into the United States and for creating an *imperium in imperio* that contradicted the demands of American national unity. In response, McGee argued that the Irish would eventually blend into American life but in the process would also help to shape the American character. "By amalgamation," he explained, "we do not understand swallowing up; we mean the union of relative natures, fit and proper to be united, in the fruits of which each constituent is represented by the good qualities he contributes to the common stock."[39]

In Canada, McGee received exactly the same criticism and responded in exactly the same way. "A unification of population would be a great gain," he wrote. "But that result must be the work of a time and times. Where there is diversity in the origin, Time can only play the part of a solvent. Such a result cannot be hurried without being delayed; it ought not, on the other hand, be hindered."[40] "We believe the fragments of all old nationalities are and ought to be politically absorbed in the new," he subsequently elaborated, "but we believe the new patriotism itself must perform the part of solvent, and by its genial and generous atmosphere mould the materials already existing on the soil. These may be by events transmuted into native forms, but they cannot be de-characterized by any abstract reasoning or preliminary setting forth of the mere grounds of change."[41] The Burkean mode of thought is clear. There was no point in arguing that the country's various ethnic groups must conform to an a priori concept of Canadianism. Gradually, through a process of interaction and accommodation, the different nationalities in Canada would produce a new synthesis that would simultaneously incorporate and transcend their original identities.

In the short run, this meant accepting that each ethnic group had a legitimate right to pursue its own interests through political means. McGee admired the skill with which English, Scottish, and French Canadians played the political game, and he urged Irish Catholics to "imitate their conduct" in the quest for equality. "We insist on our right to a proportionate representation in every department of administration, from the Cabinet to the constabulary," he wrote. "We ask no more than our just share, and shall be content with nothing – not an iota – less." Irish Catholics would then take their rightful place within a political system that was a "compromise of nationalities," where politicians from different backgrounds were compelled by circumstances "to conciliate and counter-balance, to moderate and unite."[42]

Political equality was only part of the story; equality of recognition and equality of respect were at least as important. McGee even wanted parity of place names. The Irish had settled most of Canada West, he wrote, but had been blotted off the map by English-named cities, towns, and counties – a clear case of "the under ground ramifying English prejudice of North America."[43] Another manifestation of this prejudice was the way in which Irish Catholics were being unfairly singled out and stereotyped as lawless troublemakers: "If, in any corner of the Province, or any back street of the city, a scoundrel with an Irish name commits an outrage, his crime is at once gazetted, not only as his, but as in some way or other connected with national and religious principles or causes." "We object to the new method of classifying criminals by their origins and not by their crimes," he continued; "– that it is obstructive to the ends of justice, – that it is calculated to prejudice juries, – that it is an insult to the peaceful people of the same nationality, – that it is certain to cause estrangement, heart-burnings, and mutual enmities among our peculiarly mixed population."[44] All this sounds very familiar; ethnic community leaders in contemporary Canada have been fighting much the same battle in much the same language. Everything, as the historian A.T.Q. Stewart remarked, is older than we think it is.[45]

Rather than concentrating on the negative, McGee wrote, each group should focus on the positive features of the others; generosity of spirit was central to his vision of nationalism, and Canada could not work without it. As in America, he argued that the Catholic Irish must strive to bring out the positive features in themselves and to ensure that they stay on the right moral path. Although Canada, in his view, had a more congenial climate than the United States for Irish Catholics, there were still snares waiting for the unwary.

A case in point concerned the Irish American "Indian herb doctor," Francis Tumblety, who was arrested in Montreal during the fall of 1857 for attempting to give an abortion to a prostitute. Much to McGee's chagrin, Tumblety attracted a large degree of popular support among the city's Irish Catholics. This was partly because Tumblety's herbal remedies provided a cheap and apparently effective alternative to the cost of visiting Montreal's medical elite, and partly because his arrest had been the result of entrapment; indeed, he was eventually acquitted

on these grounds. McGee attacked Tumblety as a "shameless moun-
tebank" who threatened Catholic morality, preyed on the vulnerable, and was implicated in a "heinous crime." Using the "legitimate
weapon of ridicule," McGee penned a satirical memoir of Tumblety's
life, and he applauded when the Catholic bishop Ignace Bourget publicly condemned his work.[46]

The pressure was effective. Although Tumblety later claimed that "a
delegation representing a large body of Canadian citizens" had urged
him to run against McGee in the election of December 1857, he soon
left the city.[47] After a stint in the Maritimes, he returned to the United
States and eventually left for England, where he became a prime suspect in the Whitechapel murders of 1888. If the suspicion was correct –
and the evidence cannot be dismissed lightly – then McGee's many
antagonists included none other than Jack the Ripper.[48]

By the winter of 1857–58, McGee had adumbrated a clear and consistent nationalist program. Balancing British order with American liberty, Canada would remain an integral part of the British Empire, preferably with its own monarch, but would also develop its own foreign
policy and have its own militia. Selective protectionism and the growth
of railways would integrate British North American markets and ensure a significant degree of economic independence, while measures to
promote the Canadian publishing industry would increase cultural coherence. Minority rights would be respected; this meant accepting the
reality of ethnic differences, brokering compromises, pushing for proportionate political representation, and working for a future in which
distinct groups retained their best characteristics while sharing a common national consciousness. And it meant preserving and promoting
Canada's separate school system – the main thing that had attracted
him to Canada in the first place.

Surveying the current political scene, McGee identified two major
obstacles to his vision of a pluralist and progressive Canadian nationality: Protestant opposition to separate schools and the growing power
of the Orange Order. The school question was crucial. Catholics in
Canada West may have had more control over their children's education than Catholics did in the United States, but they did not enjoy

comparable status to that of Protestants in Canada East. Catholics in English-speaking Canada had to exempt themselves annually from the common school system, and in many municipalities they had to contribute to the support of common schools. Catholic schools were not automatically entitled to a share of local funds, and they were subject to inspection from non-Catholic superintendents. The present system, McGee argued, was "unequal and unjust" and would remain so unless and until there was educational parity between Catholics in Canada West and Protestants in Canada East.[49]

Central to his position was the view that educational uniformity would undermine Catholic faith and morality and would strengthen the assimilative power of "an intolerant Anglican nationality." To counter this, Irish Catholics and French Canadians must work together; as fellow Catholics and Celts in an Anglo-Protestant empire, they had a common history of cultural resistance. McGee admired the "tenacity" with which French Canadians defended themselves, and praised their "patriotic past." "They preserved their language, their religion, and their social life, against all attempts at Anglican assimilation," he wrote, "and they will not, now that they are above a million, yield what they so well defended when scarcely fifty thousand strong."[50]

Given his view that Irish Catholics and French Canadians were natural allies, McGee was shocked to learn in January 1858 that Irish gangs had been attacking French Canadians on the streets of Quebec City. It would not be surprising, he wrote, to find French Canadians "making reprisals, repelling force by force, and rendering their own part of the city as unsafe to Irishmen, as the Irish quarter is said to be to Canadians." To prevent this from happening, McGee called on Irish Catholics in Quebec City to "frown down all such advocates of violence and hatred." The principal beneficiaries of such an "insane feud" would be the Orangemen, he argued, who would exploit the divisions within Canadian Catholicism.[51]

---

Orangeism, according to McGee, was "a primary political fact" of Canadian life.[52] In contrast to his views in 1855–56, when he had downplayed the political power and sectarian character of Canadian Orangeism, McGee now treated the Orange Order as a serious threat to Irish Canadian Catholics. When McGee in the mid-1850s was promoting his plan to bring urban Irish Catholics into the Canadian countryside, he had a vested interest in presenting Canadian Orangeism as being relatively benign. But now that he was planning to run for election in Montreal, he had an equally vested interest in magnifying its malignity; nothing could be better guaranteed to rally Irish Catholic support than some good old-fashioned Orange bashing. It seemed a classic case of McGee "subordinating the facts of a case to the fancies of his mind," as Archbishop John Hughes put it in December 1856.[53] And indeed, a certain degree of cynicism would seem to be in order.

Nevertheless, more than cynicism is needed to understand McGee's position. The Orange Order was entering a period of "unparalleled growth" between 1854 and 1860. "Almost one-third of the lodges established during the nineteenth century were created during this period," observed Cecil Houston and William J. Smyth, "and practically all of them were in Ontario."[54] Rather than fading away in the Canadian environment, as McGee had hoped, Orangeism was spreading beyond its Irish Protestant base, increasing its formal and informal political power, and tightening its grip on patronage. There were, he claimed, three Orange cabinet members, fourteen Orange MPs, twenty Orange newspapers, eight hundred Orange lodges, and at least fifty thousand Orangemen in Canada West, with increasing numbers of "English and Scotch evangelicals" joining the order.[55] Orangeism had become strong enough to "harass and oppress all liberals in detail, all Catholic liberals especially, without breaking a bone in any existing law."[56] "No wonder," he wrote, "the public men of that section of the country – even the most resolute opponents of secret political societies – hesitate before openly opposing it."[57]

McGee, then, had good reason to fear that Orangeism was becoming as powerful in Canada as it had been in Ireland, with the same negative consequences for his pluralist nationalism.[58] Most Orangemen, of course, could agree with McGee's position on the golden link of the crown, and many of them shared his views on east-west railway development and selective protectionism. But there was considerable opposition in Orange ranks to his conception of unity in diversity, especially when diversity meant separate schools and equality of status between Catholics in Canada West and Protestants in Canada East.

Instead of looking to the Canadian future with a spirit of generosity, McGee argued, the Orange Order remained mired in the Irish past and stuck in sectarianism. Even though Canada had no established church and no penal laws, the Orange Order celebrated the victory of "one race over another" at the Battle of the Boyne, and glorified a king who had paved the way for the proscription of Catholicism and the confiscation of Irish land.[59] How, he asked, would French Canadians like it if English-speaking Canadians celebrated what they wrongly called "the conquest of Canada" each year?[60] And how would Scottish Canadians react to annual celebrations of the Battle of Culloden? Would they "bear the insult more meekly" than Irish Catholics bore the "vaunting displays on the anniversary of the Boyne"?[61]

Not only was the Orange Order stirring up old hatreds; it was also a secret society and thus "intrinsically illegal."[62] In McGee's view, the central problem with secret societies – as he had argued during his pre-revolutionary Young Ireland period and again in the United States – was that they intensified communal antagonisms in an escalating cycle of ethnoreligious conflict. If Orangeism was left unchecked, it would generate a militant Catholic response in the form of rival secret societies, known under the generic term of Ribbonism. The existence of Ribbonism would drive more people towards Orangeism, which would in turn generate more Ribbonism. Once this cycle of conflict got going in Canada, it would tear the country apart and leave McGee's new northern nationality in ruins.

This must be stopped before it started, and the only way to stop it was through political confrontation, not by compromise. It was necessary to take the "evil by the throat" and crush it out of existence, as had happened with the Know-Nothing movement in the United States.[63] A good start would be to withdraw all government patronage from Orange leaders and to dismiss all magistrates and government officials who participated in Orange parades; similar measures had been taken in Ireland and should be adopted in Canada.[64]

To pursue these goals, to disseminate "true information" about Orangeism, and to prevent "new dupes" from joining the order,

McGee called for an "ANTI-ORANGE ASSOCIATION," consisting of Irish Catholics, French Canadians, and liberal Protestants. The idea was to direct opposition to Orangeism through constitutional channels; such an organization would "prevent the possibility of a revival of Ribbonism" and reduce the risk of violent clashes between Protestants and Catholics. Far from inflaming ethnoreligious conflict, McGee's proposed Anti-Orange Association was designed to damp it down.[65]

Although McGee's Anti-Orange Association never materialized, he conducted a sustained attack on the Orange Order in the columns of his newspaper, the *New Era* – most notably, in a debate with Ogle Gowan, the grand master and "Father of Orangeism in British America."[66] The two men shared a Wexford connection, Gowan by birth and McGee by upbringing. But that was about all they had in common. Gowan's father, Hunter Gowan, had earned notoriety for his ruthless repression of the United Irishmen during the 1790s. "Every Wexford Catholic shudders with horror" at his name, McGee remarked. Ogle Gowan, he added, was the "true son" of his father – corrupt, conservative, and irredeemably anti-Catholic.[67]

Responding to McGee's anti-Orange writings, Gowan defended the Orange Order as a loyal, respectable movement that stood for civil and religious liberty and believed that all people, irrespective of their religion, were equal under the law. In an age of "free thought and of free action," and under the "free Constitution" of Canada, wrote Gowan, loyal Protestants had a right to form their own society and must stand up against the "intolerant notions" of men like McGee. Irish Catholics should cast off their bitter feelings and learn from the "excellent example of their French Canadian co-religionists," who were loyal to their sovereign and who cooperated with Orangemen in the present administration.[68]

McGee would have none of it. Gowan's talk of civil and religious liberty and equality under the law was merely a smokescreen; the reality was that Orangemen held "all Roman Catholics utterly unworthy of trust, office, or employment." While Gowan played the role of moderate in the metropolis, McGee wrote, he provoked Orange bigotry in the countryside and pandered to local Orange demands for patronage. Do not be fooled by this "flimsy mask of moderation," McGee told his

Ogle Gowan. The son of John Hunter Gowan, an Orangeman from County Wexford who had played a prominent role in suppressing the rising of 1798, Ogle Gowan emigrated to Canada in 1829 and founded the Grand Orange Lodge of British North America. "I can well believe," remarked McGee, "that Mr. Ogle R. Gowan is … the true son of that Hunter Gowan, at whose name every Wexford Catholic shudders with horror." Quoted in McGee, "Address to the Catholic Public – More Especially to the Irish Catholics of Western Canada," *True Witness*, 18 June 1858. (Canadian Historical Picture Collection, Metropolitan Reference Library, Toronto)

readers; Orangeism "addresses itself only to one order of the intellect – the narrow, the distorted, and the unteachable; it builds itself on the lowest level of human nature, on the basis of unchangeable hatred and mistrust. There is nothing in it noble or generous, or attractive to good men."[69] All this added up to one thing: Orangeism, as he frequently asserted, was *radically and indefensibly* ANTI-*Canadian*."[70]

In the course of developing his nationalist program and singling out
the Orange Order as its greatest enemy, McGee moved easily between
the concept of "Canada" and that of "British North America."[71] On
the one hand, he defended the union of the Canadas against those who
wanted representation by population; on the other, he looked forward
to a wider form of British North American federalism. Once again,
he was drawing on his earlier ideas and experiences in Ireland and
the United States. In 1844 McGee had supported a federal solution to
the question of Anglo-Irish relations, and he returned to this position
during the mid-1850s. Having lived in the United States for twelve
years – more than a third of his life – McGee knew how federalism
operated in practice, and he argued that British North America was
well placed to "avoid all the dangers, and profit by all the experiences"
of the American federal system.[72]

The American experience had taught him that Canada could not
become "one indivisible state" and that the provinces must have a significant degree of autonomy:

> Each Province must retain its local Parliament for local pur-
> poses, conceding to the Federal authority such powers only
> as are necessary for the general progress and safety – for the
> superintendence of commerce, the sanctity of international acts,
> the constitution of the higher courts of justice, and for other
> common and supreme concerns. In short, these Provinces, if
> ever united, will necessarily copy the American system. Modify
> where you will, but still you must copy. That system was not
> born of Jefferson's brain, was not fed to strength by Franklin's
> providence; it existed in the *circumstances* of the Thirteen
> United Colonies.

Residual power should lie with the provinces, which would "concede"
control in specified areas to the federal government for the greater
good; at the same time, a federal union would "beget nobler thoughts,
than any local interest can ever inspire." "Never was there for a northern land a grander destiny in store," he declared; "– never was there

for man's intelligence a worthier work than to accelerate and assure that destiny."[73]

This was more than a rhetorical flourish; McGee had long believed that each nation had its own destiny, which would be realized through the work of its patriotic sons and daughters. He had discussed the nature of Ireland's destiny with Charles Gavan Duffy during their walking tour in the summer of 1845, and he returned to it regularly in his poetry, journalism, and lectures.[74] As the editor of the *Boston Pilot*, McGee had embraced the notion of America's manifest destiny, which included annexing Canada, ousting the Hudson's Bay Company, and taking over the Pacific Northwest.[75] After returning to the United States in 1848, however, he became increasingly dismayed by the way in which manifest destiny was linked to Protestant Anglo-Saxon supremacy, and eventually jettisoned the concept altogether.[76] Now, in 1857, it reappeared in a distinctly Canadian, or British North American, form. Canada, not the United States, was destined to rule the northern half of the continent, from coast to coast.[77]

Among other things, this meant that Canada's western frontier must keep pace with that of the United States – something that could only be accomplished by encouraging more immigration, which became another central component of McGee's nation-building strategy.[78] In particular, he wanted to attract Irish, French, and northern European immigrants, whom he believed were best suited to the Canadian environment.[79] Like many of his contemporaries, McGee believed that climate shaped character and that northern latitudes fostered intellectual energy and literary creativity.[80] "We are," he wrote, "a Northern people."[81]

⋯

In the United States, McGee once described himself as a "Proof-reader to the American translation of Irish ideas."[82] Now, he was engaged in the Canadian translation of Irish and American ideas. In the process, his writings became part of a British North American unionist tradition that had emerged in the early nineteenth century. McGee subsequently identified the major figures in that tradition as the Irish-born Nova Scotia politician, Richard Uniacke; the American-born loyalist, Jonathan Sewell; the Canadian-born Tory, John Beverley Robinson; and the English-born Whig, Lord Durham.[83] He also applauded Thomas Chandler Haliburton's arguments for federal union and equal status in the British Empire, just as he admired Haliburton's contribution to British North American literature.[84] But the writer with whom McGee was most impressed was the Nova Scotia journalist and poet Peter Stevens Hamilton, who published his *Observations upon a Union of the Colonies of British North America* in 1855. McGee later remarked that Hamilton's pamphlet had started him thinking about British North American union, and said that Hamilton, along with the Canadian writer Alexander Morris, had expressed the case for the "new nationality" better than he had himself.[85]

McGee probably read Hamilton's pamphlet during his trip to Nova Scotia in July 1856. Shortly afterwards, he wrote his first article on "a North British or Canadian nationality," which echoed Hamilton's arguments that confederation would enlarge the horizons of provincial politicians and produce practical benefits such as a common currency and a consolidated militia.[86] The following year, McGee's columns in the *New Era* expanded upon Hamilton's views that union would check American annexationism, promote "native literature and mechanical invention," balance the "monarchical principle" with "the essentially republican institutions of the land," and create "a compact, powerful, and *virtually independent* State" within the British Empire.[87] There were, however, some significant differences. While Hamilton preferred a legislative union of the provinces, McGee, always conscious of minority rights, insisted upon a federal arrangement. And while Hamilton waxed eloquent about the grandeur of the British Empire, McGee was conspicuously silent on the subject in 1857 – though he would have more to say later in his career.[88]

All this serves as a reminder that McGee was not as original as he retrospectively seems; his ideas about British North American union, like his writings on the new northern nationality and his cultural nationalism, were part of wider currents of thought running through British North America. Where McGee excelled was in his ability to articulate these ideas in a powerful, persuasive, and memorable way. Although he has often been criticized for changing his views, what stands out in his writings and speeches about Canada's future is the clarity and coherence of his vision – a vision that synthesized his Irish and American experiences with Canadian circumstances and with British North American unionist thought. In this way, McGee exemplified his own conceptualization of the relationship between ethnic consciousness and national identity. His earlier nationalism was being transmuted by events into a new patriotism, which simultaneously embraced and transcended his identity as an Irishman in Canada.

# PART ONE

# The Reform Alliance

I hope the time is not distant when the common voice of the Reform party throughout the Province will declare that by their politics shall men alone be known – that throwing aside all religious denominationalism, be it Protestant or Roman Catholic – (loud cheers) – and rejoicing in the common name of Reformers, having common objects in view, we shall harmoniously do battle side by side for the maintenance and establishment of our common principles.

McGee, speaking at "A Banquet at London [Canada West] to Mr. McGee," *Globe*, 17 September 1858

## CHAPTER TWO

# A Twofold Dilemma
## December 1857 – August 1858

During his first six months in Canada, McGee had articulated a comprehensive nationalist program that reached back to his Young Ireland and Irish American writings and looked forward to Confederation. At the same time, he came to Canada with clearly stated political ambitions: to become "a Member of Parliament" – a member of the Province of Canada's legislative assembly – to defend and promote separate schools, and to participate in the task of fulfilling "Canada's Future Destiny."[1] This meant working through the complex maze of mid-nineteenth-century Canadian party politics, adopting a Burkean emphasis on the possible best, and employing pragmatic means in the service of both the new northern nationality and McGee's own longstanding desire for "honest fame."[2]

The task was all the more challenging when one considers the practical political options that McGee faced in Canada. One possibility was to join the Liberal-Conservatives, led by John A. Macdonald, who were in coalition with George-Étienne Cartier's *Bleus*, the dominant party in Canada East. Within Macdonald's party there was considerable support for railway expansion and a protective tariff, both of which corresponded with McGee's national vision. Many of its members were also prepared to accept limited separate school legislation as an acceptable price of the French Canadian alliance. On the other hand, the Liberal-Conservatives were closely identified with the Orange Order – Macdonald himself was a member in good standing, albeit a moderate one – and McGee had identified Orangeism as the greatest threat to his vision of Canadian nationality. The Orange Order was divided on the educational question. While some of its leaders reluctantly acquiesced in separate schools, the faction led by Thomas Ferguson, the junior deputy grand master and Ogle Gowan's son-in-law, regularly introduced bills for their abolition.[3]

Not much joy for Irish Catholics there, it would seem. Another possibility was to support George Brown's Reform Party, which combined political liberalism with support for western expansionism. So far, so good, from McGee's perspective. But the Reform Party also stood for representation by population, which threatened to swamp French Canadians and Irish Catholics, and it attracted a number of hard-line Orangemen. One of Brown's key backers in 1857 was John Holland, the Orange grand secretary who had given blood-and-thunder speeches against McGee's earlier plans to establish Irish Catholic colonies in Canada.[4] Brown himself had been a long-standing opponent of separate schools, arguing that they enclosed Catholic children in "priestly establishments, where no ray of light could enter their minds, until it had been refracted by passing through a dense medium of bigotry and superstition."[5] Behind Brown stood the radical liberal Clear Grits, who associated Catholicism with ignorance, idolatry, and despotism, and whose opposition to separate schools appeared unshakeable. "In religious hatred," McGee commented, "the party designated 'Clear Grits' outbid and outstrip the Orangemen themselves."[6]

Caught in this "two-fold dilemma" between Orange conservatism and Clear Grit radicalism, Irish Catholics were deeply divided over political strategy.[7] For some, the best course of action was to ally with the Liberal-Conservatives, including the Orangemen, in the hope that they could be pushed further on Catholic education. For others, it made more sense to work with George Brown, in the hope of softening his opposition to separate schools, reducing the influence of Orangeism, and working out a solution to the education question.

During his first months in Canada, it was not clear which way McGee would turn. To ally with the Orangemen seemed unimaginable; to side with the Reform Party seemed unthinkable; to stand alone meant political impotence. In the first issue of his *New Era*, which he launched in May 1857, he wrote that he would support whichever party gave the best guarantee of freedom of conscience and that he would "pursue a moderate course on all political questions."[8] But his conviction that Orangeism was the most dangerous and destructive political force in Canada effectively ruled out any alliance with the Liberal-Conservatives, and he began to float the idea of a new cross-denominational party of moderates that would challenge the Macdonald-Cartier government.[9]

———•———

The opportunity to participate in parliamentary politics came six months after his arrival, when the Liberal-Conservative government called a general election for December 1857. McGee was well positioned to run. The previous month, his supporters in Montreal had held a McGee Testimonial, presenting him with a writing desk and $1,200; the idea was to raise his public profile and provide him with the resources for an election campaign.[10] His own newspaper was an important political asset, and the city's St Patrick's Society provided him with a strong organizational base. As an ethnic group, the Irish were about one-quarter of Montreal's population; most of the Irish were Catholics, with strong community networks in the district of the Quebec Suburbs and above all in Griffintown. Here, labourers in the factories along the Lachine Canal and women working as domestic servants mixed with a broad spectrum of artisans, tradesmen, shopkeepers, and publicans, who themselves shaded off into a middle class of businessmen and professionals.[11] Within this middle class were men such as the auctioneer Lawrence Devany, the merchants James Donnelly and Walter Macfarlane, and the restaurant owner Barney Tansey, all of whom helped organize the McGee Testimonial and would remain among his strongest supporters over the next decade.

Arguing, with considerable exaggeration, that the Irish constituted one-third of Montreal's population, McGee maintained that they deserved to have one representative among the city's three Members of Parliament.[12] He ran as an independent opposition candidate, on a platform that distilled the essence of his writings on the new nationality – except for the part about a Canadian branch of the Royal Family, which he prudently kept to himself for the time being. Central to his campaign was the position, endorsed by the St Patrick's Society, that Irish Catholics should vote only for candidates who passed an Orange

Winter in Montreal, mid-nineteenth century. (Notman Photographic Archives [NPA], McCord Museum, Montreal)

test and an education test. To be acceptable, a candidate must declare that he neither belonged to nor supported the Orange Order and that he opposed "any Administration that bestows place or patronage on Orangemen." The education test stipulated that a candidate must agree "to grant the same privileges to the Catholic minority in Upper Canada that is [sic] possessed by the Protestant minority in Lower Canada."[13]

Of the six men running for the three seats in Montreal, George-Étienne Cartier, John Rose, and Henry Starnes stood for the Liberal-Conservatives. McGee's fellow opposition candidates were the Reform-minded Luther Holton and Antoine-Aimé Dorion, the leader of the liberal French Canadian *Rouges*. In the ensuing campaign, the Liberal-Conservatives attacked McGee as a "stranger" and a "firebrand," and raised questions about his Irish and American past. McGee, wrote one of his critics, "labors under the imputation of being an extreme man, and the impression is so deep that it will take him years of moderation in Canada to remove it."[14] For his part, McGee accused the government of corruption and denounced its links with the Orange Order; he also criticized it for failing to support Montreal's bid to become the capital of Canada and for making false promises to Irish Catholics about improved separate school legislation.[15]

Midway through the campaign, McGee formed an electoral alliance with the other opposition candidates; meanwhile, the St Patrick's Society worked hard to get out the Irish Catholic vote. After two days of heavy polling, in a contest that McGee described as "so close, so exciting, and so important," he came in a close third, behind Dorion and Rose; Starnes and Holton had been shut out, and Cartier came last. And so, just before Christmas 1857, McGee finally realized his ambition of becoming a Member of Parliament.[16]

There was, however, a whiff of scandal about his election. This was not a matter of the seventeen charges of corruption that supporters of the defeated candidates levied against him; that kind of thing was all part of the political game and should not be taken seriously.[17] Instead, it concerned backroom manoeuvring between Dr Henry Howard, who was McGee's campaign manager and president of the St Patrick's Society, and Henry Starnes, one of the Liberal-Conservative candidates. Immediately after the election was called, Howard and Starnes, who were old friends, had discussed the possibility of a pact. If McGee would pull out of the race in favour of the Liberal-Conservatives, Starnes suggested, the party would reward him with the first country constituency that became available.

Howard, who privately favoured a joint McGee-Starnes-Cartier Liberal-Conservative ticket for Montreal, had thought the offer well worth considering. If it looked as if McGee was losing the election, here was a good fallback position, with the safety net of a country seat. To make matters still more intriguing, Howard was also engaged in similar negotiations with John Rose's camp. But when McGee delivered his election address, with its strong anti-Orange and pro-separate school position, any potential deal was off. A few days later, McGee formally

allied himself with Dorion and Holton, and publicly announced that
the ministerial candidates had tried to bribe him to their side with an
offer of a country seat.[18]

Still, a nagging question remained: Was Howard having these discussions behind McGee's back, or was he actually developing his strategy in conjunction with McGee? In January 1858 Howard declared
that McGee had known all about and approved of the negotiations
with Starnes – a charge that McGee vehemently denied.[19] Consider the
chronology, McGee told his readers. In December, during the election
campaign, Howard had publicly declared that he had not told McGee
about the negotiations. Now, in January, Howard stated that he had
indeed told McGee. Either he was lying then or he was lying now.
What had happened in the meantime? Upon discovering that Howard
preferred a Liberal-Conservative ticket, McGee had fired him as his
campaign manager and pressed him to resign as president of the St Patrick's Society. Only then, pointed out McGee, did Howard switch his
story; it smelled strongly of sour grapes.[20]

Besides, as the Montreal Catholic editor George Clerk pointed out
in the *True Witness*, it was inherently implausible that McGee would
have joined a government that he had been systematically denouncing
over Orangeism and separate schools.[21] Nevertheless, there was enough
mud for some of it to stick, and Howard's accusation could easily be
fitted into the "unscrupulously ambitious" image of McGee. Before
long, Clerk himself would be arguing that McGee had been prepared
to betray his principles in 1857 for the sake of personal power.[22]

———•———

When the dust had settled, it was clear that the Liberal-Conservatives
had won the general election, with an overall majority of seventy-
seven to fifty-three. But although the *Bleus* dominated Canada East,
their Liberal-Conservative allies were a minority in Canada West. This
meant that the "double majority" principle – that legislation should
have the support of a majority from each section – could not apply, and
thus pressure was bound to increase in Canada West for representation
by population. As McGee put it, the issue of representation by population was "the rock right in the mid-channel of Canada's career." There

Parliament Buildings, Front Street West, Toronto, 1856: After the Parliament in Montreal was burned down during the riots of 1849, the Canadian capital alternated between Toronto and Quebec City. McGee gave his first parliamentary speech in the Toronto Parliament Buildings on 3 March 1858. (City of Toronto Archives, Fonds 1498, item 10)

was no denying that numbers ought to be represented, he argued; but it would be fatal, in the Canadian context, to push the principle to excess. "Territory as well as numbers, and nationality as well as territory, must be represented," he wrote, "if we are to continue a unitary body."[23]

The parliamentary session opened in Toronto in late February. A week later, McGee made his maiden speech. It was an oratorical masterpiece, which crystallized his central arguments from the *New Era* and the election campaign. He spoke in favour of tariff reform to encourage Canadian manufactures and would later vote with the government on the issue. Everything else in his speech, though, set him apart from the Liberal-Conservatives. The government should have allowed Canadians to choose the new capital, he said, instead of referring the matter to Westminster; it also needed to strengthen the militia, challenge the Hudson's Bay Company's claims over the West, and improve Catholic education in Canada. In a brief but telling comment, he praised Bishop Armand de Charbonnel's strong stand on separate schools. Charbonnel had declared that Catholic electors and legislators who failed to support improved separate school legislation were guilty of mortal sin, and he had named several politicians, including Cartier, as being unworthy of absolution.[24]

Then, warming to his subject, McGee took on the Orange Order in general and Macdonald in particular. It was wrong, McGee insisted, for the head of the government to belong to an organization that had been the cause of "more heartburnings, quarrels, rows and riots – and of more bloodshed also – than almost any one association, secret or public, that ever existed in this province." He did not deny the right of private citizens to join the order, and he did not hold Macdonald responsible for "all the unlawful acts of the Orange body." But he insisted that "no man should abuse his high place in order to encourage what was obnoxious to the feelings and convictions of a large portion of those over whom he had been put in trust to administer the government of the country."[25]

It was not just what McGee said that impressed many of his listeners; it was how he said it. "Wit, humor, eloquence, sarcasm, excited such bursts of laughter and applause that even the Speaker forgot for a moment the decent gravity of his position in a smile," ran one report.[26] The *Globe*, after disapproving of McGee's "extreme" views on separate schools and the Orange Order, called him "the most finished orator in the House" and marvelled at the "magnetic influence" he exerted over his listeners.[27] In the *True Witness*, George Clerk – who of course fully approved of McGee's views on separate schools and the Orange Order – described the speech as "a splendid display of oratory."[28] McGee had learned his lessons well from his time as the parliamentary correspondent of the *Freeman's Journal* twelve years earlier. And he had established an immediate reputation as a man to watch as well as to hear.

---

Being a man to watch, however, came with a price; to attack Orangeism in its Toronto heartland was not necessarily conducive to one's health and well-being. Shortly after his speech, rumours spread that McGee had been shot. Two weeks later, on St Patrick's Day, he narrowly escaped from an Orange crowd that was "out to get the Griffintown papist."[29] The attack on McGee occurred in the context of violent conflict earlier in the day. It began when an Orangeman decided to drive his cab through the St Patrick's parade, in a gesture of contempt and defiance. The cabman was immediately surrounded by hostile marchers, at which point several of his friends came to his aid. A full-scale fight erupted. From around the corner on Colborne Street came Bill Lennox, tavern keeper, Orangeman, and city councilman, brandishing a pistol. As the brawl continued, a twenty-two-year-old Catholic, Mathew Sheedy, was stabbed in the groin and later died of his wounds. The police dispersed the rioters, but tensions remained high. Later in the day, a group of Orangemen assaulted a Catholic priest on Church Street, shouting "away with you, you damned Papist."[30]

That night, the St Patrick's Day events went ahead as planned. At the National Hotel on Colborne Street, directly opposite Bill Lennox's tavern, Irish Catholics – including McGee – met for dinner. Farther down the street, at Platt's Hotel, a group of Irish Protestants – including Ogle Gowan – also met to celebrate St Patrick. Although the Catholic and Protestant groups were meeting separately, there were elements of goodwill between them. A deputation from the National Hotel visited their Protestant counterparts at Platt's in a gesture of friendship and were in turn presented with a St Patrick's Day daisy.[31] The Orangemen who were gathering at Lennox's tavern, however, were in a less conciliatory mood.

Around eleven o'clock, McGee left the dinner to return to his lodgings. As soon as he entered his cab, he was surrounded by a "murderous mob" that threatened to kill him and chased him down the street. Meanwhile, the crowd started throwing rocks and bottles through the windows of the National Hotel; in response, the people inside began pelting the rioters with anything they could lay their hands on. As this was going on, Ogle Gowan ran to the hotel, climbed through a window, and offered his assistance to the beleaguered diners. Guns were fired, apparently from both sides, ratcheting up the tension. Eventually the police gained control of the situation. No one was killed, but the National Hotel had been wrecked.[32]

———·—·———

The event, and the reaction to it, had major long-term repercussions for Irish Catholics, for Catholic-Protestant relations, and, by extension, for Canada as a whole. In the short run, the most visible effect was to turn McGee into an Irish Catholic hero. Nothing, with the exception of time in a British jail, was better calculated to boost the reputation of an Irish Catholic politician than to be attacked by enraged Orangemen. When McGee returned to Montreal a week later for the Easter recess, a crowd of "not less than ten thousand" met him at the station and accompanied him home with a torchlight procession. "Rockets were discharged every few minutes," reported the *New Era*; "– windows illuminated – tar barrels burned on every open space along the route – flags and coloured lamps hung out – and one continuous cheer kept up, from the Station to the upper end of St. Antoine Street."[33]

Addressing the crowd, McGee took pains to distinguish the actions of the Orange rioters from Protestants in general. The vast majority of Toronto Protestants were appalled by the St Patrick's Day riot, he said, and should not be tarred with the Orange brush. No – it was the Orange Order and the Orange Order alone that was to blame. Its members had committed murder on the streets of Toronto and had attempted to intimidate him from speaking against them in Parliament. All this confirmed his argument that Orangeism was an "anti-loyal, anti-legal, anti-social, anti-Canadian organization." It remained to be seen, he told the crowd, whether justice in Toronto was strong enough "to reach into the darkest recesses of the lodge, and drag out the guilty even from the Grand Master's chair." But given the fact that the leader of the government was an Orangemen, there were good grounds for pessimism.[34]

McGee's pessimism turned out to be justified. No one was sent to trial for Sheedy's murder; the evidence was too confused and contradictory. The investigation into the National Hotel riot resulted in the conviction of three men, all of whom were Irish Catholics.[35] None of the Protestants arrested for their participation in the riot was convicted. The police magistrate who conducted the inquiry, George Gurnett, noted with incredulity the inability of the police to identify any of those who attacked the National Hotel, and asserted that "other obligations" had restrained witnesses from telling everything they knew.[36] There was no need to spell it out; everyone knew what he meant.

Nor, in the view of many Irish Catholics, was this an isolated incident. During an election riot in Wellington County in December, an Orangeman named William Miller shot and killed a Catholic, John Farrell, who was attacking Miller's brother with an adze.[37] Although six witnesses were prepared to identify Miller in court, the Grand Jury refused to send the case to trial; it was, according to McGee, "one of the most glaring cases of Orange conspiracy to defeat the law of which we have ever heard."[38] The implications were serious and potentially disastrous; the ground was being prepared for the very kind of escalating ethnoreligious conflict that he hoped to prevent. "Nothing," he wrote, "is so certain to produce illegal combinations as the knowledge that the law cannot be enforced, even in the most extreme cases, against the offending Brethren of the present Premier."[39]

In Toronto, something along these lines was indeed beginning to happen. In April, Patrick O'Neill, the acting editor of the Toronto *Mirror*, organized a petition to Parliament, calling for a special commission to investigate the Sheedy and Farrell murders, and insisting that Orangemen must be excluded from the magistracy and juries. If their demands were not met, more than seven hundred petitioners declared, they would "be obliged to arm in defence of their lives and properties."[40] Because Irish Catholics were a minority in Toronto, argued the *Mirror*, they must show the Orangemen that they would not be pushed around. This meant breaking with "gentlemen" like McGee who counselled caution and prudence. Such men were not fit leaders, O'Neill wrote. They had been insensitive enough to dine at the National Hotel while Mathew Sheedy lay dying and had been incompetent enough to attend the dinner without preparing to defend themselves. Rather than listening to such people, he concluded, the "plebeian" Irish must seize the initiative and exercise their constitutional right to get guns in their hands.[41]

Meanwhile, a cooper and tavern owner named Michael Murphy called together some of his friends to discuss ways to make Toronto's streets safe for Irish Catholics. Out of this meeting emerged the Hibernian Benevolent Society, which gradually evolved as an Irish Catholic answer to the Orange Order, defining itself against the threat of its enemies, functioning as a mutual benefit society and recreational association, and forming branches throughout Canada.[42] Some of its more militant members, including Murphy, established links with another, larger, movement that had also been formed on St Patrick's Day 1858 – the Irish Revolutionary (or Republican) Brotherhood, better known in North America as the Fenians. The Hibernian Benevolent Society was not in itself an "illegal combination." But it provided the perfect cover for the introduction of Fenianism into Canada. Murphy soon organized a Fenian Circle within the organization and became the Fenian head centre of British North America.[43]

—·—

Immediately after the St Patrick's Day riot, McGee attempted to channel Irish Catholic anger along constitutional lines. He unequivocally condemned the threat of force in O'Neill's petition and opposed any attempt to establish "counter organizations" to the Orange Order. At the same time, he agreed that the petition's complaints about the justice system were "as true as the gospel" and cited Police Magistrate Gurnett's report to prove his point. Nevertheless, he insisted that everyone had to work within the rule of law – and if the law failed to protect all the subjects of the Crown, then it must be reformed from within.[44] McGee shared the central objective of the petitioners – the exclusion of Orangemen from the judicial system – but rejected their methods. For his strategy to succeed, however, he had to demonstrate that constitutional resistance to Orangeism could bring results.

An opportunity to do this was already appearing on the political horizon in the form of a bill for the incorporation of the Orange Order. Although the ostensible issue was about enabling Orange lodges to hold their own property, the bill raised larger questions about the place of Orangeism in Canadian society. "Either the Orange order must advance or it must be repulsed," argued McGee in the run-up to the parliamentary debate. "It must be chartered or refused a charter, and that before six weeks have passed." He organized a petitioning campaign against the bill; some 4,500 people signed in Montreal, and there was widespread Irish Catholic support for the petition in Canada West.[45]

During his parliamentary speech against incorporation, McGee struck a low-key tone. To avoid stirring up religious animosities, he argued, the House should simply reject the bill at its first reading. "The debate in this House must be the ancestor and progenitor of endless debates throughout the country," he said. "In every country store, in every wayside tavern, at every smith's forge, without rules of order, without a moderating influence ... these discussions will go on. Is it wise to promote such controversies and heart-burnings among the people, and to sanction them by the example of Parliament?" If anyone doubted the depth of religious divisions in the country, he continued, they only needed to cast their mind back to St Patrick's Day and the different reaction he himself had received in Canada's two principal cities: "The brickbats of Toronto were by a strange metamorphosis transmuted into sky rockets at Montreal, and the rockets were certainly the more acceptable of the two." After a nine-hour debate, the House split right down the middle about giving the bill a second reading. The Speaker gave the casting vote in favour, at which point a majority voted to defer the second reading for six months. To all intents and purposes, the Incorporation Bill was dead in the water. McGee's approach, it seemed, had been vindicated – although his critics were quick to point out that the more immediate issue of Orangemen in the judicial system had not been addressed.[46]

Along with his political campaign against Orangeism, McGee attempted to defuse Protestant-Catholic tensions on the streets of Toronto and to prevent any replays of the St Patrick's Day riot. At Mathew Sheedy's inquest, the coroner – Dr. Cotter, a Catholic, who had actually got into a fistfight with Bill Lennox outside the National Hotel – suggested that "it would be better for them all if there were no St. Patrick's processions, or Temperance processions, or Orange processions among them."[47] McGee agreed. And although he obviously had no control over Orange or temperance parades, he could do something about the way in which St Patrick's Day was celebrated.

In the United States, he had criticized St Patrick's Day parades for politicizing, secularizing, and vulgarizing a religious event and for making Catholics vulnerable to a nativist backlash.[48] Now, in Toronto, he joined with leading Catholics in the Young Men's St Patrick's Association, whose president was the alderman and auctioneer John O'Donohoe, to press for a voluntary suspension of the parade. This would not only take the heat out of the situation, McGee believed, but would also contrast Irish Catholic responsibility with Orange truculence. For the next three years, there was no official St Patrick's Day march in Toronto. But this strategy could be and was interpreted as a form of cowardice and capitulation to Orange aggression. Resentment towards McGee over the parades issue began to build up, and not just in Toronto.[49]

———·———

Right from the start, then, McGee was making enemies as well as friends among Canadian Irish Catholics. Even as he argued for unity, his policies frequently met with division; in a heterogeneous Irish Catholic society, it could hardly have been otherwise. On issues such as arming for self-defence or suspending parades, he alienated a militant minority, including a number of future Fenians.[50] And on the broader question of the political alignment of Irish Catholics – the "two-fold dilemma" of whether to support the Liberal-Conservatives or the Reformers – he ran into serious opposition within the Catholic Church and the Catholic press.

Before McGee arrived in Canada, the church had generally believed that the Liberal-Conservatives, for all their faults and foot-dragging, offered the best chance for improved separate school legislation and provided the best barrier to representation by population. Catholic bishops may have been frustrated with the government, but George Brown's Reformers, with their anti-Catholic rhetoric, their hostility to separate schools, and their support for representation by population, looked even worse.

George Brown. Leader of the Reform Party and editor of the *Globe*, George Brown was the most powerful politician in Canada West. McGee described him in 1862 as "a Scotch-Presbyterian of Upper Canada – a strong anti-Catholic from educational bias, but a very able man, and no Orangeman" (McGee to T.D. Sullivan, 15 August 1862, Young Ireland Miscellaneous Letters, National Library of Ireland [NLI], MS 10,517). (NPA, McCord Museum)

McGee took a different view of the situation. He was convinced that the Liberal-Conservatives, with their increasingly powerful Orange component, were not going to move on the schools issue; they had promised much and delivered little, he believed, and could not be trusted. The fact that the ministry had refused in 1856 to support the Felton Bill, which would have established educational equality for the religious minorities in both Canada East and Canada West, only appeared to confirm his position.[51] But he also came to think that George Brown might be less inflexible than he seemed, and he gradually began to prepare the ground for a possible alliance. In February 1858, he suggested that Brown had been turned into a "bug-bear" to frighten Irish Catholics into voting for the Liberal-Conservatives; in April, he declared that Brown was "not so black as he is painted." Unless Brown wanted to be in opposition forever, McGee reasoned, he would have to win at least some French Canadian support, and the only way Brown could do that was by moderating his hard-line views on education and by navigating around the mid-channel rock of representation by population. There was room here, McGee thought, for some kind of agreement.[52]

During the parliamentary session, McGee and Brown treated each other with kid gloves, much to the chagrin of Irish Catholic Liberal-Conservatives.[53] Meanwhile, on the lecture circuit, McGee's standard topic was "The Historical and Political Connection of Ireland and Scotland," in which he argued that the two countries had common Celtic racial and linguistic origins; this was clearly designed to reduce tensions between Irish Catholics and Brown's Scottish Presbyterian supporters, and to provide a cultural basis for a political alliance.[54] Then, in the legislature on 25 May, McGee made his move towards the Reform Party. In the course of a general attack on the government, he declared that "Representation by Population could not be long resisted. – There was but one of the alternatives, Representation by Population, or Dissolution of the Union. Property should have its weight, intelligence should have its weight, but any man who on this continent and in this age of the world, did not believe that numbers should be the basis, was as little to be reasoned with as a man who believed in the philosopher's stone."[55] Barely five months earlier, he had written that territory and nationality must be factored into the electoral equation. His enemies now accused him of supporting a strategy that would turn Catholics into a permanent minority, and of simultaneously aligning himself with one of the most anti-Catholic politicians in the country.

———·•·———

The shockwaves reverberated throughout Catholic Canada. From Montreal, George Clerk sent an angry letter to McGee, "strongly condemning his declaration," and got an equally angry reply by return mail.[56] In Toronto, the *Mirror* added the emerging alliance with Brown to its list of complaints about McGee.[57] One can see why. For years, the *Mirror* had been locked in conflict with the *Globe* over separate schools, and the two-way stream of sectarian abuse was not easily forgotten. During the summer of 1856, the *Mirror* had itself tried to effect an alliance with Brown, only to run into a wall of hostility and a refusal to compromise.[58] And now, along came this newcomer who pretended to have all the answers but who clearly did not understand just how dangerous Brown was, and simply did not realize the hopelessness of his task.[59]

All this was mild compared to the treatment the Reform alliance received in Toronto's other Catholic newspaper, Michael Hayes's *Catholic Citizen*, which variously described Brown as a vampire who sucked the blood out of Catholics, a "cruel, arbitrary and immoral" opponent of separate schools, and the devil incarnate. Commenting on a by-election being held in North Leeds and Grenville that May, Hayes encouraged Catholic voters to reject the Reform Party and vote for the government candidate – who just happened to be the Orange grand master, Ogle Gowan.[60]

Upon reading this, McGee immediately wrote to John O'Donohoe, his principal supporter in Toronto, about Hayes's "infamous treachery." A meeting of the Toronto Young Men's St Patrick's Association must be called as soon as possible, McGee told O'Donohoe in a late-night letter: "No time to be lost – not an hour. In great haste and very tired." O'Donohoe followed through immediately. Within days, the St Patrick's Association "unanimously" condemned the *Mirror* and the *Catholic Citizen* for supporting the Liberal-Conservatives and strengthening Orangeism. Irish Catholics, it was resolved, should withdraw their patronage from both newspapers, and read the *True Witness* until a new Irish Catholic newspaper was established in Toronto.[61]

McGee's enemies countered that the meeting had been called at short notice and stacked with men who supported McGee's strategy. Far from being carried unanimously, they claimed, the resolutions had been passed by only one vote after a five-hour debate, and even then the result had been rigged.[62] A protest meeting the following week attracted more than three hundred people, and the *Mirror* stepped up its attacks on McGee.[63] Meanwhile, the *Catholic Citizen* went into ad hominem overdrive against the McGee-Brown alliance. In what George Clerk called a "furious article," Hayes declared that McGee had sold out his religion by supporting an anti-Catholic hate-monger like Brown. But that was just the kind of person McGee was, Hayes wrote; he was possessed by an "evil spirit" and had a "monomania for quarrel with men of his own race and creed."[64] Henceforth, Hayes would describe McGee as "the Catholic Clear Grit" or, reaching for the ultimate insult, a "Cromwellian Catholic."[65]

Normally, McGee would have countered these attacks in his own newspaper. But the *New Era* had ceased publication and may itself have been a victim of the emerging McGee-Brown alliance. While McGee was attending Parliament in Toronto, the paper had been edited in Montreal by Michael Hickey. But in April, when McGee was moving towards the alliance, Hickey resigned because of unspecified political differences with McGee. The location of the capital may have been one issue (with Hickey preferring Ottawa over Montreal), and McGee's new direction could have been another.[66] Without a Montreal editor, the paper could no longer be sustained; the last issue appeared on 1 May 1858, and McGee's long career as a newspaper editor came to an end. He had finally realized the ambition he had expressed fourteen years earlier of escaping from "type-setting as a profession."[67]

Without a newspaper, McGee answered his critics in an "Address to the Catholic Public," which Clerk generously published in the *True Witness*. Here, he restated his premise that the Orange Order, with its Liberal-Conservative connections, was the greatest menace facing Irish Catholics. It was thus essential to work with the opposition, he argued, and to recognize that George Brown and his Scottish supporters were "the controlling element, at this hour, in Canada West." "Some of our friends," he wrote, "have a *monomania* on Scotchmen, and have too often given imprudent expression to that feeling. I never could see the wisdom of making enemies of so numerous and respectable a body; and I have, without departing one inch from the line of rigid self-respect, endeavoured steadily to diminish that bitter antagonism, and to substitute in its stead a better and friendlier spirit."[68]

This was a gradual process, he continued, that required both patience and persistence. But it would only work if Brown gave "con-

vincing proofs of a different spirit, from the spirit of the *Globe* during
the late election"; the idea was cooperation, not capitulation. Clarify-
ing his position on representation by population, McGee maintained
that "a revision of our whole constitutional system cannot be far off"
and that "in any new arrangement, the representation in the popular
branch at all events, must be proportionate to population." But – and
it was a crucial qualification – there also had to be "constitutional safeguards" for Canada East, and these safeguards had to be sanctioned by
a majority of that area's population. In this way, Brown's insistence on
representation by population could be balanced with the protection
of Catholic rights. Such an arrangement, McGee argued, would settle
ethnoreligious tensions and thus "tend to hasten the advent of a genuine Canadian Nationality, co-extensive with the country, and enduring as its hills."[69]

It was an impressive defence and did much to strengthen his position
in Canada West. To disseminate his message to the widest possible Irish
Catholic audience, McGee and his supporters in Toronto's St Patrick's
Association had already started raising money for their own newspaper. In July they bought up the *Catholic Citizen*, which went down
spitting fire at "D'Arky McGee" for bringing the "curse of division"
into Canada.[70] Its replacement was the *Canadian Freeman*, published by
James Mallon and edited by James Moylan. McGee and Moylan had
first met in 1852, when McGee was petitioning US President Millard
Fillmore to take up the cause of the Irish prisoners in Australia and
Moylan was working in the Chilean Consulate in Washington. Since
then, Moylan had moved to Canada, where he taught classics and English literature at Guelph; as a former correspondent for the *New York
Times* and a long-standing admirer of McGee, he was an ideal candidate for the new editorial post.[71]

In line with McGee's position, the *Canadian Freeman* stood for separate schools and against the Orange Order. Unless the public press
resolutely opposed Orangeism, ran the paper's prospectus, "counter
Associations may spring up, to the incalculable detriment of society at
large"; the influence of McGee is unmistakable. Bishop de Charbonnel was sufficiently impressed to give the paper $100, along with his
moral support, although he insisted that the *Freeman* must be pol-

itically independent and must defend the interests of the church. In contrast, his colleague Adolphe Pinsonneault, the Catholic bishop of London, refused to endorse a newspaper that was designed to prop up "the declining popularity of Mr. McGee who has so outrageously disappointed the expectations of all Catholics by an unnatural alliance with Brown & Co." "The Catholic party is now irretrievably split up and smashed to pieces," he told de Charbonnel, "thanks to the great Orator McGee in open alliance with the *Rouges* and the *Clear grits*."[72]

The Achilles' heel of that alliance, as Bishop Pinsonneault realized, was the Catholic education question. It was one thing to find common ground on the issue of representation by population with constitutional safeguards, but quite another to overcome the seemingly insuperable differences between McGee and Brown about separate schools. The issue came up in Parliament that June, when Thomas Ferguson introduced his annual bill to abolish separate schools in Canada West. Drawing on the arguments he had been making since 1851, McGee set out to demolish the case for a common school system; his speech was so powerful that it was still being deployed in educational debates during the 1930s.[73] Such a system, he said, put the demands of the state above the needs of the family; it attempted to impose an "all-devouring uniformity" on the students; and it exposed Catholic children to teachers who despised their religion. Against the view that there was no danger in teaching children of different faiths the alphabet or the multiplication tables, McGee argued that the whole environment of common schools was morally polluted, and he insisted that "every lesson in reason, shall be accompanied by a lesson in revelation, as a rider, as a safeguard." "I, as a parent," he declared, "am not willing to risk the experiment of exercising only a Sunday revision over the imbedded errors and false impressions of the week."[74]

Above all, McGee maintained, education was the responsibility of the parents, not the state, and it was the duty of Catholic parents to ensure that their children were brought up in the One True Faith, rather than being treated as merely one "sect" among many. "I may be charged with illiberality in thus frankly stating my opinions, and those of every Catholic in communion with his Church," he acknowledged, but "there is not a Catholic layman 'in good standing,' knowing something of his own religion, on either side of the Atlantic, who does not hold unmixed secular instruction to be an evil of the most dangerous kind, fatal to the faith and morals of his children."[75]

This was not exactly music to the ears of George Brown, who voted in favour of Ferguson's bill.[76] Yet in the middle of McGee's speech, there was a potential opening for further discussion on the subject. "Nine-tenths of the Laity," he said, "are opposed, and will be opposed to the common school system, unless some such modifications could be introduced into it, as exist in the National system of Ireland. There the Priest is always the Visitor, and usually the Patron of the school, and two afternoons in the week are set apart for religious instruction. This is in accordance with the primary idea of education existing in the Catholic mind."[77] The Irish educational system, McGee believed, could provide an example for Canada West.

In Ireland, the Whig government had attempted in 1831 to solve that country's equally vexatious educational question with a non-denominational system in which children had a common education but separate religious instruction. The idea was to bring children of different faiths together while respecting their religious differences. The reality, however, turned out to be quite different. Because most Irish people preferred denominational education, the national schools soon came under attack from all sides. As the pressure mounted, the system became modified to the point at which increasing numbers of children were educated only with their co-religionists. Although mixed education existed in theory, there was a high degree of religious segregation in practice – hence McGee's favourable comments.[78] In political terms, the virtue of the Irish educational system lay in its vagueness; Brown could focus on the theory, McGee could focus on the practice, and some kind of mutually acceptable arrangement might be reached.

McGee, then, was prepared to compromise with Brown on the question of representation by population, provided that there were safeguards for Canada East. And he was prepared to consider a compromise with

Brown on the educational issue, provided that Catholic students continued to be educated in a Catholic environment. But would Brown be willing to make similar conciliatory moves? The answer came at the end of July, when Macdonald and Cartier resigned after losing a vote in the House, and the governor general, Sir Edmund Head, called on Brown to form a government. In the course of negotiations with Antoine-Aimé Dorion of the *Rouges*, Brown agreed to representation by population with constitutional guarantees for Canada East. On the question of education, Brown agreed that a modified version of the Irish National School system could settle the education controversy in Canada West. Not only that, but the supposedly ultra-Protestant bigot actually formed a cabinet with a majority of Catholics.[79]

Although he probably did not know it, McGee figured in the discussions about the new cabinet. A prominent French Canadian liberal, Joseph-Élie Thibaudeau, urged Brown to make McGee one of his ministers.[80] That did not happen, but Brown promised McGee that there would be an inquiry into the ways in which the Irish educational system could be applied in Canada, and may have planned to send him to Ireland for that purpose.[81] The Reform alliance, it seemed, was paying dividends.

And then everything came crashing down. Brown's government was defeated after only two days in office, in circumstances that drove McGee to paroxysms of fury about the Conservatives and the governor general. According to constitutional custom, new cabinet ministers had to resign and run for re-election before taking office. This meant that the Brown-Dorion administration temporarily had twelve fewer members in the House, pending their re-election. Seizing the opportunity, Macdonald and Cartier immediately defeated the government on a vote of confidence, formed a new coalition, and were invited back into power by the governor general.

This, of course, meant that the new Conservative cabinet members were themselves expected to resign and run for re-election. There was, however, a loophole; the custom did not apply to ministers who changed cabinet posts. Accordingly, Macdonald shuffled the deck so that all the Liberal-Conservative ministers had different offices. And then, the following day, he shuffled them back into their original port-

folios – and back into a government that was to last for three more
years. The Double Shuffle, it was called – "the kind of event that per-
suades historians not to write about nineteenth-century politics," as
historian Christopher Moore put it.[82] From one perspective – that of
the Liberal-Conservatives – it was simply smart politics. From another – that of the Reformers – it was a cheap and shabby trick.

In Parliament, McGee launched a blistering attack on the Liberal-
Conservatives. Arguing that the Brown-Dorion ministry could have
settled the sectarian and sectional tensions in Canada, he condemned
the Double Shuffle as an "outrage upon justice and fair play," as a "solemn farce" that had been worked out in advance between Macdonald
and the governor general.[83] Two years earlier, McGee had criticized
Edmund Head for publicly receiving Orange lodges in Toronto on the
Twelfth of July.[84] Now, McGee viewed Head's refusal to call an election after Brown's defeat as another example of prejudice from a supposedly impartial governor general.

All this was too much for Macdonald, who declared that McGee's
accusations were "false as Hell!" and asserted that McGee's attack on
the sovereign's representative in Canada was part of a pattern. "He has
carried to this country," Macdonald said, "the disloyalty which he displayed in his own."[85] For the first time in Parliament, McGee's revolutionary past was being used against him; the jibe of "rebel" and "traitor" would continue to dog his steps.

"I am as loyal to the institutions under which I live in Canada as any
Tory of the old or new school," he replied. "My native disposition is
towards reverence for things old, and veneration for the landmarks of
the past." But in Ireland, he explained, he had been moved to rebellion
when he saw "children and women as well as able-bodied men perish-
ing for food under the richest government, within the most powerful
empire of the world," and when two million lives were sacrificed for
the "bankrupt aristocracy" and the "corn buyers of Liverpool." True,
his revolutionary response had been "rash and ill-guided," he acknowledged, but he was only twenty-two years old at the time. Besides,
if Canada had experienced something similar to the Irish famine, it
would have been extremely unlikely that his fellow MPs would "tamely
submit to such a state of things." Had Macdonald "lived in Ireland in

those days," he declared, twisting the knife, "I could, no doubt, have found him among the oppressors of that people – for he is of the very timber for an Irish imitation of Toryism."[86]

---

The Liberal-Conservatives had completely outmanoeuvred the Reformers, and McGee's anger reflected the frustration of defeat. But Brown's two-day administration and the Double Shuffle had significantly altered the political landscape, not least by demonstrating that Brown, long derided as a "governmental impossibility," was in fact prepared to work with Catholics and was willing to compromise on the key issues of representation by population and religious education. The formation of the Reform government seemed to validate McGee's strategy; the circumstances of its defeat only deepened his contempt for the Liberal-Conservatives.

The Reform alliance, McGee believed, was the key to Canada's future. It could secure representation by population with constitutional safeguards for Canada East. It could settle the education question and thus lower the sectarian temperature, creating a climate in which Orangeism and Ribbonism would fade into insignificance. It could lay the groundwork for Confederation and the new northern nationality. And it could, as he later put it, "restore the Constitution shattered and debased by six years of Coalition debauchery of every description, and … place it for the future, by the application of new safeguards, beyond the power of any Cabinet, or any Governor General, to prostitute to the purposes of personal, factious, or mercenary men."[87] Over the next five years, he would attempt to realize these goals through the Reform Party, in the teeth of Orange opposition, a skeptical and increasingly hostile Catholic Church, and a small but growing Fenian movement in Canada.

## CHAPTER THREE

# An Open Debatable Space
## August 1858 – November 1859

Having committed himself to a centrist alliance that embraced Protestant Reformers, French Canadian liberals, and Irish Catholics, McGee began "working with all his might" to secure the re-election of the Reform cabinet ministers who had resigned before the Double Shuffle. John A. Macdonald was so alarmed by McGee's campaigning that he attempted to enlist Catholic clergymen to counter his influence – a somewhat unorthodox strategy for an Orangeman.[1] Meanwhile, in Toronto, an Irish Catholic meeting at St Lawrence Hall endorsed the Reform Party, despite the best efforts of McGee's old enemy Michael Hayes who stood on the chairman's table in protest, and had to be pulled down before the resolution could be passed.[2] According to the Orange press, McGee's influence over the city's Irish Catholics gave George Brown his victory in the by-election.[3] Although this was almost certainly an exaggeration, the McGee-Brown alliance and the pro-Reform Irish Catholic vote meant that Brown had a vested interest in toning down his earlier anti-Catholic rhetoric – another sign that McGee's strategy was working.

Over the next few weeks, McGee went from strength to strength, riding a wave of Reform anger about the Double Shuffle. In common with other Reformers, he directed much of that anger at the governor general, whom he blamed for orchestrating the defeat of the Brown-Dorion government. Together with Dorion and Luther Holton, McGee urged the Reform cabinet ministers to present their case to the colonial secretary, Sir Edward Bulwer-Lytton; shortly afterwards, he organized a petition for Head's recall.[4] Joining Brown on a public tour, McGee became a regular speaker at Reform banquets, denouncing the

government as "rotten and corrupt," and calling for a written constitution, a federal system of government, and a parliamentary inquiry to
settle the schools question.[5] "McGee's course has made him eminently
popular," commented Brown after reading the speech. "He is received
like a prince in every direction."[6]

———

McGee's growing popularity resulted not only from his stand against
the Double Shuffle but also from his more general activities on the lecture circuit. Since the spring of 1858, he had given dozens of talks in
cities and towns throughout Canada, attracting large audiences and receiving positive reviews. His lecture on Patrick Sarsfield in Montreal's
City Concert Hall drew over two thousand people, who responded
with "loud and prolonged cheers."[7] In Stratford, his talk on "The Future of Canada" was described as "an intellectual treat of the highest
order."[8] At St Lawrence Hall in Toronto, he delivered a lecture on
"The Political Morality of Shakespeare's Plays" before a standing-room
audience that included George Brown. Shakespeare, he argued, was "a
hater of despotism and usurpation, a lover of loyalty and order and law,
a satirist of sycophancy and meanness, a respecter of the magistracy,
the clergy, and old age" – someone who, surprisingly enough, would
have been quite at home in the Reform Party. Again, the reviews
were outstanding, with references to his "masterful ability" and "brilliant talents."[9]

As he travelled through the country, McGee established a network of
friends and supporters, and countered the rumours about his past that
had followed him to Canada. His altercations in New York with Archbishop John Hughes and his controversies with other leading American
Catholics had cast shadows of doubt about his religious integrity. Now,
through public lectures and private conversations, through the sheer
force of his personality, he reassured many of his co-religionists that he
was indeed a devout Catholic.[10]

Other compatriots were more concerned about his political history, especially the recurrent story that he had betrayed his imprisoned
Young Ireland colleagues in 1848 by publicly proclaiming their revo-

lutionary intentions while they were awaiting trial. One of McGee's admirers was so troubled by this that he wrote to William Smith O'Brien, the leader of the rising of 1848, for clarification. O'Brien replied that McGee had indeed written a public letter defending the revolutionary movement and that in doing so he had unintentionally endangered the lives of the Young Ireland prisoners. But O'Brien exonerated McGee from the charge of betrayal, praised his efforts for the liberation of the prisoners, and expressed the hope that he would rise to a pre-eminent position in Canadian politics. This kind of endorsement, which was subsequently published in the *Canadian Freeman*, could only improve McGee's career prospects.[11]

His lecture tours connected him with the St Patrick's Societies that were springing up throughout the country – a development that he welcomed and encouraged. Such societies, he said, should be formed "wherever fifty Catholics were to be found."[12] As well as strengthening a sense of Irish Catholic communal identity in different localities, they provided McGee with an informal and loose-knit organizational base in Canada West. In places such as Stratford, Port Hope, Kingston, and Perth, the societies endorsed the Reform alliance and toasted McGee as "a True Irishman, and consistent lover of his Country."[13]

Watching these developments, his Orange enemies accused McGee of establishing "a series of Ribbon Lodges, with the view of gaining control of the Roman Catholic vote for political objects."[14] The charge of Ribbonism was patently absurd, but the Orangemen were right about the Catholic character and political purpose of the societies. While McGee wanted to work with liberal Protestants, he had no problem about joining exclusively Catholic organizations. In Montreal, for example, he became the president of the St Patrick's Literary Association, which had been formed with the approval of Bishop Bourget to counter the dangerously ecumenical Irish National and Literary Association, where Catholics might be corrupted by mixing with Protestants.[15]

While the St Patrick's Societies helped to build up grassroots support, Moylan's *Canadian Freeman* disseminated McGee's message to a broad Irish Catholic audience. In return, McGee urged his friends to keep the newspaper afloat as it struggled financially during the winter of 1858–59. If the *Canadian Freeman* went under, he wrote, it would be "an irreparable loss" – "for, without organs … what are we, and where are we?"[16] He also held out the promise of patronage once the Reformers came to power. If the paper could keep going until the next election, McGee told Moylan in November 1858, its editor would have "an assured income *for life*."[17] More than eighteen months later, with no election in sight, he repeated the message: "I cannot long be kept out of my rank, but in the interim, I am most anxious to carry you with me, to final success."[18] Meanwhile, in Parliament, he was criticizing the Conservatives for giving lucrative publishing contracts to the pro-government press.[19]

All this – the lecture tours, the networking, the St Patrick's Societies, the promises of patronage – helped to build McGee's Irish Catholic base in Canada West. There was, in his view, no contradiction between his particular appeal to Irish Catholics and his wider Canadian nationalism. McGee wanted to protect and promote his religion by strengthening Catholic schools, encouraging a Catholic associational culture, and establishing Catholic political unity. As a confident and coherent ethnoreligious group, Irish Catholics could advance their interests and the good of the country by cooperating with liberal Protestants in constructing the new nationality and by ensuring that minority rights were a central component of the Canadian polity.

This project received an enormous boost in November 1858 when the Reformers and *Rouges* from Canada East, including McGee, organized a banquet in Montreal to celebrate the alliance between Brown and Dorion. In front of seven hundred guests, along with the "elegantly-attired ladies seated in the gallery," Brown made his first public appearance in Montreal and proclaimed unity between Reformers in English and French Canada. McGee was among the many speakers who welcomed Brown to the city. The Liberal-Conservatives, he argued, were rotten to the core: "Their faith is in corruption, their hope is in corruption, and their creed is corruption itself," he said to loud cheers. The Brown-Dorion alliance, he continued, would bring honest government to the country and ensure a new era of harmony between French-speaking and English-speaking Canadians. Brown appeared equally optimistic; the event, reported the *Globe*, was "a triumphant success," which dispelled ancient prejudices and energized the cause of liberalism in Canada East.[20]

————•◦•————

All this made McGee a prime target for the Liberal-Conservatives, who had a field day contrasting his earlier ultramontane writings with Brown's earlier ultra-Protestant writings. Canadian Orangemen happily caricatured McGee as the string-puller who had turned Brown into a puppet of the papists. The Brown-Dorion administration was dubbed the "McGee cabinet," and Brown was pilloried as "*the* hypocrite of the age" who would "say and do anything for the sake of office"; the same charge was levelled against McGee himself.[21]

Much of the attack focused on the schools question and McGee's plan to restructure Canadian education along Irish lines. The Irish education experiment, argued the Toronto *Patriot*, had been a disaster for Protestantism; it was "thoroughly Popish," it allowed nunneries, monasteries, and convents to take money from public funds, and it was "most distasteful to all denominations of Protestants in that country." Any attempt to implement a similar system in Canada would have similar results; the door would be open for "Popery," and McGee's Catholics would come rushing through.[22]

The most comprehensive criticism of Brown's and McGee's educational policy, however, came from Egerton Ryerson, the superintendent of schools for Canada West. In a series of newspaper letters that were eventually published in book form, Ryerson effectively demolished McGee's claim that Presbyterians, Anglicans, and Catholics supported the Irish National School system, and pointed out that the Catholic hierarchy had recently condemned the national schools "as not even yet sufficiently under their control." "The basis, therefore, of your whole scheme of School importation from Ireland being manifestly baseless," Ryerson wrote, "the scheme itself falls to the ground; and the hasty adoption of it, without any proper examination, is shown to be a grave political mistake, and very great folly." In fact, he noted, the educational system in Canada West had been modelled on the Irish system as it had originally been conceived in 1831, before it "succumbed to the

aggressions of the Roman Catholic hierarchy." And he should know;
after all, the idea of basing Canada's school system on Irish precedents had been his in the first place. By the time he had finished, Ryerson had made it abundantly clear that a compromise between Brown
and McGee on religious education was impossible. Time would prove
him right.[23]

Rather than dealing with Ryerson's specific points, McGee accused
him of being in the pocket of the government – the same government
that had bribed the press to spread lies about the Reform Party and
remained in power only through corruption. Speaking on the subject
in the legislature, McGee maintained that the government acquiesced
in the existing educational system only as a matter of expediency, and
that Ryerson's attitude to separate schools was one of "quiet discour-
agement." It was true, McGee added, that he and Brown disagreed
over separate schools, but at least they faced up to their differences and
were working to reach a solution; however, he did not say exactly how
these differences could be reconciled, just as he did not answer Ryerson's objections to the Irish National School system. Charges of corruption and a recourse to generalities were no substitute for reasoned
argument. Ironically, given McGee's comments about "facing up to
differences," the *Globe*'s coverage of his speech omitted the part in
which he disagreed with Brown. A large degree of evasiveness on the
schools question was an integral part of the McGee-Brown alliance.[24]

During the fall and early winter of 1858, the attacks on McGee emanated from the ministerial press; between February and May 1859, they
were conducted primarily in Parliament. No holds were barred; the
rules of engagement were robust, and the invective flew in all directions. McGee contended that the government's "unmeasured abuse"
was directed not only at himself but at the 300,000 Irish Catholics
whose interests he represented. His enemies quickly twisted his words
into a boast that he had 300,000 Irish men-at-arms behind him, and
ridiculed him for having delusions of grandeur.[25]

McGee's recently published *Canadian Ballads and Occasional Verses*
provided further ammunition. A book that historians and literary
scholars have viewed as a landmark of Canadian cultural national-

T. D'Arcy McGee, in full dress as General of the 300,000 Irishmen.

### D'ARCY McGEE.

#### I.

Than the sweetest, thou art sweeter—
                                    D'Arcy McGee.
Than the wisest, thou'rt discreeter—
                                    D'Arcy McGee.
For love hath thy career been noted;
Concord and peace hast thou promoted,
Ever to union's cause devoted—
                                    D'Arcy McGee.

#### II.

Hast thou made no brother weaker?
                                    D'Arcy McGee.
Has thou left alone the Speaker?
                                    D'Arcy McGee.
How many in thy snares entrapped thee?
Hath Sydney Smith, poor worm, escaped thee?
In charity thy speeches shaped thee,
                                    D'Arcy McGee.

#### III.

Oh! take in time a warning,
                                    D'Arcy McGee.
To Virtue's path returning,
                                    D'Arcy McGee.
Quit then the ranks of an unequal war,
Put not repentance off to hour afar;
If thou must shine be not a wayward star,
                                    D'Arcy McGee.

This caricature of Thomas D'Arcy McGee, combining the stereotypical Irish hat and shillelagh with a Napoleonic pose, mocked McGee's claim to represent 300,000 Irish Catholic Canadians. The poem was a parody of McGee's "God Be Praised," a favourite target of his Conservative opponents. Both the caricature and the poem were almost certainly the work of James McCarroll, an Irish Canadian satirist whose *Letters of Terry Finnegan* (Toronto, 1864) criticized McGee for his alliance with George Brown. (*The Grumbler*, 31 March 1860)

ism became in its immediate context the target of more anti-McGee invective. His poem "God Be Praised" received particular attention; McGee's description of his daughter having "eyes blue as ocean water" drew derisory laughter, as did the lines

> I have been no base self-seeker;
> With the mildest, I am meeker;
> I have made no brother weaker,
>    God be praised![26]

McGee was mocked mercilessly for bragging about his meekness and for trying to pass himself off as a poet – bragging and bad poetry being stereotypically Irish Catholic traits.[27] Other opponents went further still. One Liberal-Conservative politician described him as "a resuscitated monkey," combining simian images of the Catholic Irish with a reference to McGee's supposedly African features.[28]

All this, McGee countered, merely confirmed the anti-Irish Catholic prejudice of the Liberal-Conservatives and underlined the poverty of their position. He also tried a little mockery of his own. "Why was such singular unanimity in attacking him displayed by hon. gentlemen opposite, who agreed in little else save the desire of hanging on to office?" he asked. "He could not tell ... It was, however, similar to the direction marked on the brief sent to the barrister – 'No case, but abuse the plaintiff's attorney.'"[29] (The fact that he had just done this with Ryerson apparently did not occur to him.) More generally, McGee deplored the descent into personal attacks, even if he sometimes failed to live up to his own standards. Warning that the "spirit of disunion" was growing stronger in Canada West, McGee attributed this in part to "the imputation of motives, the convicting, arraigning and indicting by one member of another member, co-equals on the floor of the House, with a harshness and severity which would not be tolerated in private life."[30]

———•—•———

As the parliamentary session proceeded, the Liberal-Conservatives introduced a series of wedge issues, which were designed to divide the

Reformers and strengthen their own position.[31] Among these issues was the decision that the legislature would move from Toronto to Quebec City while the parliamentary buildings were being constructed for the new capital city of Ottawa. Brown and his supporters regarded the move to Quebec City as a colossal waste of money, paid for largely by the taxpayers of Canada West and designed with the crass motive of buying French Canadian support to keep the government in power – arguments that did not go down well in Canada East. For his part, McGee continued to argue that Montreal should have been made the capital, and on these grounds voted with Brown against the government.[32]

Equally challenging was Alexander Galt's bill to reduce Canada's accelerating public debt by increasing tariffs. The Reformers in Canada West complained that their section of the union would bear a disproportionate burden of the costs while Montreal's financial interests would reap the benefits. McGee, as we have seen, supported selective protectionism as part of his nation-building strategy and had voted for the government's tariff in 1858. He was still "a little of a Protectionist" but opposed some of the specifics of Galt's new bill, such as the increased tariff on tea and sugar. As with the location of the capital, he voted with Brown against the government, but for rather different reasons.[33]

The most divisive issue, however, arose from the seigneurial system, which the government had abolished in 1854 with promises of compensation for the seigneurs. But the cost of compensation exceeded expectations, opening up the problem of payment. The government decided that the financial burden should be met by Canada as a whole; in contrast, Brown's Reformers maintained that the seigneurial system was a uniquely French Canadian problem and that the extra costs should be covered entirely by French Canadians. McGee, in common with just about everyone else in Canada East, believed that the costs should be shared by all Canadians, and opposed Brown's position. Almost all the Reform and *Rouge* MPs from Canada East voted with the government, and twelve of them, including McGee, met afterwards to inform Brown of their "great dissatisfaction" with his policy.[34] This was a far cry from the euphoric display of unity among Reformers from Canada

West and Canada East when Brown had visited Montreal the previous November; the sectional stresses of the union were putting a severe strain on the Brown-Dorion alliance.

———·••·———

While the Liberal-Conservatives attacked McGee's position on separate schools, mocked his personality and his poetry, and attempted to prize apart the Brown-Dorion alliance, radical Irish Catholics criticized him for failing to take a sufficiently strong stand against Orangeism. Their complaints centred on his continuing efforts to end the St Patrick's Day parade in Toronto, and his remarks at the city's Young Men's St Patrick's Association meeting on 17 March 1859, when he congratulated the association for holding a peaceful meeting rather than "any draggletail procession through the muddy thoroughfares of this great city." Such processions, he added, "had done more to bring ridicule upon the Irish people than ever they brought good."[35]

McGee's position did indeed reduce Catholic-Protestant tensions in Toronto, but at the price of heightening divisions among the city's Irish Catholics. The main opposition in Toronto came from the Hibernian Benevolent Society, which was not yet powerful enough to challenge McGee and the Young Men's St Patrick's Association. But the Hibernians found an influential ally in Bernard Devlin from Montreal. A lawyer with a revolutionary background (he had supported the Irish Republican Union's plan to invade Canada in 1848), Devlin had met McGee at the Buffalo Convention of February 1856. He was part of the group that invited McGee to Montreal and had seconded McGee's nomination as a candidate during the election campaign of December 1857.[36] Since then, however, Devlin had become "strongly hostile" to McGee; Devlin had initially opposed the Reform alliance and believed that McGee was not promoting Irish Catholic interests vigorously enough.[37] Now, after reading McGee's St Patrick's Day speech, with its dismissive remark about "draggletail processions," Devlin went directly – but anonymously – on the attack.

"Is it thus," Devlin asked, "and with such vulgar slang, that a Catholic Irishman should designate a solemn procession, sanctified by his religion, personally participated in by the Priests of his Church, and exclusively composed of his countrymen — the people to whom he belongs?" McGee's words, he added, were "a public insult to every man, priest or layman, here or elsewhere, who ever took part in the annual procession on St. Patrick's Day." Not only had McGee disparaged processions that celebrated Irishness and Catholicism; he had also caved in to Orange threats — something that would never happen in Montreal. At the very least, Devlin concluded, McGee must publicly apologize for his offensive comments.[38]

No apology was forthcoming, of course, and McGee continued to command widespread Irish Catholic support in Montreal. Devlin and "half a dozen other grumblers are occasionally audible," he told a friend in April, "but the great unspoiled majority" were in a "good mood with their Irish Member."[39] The mood was doubtless helped by McGee's parliamentary efforts to defend Irish Catholic interests and uphold Catholic moral teaching. He had helped to turn back yet another of Thomas Ferguson's bills against separate schools, had presented sixty-three petitions to Parliament for separate school reform, and had publicized a "series of outrages" against Catholics in St Thomas, where Orangemen had attacked a priest and religious tensions remained high.[40] As a good Catholic who had upheld patriarchal family values in the United States and had attacked abortion in Montreal, McGee also took an uncompromising anti-divorce position in Parliament.

The issue arose when the House received a petition for divorce from one John McLean, whose wife had gone to the United States with another man; this meant that he could not remarry without committing bigamy. McGee sympathized with his case and said he had no doubt that McLean was "a very much injured man" whose wife was a "wretched woman"; but the sanctity of marriage was a fundamental moral principle that must never be violated by any legislative body. It was the principle that mattered, McGee insisted; if McLean's petition was granted, more petitions would follow, the marriage tie would become as weak in Canada as it already was in the United States, and the "moral welfare" of the country would be fatally undermined. McGee, along with virtually all the Catholics in the legislature, voted

against the petition; virtually all the Protestants voted in favour. The
Catholics won.[41]

McGee's political stock also remained high in Toronto, where his
popularity was enhanced by the visit of William Smith O'Brien to the
city in early May. Partly because of his role in the rising of 1848 and
partly because of his subsequent imprisonment in Australia, O'Brien
had become a symbol of Irish courage, resistance, and suffering during
the famine. Anyone who could attach himself to such an iconic figure
would reap significant political benefits. And so, before a crowd of
some three thousand admirers assembled outside the Rossin House
Hotel, the representatives of the city's different and mutually antagon-
istic Irish Catholic organizations pretended to forget their differences
and competed with one another in speeches of welcome.

James Moylan, the new president of the Young Men's St Patrick's
Association, praised O'Brien's patriotism. Up next was Patrick O'Neill,
who strongly opposed Moylan's and McGee's position on the Reform
alliance and St Patrick's Day parades; he reminded the crowd that in
1850 he had organized a petition with seventy-five thousand signatures
to set O'Brien free and that the Canadian parliament had subsequently
passed a resolution for his release. O'Neill was followed by Michael
Murphy, president of the Hibernian Benevolent Society and founder
of Fenianism in Canada, who described O'Brien as "an honoured son
of Ireland."

Returning the thanks, O'Brien spoke of his earlier efforts to encourage emigration to Canada and told the audience, "You have now in this
country that self-government for which I was contending in Ireland."
But that was as far as he got. There was so much pushing and jostling
in the crowd that his speech was disrupted; just as he resumed, another
delegation approached, accompanied by a band that drowned him out.
O'Brien had never liked these occasions and used the opportunity to
cut his speech short. At that point, McGee came to the balcony, to be
greeted with "loud cheering and waving of hats." When the noise had
subsided, he gave his own tribute to "the representative of the hospit-
able race which once had also its Halls of Legislature, and which yet
will again have its Halls of Legislature"; some of the old Irish nationalist blood was stirring. At the same time, he continued to emphasize the

The Rossin House Hotel, Toronto. Here, William Smith O'Brien addressed a crowd of three thousand Irish Canadians during his visit to Toronto in 1859. In his speech of welcome, McGee looked forward to the day when Ireland would once again have its own legislature. (City of Toronto Archives, Fonds 1498, item 12)

importance of order and decorum. Just as he wanted to avoid trouble on St Patrick's Day, McGee wanted the crowd to go home peacefully and show that they could "unite the warmest enthusiasm and the highest patriotism with the humblest deference to and obedience to the law." And go home peacefully they did, after more music and fireworks.[42]

Later that day, O'Brien visited Parliament, where he was introduced to "several of the leading members of both Houses and "invited to take a seat on the floor of each house – an honor reserved for distinguished individuals," as he informed his daughter. McGee and O'Brien had last met in July 1848, shortly before McGee had travelled to Scotland to rally support for the revolution and O'Brien had tried to raise the South. Now, in the most Orange city in Canada, they shared a few hours in the legislature – the rising Reform MP and the veteran nationalist leader, revolutionaries who in their different ways had become

Toronto from the top of the Rossin House Hotel. The view north along York Street, towards Osgoode Hall. In Smith O'Brien's estimation, the "town of Toronto is not particularly interesting as its site is not very picturesque … Like almost all other American towns of recent origin … [it] contains no anti-quarian remains that can interest a traveller." (O'Brien to his daughter [prob-ably Lucy Josephine], 16 May 1859, William Smith O'Brien Papers, NLI, MS 8653 [33]) (City of Toronto Archives, Fonds 1498, item 16)

respectable. It is not known how they got on, though their subse-quent correspondence about literary matters was cordial enough. But O'Brien's impression of Toronto was less than enthusiastic; the city, he told his daughter, was "not particularly interesting." In a detailed letter about his Canadian visit, he made no mention of McGee.[43]

O'Brien's visit coincided with the last day of the parliamentary ses-sion. Shortly afterwards, McGee returned to Montreal and reflected upon his experiences over the previous months. "There is probably no country in the world in which so many various and opposite balancing interests are combined together, and in which the problem of constitu-tional government has more serious difficulties in its way," he told his constituents.[44] During the summer, he addressed these difficulties in "Four Letters to a Friend," which were published in the *Canadian Freeman* and which served as a manifesto for the Reform alliance. "These letters," McGee told Brown, "though intended mainly to give fixity of public purpose, to my own friends – to put arguments in their mouths in defence of their and my own course, since the last Elections – and to strengthen and extend that feeling with a view to future elections – are written with all the care for the general, common strength, of the Opposition, which I could bestow on them."[45]

He began by outlining the general state of Canadian politics and what would later be called the "double minority" status of Irish Catholics – their position as a religious minority in English-speaking Canada and as a linguistic minority within the Catholic Church, occupying "an open debatable space" between the British and the French populations, and regarded by each side as subservient to its own interests.[46] How, then, could Irish Catholics negotiate their way through the "manifold intricacies" of their situation and act for themselves? In Canada East, he wrote, they were natural allies of the *Rouges*, who had established their liberal credentials by attacking Orangeism, and their Catholic credentials by voting against divorce. In Canada West, they shared the central political principles of the Reform Party: a broad popular suffrage, responsible government, economical administration, low taxation, and a long-standing hostility to Toryism.[47]

From here, McGee called for thoroughgoing constitutional reform, with representation by population, a written constitution and a Bill of Rights. Turning his attention to the schools question, he stressed the importance of approaching the subject through "a patient and thorough investigation into our own and other systems; the best possible temper in the discussion of remedies, and a high degree of moral courage." On all these counts, he added, the Liberal-Conservatives had been found wanting – which was not surprising, since the party was really "the mere external mask of a blind, insensate Orangeism." The way ahead, McGee concluded, was to give Brown a fair trial on the issue, in the spirit of letting bygones be bygones.[48]

None of this was original; McGee had made all the arguments before, in a series of public lectures, after-dinner speeches, and parliamentary debates. But this was the first time that he had set out his views in a sustained and systematic fashion – and in doing so, he opened up a full-scale debate about the Reform alliance. "The letters I think will make some stir," McGee told Moylan in June.[49] And so they did. As might be expected, Cartier's *Bleus*, Macdonald's Liberal-Conservatives, and the Orange Order completely rejected his arguments. More striking, though, was the reaction from the leaders of the Catholic Church. While Conservatives and Orangemen condemned McGee for being too Catholic, prominent figures within the church criticized him for not being Catholic enough – or for not being a true Catholic at all.

At the forefront of the Catholic campaign against the McGee-Brown alliance was George Clerk, the editor of the *True Witness*. As someone who opposed McGee's Reform strategy right from the start, Clerk had consoled himself earlier in 1859 with the belief that the alliance was inherently unstable and thus doomed to failure. On the key Catholic questions of separate schools and divorce, he pointed out, McGee and Brown had voted on opposite sides. When McGee and his colleagues in Canada East rejected Brown's position on seigneurial compensation, Clerk persuaded himself that the alliance was effectively over.[50] But as it became clear that this was not the case, he returned to the offensive; indeed, it was Clerk's attacks in the *True Witness* that had prompted McGee to write his "Four Letters" in the first place.[51]

Now Clerk launched a full frontal assault. How could McGee sustain an alliance with the Clear Grits, whom he had once denounced as being even worse than the Orangemen? How could he support George Brown, the "Prince of Orangeism" and one of the greatest enemies of Catholic education? Why did not McGee work for an independent pan-Catholic alliance that would make improved separate school legislation its top priority? Did McGee not realize that representation by population was an English-Canadian plot to revive the Protestant Ascendancy and the suppression of Popery? There was only one possible explanation: The man was driven by political ambition, by "love of self," by the desire for "a Government situation." All those rumours that McGee had been willing to support the government in 1857 were true, Clerk now believed; having been spurned by the Liberal-Conservatives, McGee was casting his lot with the Reformers. It was

Bishop Ignace Bourget, the Catholic Bishop of Montreal, who rallied the hierarchy against McGee's alliance with George Brown. In McGee's view, Bourget exemplified a French Canadian species of nativism, "which (only that it is not embittered by sectarianism), is quite as bad as Know-Nothingism" (McGee to James Moylan, n.d. [September 1859], Moylan Fonds, Library and Archives Canada [LAC], MG29-D15). (NPA, McCord Museum)

not so much that McGee was betraying his principles but that he had never had any principles to betray; the man was nothing more than "a traitor to his religion and a rank hypocrite."[52]

In taking this position, Clerk had almost the full weight of the hierarchy behind him. Bishop Bourget of Montreal issued a public letter in August, affirming his support for the *True Witness*, condemning representation by population, rejecting "a *mixed*, reformed and improved school system, to be borrowed from foreign countries," and attacking politicians who fomented "*prejudices* of race."[53] No names were mentioned, but it was clear that his targets were McGee and Moylan. Other members of the hierarchy agreed; from London, for example, Bishop Pinsonneault wrote that the McGee-Brown alliance was driving French Canadians and Irish Catholics apart and that McGee's strategy was "hostile to Catholic interests."[54] Every Catholic bishop in Canada signed Bourget's letter. As historian Arthur Monahan put it, McGee had received "one of the strongest ecclesiastical condemnations ever levelled against a Canadian Catholic politician."[55]

While all this was happening, McGee was on a speaking tour in the Maritimes; he only received the news when he returned to Montreal in mid-September. After reading Bourget's letter several times and recovering from the shock, McGee wrote to John O'Donohoe, one of his principal supporters in Toronto. On the question of representation by population, McGee stood his ground and asserted his right to dissent from Bourget's views. But on the other issues, McGee claimed to agree with the hierarchy's position, pointing out that he had unequivocally rejected mixed education in his parliamentary speeches and noting that he had worked hard to counter the "*prejudices* of race" in the country. (Significantly, he was silent about his willingness to draw on the Irish educational system for Canada.) Having presented his case, McGee asked O'Donohoe to send a copy of his letter to Bishop de Charbonnel and Vicar General Bruyère of Toronto.[56]

If anyone within the hierarchy was likely to sympathize with McGee's strategy, it was Charbonnel. Although he had signed Bourget's letter, he refused to interpret it as an attack on McGee, and had tried to persuade Bourget to take a less confrontational tone.[57] Central to Charbonnel's approach was an attempt to reduce the tensions between the anti-McGee French Canadian hierarchy and the pro-McGee Irish Canadian laity. A few days before Bourget published his letter – or "manifesto," as it was being called – Charbonnel had urged McGee to visit the clerical authorities in Montreal on a mission of peace and reconciliation. McGee had accordingly met the coadjutor of Montreal, Monsignor Joseph Laroque, to consider ways of settling the controversy with Clerk; the discussion, however, made no impression on Bourget.[58] After Bourget's letter came out, but a full three weeks be-

Bishop Armand de Charbonnel, the Catholic Bishop of Toronto, who viewed McGee as "a true, practical friend of the principles and institutions of the Church" (*Globe*, 29 September 1859) and who attempted to reduce tensions between French and Irish Catholics in Canada. (Courtesy Archives of the Roman Catholic Archdiocese of Toronto)

fore they heard from McGee, Charbonnel and Bruyère set about the difficult task of defending McGee without alienating Bourget and the other bishops.

With Charbonnel's approval, Bruyère wrote a letter to the *Canadian Freeman* in which he argued that McGee and Moylan had proved themselves to be sound Catholics on all the key issues – separate schools, divorce, religious marriages, secret societies, and Orangeism. While Bourget had explicitly endorsed Clerk's *True Witness* and implicitly attacked Moylan and McGee, Bruyère endorsed Moylan's *Canadian Freeman* and attacked Clerk. The real purpose of Bourget's letter, Bruyère argued, was to "calm angry feelings," and Clerk was particularly in need of such calming. Besides, Clerk had no business interfering in Upper Canadian affairs, about which he knew nothing. All in all, it was a remarkable performance, in which Bruyère claimed to uphold the spirit and principles of Bourget's declaration while contradicting much of its content.[59] The casuistry was not lost on George Brown. "It will be seen that Father Bruyère, while not disposed to combat the decision of the Bishops, and, in fact, professing to submit to their commands, adheres to his old ground pretty firmly," he wrote. "If the reverend gentleman were a Protestant clergyman in like circumstance," Brown added, "he would give the Bishops a piece of his mind in a way that would astonish them."[60]

As far as Charbonnel and Bruyère were concerned, McGee's alliance with the Reformers was purely tactical and involved no compromise on the core principles of Catholicism. Moreover, it had already brought results. "To Mr. McGee we are indebted, in a great measure, for the spirit of forbearance and liberality which has succeeded the bigotry and fanaticism, which but a few years ago, raged with fury in Upper Canada," Bruyère wrote.[61] Unless and until McGee "gives a vote & utters a speech hostile to the interests of the Church & Religion," he told Bishop Pinsonneault, "he ought to be supported & sustained." "Then & then only," Bruyère concluded, "will I turn my back upon him."[62] In Toronto, at least, McGee had found shelter from the clerical storm.

———·—·———

Meanwhile, his Montreal base was holding, and Irish Catholics throughout Canada were rallying to his defence. In a series of public meetings in August and September, McGee's supporters passed resolutions approving his political conduct, expressing their confidence in "his ability, integrity, and honesty, as a Statesman and a Catholic," and condemning the *True Witness* for its "unjust and unmerited persecution" of "the recognised and true representative of Irish Catholics in Canada West."[63] Clerk responded with dismissive contempt; such meetings, he snorted, were full of "bad Catholics, and rabid Protestants."[64]

But it was clear that Clerk was losing the battle. In September, Bruyère informed Pinsonneault that the *True Witness* was "morally dead" in Canada West and that Bourget's declaration had "killed it completely" in Toronto. McGee was getting similar information and reckoned that Clerk's editorial career would be over by the end of the month.[65] Two-thirds of the Irish Catholics in Canada West supported the McGee-Brown alliance, he told Brown, and would vote for the Reform Party in the next election.[66]

The public meetings of the summer culminated in a pro-McGee banquet in Toronto at the end of September. The head table consisted entirely of Catholic priests, endorsing a man whom most of the hierarchy and the *True Witness* had attacked. Charbonnel did not attend, but he issued a statement describing McGee as "a true, practical friend of the principles and institutions of the Church." From the head table, Bruyère said that McGee had "never cast a vote, or uttered a speech, hostile to the interests of his church, or adverse to the known intentions of his ecclesiastical superiors."[67]

This was not only an expression of majority Irish Catholic opinion in Canada West; it also reflected growing resentment in English-speaking Catholic Canada about French Canadian control. Privately, McGee believed that conservative French Canadians were subjecting Irish Catholics to "a sort of *Nativism*, which (only that it is not embittered by sectarianism), is quite as bad as Know-Nothingism."[68] The same kind of anger and frustration about French dominance that fuelled George Brown's Reformers could be found within the Catholic Church in Canada West. Hence Bruyère's comment that Clerk should keep his nose out of Upper Canadian affairs; hence also his private remarks to Pinsonneault: "As long as the unnatural union of both sections will last, there will be discord, division, antipathy. The sooner the frail link is snapped asunder, the better for Religion, peace & charity ... No wonder that the laity & inferior Clergy are at variance, since the Bishops themselves of the Eastern & Western sections disagree among themselves. So it will be until the apple of discord is removed by the severance of a discordant Union."[69] McGee, of course, had also identified the problem, but he rejected Bruyère's separatism in favour of federalism – a solution that increasingly appealed to George Brown as well.

Just as there were divisions within the Catholic Church, the Reform Party contained its own competing factions. At one pole was John Sandfield Macdonald, the powerful MP for Cornwall, who believed that the "double majority" principle offered the best answer to tensions between Upper and Lower Canada, and who had already clashed with Brown on the issue. At the other pole were the Clear Grits, who thought that Brown was getting far too close to the Catholics, feared a sellout on the key questions of French domination and separate schools, and wanted to dissolve the union. As part of his effort to make the alliance work, McGee tried hard to avoid alienating either camp. In the case of Sandfield Macdonald and the double majority principle, this was relatively straightforward. McGee argued that the double majority was only a short-term solution to the sectional crisis in Canada, insisted that it should not be turned into an "invariable rule," and continued to support federalism as the ultimate goal.[70] But in the case of his relationship with the Clear Grits, the task proved much more challenging.

The closer McGee was to the hierarchy, the more unpopular he became with the radicals. In this sense, Bourget's letter did him a favour with the Clear Grits; anyone who incurred the wrath of the bishop of Montreal could not be all bad. Conversely, McGee's attempt to rehabilitate himself with the church reignited Clear Grit hostility and deepened the stresses within the Reform Party. The dilemma was particularly acute during the lead-up to the McGee banquet in September. On the one hand, McGee wanted to clear his public statements with Charbonnel and Bruyère; on the other, he wanted to conceal the fact that he had sought clerical approval, since he could not appear to be under the control of the Catholic Church.[71] For similar reasons, he oscillated between wanting the clergy to attend the banquet and wanting them to stay away. If the priests attended, it would strengthen his position within the Catholic Church; if they stayed away, he would be able to attract leading Reformers to the banquet.[72] In the event, of course, the priests came out in full force and the leading Reformers stayed at home. Writing to Luther Holton two weeks later, Brown observed that McGee "had a very successful ovation – but the array of priestcraft hurt him somewhat with the Protestant population."[73]

—·—

Nevertheless, the McGee-Brown alliance remained intact, and it became even closer when Brown set out to make federation the central policy of the Reform Party. The *Globe* had been pushing a strong federalist line since the summer, and Bourget's anti-McGee "manifesto" provided Brown with yet more evidence that fundamental constitutional changes were needed. Not only was Bourget's letter a "wanton exercise of unwarranted authority by clergymen," Brown argued; it had also condemned "the entire policy of the Brown-Dorion cabinet." Given that the Catholic Church commanded three-quarters of Lower Canada's population, and that its opposition to representation by population was shared by Lower Canadian Protestants and "a considerable section of Upper Canadians," there was no hope of attaining reform within the union.

What, then, was to be done? "A separation of the existing union between Upper and Lower Canada, and a confederation of the two with the North West territory," the *Globe* concluded, "are the only measures which will rid us of the baneful domination of Lower Canada, while securing all the commercial advantages of the present union."[74] To commit his party to this solution, Brown organized a Reform Convention for November in Toronto; it would become, in the words of J.M.S. Careless, "one of the most significant party gatherings in Canadian history."[75]

In preparing the ground, Brown needed the support of the liberals in Canada East, the men who had invited him to Montreal the previous year. McGee was more than willing to cooperate; here was a golden opportunity to advance the federalist cause that he had been advocating since the summer of 1856.[76] In October, the leading Canada East liberals met to formulate their position. Some of the "more advanced Rouges" wanted to continue the fight for representation by population within the union, fearing that under a federal system they would be isolated in a clerically dominated Quebec. Others wanted more time to consider the issue. But McGee, along with Dorion, Louis-Joseph Papineau, and Lewis Thomas Drummond, "pronounced themselves emphatically and unreservedly in favor of Federation," and it was their position that prevailed.[77] Just before the Reform Convention, McGee, Dorion, Drummond, and Louis-Antoine Dessaulles published a pro-federation manifesto in Canada East, advocating a decentralized arrangement in which "the power to legislate on all matters not specially devolving to the Federal Government – would be lodged in the government of the separate provinces."[78] Partly thanks to McGee, Brown's eastern flank was secure.

Immediately before the convention, McGee wished Brown success while expressing the fear that some of the "deplorable feuds" that had divided Catholics and Protestants would resurface. He was particularly worried about reports that the Reformers were trying to draw Orangemen into their party. "If they join the Reform movement, as reformers, we ought all to rejoice over their accession," he wrote; "but if they ask to come in as Orangemen, my friends, of course, could not act with them, for an hour." The best way to proceed during the convention, McGee advised Brown, would be to concentrate exclusively on constitutional questions, thus avoiding the divisive issue of education.[79]

As it turned out, McGee's concerns were unfounded. The Reform Convention focused on the resolution for "the formation of two or more local governments, to which shall be committed the control of all matters of a local or sectional character, and a general government charged with such matters as are necessarily common to both sections of the Province." Speaking for the resolution, Brown supported a written constitution and a division of powers in which "everything that could possibly be left to the local governments should be left to them, and as little as possible to the general government"; his views on both counts were indistinguishable from those of McGee. After a tough and tense debate between those who wanted to dissolve the union and those who supported federalism, a compromise was reached in which the words "general government" in the resolution were replaced with the phrase "some joint authority." This was sufficiently vague to prevent the party from splitting, and the amended resolution was passed with overwhelming support.[80] Subsequently, Brown interpreted "some joint authority" as a licence for federation, which he would make a priority in the next parliamentary session.

————·————

Despite his vicissitudes, McGee remained a powerful figure within Irish Catholic Canada and the Reform alliance at the end of 1859. If a man is known by his enemies, the task of understanding McGee would be particularly challenging. He was attacked by Orangemen for being too Catholic, and by prominent Catholics for not being Catholic enough; he was attacked by the Clear Grits for being too conservative, and by the Liberal-Conservatives for being too radical; and he was attacked by the Hibernian Benevolent Society and Bernard Devlin for failing to take a strong enough stand against Orange bigotry and belligerence.

If this was the price of political moderation, it was one that he was willing to pay – and also one that he could afford to pay. His lecture tours, his links with the St Patrick's Societies and the reflected glory of Smith O'Brien's visit all enhanced his reputation among Irish Catholic Canadians, many of whom supported his alliance with George Brown. The alliance had its own problems, of course, with McGee and Brown voting against each other on such issues as divorce, seigneurial compensation, and, above all, separate schools. Only by drawing a veil of ambiguity over the schools question was it possible to avoid a split over the issue. When Egerton Ryerson ripped the veil off and ruthlessly exposed the contradictions, McGee had no effective answer, charging Ryerson with corruption and taking shelter in the hope that some kind of compromise could be sorted out in the future. On the issue of representation by population, in contrast, McGee and Brown were on the same wavelength; the idea of building constitutional guarantees for Canada East pointed in the direction of federalism, and by the end of 1859 this was now on the parliamentary agenda.

Bourget and the French Canadian hierarchy continued to fear that any compromise on separate schools and representation by population would pave the way for Protestant domination. In Canada West, however, and particularly in Toronto, things looked different. Here, McGee had the crucial backing of the *Canadian Freeman* and Bishop de Charbonnel on the grounds that McGee's policies had reduced sectarian tensions and that his voting record showed that he would not retreat on core Catholic issues. Besides, if the Irish Catholics abandoned the Reform alliance, they would have all of Protestant Canada West against them, and that would hardly improve their situation. The strong show of clerical support at the McGee banquet of September 1859 vindicated his religious reputation, just as Brown's success at the Reform Convention of November vindicated his political strategy. Both would be severely tested in the years ahead.

## CHAPTER FOUR

# The Shield of Achilles
## December 1859 – March 1861

If we step back and consider the trajectory of McGee's early Canadian career, three dominant themes emerge. First, there was his attempt to lower the ethnoreligious temperature in the country. In the late 1850s and early 1860s, he believed that this could be accomplished by bringing Irish Catholics and Protestant liberals together in the Reform alliance, by reducing the political and social power of the Orange Order, and by marginalizing the radical elements within Irish Catholic Canada. Second, there was his commitment to federalism, both as a way out of the sectional conflict between Canada West and Canada East, and as a fundamental component of the new northern nationality. He remained convinced that Brown's Reformers offered the best means to this end, especially after the Reform Convention of November 1859. And third, there was his effort to protect and promote the interests of Irish Catholics in English Canada, particularly through improved separate school legislation. Here again, he bet on Brown rather than on the Liberal-Conservatives, though he also made it known that the issue transcended party allegiances; in the unlikely event that the Liberal-Conservatives would support improved separate school legislation, McGee wrote, he would vote with them.[1]

These themes were not, of course, the only ones that preoccupied McGee, and focusing exclusively on them would obscure many of his other activities during this period. He had become an apprentice in Edward Carter's Montreal law firm in June 1858, enrolled in McGill University's Law School that autumn, and for the next two-and-a-half years combined his political career with legal studies. When he received his law degree in May 1861, McGee fulfilled another of his

Mary McGee. Her few remaining letters indicate that she experienced periods of intense loneliness while her husband was away and that she tried to curb his heavy drinking when he was at home. They also bear out the views of contemporaries who commented on her strength of character. Although their marriage had its share of stresses, it is clear that Mary and Thomas cared deeply for one another. (NPA, McCord Museum)

long-standing ambitions, reaching back to his plan in 1844 to study law in Cincinnati and his intention a year later to take a law degree at Trinity College Dublin.[2]

   While McGee was studying law at McGill, he was also ensconced in the parliamentary library, writing his two-volume *Popular History of Ireland*, and keeping his friends informed about his progress. "I arrest my pen in the midst of the IXth Century," he told John O'Donohoe in January 1859, "when our ancestors were dealing with the Danes, to descend into things present."[3] In addition, he found time to write a play, *Sebastian, or, The Roman Martyr*, to be performed in Christian Brothers' schools and intended to inspire the new generation with the example of men who willingly sacrificed everything, including their own lives, for the Christian faith.[4] Meanwhile, he was frequently on tour, giving lectures in the United States and Canada; this was one of his major sources of income. At times, the pace caught up with him; on one occasion, he wrote that he needed three days of solid rest to "restore the equilibrium of mind first lost, through the exhaustion of the body, in six weeks of nightly vigils."[5]

All this took its toll on his family life. Mary was prone to illness and suffered from bouts of depression; according to one acquaintance, the death of their children Martha Dorcas, Thomas Patrick, and Rose "was an affliction she felt keenly and saddened her after years." Mary was variously described as "very retiring and domestic in her life" and as "a woman of much force of character" who was "fitted to shine in society by her brilliant conversation and fine wit"; there was general agreement, though, that she was a "true helpmate" and "wise and prudent counsellor" to her husband. It is difficult to see how her husband could have provided her with close emotional support, given his continual absences and his growing addiction to whisky. Much as McGee's admirers liked to portray an idealized image of domestic bliss, and for all the love and affection that McGee's poems displayed for Mary, her life could not have been easy.[6]

Despite and to some extent because of McGee's best efforts, ethnoreligious conflict in Canada West continued to flare up during the early 1860s. His continuing attempts to curb the political influence and patronage machinery of the Orange Order ensured that he remained a hate figure for many Orangemen. When the Bradford Literary Society invited him in January 1860 to give his standard lecture on "The Historical Relations between Ireland and Scotland," the local Orange lodge decided to take a stand. This was Orange territory, the home of Thomas Ferguson's "Simcoe Lambs" and no place for a "*poor, miserable, and single-handed traitor*" like "*the unrelenting arch rebel McGee.*"[7] To prevent him from speaking on their home turf, some three hundred Orangemen, acting under the licence of Ferguson, their MP, converged on the town; many were armed and threatened the use of force. The literary society was divided about how to respond. In principle, its members believed that McGee should attempt to deliver his lecture; but in practice, they could not guarantee his safety. After a heated debate, they sent a deputation to Toronto, requesting him to cancel the lecture.[8] The "rough voices of angry backwoodsmen," declared the ministerial *Colonist*, had carried the day against one of the most "dangerous foes of British institutions."[9]

McGee's supporters were furious. This was nothing less than Orange mob rule, sanctioned by an MP and supported in the ministerial press, wrote George Brown; the Simcoe Lambs had trampled freedom of speech into the ground.[10] James Moylan had no doubt about the composition of the crowd, contending that "nineteen out of every twenty" of them were "North of Ireland brethern [sic], of the lowest stamp." The "low North of Ireland Orangeman," he explained, "never was a freeman, and has no conception of what freedom is."[11]

Nevertheless, Orange-Green relations were not quite as stark as the "Bradford Outrage" might suggest. While most Orangemen endorsed the actions of the Simcoe Lambs, a minority did not; the Orange Lodge in Guelph, for example, registered its disapproval. Within the Bradford Literary Society, a number of prominent Orangemen were among those who had extended the invitation to McGee in the first place.[12] Moreover, although Ferguson and McGee were political enemies, they got on well with each other personally, drinking whisky and water together after parliamentary debates.[13] Even in political terms, there was some common ground between them; in a lecture delivered in Oshawa shortly after the Bradford Outrage, McGee praised William III for resisting James II's attempts to overturn "established laws of the realm" and impose Catholicism on his subjects. Consciences, McGee noted, could not be coerced. "Certainly," remarked Moylan, "the most devoted worshipper, of the hero of 'glorious, pious, and immortal memory,' could not take the least exception to Mr. McGee's portraiture of William of Orange."[14]

None of this, however, meant any let-up in McGee's political campaign against Orangeism. Having helped to defeat the Orange Incorporation Bill two years earlier, McGee in March 1860 introduced a resolution in the House that "no avowed leader or chief of any exclusive Secret Politico-Religious Society ought to be entrusted with the prosecution of justice on behalf of the Crown, in this Province." To all intents and purposes, he declared, there was only one such society in Canada – the Orange Order.

In a speech delivered before largely empty ministerial benches, McGee condemned Orangeism as a divisive and disruptive force, and noted that Edmund Burke, "the personification of all that was Conservative in the last ten years of the last century," disapproved of the Orange Order. It was impossible, McGee contended, for Orangemen to administer justice impartially. They were politically partisan, turning out in large numbers to support Liberal-Conservative candidates; they intimidated Catholics with their parades; they suppressed freedom of speech, as he himself had experienced in Bradford; and they put their obligations to the order above the law of the land. No public confidence could be placed in such people, and the fact that they were encouraged "by persons in high places" would almost certainly result in "the establishment of counter-associations – a thing which would be very much deplored as the evil would thereby be increased and perpetuated."[15]

All to no avail. In a parliamentary rerun of the earlier debate in the New Era, Ogle Gowan denied that the Orange Order was a secret society, argued that some of the most peaceable counties in Canada were Orange strongholds, reminded McGee that the Orange Order had been on good terms with loyal Catholics such as Bishop Alexander McDonell of Kingston, and rejected the view that Orangemen were inherently incapable of administering justice. And it was Gowan who won. Almost two-thirds of the MPs present voted against McGee's resolution – including George Brown, who felt that it was "inadvisable to single out a particular class of persons by the Legislature" and that appointments to public office should be handled on a case-by-case basis.[16]

The comprehensive defeat of McGee's resolution did nothing to help his constitutional strategy for the redress of Catholic grievances. From Montreal, George Clerk declared that the result would only confirm the view of Upper Canadian Catholics that the "law, as actually administered in their section of the Province, is but a powerful instrument of wrong, fraud and oppression; – that ... it is a shield behind which the Orange culprit, no matter how clear and atrocious his guilt, is always sure to find protection."[17] In Toronto, the Young Men's St Patrick's Association was still strong enough to keep the lid on popular protest. "I take it for granted there will be no street parade – as there assuredly ought not to be," McGee wrote to Moylan just before St Patrick's Day.[18] But although there was no parade, the Hibernian Benevolent Society, which was already developing links with the Fenian Brotherhood, organized its own festivities – including a two-hour Gaelic football match with "an immense number of spectators." "There is hot Irish blood in Toronto," reported the New York *Phoenix*.[19]

———————

Meanwhile, the politicians in the makeshift parliamentary buildings in Quebec City were turning their attention to the question of Canadian federation. Building on the momentum of the Reform Convention of November 1859, Brown announced that he would introduce resolutions during the parliamentary session on a federal union of the Canadas. In doing so, however, he precipitated a crisis within his own party. Sandfield Macdonald continued to support the double majority principle, while the Clear Grits wanted either representation by population or a straightforward dissolution of the union. There were also divisions within Lower Canadian Reformers; Dorion and McGee supported Brown, while others feared the prospect of becoming a permanent minority in a conservative and Catholic Canada East. In a stormy five-day caucus meeting, the Upper Canadian Reformers came close to splitting. "If the *private* breach once becomes *public*," McGee told Moylan, "... then I fear this will result in the triumph of the Orange Conservatives of Upper Canada, in the next General Election."[20] Partly because Brown threatened to resign and partly because dissidents such as Michael Foley and Skeffington Connor pulled back from the brink, a semblance of unity was maintained. But it was clear that federalism was a deeply divisive issue within Reform ranks and that the Liberal-Conservatives were eagerly expecting their opponents to self-destruct.[21]

In these unpromising circumstances, Brown eventually introduced his resolutions on 30 April, following them up with a four-hour
speech. Two days later, on 2 May, McGee entered the debate. Adopting
a Burkean perspective, he argued that Canada's constitutional evolution had been the product of changing circumstances. In the light of
time and experience, the Quebec Act of 1774 had given way to the constitution of 1791, which was itself replaced with the union of the Canadas that had been drawn up in 1840, to be implemented the following year. But the constitution of 1840, he continued, had been hastily
cobbled together by imperial statesmen in the immediate aftermath
of the Rebellions of 1837–38. "There is no sanctity of age about this
Constitution of ours," he said; "we cannot invoke its provisions as 'the
wisdom of our ancestors!'" On the contrary, time and experience had
only revealed its shortcomings, especially in the light of Canada's rapid
growth during the mid-nineteenth century. The constitution of 1840,
McGee declared, "now hangs in tatters upon the expanding frame of
this colony." Among its many faults, the most egregious was the equality of representation between Canada East and Canada West, a policy
that had been designed "for the purpose of 'swamping the French.'"
"It was a deliberate conspiracy against the rights of one set of people –
flagitious in the conception, and wholly indefensible in the enactment,"
he asserted. "Why, then, should it be maintained and enforced against
another set?"[22]

This state of affairs could not continue, he said; some kind of major
constitutional revision was essential. McGee quickly disposed of the
argument for "dissolution, 'pure and simple.'" It was "altogether re-
trograde" to create parochial political units; the British government
would oppose the idea, and dissolution would inexorably culminate
in American annexation. The best remedy would be "a bold application of the federal principle," preferably incorporating all the British
North American colonies. It would, McGee recognized, involve difficult, protracted, and complex negotiations. "Much time for deliberation, and many mutual conferences, will be necessary," he said. But,
he asked, quoting Oliver Mowat, "What are statesmen fit for, if not to
overcome difficulties?"[23] He added that, beyond the commercial ad-

vantages, federation would "enlarge our horizon, and open before us new fields of labour and of honour," attracting men with "a wider vision and better aspirations." And then, in his peroration, McGee presented his own vision and aspirations:

> I look to the future of my adopted country with hope, though not without anxiety; I see in the not remote distance, one great nationality bound, like the shield of Achilles, by the blue rim of ocean – I see it quartered into many communities – each disposing of its internal affairs – but all bound together by free institutions, free intercourse, and free commerce; I see within the round of that shield, the peaks of the Western mountains and the crests of the Eastern waves – the winding Assinaboine, the five-fold lakes, the St. Lawrence, the Ottawa, the Saguenay, the St. John, and the Basin of Minas – by all these flowing waters, in all the valleys they fertilise, in all the cities they visit in their courses, I see a generation of industrious, contented, moral men, free in name and in fact, – men capable of maintaining, in peace and in war, a Constitution worthy of such a country.[24]

These words have echoed through Canadian history as the most eloquent expression of British North American nationalism ever made; they have been reprinted in school textbooks, quoted in biographies, speeches, and anthologies, and reproduced in TV and radio documentaries. They are the best-known words that McGee spoke. It was not the first time, though, that he had employed the "shield of Achilles" image. In 1856, while he was living in New York, he told the readers of his *American Celt* that he had recently received a map of the High Kings of Ireland. "I looked abroad on that shield-shaped Island," he wrote, "round which roll the subject waves, like the old ocean round the shield of Achilles." The same image appeared at the beginning of his *Popular History of Ireland*.[25] Canada had become McGee's New Ireland.

When McGee finished his speech, it was reported, he "resumed his seat amidst loud and general applause."[26] Reactions in the press were equally positive. The *Montreal Herald* declared that McGee had "surpassed himself," the *London Free Press* described it as "the speech of the session," and even the conservative *Leader* praised McGee's oratory, while distancing itself from his message.[27] This was all well and good, but it had little or no immediate political impact. The Liberal-Conservatives opposed Brown's resolutions, as did the vast majority of MPs from Canada East; within Brown's own party, there were major doubts, reservations, and misgivings. For all the fine words, federation was decisively defeated by a vote of seventy-four to thirty-two – roughly the same margin by which his resolution against Orangemen in the judiciary had failed.[28] In his peroration, McGee had viewed the future "with hope, though not without anxiety." Hope belonged to the long run; in the immediate context of 1860, there were good grounds for anxiety.

————

This was also true of McGee's other major preoccupation, the school system in Canada West. In March 1860, Richard Scott, a Liberal-Conservative MP from Ottawa, introduced the Separate Schools Bill, which was designed to make it easier for Catholics in Canada West to establish, organize, and sustain their own schools; among other things, it would have enabled Catholics in adjacent municipalities to pool their resources and send their children to the same school.[29] All in all, it was a rather modest bill, which failed to meet the larger demand of parity between Catholics in Canada West and Protestants in Canada East. Nevertheless, any changes to the separate schools system had the potential to escalate ethnoreligious tensions, and McGee wanted to draw as little attention as possible to Scott's bill. He advised Moylan to take the same approach, asking him "not to make much of it either – *till it is passed.*"[30] Moylan followed his advice; the *Canadian Freeman* described the bill as "meagre in its provisions," while adding that it was "a decided improvement upon the existing law."[31]

Yet even Scott's limited proposals failed to get off the ground. His bill did not receive its second reading until the end of the parliamentary session, when many MPs had already left Quebec, and most of those who stayed preferred to discuss other business. For McGee, this was yet more proof that the government had no intention of strengthening Catholic education in Canada West. In his last speech of the session, he "complained that the Bill had been twice delayed at the instigation of the Administration, who ... were simply going through the farce of ordering up the Bill only to throw it out five minutes afterwards."[32] Subsequent events appeared to bear out this interpretation. When Scott insisted on proceeding with the bill, he was sharply rebuked by John A. Macdonald for blocking the remaining business of the House. To prevent Scott from going ahead, Macdonald said that he would vote against the bill, however much he supported it in principle. Not surprisingly, Scott backed down.[33]

All this seemed to fit into a well-established Liberal-Conservative pattern – attracting the Irish Catholic vote by promising change, while keeping the Orange vote by doing nothing. The Catholic hierarchy and the *True Witness* continued to hope that the Liberal-Conservatives would eventually deliver, while McGee remained convinced that they would not. In taking this position and in siding with the Reform Party, McGee retained the support of most Irish Catholics, the *Canadian Freeman*, and Bishop Charbonnel.

But in the spring of 1860 the clerical ground began to shift under McGee's feet. After ten years as Toronto's bishop, Charbonnel resigned and returned to his native France. His successor was the Irish-born John Joseph Lynch, who had served in Texas, Missouri, and upstate New York before arriving in Toronto. And Lynch, like the rest of the hierarchy, believed that the Liberal-Conservatives would indeed improve the separate school system; it was time, Lynch decided, to abandon the Reform alliance.[34]

This was, in McGee's view, a disastrous course of action. Irish Catholics in Canada West already incurred the hostility of the Orange Order; Lynch's policy would ensure that the Reform Protestants would turn against them as well. "There has not been a moment for years when there was such imminent risk of a great Protestant combination sweeping over Upper Canada, and leaving the Catholics, as the Yankees say – 'nowhere' – as at this moment," he told O'Donohoe. "Of course, if His Lordship is ready for a great anti-Protestant war," he added, "he has only to say 'let it come.' For my part, as a Catholic publicist, I am not, and *cannot* be, a party to it. But it is not one season off, if things go on, as they are now doing." To make matters worse,

Bishop John Joseph Lynch. After becoming the Catholic Bishop of Toronto in 1860, he rejected McGee's Reform alliance and believed (correctly, as it turned out) that the Liberal-Conservatives were a better bet than the Reformers for improved separate schools legislation. Later in the decade, McGee and Lynch also differed over Fenianism; while McGee was unequivocal in his denunciations, Lynch had a more ambivalent attitude towards the movement. (Courtesy Archives of the Roman Catholic Archdiocese of Toronto)

Lynch's strategy would fail on its own terms, McGee believed; Lynch had been "taken in" by Cartier's false promises about separate schools, just as Charbonnel had been deceived before seeing the light. If Lynch's position prevailed, Irish Catholics would end up with the worst of both worlds – they would have alienated Protestants from across the political spectrum without making any advances on the separate schools issue.[35]

It was imperative, then, to "undeceive" Lynch as soon as possible.[36] In no circumstances should this campaign be conducted publicly. McGee was in no mood to repeat the mistakes he had made in confronting Bishop Hughes of New York.[37] Instead, he wanted to arrange a private meeting in which Irish Catholic Reformers would persuade Lynch to judge Cartier by his actions rather than his words. Had not Cartier assured Lynch that he supported equal rights for Upper Canadian Catholics? Very well. Let Cartier prove it by doing three things during the next parliamentary session: replace Ryerson as superintendent of education; support educational parity for religious minorities in Canada East and Canada West; and refuse to lead any cabinet that included Orangemen. "Will he do this?" McGee asked. "Nothing of the kind. Will he promise to do it? Perhaps – probably." McGee hoped that by the end of the next session, Cartier's hypocrisy would have been exposed and Lynch would have been put back on the right track.[38]

In the meantime, McGee wrote a long letter to Lynch, vindicating his strategy and defending Moylan's Canadian Freeman against its Orange and clerical detractors. He began by contrasting the position of Irish Catholics in 1857–58 with their current condition. When he had arrived in Canada, McGee wrote, priests were insulted and assaulted on the streets of Toronto and Catholic churches were being attacked while the Orange police looked the other way. Although "the ruffianism is not all extinct," he continued, doubtless with a backward glance to Bradford, the situation had improved significantly. Priests were now respected, the police force had been reformed, the Orange Incorporation Bill had been defeated, attempts to abolish separate schools had been turned back, and the effort to permit divorce had failed.

What accounted for these "advances"? Nothing less than "the new policy of conciliation, and moral courage" that McGee and Moylan had advocated – code language for the Reform alliance. But the Canadian Freeman was being squeezed from two directions: John Hillyard Cameron of the Orange Order was suing Moylan for libel, while the French Canadian "ruling class" – the same class, McGee added, that had opposed immigration and resisted the establishment of St Patrick's Church in Montreal – was trying to break Moylan and his newspaper. "That an amiable, able, honest, well-bred man, an Irishman to boot, should suffer through his friendship for me, I confess touches me to the quick," McGee wrote. Without the bishop's support, the combined force of Orangeism and narrow-minded French Canadian conservatism would succeed in destroying the *Canadian Freeman*, leaving Irish Catholics in Canada West back where they were in 1857.

"I write feelingly and as you see, with heart in hand," McGee told Lynch.[39] But for all the passion and all the reason, his appeal did not work. Lynch remained convinced that the French Canadians in Parliament would support new separate schools legislation and that enough of their English Liberal-Conservative allies would vote with them to ensure its success; all that was needed was patience and perseverance, rather than McGee's bizarre alliance with George Brown's Protestants. McGee's strategy had suffered a serious setback.

———·———

Serious, but far from fatal. He still enjoyed widespread support in Irish Catholic Canada, and Moylan's *Canadian Freeman* continued to disseminate his ideas. Moreover, his Orange enemies were pushed onto the defensive later that summer when the Prince of Wales toured through Canada, accompanied by the colonial secretary, the Duke of Newcastle. Orange parades had been banned in Ireland since 1850, and the British government had recently introduced a bill at Westminster to suppress Orange flags and emblems.[40] Accordingly, Newcastle was determined not to give the Orange Order in Canada the least semblance of public recognition or approval. He made it clear that the prince would not walk under any Orange arches and would not visit any town where Orangemen turned out in their official capacity.[41]

In Orange eyes, this was nothing less than betrayal – yet another example of British ingratitude to the most loyal subjects in the empire. It also meant dashed hopes; Orangemen had looked forward to meeting the prince, receiving his recognition, and boosting their prestige in the province. Faced with Newcastle's snub, they were divided about how to react. Some counselled caution; others preferred a course of defiance and direct confrontation.

When the prince's ship approached Kingston on 4 September, the wharf was lined with several thousand Orangemen in full regalia, with their bands playing and banners flying. Newcastle told the mayor that the prince would not land unless the Orangemen dispersed; the Orangemen refused to move. After a two-day standoff (subsequently

Orange Parade, Toronto. Orangemen in Toronto celebrating the anniversary of the Battle of the Boyne. Toronto was so Orange in complexion that it was known as the "Belfast of Canada." (*Canadian Illustrated News*, 1 August 1874)

magnified into the "Siege of Kingston" in Orange mythology), the prince's ship raised anchor and headed up Lake Ontario to Belleville. But the Orangemen got there first, having taken the train from Kingston, and the prince was forced to continue to Cobourg. This time, though, the Orangemen were nowhere to be seen. "By some curious *accident* (which will sometimes happen when the Government has the road in its own hands) the train has broken down in a wild part of the line," Newcastle informed Queen Victoria.[42]

And so the entourage continued to Toronto, the bastion of Canadian Orangeism. After receiving assurances from the mayor, Adam Wilson, that there would be no Orange displays in the city, the royal party travelled through the streets, only to pass beneath an arch adorned with a portrait of King William III. An incensed Newcastle demanded an apology, described the mayor as a "damned blackguard and liar," and commented that "if Canada could only be kept on such terms as dealing with fellows like him, it was not worth keeping."[43] Two days later, an Orange crowd attempted to commandeer the royal coach, with the prince and the duke inside, and steer it underneath the Orange arch. Such an action was hardly likely to endear the Orangemen to the imperial authorities; Newcastle remained in a black mood, and the relationship between the Canadian Orange Order and the British government reached its lowest point of the nineteenth century.

None of this had been anticipated by McGee. Initially, he feared that the visit would become a publicity stunt to prop up the governor general and the government; in which case, he argued, "it were really better that His Royal Highness should not visit the Province."[44] His comments unleashed a storm of criticism, in which McGee's revolutionary past was once again dug up against him; the traitor of 1848 was supposedly showing his true colours and insulting the Royal Family and its representative.[45] McGee's past also came back to haunt him when the Prince of Wales arrived in Montreal. He had been invited by the Grand Trunk Railway to make a speech at the inauguration of the Victoria Bridge, the centrepiece of the royal tour. But Newcastle vetoed the plan, on the grounds that a former rebel should not address the prince. If McGee accepted the invitation to speak, Newcastle told him, the prince would not attend the inauguration.[46] It was not only the Orangemen who were snubbed in 1860.

Nevertheless, the events in Kingston, Belleville, and Toronto appeared to play directly into McGee's hands. As Orange stock fell, it was only natural to assume that Irish Catholic stock would rise. "I cannot describe to you the state of feeling here, in relation to the Kingston proceedings," he wrote to Moylan from Montreal. "Every one is congratulating *us* on the good *sense* displayed by *our* people in Upper Canada." To press home the advantage, McGee urged Moylan publicly to request from Newcastle "a *Royal Commission*, similar to that sent three years ago to Belfast, *to inquire into the disastrous effects of Orangeism in Upper Canada*." Shortly afterwards, Moylan followed McGee's advice with an open letter to the colonial secretary, making the same point in much the same language.[47] Newcastle did not reply.

Immediately after the Kingston standoff, McGee believed that the Orangemen had "irretrievably damaged themselves." A week later, though, he came to feel that "the enemy had been 'scotched not killed'" and that they would "make desperate attempts to recover lost ground, or to be revenged of the Catholics."[48] To prevent this from happening, he encouraged the formation of local Catholic committees and floated the idea of a Catholic Convention to mobilize the vote during the next election – an event that could not be far off, in his estimation. The Liberal-Conservatives were in a state of disarray, and Macdonald had been "hopelessly inebriate for weeks"; he "wants to retire & colleagues want to get rid of him." But although Irish Catholics had to organize themselves, they must not be seen to be organizing themselves, warned McGee; a Catholic Convention must meet in conditions of the tightest secrecy to avoid a political-religious backlash. In any case, it was essential to maintain a united front against a weakened but angry and therefore dangerous Orange enemy.[49]

---

It seemed, then, that events had turned significantly in favour of Irish Catholics and the Reform alliance and against the Orange Order and the Liberal-Conservative Party. In practice, however, any Irish Catholic advantage proved to be ephemeral, and the Orange Order suffered no long-term damage from the royal visit. A few months later, Grand Master John Hillyard Cameron presented a petition to Queen Victoria from 150,000 Canadian Orangemen in protest against Newcastle's actions. The fact that Victoria received the petition was claimed as a great triumph, while the fact that she ignored its contents was quietly passed over. Not for the last time in the history of Orangeism, symbols counted for more than substance and defeat was dressed up as victory.[50]

Ironically, and unexpectedly, the royal tour put at least as much strain on McGee's Reform strategy as it did on the Orange Order. The reason for this lay in the *Globe*'s growing conviction that the prince's refusal to meet Orangemen was symptomatic of encroaching and excessive Catholic power on both sides of the Atlantic. Newcastle's objection to Orange arches in Toronto, asserted the paper, demonstrated that he was "completely under the thumb of the Pope's brigade in the House of Commons."[51] The same dynamic was supposedly at work in Canada, where a government dominated by French Catholics fully supported Newcastle, while John A. Macdonald cowered in the background. The upshot was that the prince visited Catholic institutions in Quebec and praised "the exertion of the nuns in the cause of education," but was prevented from greeting his most loyal Orange supporters.[52] Genuine Orange loyalty was spurned, and feigned French Catholic loyalty was embraced; after all, asserted the *Globe*, everyone knew that French Canadians only supported the Protestant British Empire insofar as it protected and promoted their privileged position.[53] The message was clear: Orangemen had been betrayed by a hypocritical government and should come into the Reform fold.

Not surprisingly, this position put an enormous strain on the Catholic-Protestant alliance within the Reform Party and threatened to undermine McGee's entire strategy. Nevertheless, Brown and McGee needed each other and continued to work together. Insisting that he wanted religious and political equality rather than Catholic or Protestant domination in Canada, Brown responded to an anti-McGee heckler at a speech in Galt with a ringing endorsement of his ally: "I would a thousand times rather act with Mr. McGee than with the dough-faced Protestants that misrepresent Upper Canada. I have found in him an uprightness of character and a manly straightforwardness, which have won for him my highest respect and esteem."[54]

After reading the speech, McGee thanked Brown for his "excessively kind" remarks and then urged him to cut out the anti-Catholic rhetoric. "Why cannot the *Globe*, state its own strong case, without using offensive *epithets*, such as 'Priestcraft' 'Popish' 'Romish' 'Jesuits' &c. &c.," McGee asked. "Let the general ground of the exclusion of all clerical influence be taken, if you choose; but don't let the writers for the organ of the party, use epithets which irritate and estrange many, without any commensurate gain. There are surely facts enough to pelt these people out of power with, without dipping into the *odium theologicum*."[55] There was a certain amount of disingenuousness here; McGee had no objection to clerical influence, provided that it came from priests who agreed with him and provided that it was applied surreptitiously.[56] There was also a degree of exaggeration; the epithets McGee mentioned were few and far between in the *Globe*, although there was no mistaking the paper's hostility to Catholic education and its anger about perceived Catholic privilege.

But while McGee persisted in his effort to maintain the Reform alliance, James Moylan was among those who were irritated and estranged by Brown's attitude to the Catholic Church. The *Globe*'s coverage of the royal tour in Quebec, Moylan wrote, was characterized by a "depth of malice, a rankling spirit of petty vindictiveness," and a sneering attitude to Catholic institutions. While McGee preferred to put the blame on the paper's writers rather than Brown himself, Moylan was convinced that Brown bore full responsibility, and he began to have serious doubts about the Reform alliance.[57] Moylan also knew that Bishop Lynch backed the Liberal-Conservatives and that the continuing success of the *Canadian Freeman* – which always had a precarious existence – owed a great deal to the bishop's support. In these circumstances, Moylan's commitment to McGee's policies became weaker and weaker. In November it snapped.

McGee was taken completely by surprise. He knew nothing about the change in Moylan's position until he read the *Canadian Freeman*'s coverage of the upcoming elections for the legislative council. An editorial attacked a Reform candidate who was equivocal about separate schools and endorsed his prospective Liberal-Conservative rival, who had committed himself to educational equality between Catholics in Canada West and Protestants in Canada East. "We want no more," Moylan declared, "and will cordially support the man who will grant so much."[58]

Writing in a "paroxysm of feeling" that arose from a sense of personal betrayal and impending political disaster, McGee fired off a letter to Moylan. "I cannot tell you with how much regret, I have read the *Freeman* of this day," he wrote. "Considering our relations all along, I think I ought to have been consulted, before so positive a declaration of change of *policy*, was *editorially* announced." "To go back to Cartier, is, at this moment, suicidal," he continued; "it is for the Catholic one-sixth, to invite the hatred and to make sure of the contempt, of their Protestant neighbors, and for what – and for whom? It is not only a policy immoral in itself, but utterly insane ... Twelve months will show its futility, but twelve years may not exhaust the hatreds and estrangement, it is certain to create. Let the Catholics of western Canada date their darkest day, in this decade on which we have lately entered, to the day of its enunciation."[59]

It was essential to stay the course. "I will be dragged at no Bishop's chariot wheels, into the policy of the Crawfords, the Elmsleys, the J.A. MacDonalds and G.E. Cartiers," McGee told O'Donohoe the next day. "When will we get our political alphabet – when will we show ourselves steady under the fire of the bigoted few, whose delight it would be, to buff us out of the Reform ranks? When will we learn that there is no such thing as taking a *single* step in politics – that each step must be one of a series, forward or backward?" The only explanation for this about-face, McGee believed, was that Moylan had been misled, presumably by Bishop Lynch.[60]

Despite his anger, McGee hoped that he and Moylan could remain on good terms: "Let us seperate [sic] as we have acted," he wrote, "in mutual good feeling."[61] Shortly afterwards, he left Montreal for a lecture tour in New England, after which he visited Toronto. Before arriving, he sent a note to Moylan, apologizing for the heated tone of his previous letter and asking for a meeting. "A full and friendly conversation can do no harm," he wrote, "and if we neither of us convince each other, on a point of policy, I hope we shall not part the worse friends."[62] Although they were not able to convince each other, they were able to prolong their friendship well into the New Year. The split remained private rather than public, and the *Canadian Freeman* continued to publicize McGee's lectures, print his letters, and defend him from attacks in Cartier's *La Minerve* and Clerk's *True Witness*.[63] He may have lost the support of the newspaper that he had helped to establish, but he had managed to avoid making a direct political enemy – at least for the time being.

---

By the end of 1860, McGee's alliance with Brown had alienated the entire Catholic hierarchy and the two major English-language Catholic newspapers in Canada. For someone who had initially been drawn to Canada by his ultramontanism, this was quite an achievement. During the early 1850s, McGee had written that Catholic politicians should conform to "an exact Catholic standard" and that Catholic bishops should have formal political power in a Home Rule Ireland.[64] Now, he was at odds with the hierarchy over the strategy to attain educational equality and was defying the French Canadian bishops on the question of representation by population. In the process, he was beginning to sound like his pre-ultramontane self. "While I remain in public life, using all its opportunities of observation," he declared in April 1860, "I shall never consent to abandon one single conviction, at the dictate of any authority, that does not reach me through that reason, which is at once the charter and the chart of the tempestuous voyage of public life."[65]

When George Clerk read these words, he went for the jugular. This was clear proof, he contended, that McGee was elevating private judgment over the teachings of the church. "This is, and ever has been," Clerk wrote, "the language of all heresiarchs, of all renegades, and apostates, since the days of Luther."[66] It was a serious charge, which McGee was anxious to refute. All he meant, he assured Moylan, was that any criticism of another person's political position should be made with "a due regard to reasonable proof & surrounding circumstances; – not a mad, and murderous imputation of motives and intentions." Rather than elevating private judgment over Catholic morality, he was simply protesting against the "dictatorial and denunciatory style" that characterized the columns of the *True Witness*.[67] Maybe so, but there was a large gap between what he actually said and what he supposedly meant; the tension that had struck one observer fifteen years earlier between McGee's active mind and Catholic orthodoxy was still in existence.[68]

The erosion of his ultramontanism was evident not only in McGee's political independence from the hierarchy but also in his attitude to Protestants. Between 1851 and 1854 he had attacked Protestants, including Canadian Protestants, as heretics, bigots, and persecutors who were leading society into the abyss of anarchy. Yet in Canada he was politically allied with the Reform Party and had developed close personal ties with Protestants. During the parliamentary sessions of 1858 and 1859 in Toronto, he had stayed at the Rossin House Hotel with some twenty or thirty Protestant politicians. "I found among these Protestant gentlemen, with many educational prejudices of course, a genuine regard for the rights of others, (aye, even for the special rights of Lower Canada)," he wrote. "I found among them great natural virtue, very acute religious susceptibilities, and a settled tolerance of temper, which made them deplore and condemn everything like theological rancour."[69]

He had had similar experiences on his travels, where his Protestant hosts and Protestant audiences had treated him with respect and courtesy, despite his strong Catholic beliefs and his Irish revolutionary background: "I have been the guests of some of the most influential among them, who, when they were about to join in their family prayers, have with an inexpressible delicacy provided me with a book, and withdrawn from the room. I have sometimes been driven two or three miles on a Sunday morning by my kind Protestant host, at the risk of being late for his own service, to the nearest Catholic Church."[70] There is little doubt that McGee still regarded Protestants as wrong, although he prudently kept that opinion to himself. But the old stereotype of Protestants as persecuting bigots who were destroying the social fabric had fallen by the wayside.

This was another source of tension between McGee and Clerk. In language that paralleled McGee's earlier ultramontane writings, Clerk described Protestantism as "the common sewer of the Church." All McGee's talk about nice Protestants was just so much "unmeaning verbiage," argued Clerk; the fact remained that Protestants had a long history of oppressing Catholics, and they currently supported state schools that had "done more to pervert Catholics, and therefore to consign souls to hell, than have all the brothels and gambling houses on this Continent."[71] Catholicism was God's true religion; anything that contradicted God came from the Devil; Protestantism contradicted God; therefore Protestantism was the spawn of Satan. If anyone required further proof, Clerk continued, all they needed to do was read McGee's *History of the Protestant Reformation*, with its long and detailed catalogue of Protestant persecution. The ultramontane McGee of 1853 was being used to discredit the liberal McGee of 1858–61.[72]

In attacking Clerk, McGee was demonstrating the distance he had travelled over the previous decade. Clerk's inflammatory and intolerant language, McGee argued, was threatening to poison Protestant-Catholic relations in Canada and was hurting all those "Irish Catholics, who are in any way dependent on the good offices and good opinion of Protestant neighbors, Protestant employers, or Protestant public opinion."[73] Clerk, who had initially been brought up in the Protestant faith, was manifesting the extremism of the convert: "Remember – do remember – that if you have had a *personal quarrel* with your former religion, we have had none," McGee wrote. "Catholics of English, Irish, and Scottish origin, when not inflamed by such articles as yours, are desirous to live on the best terms with their Protestant neighbours."[74]

McGee, of course, had his own personal experience of this dynamic, both in political and religious terms. In 1849 he had converted from revolutionary to liberal nationalism and had emerged as an extreme opponent of physical-force republicanism. And in 1851 he had converted from liberal Catholicism to ultramontanism and exhibited exactly the same kind of intolerance that he currently condemned in Clerk. Now, McGee was a political and religious moderate – something that was completely unacceptable to Clerk. "We would rather be a dog than a '*moderate Catholic*,' or an avowed infidel than a '*moderate Christian*,'" Clerk wrote in response to McGee's criticisms. "Truth, not moderation, is the one attribute of which we are emulous; and our title is not 'THE MODERATE,' but 'THE TRUE WITNESS.'"[75] McGee himself could have written these words in the mid-1850s, when he first met Clerk and worked with him at the Buffalo Convention. But McGee now inhabited a different world, while Clerk manifestly did not.

In his attempt to enlarge the middle ground while advocating federalism and working for educational equality between Protestants and Catholics, McGee had alienated not only militant Orangemen, anti-Catholic Clear Grits, the Catholic hierarchy, and George Clerk, but also Bishop Lynch and James Moylan. Yet he survived the storm. While the *True Witness* hovered on the brink of bankruptcy, McGee remained unassailable in Montreal and was, Clerk reluctantly concluded, "all-powerful" in Canada West.[76] Although this was an exaggeration, McGee still commanded considerable support among Irish Canadian Catholics. After all, he was sound on the separate schools question, he had become Canada's most eloquent proponent of federalism, and – probably most important of all – he had continued his campaign against the Orange Order in the teeth of the Bradford Outrage.

Having failed to persuade his fellow MPs to remove Orangemen from the judiciary, McGee attempted to short-circuit the Canadian legislature by appealing to the Duke of Newcastle for a royal commission on Canadian Orangeism. In effect, he was attempting to engage British imperial power against local Canadian autonomy in the service of ethnoreligious equality. This approach had Irish historical precedents. During the early 1790s, the Catholic Committee in Ireland had tried to enlist the support of Westminster against the Protestant-controlled Irish House of Commons. Ultimately, in Ireland, the strategy had been superseded by the militant nationalism of the United Irishmen; in Canada, it would be challenged by radical Irish nationalists, who dismissed McGee as an ambitious adventurer and preferred direct action over and above appeals to Westminster. Such people were very much a minority at this stage, but their influence was increasing. In 1861 the St Patrick's Day parade in Toronto was cancelled for the third year in a row. But the pressure was building to return to the streets, and it was unlikely that it could be resisted for much longer.

Nevertheless, as McGee had told Bishop Lynch, Irish Catholics had scored some significant successes. Attempts to incorporate the Orange Order, to allow divorce, and to abolish separate schools had all been turned back, and municipal reform in Toronto promised to reduce the power of Orangeism in the police force. More generally, McGee argued, the Reform alliance had helped to defuse ethnoreligious tensions in Canada West, as had his personal efforts to counter religious bigotry in the press, whether in the *Globe*'s coverage of the royal tour or the *True Witness*'s much more strident anti-Protestantism. In Canada, it seemed, the centre had a good chance of holding – even of expanding. In the United States, however, it was a different story altogether.

## CHAPTER FIVE

# Democracy Armed and Insolent
## April 1861 – May 1862

While McGee was working to bring Canadians together, the United States was falling apart. In a crisis of continental expansion, set in motion by the Mexican war and the thrust into the southwest, deep divisions emerged over the status of slavery in the new American territories. At stake was the balance of power between the slaveholding South and the free-labour North. Most white Southerners construed attacks on slavery in the southwest as attacks on their way of life and feared that the exclusion of slavery there would reduce their society to an isolated and vulnerable minority in the United States. Northerners who opposed the extension of slavery were not necessarily abolitionists – for many, the great attraction of free soil was that it would keep Afro-Americans out of the west – but they believed in the superiority of their own social system and wanted to ensure its dominant position in the country.

As the United States lurched through a series of crises during the 1850s, the sections became increasingly polarized; in a climate of distrust and recrimination, each side increasingly believed the worst of the other. For many Southerners, the election of Abraham Lincoln as president in 1860 was the last straw; unless they took swift and radical action, they would be governed by a man who viewed slavery as a great moral wrong. Swift and radical action was forthcoming: South Carolina voted to secede from the Union, and six other southern states quickly followed suit. With the failure of attempts to cobble together a compromise, and with secessionists taking over federal institutions in the South, the crunch came in April 1861, when the Confederates opened fire on the federal stronghold of Fort Sumter. "That shot fired at Fort Sumter," wrote McGee, "was the signal gun of a new epoch for North America, which told the people of Canada, more plainly than human speech can ever express it, to sleep no more, except on their arms."[1]

As a "continental people," in McGee's phrase, Canadians were vitally concerned with the crisis in the United States.[2] Within British North America, there was widespread support for abolitionism, and as long as the conflict was viewed through the lens of slavery, Canadians generally sympathized with the North. But as it became clear that the federal government was fighting against secession rather than slavery, the moral case for supporting the North became harder to sustain. Interpreting the Civil War as a struggle between rival economic sections rather than a crusade against slavery, leading Canadian conservative newspapers began to side with the South. Other fears bubbled to the surface; the United States government might provoke a war with Canada to unite Americans behind a common foe, or the Civil War might serve as a prelude to the annexation of Canada. Although Canadian opinion was fragmented and crossed party lines, the mood became increasingly anti-northern during the spring and summer of 1861. In the process, traditional loyalist stereotypes about the United States acquired new force.

According to S.F. Wise, most politically involved Canadians viewed the Civil War as "the inevitable outcome of the weaknesses of government in the United States and as a satisfactory vindication of British American forms and ways."[3] The central "weakness of government," from the loyalist viewpoint, was an excess of democracy; the United States was synonymous with political factionalism, populist prejudice, endemic instability, and moral degradation and was now being destroyed by the very anti-authoritarian spirit that had attended its birth. Canada, in contrast, had found the right balance between authority and liberty and was characterized by peace, order, and stability.[4]

It was only natural to expect that McGee would respond in the same way. During the mid-1850s he had argued that American society was coming apart at the seams, with excessive individualism and materialism, the breakdown of the family, a culture of constant nervous excitement, amoral celebrity worship, urban squalor, exploitation, and violence. McGee had become disillusioned with both the Demo-crats and the Whigs, disgusted by the Know-Nothing movement, and dismayed by the demagoguery of American life. He was also a major critic of American expansionism, sympathizing with the Native people who were swept aside by white settlement, and condemning filibus-tering expeditions in Central America.[5] Having voted with his feet and crossed the border, McGee praised Canada for its healthier social environment, its respectful attitude to the Catholic Church, and its freedom from the taint of slavery. All this would seem to place him squarely in the Canadian tradition of anti-Americanism, in which the Civil War appeared as divine retribution for rebellion and continental imperialism.

Yet there was not a trace of vindictiveness or *schadenfreude* in McGee's reaction to the Civil War. On the contrary, he was appalled by signs of Canadian satisfaction at America's conflict and rejected the view that the Civil War demonstrated the bankruptcy of America's republican institutions. "All this wretched small-talk about the failure of the Re-publican experiment in the United States ought to be frowned down, wherever it appears, by the Canadian public," he said in July 1861, just before the first Battle of Bull Run.[6] As the conflict intensified, so did McGee's revulsion towards those Canadians who exulted in Amer-ica's misery. "I cannot conceive the perversity of nature, the hopeless skepticism in man's self-government," he said, "which could make any one applaud at such a national tragedy – at the miserable prospect of a whole continent given over to bloodshed, rapine, and revolution."[7]

Rather than denigrating the United States, McGee described its system of government as "the product of the highest political experi-ence of modern times," and believed that it would emerge from the conflict even stronger than before.[8] And rather than seeing the Civil War as punishment for the "inordinate ambition" of a predatory fed-eral government, he maintained that the southern states were the dom-inant force behind American expansionism. "We should remember on this head," McGee wrote, "that the invasion of Texas – the Santa Fe expedition, the descent on California, the filibuster forays into South America, were mainly acts of the floating, turbulent Mississippi popu-lation, who are the chief authors of the present insurrection." The conflict, in McGee's view, had nothing to do with any inherent weakness of republican institutions or with payback for American imperialism, and everything to do with the rebellious proclivities of the South and the impossibility of combining "social slavery" and "political liberty" in the same state. Instead of exhibiting "ungenerous exaltation" at the troubles of the United States, Canadians should side with the forces of liberty and support the Americans in the "defensive and justifiable war of their Revolution."[9]

Why did McGee, who had been one of the severest critics of the United States and was emphatically not a republican, take this position? Part of the answer lies in his long-standing attitude towards American unity. Throughout his earlier American career, McGee had opposed anything that might lead to the breakup of the United States. Much of his social and political criticism, in fact, had been directed against the putative anarchical tendencies of American life and had been intended to keep the country together. The same dynamic had influenced his attitude towards slavery in the United States. Convinced that abolition would plunge the country into civil war, he had denounced *Uncle Tom's Cabin* as a dreadful and dangerous book, and supported the Fugitive Slave Law of 1850.[10] In the United States, there had been a fundamental contradiction between national unity and abolitionism; forced to choose between the two, McGee had come down on the side of national unity.

In Canada, however, national unity and abolitionism were perfectly compatible; indeed, anti-slavery sentiment could function as a cohesive force, through which Canadians could assume the moral high ground and define themselves against Americans. This view found expression in McGee's poem "Along the Line!" in which he imagined the thoughts of Canadian volunteers as they prepared for the impending American invasion of 1812:

> We have never bought or sold
> Afric's sons with Mexic's gold,
> Conscience arms the free and bold,
> Along the line! along the line![11]

Reading these words, some Canadians have assumed that McGee left the United States because he was appalled by slavery and was impressed by its absence in Canada.[12] In fact, McGee's reaction to slavery in the United States had been one of ambivalence rather than abhorrence, and had nothing to do with his decision to leave the United States.

Having moved north, McGee no longer had any reason to be ambivalent about slavery. The contrast came through clearly in his different responses to runaway slave cases in the United States and Canada. In the United States in 1851, he had been furious when a group of Afro-Americans defied the Fugitive Slave Law and rescued the escaped slave Shadrach Minkins from a Boston courtroom.[13] In Canada nine years later, McGee opposed the extradition of another escaped slave, John Anderson, who had killed a Missouri farmer during his flight to freedom.[14]

What had changed was not so much McGee's attitude as his location. Because he considered that the Fugitive Slave Law was essential to American unity, it must be upheld in the United States; the alternative was a prospective civil war and its attendant bloodbath. In Canada, where such considerations were irrelevant, he believed that escaped slaves should be given sanctuary. But although McGee had avoided the contradiction between national unity and slavery in Canada, he recognized its continuing force in the United States and empathized with those Irish Americans who were torn between their oath to uphold the federal constitution and their moral objection to slavery, just as he had been torn himself.[15]

After Fort Sumter, though, everything was different. During the 1850s, McGee had attacked American abolitionists on the grounds that their actions would detonate a civil war. Now, he attacked the slave states for actually starting one – and for doing so despite the Fugitive Slave Law, the Dred Scott decision, and the adoption of Stephen Douglas's principle that the new territories could join the Union with or without slavery as they chose.[16] McGee still believed that these concessions constituted an acceptable price for American unity; the problem was that the South had refused the terms.

With that refusal, McGee could now express freely and fully views that had previously been half-hidden. The South, he declared, was attempting to establish a state based on "the monstrous doctrines of the innate diversity of the human race, the incurable barbarism of the black, and the hereditary mastership of the white ... Build a government on such a basis; accept 300,000 whites as the keepers and lords of life and death over 4,000,000 blacks; erect an entire social and political superstructure on that foundation, and contemplate, if you can, without horror, the problems and the conflicts you are preparing for posterity!"[17]

Among the other factors that shaped his response to the Civil War, McGee's personal connections in the North should not be overlooked. He had lived and worked in Boston, Buffalo, and New York and travelled extensively in the northern states. Despite his antipathy towards American society, he still had many friends in the North and continued to conduct speaking tours in the region. Personal ties mattered to McGee, even though he was prepared to break them when fundamental political differences got in the way. But in the summer and autumn of 1861, the differences between Canada and the United States were being contained, and McGee's American experiences and friendships meant that he could not look on the Civil War with indifference or complacency. Nor, as a conservative in the Burkean tradition with a strong aversion to revolution, was McGee likely to welcome what he called the South's "wanton assault on the legitimate central authority" in the United States.[18]

There was also an important Canadian dimension to his position: it was not in Canada's self-interest to alienate the North by supporting or sympathizing with the South. Since the North was the dominant military force on the continent and would ultimately defeat the Confederates, McGee reasoned, Canada should keep in its good books and reduce the risk of armed invasion or economic retaliation. The Reciprocity Treaty was up for renegotiation in 1865; should an aggrieved Congress refuse to renew it, the economic consequences would be disastrous for Canada. And what would happen in the unlikely event that the North did not prevail and the United States split? The North and the South would become two hostile powers, ushering in an era of "standing armies, of passports, of espionage, of fluctuating boundaries, and border wars." They would also be diplomatic rivals; if Britain became the ally of the South, France would become the ally of the North. As the continent became permanently militarized and destabilized, British North America would become drawn into geopolitical rivalries beyond its control – a prospect that no Canadian could welcome.[19]

On the grounds of both enlightened self-interest and political morality, then, Canada had every reason to support the North. McGee's earlier position on American unity was brought into phase with his Canadian nationalism, and his anti-slavery sentiments became more pronounced. The key to his outlook lay in his response to changing circumstances, rather than any profound ideological shift. What is most striking about McGee's attitude to the United States during the first months of the Civil War is not its absorption into the Canadian loyalist tradition but its underlying consistency with his earlier views.

———

Against the background of Civil War in the United States, McGee kept working for solutions for Canada's own sectional tensions. In the face of Clear Grit assertions that annexation to the United States was preferable to the French domination of Canada West, and amid warnings that Canada was on the brink of a "war of race," McGee tried to dampen the kind of inflammatory rhetoric that would "drive moderate men into extremes." Drawing on Daniel O'Connell's complaint that Irish constituencies had been underrepresented in Britain's House of Commons, he continued to press for equal representation with minority safeguards in Canada and for the ultimate goal of British North American union.[20] But when McGee asked Cartier in the legislature if the government was prepared to work towards federation, he was met with a terse, "It is not."[21]

Knowing that he would hit a brick wall on this issue, McGee had already discussed other methods of strengthening and uniting Canada. Establishing a hereditary monarchy in Canada was one possibility, and colonial representation at Westminster was another; the closer the connection with Britain, the greater the security of Canada. And if federation was not on the political agenda, he was prepared to support the concept of the double majority, provided that it was not turned into "a rule or principle."[22] There was a good reason for this proviso; if the double majority became a fixed principle, there was little or no chance of getting improved separate schools legislation through Parliament, where it would encounter strong opposition from Upper Canadian representatives.

On the same day that McGee asked Cartier about federation, he asked Macdonald whether the government intended to introduce a separate schools bill in the current session. The answer was an equally terse no; with an election coming up, there was no way that Macdonald would sponsor any measure that might cost him Protestant votes.[23] When Richard Scott reintroduced his bill for improved separate schools legislation in May, it was frozen out for the second time.[24] Yet Macdonald in the spring and early summer of 1861 had secretly assured the hierarchy that he would support a separate schools measure once the election was over.[25] It is not clear whether McGee was aware of this promise. Even had he known, he would not have believed it.

———

The long-awaited election was called in the summer of 1861. McGee was on firm ground in the newly created constituency of Montreal West and easily regained his seat – although George Clerk bitterly complained that McGee's opponent had withdrawn after being intimidated by a mob of "Irish rowdies."[26] In Canada West, where Irish Catholics had become increasingly divided about the Reform alliance, many of them were turning with Moylan towards the Liberal-Conservatives, much to McGee's disgust. The depth of his anger became clear when, immediately after his acclamation in Montreal, he received letters of congratulation from Irish Catholics who were planning to vote for John A. Macdonald in Kingston. "I cannot understand – I tell you frankly – this double-dealing folly," he wrote to Daniel MaCarow, a prominent Kingston Irishman. "Do these gentlemen take me for a fool? ... Tell these trimmers and double-dealers from me, that I recognize no communion with men who desert their principles, in the hour of trial and that I beg them to spare me in future the humiliation of their congratulations." "I write with feeling, bitterly, but honestly," he concluded, adding a parting shot about "these gentlemen who cannot walk a chalk line for an hour" – ironically, a charge that had been frequently levelled at McGee himself and one that would be raised again in the near future.[27]

The key battle took place not in Kingston but in Toronto, where George Brown was challenged by the Liberal-Conservative candidate John Crawford. A Protestant who was married to a Catholic, Crawford enjoyed the support of Bishop Lynch, Moylan's *Canadian Freeman*, and Michael Murphy's quasi-Fenian Hibernian Benevolent Society. McGee's allies, such as John O'Donohoe, Thomas McCrossan, and William Halley – the same men who had originally helped to establish the *Canadian Freeman* – continued to support Brown and the Reform alliance.

From Montreal, McGee offered encouragement, advice, and strategic support to the "faithful band" of Irish Catholic Reformers.[28] As well as reiterating his earlier views – asserting that "Mrs Crawford's husband" would never initiate improved separate schools legislation, and that Irish Catholics would become an isolated and vulnerable minority if they voted Conservative – McGee resorted to some old-fashioned Orange bashing. Irish Catholics, he informed O'Donohoe, should be told that Conservative candidates such as John Beverley Robinson had secret plans to establish an Orange militia, "a project so fraught with evil to Catholics in Upper Canada, that I think if properly presented to our friends, they would revolt against its advocates and representatives."[29] Whether or not such plans actually existed was irrelevant (they almost certainly did not); the idea was to play on traditional Irish Catholic fears of Orangeism and thus hit the Liberal-Conservatives at their weakest point. In effect, McGee was exploiting ethnoreligious fears as a means of safeguarding the Reform alliance; it was not, it must be said, his finest hour.

McGee also endorsed O'Donohoe's plan to call an Irish Catholic convention in Toronto to rally support for Brown.[30] But the city's Irish Catholic Reformers were being squeezed between clerical support for the Conservatives and the more militant tactics of Michael Murphy's Hibernian Benevolent Society. At a political gathering in St Lawrence Hall, Murphy's supporters rushed the stage when Brown started speaking, and Murphy was charged with assault after hitting Brown over the head from behind with a cudgel.[31] Just over a week later, at a pro-Reform Irish Catholic meeting, Murphy and the Hibernians shouted down O'Donohoe at the front of the room while Moylan stayed at the back, reportedly blowing cigar smoke "in respectable people's faces in the most disgraceful manner."[32]

Despite these events, McGee still expected Brown to keep his seat.[33] Yet for all McGee's arguments, scaremongering, and exhortations, Irish Catholics in Toronto were abandoning the Reform alliance in droves. In the event, Brown was defeated by an unholy but effective alliance of Irish Catholics and Orangemen. Bishop Lynch had encouraged his flock to vote not only for Crawford but also for John Hillyard Cameron, the grand master of the Orange Order, who was running for Peel. Crawford, Cameron, and Robinson were all elected.

"A section of the Roman Catholics, liberals at heart, stood by the Opposition," reported the *Globe*, "but they were almost always few in number, and in the vast majority of cases the whole Irish Roman Catholic vote was thrown for the Ministerial candidate. The old bitterness against Orangeism was entirely discarded ... Papal and Orange influences [were] going hand in hand against us."[34] If McGee had retained his powerful grip on Montreal, where the school question was not a pressing issue for his constituents, his attempt to unite Irish Catholics in Canada West behind the Reform Party had manifestly failed. Macdonald's Liberal-Conservatives won thirty seats in Canada West (up from twenty-eight in 1857), while Cartier's *Bleus* won thirty-five (down from forty-eight in 1857) in Canada East – just enough to stay in power.[35]

---

Over the rest of the year, McGee sought to recover the ground he had lost in Canada West. His task was made harder by his split with Moylan, which had deepened and widened under the pressures of the election campaign. Amid mutual recriminations, Moylan refused to print McGee's letters in the *Canadian Freeman*, effectively shutting him out of the newspaper he had helped to start and severing him from its Irish Catholic readership. In response, McGee resorted to printed circulars and planned to form a Loyal Irish Society of Canada that would "diffuse sound political information among our countrymen."[36] But printed circulars were a poor substitute for newspaper columns, and clerical opposition hobbled the Irish Society right from the start. When McGee and his supporter Frank Smith attempted to hold an Irish Society convention at a Catholic schoolhouse in London, they were ejected by the priest and forced to reconvene above Smith's store.[37]

Conservative Irish Catholics denounced the Irish Society as a propaganda machine for George Brown's bigotry and criticized it for being open to all men, whether Irish Catholic or not; even "Germans or Niggers" could join, complained one of Moylan's correspondents.[38] Moylan argued that McGee claimed to speak for Irish Catholics while attacking the views of their religious leaders, thus arrogating to himself a superior role to that of the bishops and priests. It was useless for McGee to pretend that his Irish Society was a secular organization, Moylan wrote; the "vital questions of Catholic education and emigration" were not purely secular, and the church had the right and duty to involve itself in such matters. All in all, he concluded, "the whole affair is a threadbare and flimsily concealed device on the part of Mr. Thomas D'Arcy McGee to galvanize his decayed prestige and to recover his lost influence over the Catholics of Western Canada."[39]

The previous year, McGee and Moylan had tried to maintain their friendship despite their political differences; now, the conflict became bitter and personal. After the election, while on vacation at the fashionable resort town of Cacouna in Canada East, Moylan supposedly said that he had received $3,700 in return for supporting the Liberal-Conservatives. The story was picked up by Thomas McCready and James Donnelly, two of McGee's major supporters in Montreal. When they told McGee, he penned a circular that was printed in the Toronto *Mirror* and the *Globe*.[40] Pointing to the "late extraordinary change in the principles and conduct" of the *Canadian Freeman* and claiming that the paper had "turned a sharp angle on the eve of the election," McGee declared that Moylan had sold himself to the government, and for the price of $3,700 was spewing out "slanders and insults against his old friends and patrons"; it was an act of betrayal, "an exhibition of the workings of the viler species of human motives." Privately, McGee

was just as scathing. It was, he told O'Donohoe, "one of the most fla-
grant cases of bargain and sale, that ever disgraced any press, *secular* or
*religious*."[41]

With that, the gloves were off. Moylan replied that the accusation
was "characteristic of the disposition manifested by the writer, of
late – truculent, false, vindictive." George Clerk had been right after
all, Moylan wrote: McGee was a self-serving hypocrite, who had been
prepared to sell himself to the Liberal-Conservatives during the 1857
election and had formed an alliance with Brown merely to advance
his own career. Now, here he was, making frothy speeches about separate schools while working for a party whose slogan was "No Sectarian Education!" The same double standard applied to McGee's personal life; publicly, he denounced the Orange Order, but privately he
hobnobbed with the brethren in Orange lodges. This was all part of
a pattern stretching back to 1848, Moylan asserted, when McGee had
committed "treason and treachery of the blackest type towards his compatriots." All the old charges were trotted out and used against him.[42]

The attack was patently unfair, and it is not surprising that some
of McGee's Toronto allies tried to bring down Moylan's newspaper
by suing for libel.[43] But it was no more unfair than McGee's allega-
tion that Moylan had been bought by the government. Moylan had
changed his views about the Reform alliance the previous November,
and McGee knew it; there were no sudden "sharp angles" or "extraordinary changes in policy" before the election. There is also evidence
to suggest that McGee rushed to judgment by taking unsubstantiated
rumours at face value. In September he asked McCready and Donnelly
for "explicit written letters" about Moylan's statement in Cacouna and
even drew up a template of the intended letters for publication in the
*Globe*.[44] It is significant that McGee sought written verification well
after he had made his initial charges and that no letters from McCready
and Donnelly ever appeared in the *Globe*.

Moylan could have added, but did not, that McGee himself had
helped to raise money for the *Canadian Freeman* and had privately
assured Moylan of an income for life if he stayed the course and continued to support the Reform Party.[45] From McGee's perspective, this
money would be Moylan's reward for sticking to his principles, while

the money Moylan supposedly got from the government was a bribe that made him abandon those principles. A double standard was operating: McGee publicly condemned patronage when in opposition but privately signalled his willingness to use it when in power. That was how the world worked; that was how McGee worked. But it was not simply a matter of cold political calculation. His use of Orange scaremongering tactics, his outburst against the Kingston Irish Catholics who praised him while voting for Macdonald, and his impetuous charges about Moylan's supposed betrayal were all symptomatic of deep political passions and an intense conviction that the Conservative alliance would lead Irish Canadian Catholics into the social and political wilderness.

While the combined attacks of the hierarchy, the Catholic press, the Orange Order, and the Hibernian Benevolent Society were forcing McGee onto the defensive in Canada West, developments in the United States were challenging his position on the Civil War. It was increasingly difficult to argue that Canada should stay on good terms with the North when newspapers such as the New York *Herald* were advocating annexation, when Secretary of State William Seward seemed to share their sentiments, and when the Union army was expanding at an unprecedented rate.[46] Canadian-American relations approached the crisis point towards the end of the year, when a Union ship intercepted the *Trent*, a British mail packet, and seized two Confederate agents who were en route to Europe. As far as the British government was concerned, this was an act of piracy; Lord John Russell sent an ultimatum to Washington, demanding the release of the prisoners by 26 December. The scenario that had long haunted Canadian politicians appeared to be unfolding: Britain and the United States were moving towards war, and Canada would be the first casualty.[47]

This prospect was particularly appealing to Irish American nationalists, who saw an opportunity to strike back at the British Empire through Canada and convinced themselves that Irish Canadians would welcome an American invasion force. Nothing could be further from the truth, McGee replied; on the contrary, he and his fellow Irish Canadians would fight "as one man in defence of the Canadian Constitution and the Imperial Connexion."[48] His own brother was a captain in the Union army, he said, but "if he comes here as an enemy – if he comes here to trample upon the rights of Canada, let him meet the fate of an enemy and an invader. Our first duty is to Canada."[49]

Three days before the ultimatum expired, McGee held a public meeting in Montreal to demonstrate Irish Canadian loyalty and to call for an Irish regiment to defend the country. Things did not, however, go as smoothly as he had hoped. Among the crowd were members of Bernard Devlin's militia company, along with a group of Fenians who had come from Vermont especially for the occasion; encouraged by Owen Devlin, Bernard's brother, they began to heckle and hiss the speakers. Their intention, as McGee realized, was to show that Irish Canadians were divided on the defence of Canada and that some of them would indeed welcome an American invasion. To force his opponents into the open, McGee called for a division of the whole meeting. The tactic worked; rather than reveal themselves, the dissidents moved with the majority, and the resolution calling for an Irish regiment passed unanimously.[50]

This event, relatively minor in itself, anticipated some of the central characteristics of Irish Canadian political conflict later in the decade. On the one hand, radical Irish Canadian nationalists, some of whom were in the militia, joined forces with their American allies to attack Irish loyalists and repudiate the imperial connection. On the other hand, McGee confronted the challenge through a strategy of polarization that was designed to identify and isolate his republican enemies. This was to be a recurring pattern over the next seven years, with one crucial difference: radical Irish nationalists in Canada became increasingly organized, influential, and militant, to the point where McGee's strategy of polarization began to backfire on him.

Although McGee was powerful enough to face down the radicals in the winter of 1861–62, he was concerned about their potential for growth. During his first four years in Canada, his opposition to secret societies had focused on the Orange Order; now it seemed that Fenianism was beginning to get a foothold. In Toronto, Fenian circles were already forming under the umbrella of the Hibernian Benevolent Society, and McGee wanted to prevent something similar from happening in Montreal. Shortly after the meeting in Montreal, he fired a warning shot in the *Montreal Herald*. Writing under the pseudonym *Civis Canadiensis*, he pointed out that anyone who organized a seditious secret society in Canada East faced twenty-one years in jail, and that anyone who joined such a society could get up to seven years.[51]

This confrontational approach, together with his unequivocal loyalism, made him the most hated man among Fenians on both sides of the Atlantic. Writing to McGee from Dublin in the aftermath of the *Trent* crisis, Timothy Daniel Sullivan noted the "bitterly anti-English spirit" of the Fenians and their contempt for anyone, priests and patriots included, who refused to join the movement. "Towards any who may have made themselves particularly obnoxious," Sullivan wrote, "they take every means of manifesting their bitter enmity." And among those who were "particularly obnoxious," he added, was McGee himself, the former rebel who was now supporting the "English connection in Canada."[52] The lines had been drawn for the biggest battle of McGee's life.

⸺

As it turned out, Governor General Monck rejected McGee's plan to form a Montreal Irish regiment, on the grounds that Canadian defence forces should transcend specific nationalities.[53] In any case, the United States backed down over the *Trent* crisis and agreed to release the Confederate agents: "One war at a time," Abraham Lincoln told his cabinet.[54] But if the immediate danger had lifted, the broader issue of Canadian defence remained. Across the Atlantic, the *Trent* crisis had strengthened the position of Little Englanders such as Richard Cobden and John Bright, who argued that the cost of defending Canada far exceeded any benefits to Britain. Canada was a diplomatic liability as well, which provided the United States with a potential hostage in the event of deteriorating Anglo-American relations. All in all, it was better to cut the cords and let Canada fend for itself or drift into the United States.[55]

Against these arguments, McGee asserted the indivisibility of the empire. The people of Canada, Britain, and Ireland, he wrote, were fellow subjects, sharing a common political heritage; such an arrangement could not be reduced to "the scales of a cash balance." An attack on any part of the empire was an attack on the whole: "Those who talk, therefore, of it being unreasonable to expect the Empire to defend Canada, forget that Canada *is* itself the Empire in North America." With Canada's proximity to "democracy armed and insolent," the vast imbalance in power and population between Canada and the United States, and the Union's military buildup, it was impossible for Canada to stand alone against American aggression. But as part of a united British Empire, the imbalance could be redressed, and Canada could avoid being absorbed into the United States. Implicit in his position was the strategy of deterrence; a strong and unequivocal imperial commitment to Canada would prevent Americans from marching northwards in the first place. Conversely, the anti-colonial views circulating in Britain imperilled Canada by giving "a new hope of spoliation to our irritated neighbours."[56]

At the same time, McGee insisted that Canadians must take an active role in their own defence; they were, after all, equal members of the empire and should behave as such. This meant, at its most obvious level, that they should start arming themselves. But it also meant creating a common identity, a common purpose and a sense of cooperation, to engage all Canadians in the struggle for survival, freedom, and prosperity. "If we would make Canada safe and secure, rich and renowned," he wrote, "we must all liberalise – locally, sectionally, religiously, nationally. There is room enough in this country for one great free people, but there is not room enough, under the same flag, and the same laws, for two or three angry, suspicious, obstructive 'nationalities.'"[57]

External security was contingent not only on imperial support but also on domestic harmony. "A Canadian nationality, not French-Canadian, nor British-Canadian, nor Irish-Canadian – patriotism rejects the prefix – is, in my opinion, what we should look forward to," he wrote; "that is what we ought to labour for, that is what we ought to be prepared to defend to the death." It is one of McGee's most frequently quoted – and most frequently misunderstood – statements. Rather than calling for Canadian homogeneity – something that he felt was both unattainable and undesirable – McGee was continuing to advocate a form of nationality that superseded but did not abolish ethnoreligious identities. In the same speech, McGee insisted on the importance of "giving full credit to all the elements which at the present day compose our population," as long as those elements were free of former feuds. "All we have to do," he said, "is, each for himself, to keep down dissensions which can only weaken, impoverish, and keep back the country ... to lift ourselves to the level of our destinies, to rise above all low limitations and narrow circumscriptions, to cultivate that true catholicity of spirit which embraces all creeds, all classes, and all races, in order to make of our boundless Province, so rich in known and unknown resources, a great new Northern nation."[58]

---

One way to strengthen Canadian nationality was to attract more people into the country – and this became one of McGee's major preoccupations during the parliamentary sessions of 1861 and 1862. "I can say for myself most truly," he declared in April 1862, "... that if I were quitting public life or personal life to-morrow, I would feel a far higher satisfaction in remembering that some honest man's sheltering roof-tree had been raised by my advocacy, than if I had been Premier or Governor of the Province. Let it be the mad desire of others in Europe and America to lay waste populous places; let it be our better ambition to populate waste places."[59] What was good for settlers was good for the country. By closing the population gap between Canada and the United States, immigration would increase Canada's capacity for survival and self-defence. If more immigrants came into Canada East, the demographic imbalance in the province would be redressed, and sectional tensions would be reduced.[60] That, at any rate, was the theory. In practice, most French Canadian politicians were hardly likely to promote non-French immigration in Canada East, for the obvious reason that it could threaten their majority status in the region.

As chairman of the Select Committee on Immigration, McGee argued that the crisis in the United States, along with the Maori war in New Zealand, would induce more emigrants to choose Canada as their new home; America's and New Zealand's difficulty, one might say, was Canada's opportunity.[61] But if the opportunity was to be seized, more had to be done to attract immigrants and keep them in the country once they arrived – abolishing the tax on immigrants who intended to stay in Canada, constructing an "enclosed landing-place for emigrants" arriving in Quebec City (modelled on New York's Castle Garden), building more colonization roads in Canada East, and breaking up monopolies that controlled access to land. All these reforms should be coordinated by a new Department of Agriculture and Emigration, to replace the existing ad hoc administrative structure.[62]

The program was ambitious – and was meant to be. As someone who had traversed the Atlantic four times and had spent much of his time in Boston and New York trying to improve the condition of Irish immigrants, McGee had extensive first-hand experience of the issues involved. One of the most striking manifestations of this was his awareness that immigration to the United States and Canada could only be properly understood in a continental framework, and that cross-border flows must be factored into the analysis; this was why he called for a Canadian agent in New York, who would direct new immigrants north and encourage native Canadians to return home.[63]

Above and beyond his specific recommendations, McGee believed that Canadian institutions were the single most important factor in drawing emigrants into the country. Despite the problems in Canada, these institutions were "the most desirable in the world" and would remain attractive as long as moderate Canadians succeeded in overcoming religious and political bigotry.[64] All roads, it seemed, looped back to the question of religious tolerance, which was an essential prerequisite both for a successful immigration policy and for Canadian solidarity in the face of American expansionism.

———

The litmus test of religious tolerance, in McGee's view, remained improved separate schools legislation; as well as preserving and promoting the Catholic faith, it would remove the principal source of religious tension in the country, he believed. But it was still not clear whether

Upper Canadian Protestants would agree with McGee's minimum demands, and his distrust of the Liberal-Conservatives remained as deep as ever.

Yet Macdonald did indeed make good on his secret pre-election promise to advance the cause of separate schools in the province. In March 1862 he gave Egerton Ryerson the green light to open discussions with Bishop Lynch; the two men found a significant degree of common ground, after which Ryerson drew up proposals for new legislation.[65] By this time, however, the indefatigable Richard Scott was preparing his third Separate Schools Bill, which attempted to ensure that "the Roman Catholics of Upper Canada should be treated with the same liberality as the Protestants of Lower Canada," and which went much farther than both his previous efforts and Ryerson's current proposals.[66]

As the politicians debated whether to proceed with Scott's bill, one of the strongest expressions of support came from an apparently unlikely quarter – John Beverley Robinson, the Liberal-Conservative MP from Toronto West, who had recently been re-elected with the backing of both Irish Catholics and the Orange Order.[67] In contrast, some of McGee's fellow Reformers came out strongly against the religious segregation of education. "Were the measure granted," one of them asserted, "we might have every other sect making similar applications": High Anglicans would request their own schools, other denominations would follow suit, and the entire common educational system would start to unravel. Religious instruction belonged at home, not in the schools, they argued; besides, separating Protestant and Catholic children would only accentuate differences and destroy the harmony that should exist among all religious groups in the country.[68] Such views were beginning to gather momentum, and there was a distinct possibility that a majority of Reformers would reject Scott's bill.

McGee had feared as much, and he had his reply ready. The bill, he claimed, was "not demanded so much by the clergy as by the laity" and was not "the result of ecclesiastical dictation" – technically true, perhaps, but something that conveniently omitted the considerable clerical input. The principle of separate schools had already been established by earlier legislation, McGee said; Scott's bill was simply designed to make the system work more efficiently and equitably – especially by helping Catholics in rural areas to have their own schools. And there were more Catholics in rural areas, he noted, than there were in the cities of Upper Canada – a point that subsequent historians of the Irish in Canada often overlooked.

All these arguments had been made before. But there were two elements of McGee's speech that sent shockwaves through the Reform ranks. First, he declared that anyone who opposed Scott's bill "would write himself down as an enemy of religious freedom, and those members who gave it their support would proclaim a true liberality whatever be the partizan names they bore." There was no mistaking his meaning: Opposition to the bill stemmed from religious bigotry, and much of this opposition came from within his own party. Second, McGee looked the political implications of his position directly in the face. If the debate demonstrated that Catholic religious liberties in Upper Canada were safer in the hands of the Liberal-Conservatives than the Reformers, then he would have no hesitation in supporting the Liberal-Conservatives, "however painful it might be to him personally" and however much he disagreed with them on other issues. Over the previous years, he continued, he had believed that the Reformers were more open to separate schools reform than the Liberal-Conservatives were; now, when it came down to a "practical test," too many of his colleagues were found wanting.[69]

It was a remarkable performance, which stunned many of his listeners and left no doubt about his priorities. Improved separate schools legislation was more important than the Reform alliance; indeed, the Reform alliance was, among other things, a means to the end of improved separate schools. If the means contradicted the end, he would employ different means, through supporting the Liberal-Conservatives. During the debate, Thomas Ferguson remarked that McGee's "love of the Opposition was growing cold, and that he was a species of political commodity open for sale." This was a caricature; it was a matter of principle, not price. But the comments of other politicians that McGee had threatened to desert the Reformers were right on the mark.[70]

The following day, McGee sent a note to Luther Holton explaining that he had informed the Reform leaders of his position before he spoke and that his intention was to ensure that Reform supporters of separate schools, such as Michael Foley and Adam Wilson, would not be isolated in Canada West. "It was, I felt, a bold, and even a defiant course to take, but I am rejoiced to see that the event has justified the risk – 15 sustaining Foley, 10 going the other way – and a few being absent, or out of the House."[71]

Holton was not convinced. "I think he made a great error in uttering the threat he did and I propose telling him so when I see him," he told George Brown. "He has been behaving remarkably well this session and is rapidly taking a high position. *For his own sake* as well as ours I hope he is not going to throw himself away."[72] Shortly afterwards, the two men had a "plain talk," in which McGee spoke of the peculiar position he was in as a Catholic in the Reform Party, and said that he would have been "frankly embarrassed" if a majority of his colleagues had refused to consider Scott's bill. It seems to have had some effect; Holton agreed that "allowances must be made for the exigencies of his peculiar position."[73]

Brown, however, was in no mood to make any allowances and was particularly incensed by McGee's assertion that anyone who opposed Scott's bill must be an enemy of religious liberty. This was not so, Brown argued. True liberals believed that Catholic and Protestant children should be educated together in schools where their religious beliefs would be respected, and not that they should be prized apart by the dictates of the Catholic Church. From this perspective, McGee's rejection of common schools was the product of "bigotry, intolerance and narrowness of mind." But McGee was right about one thing, Brown acknowledged; the Liberal-Conservatives were more likely than the Reformers to support separate schools. The Liberal-Conservatives, after all, contained High Anglicans who wanted their own separate schools, along with unprincipled and ambitious men who would do anything to stay in power, such as pandering to French Canadians and Irish Catholics on the education issue.[74]

At last, the tensions between McGee and Brown on the separate schools issue had come into the open; the previous four years of fudging, evasion, ambiguity, and papering over the cracks could no longer be sustained, and the contradictions that Egerton Ryerson had exposed were now recognized and admitted by the Reformers themselves. And as the gap between McGee and Brown widened, the gap between McGee and Moylan began to narrow. Far from viewing McGee's speech as an "error," Moylan believed that he had finally seen the light and was belatedly coming round to the position that the *Canadian Freeman* had adopted in November 1860. Even George Clerk and the *True Witness* praised McGee's speech in support of Scott's bill – and when this happened, it was clear that the ground was shifting.[75]

When it came to the vote, a large majority decided to proceed with Scott's bill, which was then amended in committee to restrict the influence of priests and to limit the power of school trustees.[76] When it came back to the House at the end of May, Ryerson successfully insisted on further administrative changes as a condition of his support.[77] None of this sat well with Moylan and Clerk, who both pointed out that the amended bill fell far short of educational equality between Catholics in Canada West and Protestants in Canada East.[78] But McGee had anticipated the amendments and was prepared to accept them as a reasonable compromise.[79] Scott felt the same way and supported the amended bill in Parliament. The amendments, however, did nothing to conciliate Thomas Ferguson and his supporters, who dug in for a long debate; as a result, Scott reluctantly concluded that the bill would have to be withdrawn until the next session.[80] Yet again, the campaign to improve separate schools had died on the floor of the House.

———

By this time, though, the separate schools question had been eclipsed by a major political change – the defeat of the Liberal-Conservatives and their replacement by a Reform administration under Sandfield Macdonald and Louis-Victor Sicotte. The shift in power was occasioned by the Militia Bill of May 1862, which was the product of broader concerns about Canadian defence requirements during the Civil War. Amid rumours that the North was planning to invade Canada, British military strategists reckoned that it would take at least 100,000 men to defend the colony from an American attack. Such numbers were beyond Britain's capacity to supply, and the very act of bringing in so many soldiers ran the risk of provoking American countermeasures and precipitating a war that might otherwise be avoided. Far better, then, to rely on domestic Canadian forces; besides, it seemed only reasonable that Canadians should play a leading role in defending their own country. Accordingly, Britain put pressure on the Canadian government to shoulder more responsibility and strengthen its militia.[81]

In these circumstances, Macdonald's government introduced the Militia Bill, with its aim of enlisting 50,000 men – a goal that probably could not have been reached without conscription and would certainly have meant increased taxation. The projected costs were staggering; 10 per cent of Canada's entire revenues would be required simply for training the troops, let alone anything else – and even then, the proposal fell far short of British expectations. Macdonald must have known that his bill would provoke an outcry; conscription and higher taxes were hardly likely to win mass popular support. Not coincidentally, he hit the bottle hard after his first speech on the subject and spent the next few weeks on an alcoholic binge. His biographers suspect that he and his government had run out of ideas and that Macdonald was using the Militia Bill "to provide a discredited government with a dignified exit," as Robin Winks put it.[82] Whether or not this was the case – and the evidence is far from conclusive – the government did indeed fall on the issue. When, on 20 May, the bill came up for its second reading, fifteen *Bleus* switched sides and voted with the opposition. The government resigned the next day, leaving the way open for Sandfield Macdonald.[83]

And so, four years after the Double Shuffle, the Reformers – and McGee with them – were finally in power. McGee's own role during the controversy over the Militia Bill had been uncharacteristically muted; he did not participate in the debates, probably because of his ambivalence about the situation. On the one hand, here was a clear opportunity to defeat the government; on the other, McGee believed that Canada's defences did indeed need to be strengthened, and strengthened quickly. Consequently, as he admitted shortly afterwards, he had "some difficulty" in voting against the Militia Bill. But vote against it he did, on the grounds that it was "cumbrous and costly" and opened the doors to corrupt contractors. Taken in conjunction with Alexander

Galt's budget, which had failed to reduce the deficit or protect Canadian industries, it was enough to warrant the government's downfall.[84]

———•———

By bringing the issue of defence into sharp relief, the Civil War had revealed deep divisions between Canada and Britain, and exposed severe strains between the Liberal-Conservatives and the *Bleus*. In McGee's own case, the Civil War helped to resolve his earlier tensions between American national unity and slavery, and demonstrated his support and sympathy for the North. But in doing so, it created new tensions between his hope for a northern victory and his awareness that many Northerners wanted to annex Canada. As a good Canadian nationalist, there was no doubt where McGee's loyalties lay. When he spoke of being prepared to fight his own brother in defence of Canada, he meant what he said. Nor was there any doubt that McGee wanted to strengthen the militia, as his attempt to raise a Montreal Irish regiment attests.

At the same time, the Civil War increased McGee's sense of the connection between Canadian defence and Canadian identity. Defence was not only a matter of military preparation, important as that was; it also involved uniting Canadians behind a common sense of purpose and building a country that was worth fighting for. This meant bringing in more people, and bringing them together – goals that could be accomplished by encouraging immigration and settling the separate schools question. It also meant challenging those elements in Canada which were deemed to threaten ethnoreligious harmony – Thomas Ferguson's Orangemen, Michael Murphy's Fenians, and those of his fellow Reformers who rejected Richard Scott's Separate Schools Bill. These goals and challenges were not new, but by the spring of 1862 the Civil War had brought them into sharper focus. And it appeared that McGee, as a leading figure in the new administration – the minister responsible for agriculture and immigration, perhaps? – would be well placed to deal with them.[85]

## CHAPTER SIX

# A False Position
## June 1862 – May 1863

It should have been a turning point in McGee's career – and in some respects it was, though not in ways that he anticipated. After sixteen years as a journalist and almost five years as an opposition MP, McGee had finally moved from protest to power. Yet he was never entirely at home in Sandfield Macdonald's Reform administration. In part, it was a matter of personality – Sandfield Macdonald's irascible temperament versus McGee's swashbuckling style. But there was much more to it than that. Sandfield Macdonald took a cautious, safety-first approach, focusing on retrenchment, a balanced budget, and fiscal and administrative reform. McGee was a big-frame thinker, with his plans to establish a "great commercial northern nation" characterized by federation, railway development, western expansion, and increased immigration. "I know it is said, the motto of our Government is, and ought to be, the one word, 'Retrenchment!'" McGee declared. "Gentlemen, that is an excellent word – *Retrenchment* – but I will follow it with another, not hostile, not inconsistent with it, the word *Development*."[1] But the policy of development was indeed inconsistent with the policy of retrenchment – as both radical and conservative critics of the government were quick to point out.

On the key questions of representation, defence, and immigration, McGee was constricted rather than liberated by his position in the government. Sandfield Macdonald believed that the double majority principle was a reasonable way of accommodating ethnoreligious differences and preserving the economic unity of Canada; McGee remained deeply skeptical about its practicability and still saw federation as the solution to Canada's constitutional problems. "This constitutional expedient would not have been my own preference if I were in a position to present a remedy for the incongruities of the Act of Union," he said in June 1862. But since he was "with very few individual exceptions, politically alone in Lower Canada" on the issue, he felt that he had little choice but to acquiesce in the policy.[2]

McGee was also politically alone on the question of defence, which continued to produce severe tensions between Canada and Britain. In response to mounting criticism in Britain that the Canadians were shirking their responsibilities, Sandfield Macdonald tripled the defence budget and increased the size of the militia to ten thousand men. But these measures still fell far short of British expectations, and the criticisms kept coming. Lord Monck, the governor general, regarded Sandfield Macdonald as a mediocre politician and described his cabinet ministers as a "wretched lot" who were not "capable of rising above the level of a parish politician."[3] In considering ways to reconcile Canadian costs with British demands, McGee put forward an imaginative proposal that went far beyond anything envisaged by Sandfield Macdonald – or by the British government, for that matter: an international agreement to make Canada a neutral North American power, drawing on the European precedents of Greece and Belgium earlier in the century. "With such an arrangement," McGee argued, "our own militia would be quite adequate for an internal defence, and Great Britain would be honorably relieved from the anxiety and outlay of her Canadian garrisons."[4] But his idea got nowhere fast; his fellow Reformers simply ignored it, while the Liberal-Conservatives dismissed it as being impractical and "visionary."[5]

Even more frustrating, from McGee's viewpoint, was the government's position on immigration. He had chaired the Select Committee on Immigration since 1860, and continued to gather information about opportunities for settlement in the Northwest.[6] When he ran for re-election in Montreal in June, McGee said that his "highest ambition" was to bring more settlers into the country, and Sandfield Macdonald had promised him the immigration portfolio in the cabinet.[7] But although the promise continued to be dangled in front of him, he was not given the position, and the government failed to pursue a vigorous immigration policy. French Canadians who feared being swamped

7383

Thomas D'Arcy McGee, president of the Executive Council, 1862 (NPA, McCord Museum)

by English speakers did not want McGee in charge of immigration, and there was little love lost between McGee and the Clear Grits in Canada. "The radicals," he wrote, "are a poor pack – their spite is not a whit smaller than their politics."[8] Instead of realizing his highest ambition, McGee was appointed president of the Executive Council, with responsibilities for the administration of government.

He carried out these responsibilities with characteristic thoroughness. One of his major achievements in office – arguably, his only major achievement – was to prepare a detailed and rigorous report on government departments, which was the first serious and systematic attempt to analyze and rationalize the civil service under the union of the Canadas. As well as highlighting existing inefficiencies and wasteful spending, he presented detailed plans to establish clearly defined departmental functions and to develop more efficient policies for recruitment and promotion. The Board of Statistics came in for special attention; it should be remodelled along the lines of the Dutch Statistical Commission and divided into different sections that would provide accurate and comprehensive information about immigration and settlement, arts and manufactures, fisheries, mining, patents, and the composition of Canada's population. As Bruce Curtis notes, his recommendations were "very unevenly implemented" under Sandfield Macdonald's government, but his statistical proposals would assume much greater importance later in the decade.[9]

Had he been given the immigration portfolio and had he been able to emphasize development over retrenchment, things might have been different. But instead of producing exhilaration, McGee's position in the new government was characterized by feelings of frustration and powerlessness. During the summer, he sank into something of a depression, complaining of "a sluggish state of the system" and suffering from a "bilious attack."[10] His mood was not helped by news that two of his Irish friends had died – the Celtic scholar Eugene O'Curry, who had been one of his mentors; and the Young Ireland poet Richard D'Alton Williams. "By what fatality the Elegiac Harp has so often come into my hands of late," he wrote, "I cannot explain."[11]

What pulled him out of his dejection and renewed his sense of purpose was the Intercolonial Convention at Quebec City in September, where government leaders from Canada, New Brunswick, and Nova Scotia met to discuss a railway link between the Maritimes and Canada, trade connections between the regions, and the possibilities of British North American union – all issues that were of central importance to McGee. The meeting had been encouraged by the Duke of Newcastle, who as colonial secretary believed that an Intercolonial Railway linking Halifax and Quebec City would strengthen British North American defences.

During the *Trent* crisis in December 1861, Britain had sent over 11,000 troops to British North America – just in time for the Canadian winter. Only one troopship made it to the St Lawrence; the others landed in Halifax and Saint John. From there, the soldiers had to sled and slog their way through New Brunswick to Canada East, before reaching the Grand Trunk Railway at Rivière-du-Loup. Had an Intercolonial Railway line been in place, the troops could have been brought into Canada much more quickly and effectively. And if such a railway facilitated the political union of the British colonies, Newcastle reasoned, so much the better. A united British North America would become an essential "makeweight in the balance of power on the American Continent." If the colonists took the initiative, Newcastle would support "any well-considered plan which has the concurrence of all Parties concerned."[12]

In response, the Nova Scotia premier Joseph Howe contacted the governments of New Brunswick and Canada to sound out the possibilities of closer intercolonial cooperation.[13] Although Sandfield Macdonald emphasized retrenchment and although many of his supporters had reacted strongly against the corruption associated with the Grand Trunk Railway, he had good reason to discuss plans for a railway connection with the Maritimes. Here, it seemed, was an effective way to blunt British criticism of his defence policy: Canadian support for an Intercolonial Railway could be presented as a major contribution to imperial defence, making it easier for the Reform government to resist British pressure for an even larger militia force.[14] Behind the scenes, further support for the railway came from Montreal business interests and from the new president of the Grand Trunk Railway, Edward Watkin. McGee and Watkin quickly became close friends and allies; in 1865 McGee would dedicate his *Speeches and Addresses, Chiefly on the Subject of British-American Union* to Watkin, in appreciation of his contribution to "the material future of British-America" and his "high-spirited advocacy of a sound colonial policy."[15]

And so fourteen politicians from Canada, New Brunswick, and Nova Scotia came together in Quebec City. Among them were Sandfield Macdonald, Louis-Victor Sicotte, Leonard Tilley, and Joseph Howe; unlike later meetings on Confederation, members of the opposition parties in each colony were excluded. Over four days, with McGee in the chair, they discussed the long-range prospects for British North American economic union and the immediate issue of railway development.[16] After debating the details, they agreed to share the costs of the Intercolonial Railway, provided that they could secure financial backing from Britain. To negotiate a deal, they sent a delegation to the British government in London.

Although there was significant support for the plan in the Maritimes, it generated widespread opposition in Canada. Antoine-Aimé Dorion resigned from the cabinet in protest, on the grounds that the costs of the projected railway far outweighed any potential benefits. Other French Canadians feared that the Intercolonial Railway presaged a political union that would turn them into a permanent minority and "swamp their nationality."[17] In Canada West, the *Globe* argued that a government elected on the basis of retrenchment was paving the way for a wild spending spree that would plunge the country into debt and finance an orgy of corruption; Canadians, it insisted, should have nothing to do with the "mad proposition."[18] The paper also rejected the position that an Intercolonial Railway was necessary for defence; large sections of the line would run close to the American border and could easily be attacked in the event of a conflict. If a railway was to be constructed, the *Globe* had long maintained, it made much more sense to open up the Northwest rather than embarking on an unprofitable and unjustifiable line to the East.[19]

Taking stock of the situation, McGee told Sandfield Macdonald that there was a "very general, though very vague dread of our policy," with "fixed opposition" coming from the French.[20] Much of the opposition was focused on McGee himself, who was caricatured as "an enemy of our race."[21] When, over the winter, he delivered a lecture that contrasted British constitutional liberty with French revolutionary terror, his French Canadian opponents chose to interpret his words as further evidence of his "anti-French" attitude. Such an accusation completely distorted his views and had more to do with political mudslinging than historical analysis – but it was no less effective for that.[22]

Although French Canadian opposition to the Intercolonial appeared immovable, McGee believed that there was room to manoeuvre within English-speaking Canada. Much depended on the financial negotiations in Britain and on the extent to which the British government accepted the railway as a contribution towards colonial defence. He had reason to believe that the talks would succeed; George Brown, who was visiting Britain, reported that Newcastle and his colleagues – with the important exception of William Gladstone, the chancellor of the exchequer – were in favour of the Intercolonial Railway. Knowing this, McGee told Sandfield Macdonald that the delegates in London should "stick out for the best possible *Canadian* terms."[23]

Within English-speaking Canada, McGee believed that the railway could win popular support only if it was connected to "the great question of defence."[24] Accordingly, after the convention he accompanied Joseph Howe and the New Brunswick delegate Peter Mitchell to a Reform Party rally at Port Robinson in the Niagara peninsula. Howe told the audience that he had been working for an intercolonial railway since 1850, and Mitchell said that a railway would promote commercial and political unity in British North America. When it was his turn, McGee countered British criticism of Canada's defence policy and spoke to a sense of Canadian nationalism. "If we were to be an Imperial people," he declared, "… let us continue an Imperial people, but not to be an Imperial puppet, to be petted at one moment, and whipped and stigmatized before the world at another." As equal members of the empire, Canadians would make a reasonable and fair contribution to the costs of imperial defence, but they would never take "insult and opprobrium" from the English people.[25]

Three weeks later, he returned to the subject in a speech to the St Patrick's Literary Society in Ottawa. The choices facing Canada, he said, were annexation, independence, or the continuation of the imperial connection. Hardly anyone wanted annexation, and hardly anyone wanted independence, so those options were out. How, then, could the imperial connection be preserved? The best way was to build the Intercolonial Railway and thus demonstrate that Canada was serious about its own defence. At the same time, the railway would have significant commercial benefits. Intercolonial free trade would provide Canada with 700,000 more customers and would shelter the economy if the Reciprocity Treaty with the United States was not renewed in 1865. Once the Intercolonial was built, the line could be extended westwards, connecting the Atlantic with the Pacific and establishing the foundations of a "great country," with Ottawa becoming the capital of a "United British America."[26]

This was all very well in theory. In practice, however, the British North American delegates to London ran into serious difficulties. Contrary to McGee's expectations, the British government was in no mood for concessions. Newcastle rejected as a "monstrous proposal" the argument that Canadian contributions to the Intercolonial Railway should be counted towards the cost of defence.[27] After Gladstone insisted on stringent financial conditions that the Canadian delegates refused to accept, they returned home without an agreement, leaving their Maritime colleagues in the lurch. Sandfield Macdonald subsequently agreed to participate in a preliminary survey of the route, but the departure of the Canadian delegates put a severe strain on Canadian-Maritime relations and was a serious setback to McGee's nation-building strategy. He pressed for further talks with Britain and continued to hope that a reasonable compromise could be reached; his colleagues, however, were less enthusiastic, and the immediate prospects for success were not encouraging.[28]

———

McGee's frustration about the Intercolonial Railway was offset by a major breakthrough in the much-debated and oft-delayed issue of separate schools legislation. In March 1863, Richard Scott's bill was carried over into the new parliamentary session, where it once again became the focus of intense controversy. As he prepared for the debate, McGee found himself fighting against those who thought he was going too far and those who thought he was not going far enough. Most of his fellow Reform MPs fell into the former camp, arguing that Scott's bill would further undermine the common school system. Meanwhile, Moylan's *Canadian Freeman* attacked McGee for abandoning his earlier principle of educational parity between religious minorities in Canada West and Canada East, and for allying himself with men who rejected separate schools.[29]

McGee had indeed abandoned the principle of educational parity, on the grounds that it was unattainable; he would not sacrifice the Scott bill by holding out for the impossible. Instead, he sought to avoid polarization and to reach a workable compromise between liberal Protestants and Catholics – tasks that were made more difficult by Moylan's anti-Reform editorials, which McGee believed were alienating "the really friendly Protestants." He complained to Bishop Lynch about "the mischief that the so-called Catholic press is doing," clearly hoping that Lynch would persuade Moylan to tone down the rhetoric.[30] Whether Lynch did so remains an open question; the *Canadian Freeman* continued to stress the shortcomings of Scott's bill, but subsequently dropped its criticisms of McGee and apologized for arguing that he had taken an "un-Catholic" position on the schools question.[31]

All this made no difference to McGee's fellow Reformers, most of whom remained opposed to the bill and impervious to his best oratorical efforts. For the most part, McGee's parliamentary defence of the bill went over familiar ground. But in two respects, his speech marked a significant departure from his previous position. First, McGee no longer believed that the Irish educational system could provide a model for Canada. Implicitly conceding the criticism of Egerton Ryerson four years earlier, he admitted that the Irish attempt to establish "common secular, and separate religious instruction" had not worked, and that there was no point in importing a failed educational experiment into Canada. And second, McGee now explicitly incorporated non-

Christians into his conception of religious freedom. "As long as any body of people, Pagan or Christian, render the *minimum* of obedience to the civil power, as long as they dwell in peace within the precincts of the constitution anywhere," he declared, "they are entitled to the *maximum* of freedom in the exercise of their religious practices, doctrines, and worship." Through the specific struggle for Catholic educational rights, McGee was establishing arguments for minority educational rights in general.

Once these rights had been secured, McGee argued, Protestant-Catholic tensions would subside, and religion would be taken out of politics; educational difference would promote political unity. "The exclusion of this question from the arena will restore the rule of legitimate politics," he said. "It will no longer be possible for unfit and insincere men to find their way into the House, with the certificate of a Catholic Bishop in one pocket, and the card of an Orange Lodge in the other." Scott's bill, it seemed, would settle the educational problem in Canada once and for all. Although McGee obviously could not speak for the Catholic clergy and bishops, he thought that they "sincerely desire this thing to be put out of politics – that they desire a final settlement, and I believe they will accept this measure, as such settlement." "I can only say for myself," he added, "that I will endeavor to the utmost of my power to make this settlement final, and so far as I am concerned, I will be no party to re-opening the subject, either in the House or the country."[32]

When the debate was over, Richard Scott's bill passed by seventy-six to thirty-one votes. In Canada East, support was unanimous; but in Canada West, a clear majority of thirty-one to twenty-two came out against the legislation.[33] There were different ways of looking at this. From one perspective, MPs from Canada East were protecting the rights of a minority from an intolerant majority; from another, Canada East had trampled on the democratic rights of Canada West. Either way, the vote clearly contradicted the principle of the double majority.

Sandfield Macdonald resorted to splitting hairs. Scott's bill, he pointed out, had been introduced by a private member with cabinet support and had not been initiated by the government; as such, he said, the double majority principle did not apply.[34] It is doubtful whether McGee lost any sleep over the issue, since improved separate schools legislation had always been his priority, and he had never put much stock in the double majority to begin with. More troubling, from his viewpoint, was the fact that almost all the Reform MPs from Canada West had rejected the bill. McGee's strategy of coaxing Reformers into supporting separate schools had failed. It turned out that Moylan had been right to back the Liberal-Conservatives after all.

The other side of the coin was that most of the twenty-two Canada West MPs who supported Scott's bill were Liberal-Conservatives, and several were Orangemen − a fact that requires some explanation. In part, their vote reflected the political realities of Canadian life − the need to operate within a party system in which no single ethnoreligious group could impose its will on the others, and in which politics consisted of hard bargaining and compromises. Since the early 1850s, those Orangemen who joined or supported the Liberal-Conservatives had been part of a coalition that included French Canadian Catholics − a position that had produced a major split in the Orange Order in 1853.[35] The tensions between pragmatists and purists persisted into the 1860s, with rank-and-file Orangemen accusing those who voted for Scott's bill of "bartering away our Protestant principles."[36]

In response, the pragmatists countered that the principle of separate schools had already been conceded in Canada West, that Scott's bill simply rationalized the existing system, and that Protestants were not being compelled to finance Catholic education. Besides, some Orangemen wanted to extend separate schools to other denominations, such as High Anglicans. Others wanted to ensure that the Protestant Bible would be used in public schools and realized that this would not happen if Catholics were in the system.[37] Hence the outcome: while most of McGee's political allies in the Reform Party rejected separate schools, some of his leading Orange Conservative opponents had demonstrated that they could and would cut a deal on a measure of paramount importance to Catholics.

At the start of his Canadian career McGee had identified the two great threats to the new nationality as a standardized state school system and an increasingly powerful Orange Order. Now, with the resolution of the separate school question, the first of these threats had been removed – and had been removed with the help of some of those very Orangemen who had supposedly constituted the second threat. New possibilities were appearing on the horizon. The man who had been denied the immigration portfolio, who had been frustrated by the negotiations over the Intercolonial Railway, and who had been marginalized in his own party over the vital question of Catholic education might well find that he had more in common with John A. Macdonald's Liberal-Conservatives than with Sandfield Macdonald's Reformers.

But although the more pragmatic Conservative Orangemen were reaching an accommodation with Catholic political and religious leaders, serious ethnoreligious tensions continued to operate on the ground. On 17 March 1863, only four days after Scott's bill was passed, an armed Orange crowd in Peterborough trained a cannon on the Catholic church, blocked the streets, and prevented the town's Catholics from holding their first St Patrick's Day parade. McGee's half-brother, John Joseph, was among those who felt the full force of populist Orange intimidation.[38] With many Irish Catholics denouncing Orangemen as "semi-savages" and the "very dregs of society," there were calls to form a provincewide counter organization that would stand up to Orange bullying and bigotry. The Hibernian Benevolent Society seemed particularly well placed to take the lead; the only reason that similar scenes had not been enacted in Toronto, its supporters insisted, was because Orangemen knew that the city's Catholics would stand their ground and fight back.[39]

By this time, the Hibernian Benevolent Society had become the dominant Irish Catholic association in Toronto, pushing aside the pro-McGee Young Men's St Patrick's Association. The turning point had come in the winter of 1861–62, when Michael Murphy and Patrick Boyle requested Bishop Lynch's support for the resumption of St Patrick's Day parades in the city. Lynch replied that they should use their own judgment, in effect giving them his permission. Fearing a return to the sectarianism of 1858, and arguing that the suspension of St Patrick's Day parades had produced "great public good," McGee's supporters petitioned Bishop Lynch in protest. But they gathered only sixty-five signatures, and their arguments were ignored.[40]

The parade went ahead in 1862 and was a great success. More than a thousand people marched to the music of three bands; two detachments of the Toronto police force joined in, and the sidewalks were crowded with spectators. That night, there was a large dinner, attended by numerous politicians, including Ogle Gowan of the Orange Order. There were enthusiastic toasts to Her Majesty the Queen, to the British soldiers stationed in Canada, to the empire, and to "the land we left and the land we live in." It was all very respectable and orderly, without a trace of tension or of Irish nationalist politics. As such, declared Murphy, it was an impressive answer to "a certain politician from Montreal and other would-be leaders in Toronto" who wanted "to put down processions on St. Patrick's Day."[41] Murphy and Boyle had greatly increased their public influence in the city without displaying the slightest hint of their Fenianism. That, however, would soon change.

Building on the momentum, the Hibernian Benevolent Society established its own newspaper in January 1863 – the *Irish Canadian*, edited by Patrick Boyle. Initially, the paper took a careful, middle-of-the-road approach, with articles emphasizing the political loyalty of Irish Catholic Canadians and praising the Catholic bishop, Michael Power, who had died helping the famine victims of 1847.[42] Gradually, though, it assumed a more radical stance, combining declarations of loyalty to Canada with support for revolution in Ireland. The St Patrick's Day proceedings of 1863 were very different in tone and temper from those of the previous year. As the *Irish Canadian* approvingly reported, Michael Murphy denounced Britain's "tyrannical" government of Ireland, invoked the example of the Polish people, who were "determined to fight, and die, for their freedom," and spoke of an international organization that was preparing to liberate Ireland – and although he did not name it, there was no doubt that he meant the Fenians. There were, he said, "twenty thousand thorough nationalists in Canada who would not hesitate to sacrifice their lives if their country would demand the offering. Ireland's liberty must be obtained only by blood, and ... a million lives would not be sacrificed in vain to purchase her freedom; three fourths of the Catholic Irish of this country would offer themselves as an offering on the altar of freedom, to elevate their country and raise her again to her position in the list of nations. Nothing would resist the Irish pike when grasped by the sinewy arms of the Celt."[43]

When newspapers such as the *Globe* attacked such "disloyal sentiments," the *Irish Canadian* countered with a vicious diatribe against the "Scotch" in Canada and continued with a steady stream of sectarian invective against Scottish Protestants, who were described as a "set of harpies" and the "very scum of humanity." Their "scrubby creed" was nothing more than the "offal of religion," a "moral stench which taints the atmosphere," and a "low-bred, narrow-minded, God-forsaken John Knoxism." George Brown himself was merely a "disciple of oatmeal and predestination."[44]

Meanwhile, in Montreal, the Fenians were also making progress, albeit in a more surreptitious way. The key figure was Francis Bernard McNamee, a contractor and crimp who had long been involved in Reform politics and who was a prominent member of the city's St Patrick's Society. In the fall of 1862, McNamee visited the Fenian headquarters in New York, met with the head centre John O'Mahony, and returned to Montreal with a warrant to establish a Fenian circle in the city. After a regular meeting of the St Patrick's Society, McNamee invited a handful of like-minded individuals to his house, where they established the Hibernian Society, agreed to follow the orders of the Fenian Brotherhood in New York, and pledged to "assist Ireland in the revolutionary movement then in progress." Like their counterparts in Toronto, they focused their attention on Ireland rather than on Canada; their chief activity was raising money to buy arms for an Irish revolution, and their immediate aim was to infiltrate the St Patrick's Society and turn it into a Fenian front organization, with links not only to the United States but also to sister societies in Canada.[45]

All this was politically and morally repugnant to McGee, a source of danger that had to be driven back. To advocate violent revolution in Ireland, he believed, was to attempt the impossible. By doing so, the Fenians were setting back the cause of reform and opening the way for repression. In Canada, support for the Fenians made Irish Catholics vulnerable to charges of disloyalty and thus threatened their social, economic, and political position; anything that exacerbated ethnoreli gious tensions could only hurt the Irish Catholic minority. Moreover, the reaction of the Hibernian Benevolent Society to Orange violence was making a bad situation worse, and the visceral anti-Scottish and anti-Presbyterian writings of the *Irish Canadian* were undermining his efforts to promote ethnoreligious cooperation. Not only that, but Fenianism contradicted the Catholic Church's teachings against secret societies and deserved condemnation on those grounds alone.

The Orange Order had long been in McGee's sights, and he continued to attack the organization for its secrecy and its anti-Catholicism. But he had also said that he would attack any Catholic or Irish nationalist secret societies that might emerge in Canada. Now, with the *Irish Canadian* spreading the Fenian message, and with the Fenians gaining a foothold in his own backyard, McGee made good on his word. Revolutionary Irish nationalism, he believed, was becoming even more dangerous than Orangeism to Irish Catholics. At least Orangeism had some moderate elements, which might be cultivated; the separate schools vote had demonstrated that. But the growth of Fenianism, which McGee saw as an extreme revolutionary force fuelled by a sense of absolute moral certainty, could have catastrophic consequences for Ireland and for Irish Catholics in Canada. Compromise with such a movement was out of the question.

An opportunity to alert his countrymen about Fenian activities in Montreal arose in May 1863, when a deputation from the city's St Patrick's Society thanked McGee for steering a bill of incorporation through the legislature. In reply, McGee said that "there were several good Societies in the city, which any good Irishman or Catholic could join." But he had "heard with the greatest regret and astonishment that emissaries were abroad attempting to introduce a secret treasonable society into Montreal." If they succeeded, they would "see re-enacted in Canada the treachery, ruin and disunion which, flowing from precisely similar causes, had so long cursed their native land." To deter any prospective Fenians, he reminded his audience that there were serious penalties in Canada East for anyone who joined a secret seditious society.[46]

In Toronto, the *Irish Canadian* took note. "We would humbly advise the hon. gentleman to be a little more guarded in his expressions," it commented, "as if he should continue obstinate, possibly he may find, when he visits the Upper Province, his popularity growing small and beautifully less."[47] In Montreal, the incipient Fenian movement continued its plans to take over the St Patrick's Society and to undermine popular support for McGee.

---

McGee's popularity was already taking a hit, for reasons entirely unconnected with Fenianism. To understand why, we must reopen a forgotten but fascinating episode that became a *cause celèbre* for many Irish Catholic Canadians – the Aylward affair. Ostensibly, what happened was straightforward enough, if somewhat gruesome. In May 1862, on the Hastings Road north of present-day Bancroft, two farming families, the Aylwards and the Munros, got into a heated argument over Munro's hens, which had been straying onto the Aylwards' land and eating the grain. After Richard Aylward shot at one of the hens, an incensed William Munro came round to the farm to complain. As the argument turned violent, Richard's wife, Mary, struck William with a newly sharpened scythe, leaving a three-inch-deep gash in the side of his head; after twelve days of agony, he died.

At the trial, which was held in Belleville the following October, the testimony against the Aylwards was damning. According to one witness, Mary Aylward had said beforehand that she planned to kill Munro by enticing him into her house and shooting him. Other witnesses testified that immediately after the murder, Mary had boasted of her deed, proudly displaying the bloody scythe to a neighbour and saying that she had tried to decapitate Munro. Later, when she heard of Munro's suffering, she said, "May God Almighty increase his pain!" The defence counsel, James O'Reilly, contended that Mary was trying to protect her husband, that she struck the blow in "a moment of phrenzy," and that her words afterwards were the "babbling of a maniac" whose mind had been shattered by the shock of her action. The verdict, he argued, should be manslaughter for Mary and an acquittal for Richard.

In response, the prosecuting attorney, Adam Wilson, who was now the solicitor general, declared that he had "never met with a case combining so much atrocity … as the almost demoniacal fury with which the prisoners at the bar, gloried in their work of death," and he insisted that the case for the premeditated murder of Munro was "beyond doubt." After a two-hour deliberation, the jury found the Aylwards guilty, "with a strong recommendation to mercy." Sentencing the couple, Chief Justice William Draper pointed out that the only penalty for murder was death but said that he would transmit the jury's recommendation to the government.[48]

This was far from the end of the matter. After the trial, questions were raised by Irish Catholics in Belleville and beyond. The Aylwards were Catholic; Munro was Protestant. Could that have been a factor in their dispute? And could the Aylwards' religion have affected the outcome of the trial? Stories began to surface that William Munro had a long history of taunting the Aylwards, throwing stones at them and calling Mary a "damned whore"; and Mary suspected that he had put a dead dog in their well. There were also suggestions that one of the key prosecution witnesses had been equally provocative and that another had lied at the trial. Richard had taken his gun and pistol to defend himself, it was argued; William had threatened to shoot Richard with his own gun and was trying to take it for that purpose when Mary rushed forward to protect her husband. There was nothing premeditated about it at all, it seemed; the correct verdict for Mary should have been manslaughter, and the Aylwards did not deserve to hang.[49]

Their cause was taken up by the Catholic priest in Belleville, Michael Brennan, who visited them regularly in jail and became convinced that they were not guilty of murder. Together with John Finn, one of the Aylwards' attorneys, he circulated petitions for the commutation of the death sentences. More than a thousand people signed (Protestants as well as Catholics, Brennan pointed out). The petitions were sent to the Executive Council; it was hoped that McGee, in his capacity as president of the council and as the leading Irish Catholic in the cabinet, would exert his influence to commute the death sentences. But on 6 December, when the council reviewed the petitions and the papers, McGee was nowhere to be seen. The government decided to let the law take its course, and McGee concurred with its decision. Two days later, in front of a crowd of more than five thousand people, the Aylwards were hanged.

From here, the Aylward affair rapidly assumed a highly charged symbolic significance. The fact that Mary had dictated a heart-rending letter to her three young daughters only increased the sense of anguish and anger among those who had campaigned for commutation.[50] In French Canada, the executions became a symbol of English Canadian injustice; there were riots in Quebec City, during which McGee and Lord Monck were hanged in effigy. Among many Irish Catholics, the executions were seen as symptomatic of Orange and Protestant bigotry, and Mary Aylward was reconstructed as a "courageous and faithful wife" who had tried to protect her husband from the wrath of a "rabid Orangeman."[51] For the Liberal-Conservatives, the executions became a convenient club with which to beat the Reform administration. And in the middle of it all was McGee, taking heat from all sides.

During an impassioned and angry parliamentary debate in February, he fought back, asserting that there had been "great misstatements of facts on this subject" and condemning the "inflammatory" arguments emanating from politically motivated newspaper editors. Five members of the jury were Catholics, he said, as were three of the four prosecution witnesses; it was simply wrong and irresponsible to reduce the verdict and sentence to a matter of "religious feeling." He also noted that the defence had chosen not to appeal the jury's decision, which it surely would have done if it had a stronger case. To those who attacked him for failing to make any special efforts for his co-religionists and compatriots, McGee replied that he "did not sit at the Council Board to act partially towards any class in the country"; his job was "to do justice, and not to advise His Excellency as a Roman Catholic in religion, or as an Irishman in origin."[52]

His words did nothing to stop a barrage of Catholic Irish Canadian criticism. The *Canadian Freeman* claimed that "religious feeling" was a red herring and that the real issue was the heartlessness of the government. Meanwhile, in Montreal, the *True Witness* contended that religion was of central importance and that the Aylwards were victims of Protestant prejudice.[53] Interestingly, the *Irish Canadian* did not comment on the affair at this stage – although it later entered the controversy with a vengeance. As McGee stepped up his attacks on the Fenians, the *Irish Canadian* repeatedly flung the Aylward affair back in his face. McGee had abandoned the Aylwards to the savagery of "Orangemen and Scotch fiends," the paper argued; he would go to any lengths, including "judicial murder," to "keep in with the Protestant ascendancy party," and had earned "the scorn and contempt of the entire community."[54] The same charges were again made during the Montreal election campaign of 1867, when Bernard Devlin declared that McGee had been complicit in the murder of the Aylwards and that no Irish Catholic could or should vote for the man who had committed such a crime.[55]

The extent to which the Aylward affair damaged McGee's political reputation can easily be exaggerated. Many Irish Catholics in Canada West continued to support him, and his base in Montreal remained intact during the elections of 1863 and 1864. But by the middle of the decade, at the height of McGee's fight against the Fenians, his enemies were more than willing to use it against him and to fit the story into their narrative of McGee as an unscrupulous, self-seeking, and ambitious adventurer who would sacrifice anybody and anything – innocent victims of Protestant injustice or the Irish nation itself – in the relentless pursuit of political power. If the Aylward affair made little difference to the breadth of anti-McGee feeling in Canada, it certainly contributed to its depth.

———

The controversy over the Aylwards fed into a political crisis that strained and snapped McGee's already tenuous relationship with Sandfield Macdonald. The government was finding it increasingly difficult to hold together its English-speaking and French wings, as the vote on separate schools had demonstrated. When George Brown re-entered the House after winning a by-election in March, his increasing influence over the Reform Party began to alarm its French Canadian wing. Sensing their opportunity, the Liberal-Conservatives moved a nonconfidence resolution against the government, citing among other things its failure to secure the Intercolonial Railway, its Militia Bill, and its handling of the Aylward affair.[56]

In the course of a five-day debate, all the leading figures in the government defended its record – all of them, that is, except McGee, who was getting drunk with friends when he was scheduled to speak. Although he showed up for the vote itself and duly supported the government, his erratic behaviour was symptomatic of his deeper disillusionment with the Reform Party.[57] Sandfield Macdonald's immediate reaction has not been recorded, but it seems safe to say that he was not impressed. He was even less impressed with most of Louis-Victor Sicotte's supporters, whose defection to the Liberal-Conservatives meant that the government was narrowly defeated and that a new election would be called.

To salvage the situation and reconstitute his party, Sandfield Macdonald opened up secret negotiations with George Brown and Oliver Mowat from Canada West and with Antoine-Aimé Dorion and Luther Holton from Canada East. Dorion, whose supporters had continued to back the government during the non-confidence debate, was now the key figure in Canada East, just as Brown was in Canada West. Both men agreed that a new Reform government must abandon the Intercolonial Railway and that there would be no place for McGee in the new cabinet. Sandfield Macdonald concurred; McGee was a loose cannon, whose position on separate schools had alienated the Clear Grits, whose support for increased immigration had alienated the Rouges, and whose endorsement of the Intercolonial Railway had alienated both the Clear Grits and the Rouges. For the key figures in the Reform Party, McGee had become a political liability.[58]

When Sicotte resigned, partly because he refused to play second fiddle to Dorion and partly because he feared excessive Upper Canadian influence in the reconstituted Reform Party, McGee followed suit – as did all the other ministers from Canada East.[59] Although McGee moderated his statements in public, he was privately furious about the way in which he had been treated. It was not simply that Sandfield Macdonald had behaved with "dour dogmatism" and had treated his Lower Canadian ministers with "the most offensive disrespect," McGee told

John Sandfield Macdonald. Increasingly viewing McGee as a political liability, Sandfield Macdonald ousted him from the cabinet in May 1863. The clandestine way in which it was done was as offensive to McGee as the act itself.
In McGee's view, Sandfield Macdonald and his allies had stabbed him in the
back; he never forgot or forgave this "betrayal." (LAC, PA-012855)

John O'Dohonoe. What made it even worse was the fact that Dorion
and Holton had been conducting the negotiations "*without ever once
letting me know,* their position, or agency in the intrigue." McGee felt
strongly that he had been stabbed in the back by his "old colleagues."
"Just at the last moment," he continued, "… they called on me, as I
was packing up, with a view to soothe my wounded sense of fairness &
fellowship, but I told them, frankly, that 'we were quits' – so here I am,
an '*independent candidate.*'"[60]

And there he was indeed, back in the position that he had occupied
at the beginning of his political career in Canada – running for election

as an independent. The Reform alliance that he had cultivated when he first arrived in the legislature and had defended in the teeth of criticism from the Catholic hierarchy and the Hibernian Benevolent Society was now in ruins. In the short run, that alliance had helped to lower the sectarian temperature of Upper Canadian politics and had broadened the support for Brown's federation proposals in 1859 – proposals that McGee eloquently defended in Parliament the following year. It had been strong enough to withstand differences over such matters as divorce and seigneurial compensation, though it suffered a severe shock during the royal tour of 1860 when the *Globe* defended the Orange Order and fumed against "papal influence" in Canada and Britain. But its most vulnerable point had always been the issue of Catholic education, and despite McGee's best efforts, Brown and the Reformers had repeatedly rejected Richard Scott's separate schools bills. Nevertheless, McGee and Brown continued to respect one another, despite their differences. When Brown embarked on his trip to Britain and Ireland in the summer of 1862, McGee gave him advice about places to visit and wrote a letter of introduction to T.D. O'Sullivan, describing Brown as "a Scotch-Presbyterian of Upper Canada – a strong anti-Catholic from educational bias, but a very able man, and no Orangeman." For his part, Brown continued to speak highly of McGee.[61]

The same could not be said about McGee's relationship with Sandfield Macdonald. The Reform victory in May 1862 had opened up the prospect of power, and McGee had hoped to exert influence on the issues of immigration and the Intercolonial Railway. But the hopes failed to materialize; he did not get the immigration portfolio, the Intercolonial Railway had been stalled, and his civil service reforms had not been fully implemented. Nor was Sandfield Macdonald willing to pursue the option of federalism, McGee's central objective, despite the impracticality of the double majority and widespread French Canadian hostility towards representation by population. If McGee had become surplus to Reform requirements, it was also true that the Reform alliance had become an obstacle to his own.

Even through his anger, he felt a sense of release. "After a year's self-denial in office, where I had the name, without the reality of power," he told O'Donohoe, "I find myself personally relieved, by quitting a false position – into which I had fallen from want of accurate knowledge of some of my *confrères* – and from which there was no escape, but resignation."[62] This did not, however, mean that McGee could easily bring himself to join the Liberal-Conservatives. He had an "ugly little altercation" with John A. Macdonald earlier in May over the issue of corruption and declared after his resignation that if push came to shove he would vote for the Reformers rather than restore the "greater evil" of the old Liberal-Conservative government.[63]

But if there was no going back to the Reformers and if to remain an independent meant sitting on the sidelines, then there appeared to be only one option left – to form a new alliance between disillusioned Reformers and moderate Conservatives, in the hope of establishing a revamped party whose policies matched his own position.

Meanwhile, John A. Macdonald watched and waited.

# PART TWO

# Conservatism and Confederation

It may be said that it is rather strange for an Irish man,
who spent his youth in resisting that government in his native country,
to be found among the admirers of British constitutional government
in Canada. To that this is my reply – if in my day Ireland had been
governed as Canada is now governed, I would have been as sound a
constitutional conservative as is to be found in Ireland.

McGee, "The Future of Canada,"
*Ottawa Citizen*, 1 December 1863

## CHAPTER SEVEN

# A Constitutional Conservative
## June 1863 – February 1864

As an independent candidate, McGee's immediate task was to get back into Parliament. To stop this from happening, the Reformers enlisted John Young, a leading Montreal businessman, to run against him. As part of their effort, Sandfield Macdonald, Holton, and Dorion decided to engage in a little *quid pro quo*; they promised to pay the Grand Trunk Railway $150 a mile for postal services as long as the company used its influence to back Young. Charles Brydges, the superintendent of the Grand Trunk, would not bite; he did not trust Sandfield Macdonald, and he valued McGee's support for the Intercolonial.[1]

When the story came out later in the summer, it produced a storm in the legislature, with the Reformers loudly and unconvincingly protesting their innocence, and the Liberal-Conservatives indignantly denouncing their enemies for the same kind of political bribery that they practised themselves.[2] It is possible that the Grand Trunk actually worked for McGee's re-election behind the scenes; Holton certainly thought so, and similar charges would be made during the election of 1867.[3] Some of McGee's detractors believed that he was in the pocket of the railway company – an accusation that seemed to be strengthened by his continual hobnobbing with the Grand Trunk's leaders. This is, however, to mistake cause for effect. McGee's belief that railways were an essential element of nation building went right back to his Young Ireland days and had long been central to his program for British North America.[4] His nationalism was not a "front" for the Intercolonial; the Intercolonial was a key component of his nationalism.

During the election campaign, McGee's strategy was to highlight his contributions to the previous Reform administration while attacking Sandfield Macdonald for abandoning his principles and betraying his friends. At the hustings, McGee reeled off his major activities in government – initiating civil service reform, helping to pass the Scott bill, supporting the Intercolonial, and encouraging immigration. Against this, he accused Sandfield Macdonald of acting in "bad faith" over the Intercolonial negotiations and of harbouring a deep antipathy to Irish Catholics.[5] After all, McGee argued, this was the man who had once made disparaging remarks about the immigrants who were "*whitewashed* at Grosse Ile" and who had excluded Irish Catholics from his cabinet. "If the rule is to be established '*No Irish Need Apply*' it is well we should know it," he told John O'Donohoe. "Once established, it will be hard, indeed, to break it down, either with Protestant Upper Canada, or French Lower." This was an issue that was bound to resonate with his Irish constituents. "The School question being settled," he wrote, "I say our test should be – *Are you in favor of a fair representation of all classes of the people of Canada, in the Executive Government of the Country*'?"[6]

To those who charged him with inconsistency, he replied that it was Sandfield Macdonald who had changed position for the sake of power. And indeed, McGee's national policy in 1863 was substantially the same as that of 1857–58: conciliating "different creeds and classes," developing railway connections among the British North American colonies, bringing in more immigrants, opening up the West, and creating a new national identity for a northern people.[7]

What was different, of course, was the nature of McGee's political alliances. During the campaign of 1857, he had supported Dorion and Holton over Cartier and John Rose. Now the positions were reversed, with McGee advising those outside his constituency to support the Liberal-Conservative candidates, and with Cartier and Rose coming out in favour of McGee. It proved to be an unbeatable combination. McGee easily defeated Young, and the Reformers were completely shut out of the city.

Elsewhere, however, the results were mixed; the Reformers were a minority in Canada East but had a strong majority in Canada West. The result in Canada West, declared the *Globe*, was a "crushing condemnation of John A. Macdonald and his partizans." True enough; but

the result in Canada East was also a condemnation of Sandfield Macdonald and his partisans, and the new Reform administration clung
to power with a slender majority.[8] Something, McGee argued, had to
give: Canada West was telling Canada East that "the present state of
things between you and us cannot continue"; Britain was telling its
North American colonies the same thing; and the American Civil War
meant that "the former state of things on this continent is closed, and
a veritable new era opened." "Can it be premature then," McGee won-
dered, "for us to ask ourselves, what is to become of Canada and her
sister Provinces in the new arrangements, of these new times?"[9]

---

In considering the question, McGee insisted that any new political
arrangements must find the right balance between authority and liberty. "I do not undervalue the democratic principle as one of the living
and essential forces of every free society," he wrote, "but it must have a
counterpoise even for its own sake, otherwise it runs wild into anarchy,
to be caught and tamed down by the first strong-handed despot who
may arise." Accordingly, he revived an idea that had initially appeared
in the pages of his *New Era* – making Canada a constitutional monarchy, with a royal prince on the throne. As a further check on excessive democracy, he also argued that Canada should have a hereditary
upper house.[10]

After broaching the subject in 1858, McGee had said little about
establishing a monarchy in Canada; now he raised the issue at every
opportunity. In part, the change in emphasis came from his concern
about the creeping Americanization of Canada; unless Canadians embraced monarchy and aristocracy, and formed a Burkean alternative
to Paineite democracy, they would fall victim to the tyranny of the
majority and the corrosion of social values that he had long associated with the United States. McGee had come to Canada to escape the
American way of life; if the American way of life came to Canada,
he would "commit his family, and all he held dear, once more to the
deep and seek a home under the Southern Cross" – joining his friend
and mentor Charles Gavan Duffy in Australia, as far away from North
America as possible.[11]

But the other factor behind McGee's return to monarchy was situational rather than ideological. It was no coincidence that he had first advocated a Canadian monarchy as an independent MP shortly after his election in 1857 and that he had renewed the argument as an independent MP shortly after his election in 1863. During the intervening years, when he was in the Reform alliance, McGee could not have campaigned for a Canadian monarchy without alienating his colleagues. Many Liberal-Conservatives would doubtless have approved of his idea, but McGee had associated them with Orange bigotry and opposition to separate schools – opinions that he had subsequently revised in the light of experience. Now that the Reform alliance was over, he was free to speak his mind on the subject. Given his conviction that the status quo was no longer an option, the time was right to advocate for a monarchy in Canada, and preferably in British North America as a whole.

Predictably, McGee's monarchism generated fierce controversy among British North Americans, most of whom mistakenly believed that he was coming to the idea for the first time. The most effective reply to McGee's position came from Timothy Warren Anglin, the former Irish revolutionary who was now a leading newspaper editor in New Brunswick. In much the same way that Paine had criticized Burke, Anglin pointed out that a hereditary monarchy did not mean hereditary virtue; even if a royal prince was just, humane, and popular, there was no guarantee that his successors would be the same. And any kind of appointed upper house, whether its members were hereditary or appointed for life, would create a politically privileged "aristocracy of wealth." Nothing could be better calculated, Anglin argued, to drive British North Americans into the arms of the United States.[12]

While McGee's monarchism alienated many of his former allies, it also made him new friends in new places. In the Maritimes, Anglin's antipathy was countered by loyalist newspaper editors who admired McGee's conservatism and his willingness to stand up against democratic populism.[13] In Canada West, Orangemen noted with surprise that a former Irish rebel had become "the first man in Canada to demand for the monarchical principle a fair trial, in this part of the world."[14] Even before McGee renewed his call for a Canadian mon-

Timothy Warren Anglin. A republican revolutionary in Ireland, Anglin emigrated to New Brunswick in 1849, where he founded the *Saint John Weekly
Freeman* (renamed in 1851 the *Morning Freeman*) and became a leading Liberal politician. Strongly opposed to McGee's position on monarchy, the Inter-
continental Railway, Confederation, and Fenianism, Anglin hoped to replace
McGee as the dominant figure in Irish Canadian politics. (LAC, PA-026339)

archy, one of his speeches associating England's "Glorious Revolution"
of 1688 with civil and religious liberty had caught the attention of his
old Orange antagonists. When Ogle Gowan read McGee's words, he
jocularly "warned the County Master to be in his place at the next
Grand Lodge meeting, lest Mr. McGee might be a candidate for the
position of Grand Master."[15]

Nevertheless, McGee's monarchical views cut against the democratic grain of Canadian politics and had little chance of winning general acceptance.[16] The divided reaction to his suggestion was, in fact,
the main reason why it would not work. A Canadian monarchy would
remain impossible without broad consensus, and that was never going

to happen. McGee's proposal was, in its own way, as unrealistic as his attempt in 1847 to convert the Irish Confederation to his views about the "Compact of 1541" and the "golden link of the Crown."[17]

————·•·————

The theme of monarchy figured prominently during McGee's visit to New Brunswick and Nova Scotia that summer. This was his third trip to the Maritimes. Leaving aside a brief stopover in Halifax in 1845, he had stayed in the region during the summers of 1856 and 1859, giving lectures on literature and politics to small but enthusiastic audiences.[18] McGee had personal connections with the Irish in Saint John, many of whom came from his native Carlingford, and he moved easily through familiar and friendly circles in the city.[19] There had also been a political component to his travels. In 1859 he had spoken on the "necessities for a British American Union" and had met two future Fathers of Confederation, Leonard Tilley and Charles Tupper, as well as Peter Stevens Hamilton, whose writings in support of colonial union had impressed him so much.[20]

McGee's links with the political leaders of Nova Scotia and New Brunswick had been strengthened during his chairmanship of the Intercolonial Convention in Quebec City. Now, in July 1863, he carried his message to a wide range of politicians, businessmen, and journalists at public lectures in Halifax and Saint John. Two days after his Halifax lecture, he spent a convivial night at the Ten Mile House, Bedford Basin, with "about fifty of the leading men of Nova Scotia, including the chiefs of both parties."[21] In the same spirit, a "brace of Editors, Lawyers, Doctors, [and] Merchants" from Saint John took him on a railway trip to Moncton and treated him to an "excellent dinner."[22] During the early 1860s, no Canadian politician knew more about the Maritimes, and knew more Maritime politicians, than D'Arcy McGee. And no Canadian politician pushed the case so vigorously in the Maritimes for constitutional monarchy, British North American union, and the Intercolonial Railway.

"If I am right," McGee said during his lecture in Saint John, "the railroad will give us Union, Union will give us nationality, and nationality a Prince of the blood of our ancient kings." The railway would promote trade among the British provinces, improve their defensive capabilities, and provide the basis for political unity; trade barriers would fall, and a common sense of patriotism would prevail. With railway links, free trade and a new national consciousness, British North America would become more prosperous and more attractive to immigrants; with its own monarch, it would strengthen its position within the British Empire, assert the principle of authority over anarchy, and push back the rising tide of Americanism.[23]

Although McGee's speeches attracted a great deal of attention, their impact should not be exaggerated. Large-scale audiences did not necessarily mean large-scale agreement, and personal popularity did not necessarily translate into political support. As Anglin pointed out, people attended McGee's lectures for a variety of reasons – because of his reputation as an outstanding orator, because his fellow Irishmen wanted to hear one of their own, or because people in general wanted to discuss the Intercolonial Railway.[24] McGee's ideas about a British North American monarchy were as controversial in the Maritimes as they were in Canada, and his views on colonial union ran into serious resistance.

Hard questions were asked. How would political unity strengthen the defence of British North America? American military power would still be much greater than that of the combined British colonies, and the real guarantee of colonial security would still be their membership of the British Empire. What were the commercial advantages of colonial union? The Maritimes already had good markets for food and fish but needed to protect lumber and shipbuilding interests from Canadian competition. Why did the Intercolonial Railway need to be part of a political unity package? And what were the benefits of ceding local political control to a distant government in Ottawa? There might be advantages for self-important politicians who wanted to strut their stuff on a larger political stage, but there was nothing here for "plain, practical, common sense" people.[25] Ironically, one consequence of McGee's visit was to provide a focus for anti-Confederation arguments in the Maritimes.

On the other hand, McGee's speeches inspired and impressed many of his listeners. He was praised for rising above the "rabid Partizanship" of provincial politics and for his British North American nationalism.[26] McGee "does not live in Canada alone: we are sure of that

... He lives in British America," commented the *Acadian Recorder*. In Prince Edward Island, Edward Whelan wrote that if McGee's plans succeeded, he would deserve "the first federal premiership of these Colonies."[27] McGee was building a fund of personal and political goodwill that might pay political dividends in the future. Although such goodwill might mean little or nothing in the face of fundamental regional disagreements over the Intercolonial Railway, it could mean a great deal when circumstances changed and the possibility arose of political convergence between the Maritimes and Canada.

During his visit, McGee did more than present a Canadian case for federation; he also attempted to explain the Maritimes to Canada. With this in mind, he penned two letters to the *Montreal Gazette*, describing the "population, resources, and prospects" of New Brunswick and Nova Scotia. He enthused about the hospitality he had received in Halifax, putting in a special word for the beauty, style, and grace of the city's women; he saw great potential in the region for agriculture, mineral extraction, and deep-sea fishing, adding that local railways were connecting communities; and he asserted that enlightened opinion supported Maritime union. Canada would benefit from closer social and economic ties with the Atlantic colonies, and Maritime union could open up the possibility of wider political unity. If Canadians failed to seize the opportunity, he wrote, they would have no one to blame but themselves.[28]

After leaving the Maritimes, McGee travelled to Toronto. Here, he joined Edward Watkin and Charles Brydges of the Grand Trunk on an excursion to Niagara Falls, along with a group of American businessmen – further evidence of his close connection with the railway company.[29] During the visit, they decided to attend a Reform meeting at Welland. McGee was spotted in the audience, brought up to the platform, and put in the awkward position of speaking to a party that he had left. He handled the situation with tact and humour, making some self-deprecating remarks about his physical appearance, talking in general terms about "the union of all British America," and refusing to be drawn about his resignation from the government. It was the last time he would appear at a Reform rally.[30]

A week later, McGee was in Quebec City for the opening of Parliament, bristling with anger and ready for action. In some respects, his position was analogous to that of 1857–58, when he had entered the legislature as an independent and advocated a centrist party that united liberal Protestants, Irish Catholics, and French Canadians.[31] Now he was calling for an alliance between the liberal opponents of Sandfield Macdonald and the Liberal-Conservatives who had been elected in June.[32] During the spring of 1858, McGee had gradually moved towards George Brown on the grounds that he was not as bad as he had been painted and that he was prepared to compromise on the key constitutional and educational questions facing Canada. Now McGee was gradually moving towards John A. Macdonald on the grounds that he was not as bad as he had been painted (or as McGee himself had painted him), that he had already supported Catholic educational demands, and that he could be equally accommodating on the issue of constitutional change.

In 1858 McGee had thought that Brown could exert a moderating influence over the Clear Grits and had viewed the Orange Order as the greatest threat to Canada's future. Now McGee thought that John A. Macdonald could exert a moderating influence over the "kick the Pope" elements within the Orange Order; he also knew that many Orangemen agreed with his views on monarchy and a hereditary upper house and that some of them had voted for improved separate schools legislation. The greatest threat to Canada's future, McGee now believed, came from the Clear Grits, with their opposition to separate schools and their attempt to inject American-style democracy into Canada.

But more was going on than an intellectual reappraisal of political circumstances and prospects; the emotional undercurrents ran deep, and their importance should not be underestimated. The pent-up frustration of McGee's experiences in Sandfield Macdonald's cabinet and his bitterness about the "betrayal" in May meant that he turned on the government with a vengeance. As the parliamentary session proceeded, McGee's drinking began to spin out of control – reflecting and reinforcing his underlying sense of rage.[33]

At the first possible opportunity, McGee lit into Sandfield Macdonald for the "scandalous" way in which he had dumped the men who had helped him into power, and he attacked Dorion and Holton for plotting behind his back.[34] When Sandfield Macdonald insinuated that McGee had a long history of breaking faith with political allies, McGee responded with defiant fury; whatever else he may have done in the course of a long career, McGee said, he had never "betrayed a friend or intrigued against an associate."[35]

McGee followed up his attack with scathing criticism of the government's position, or lack thereof, on immigration and defence. Despite the recommendations of his Select Committee on Immigration, the immigration sheds in Quebec were not being used, there was no one to advise immigrants when they arrived in the city, and there was still no Canadian agent in New York to guide immigrants northwards.[36] The same kind of complacency characterized the government's attitude to defence, he argued, but with much more dangerous implications. Early in August, McGee had learned that the US government had contingency plans to send 100,000 troops into Montreal in the event of war, and there was hard evidence that the American military was reinforcing the strategically important fort at Rouse's Point, on the border with Canada.[37]

Although his opponents accused him of alarmism and opportunism, and although there may have been an element of truth in these charges, McGee's concerns were deeply rooted in his earlier American experience. Having lived in the United States and having criticized the periodic "excitements" that gripped American public opinion, McGee knew "how easy it was to get the people excited in any direction, if it were necessary, in order to make sure of carrying the next Presidential election." Anyone who wanted to whip up anti-Canadian feeling, he said, would have plenty of material to work with: northern capitalists who made large profits from the carnage of war; New Englanders who hated "Popery and the French"; and Irish Catholics who had been misled by "artful demagogues" into thinking that Canada was as oppressed as Ireland. "It would indeed be a curious coincidence," he said, "if we should live to see the children of the Puritans, and the descendants of the Catholic Celts of Ireland, marching shoulder to shoulder in the same army, to the pillage and subjugation of a people, out of whom they have chosen to create to themselves imaginary slaves, and imaginary enemies. But it is possible; it *is* possible." American volatility meant Canadian vulnerability, and the government was taking no steps to counter the danger.[38]

———•·•———

All this was too much for Sandfield Macdonald. Here was this Irish Catholic adventurer who pretended to have a monopoly on patriotism, who passed himself off as "the great oracle of the country," and who incessantly lectured the government about its duties. "His coming here and telling native-born Canadians what they ought to do and what not," Sandfield Macdonald countered, was "ridiculous in the extreme."[39] This was a telling remark; McGee had spent years in the United States fighting the Know-Nothing movement, and he recognized nativism when he heard it. In criticizing immigrants for participating in Canadian politics, McGee countered, Sandfield Macdonald was "spitting on the grave of his grandfather."[40]

The Irish Catholic press agreed wholeheartedly. According to the *Irish Canadian*, Sandfield Macdonald had "unwisely attacked the nine-tenths of the people of this Province in the person of the Hon. Mr. McGee." James Moylan's *Canadian Freeman* pilloried Sandfield Macdonald as "a Canadian Know-Nothing," adding that McGee's ejection from the cabinet was "a chapter of duplicity, deception, and paltriness … unparalleled in the history of British or Canadian statesmanship."[41] The old wounds between McGee and Moylan over the Reform alliance and Catholic education were healing, just as the new wounds between McGee and Sandfield Macdonald were deepening. From Moylan's perspective, McGee was finally catching on to the position that the *Canadian Freeman* had adopted more than two years earlier – that the Reformers were a lost cause and that Irish Catholic interests were best served by an alliance with the Liberal-Conservatives.

As this was happening, the leading Canadian newspapers changed places in their attitude to McGee. When McGee was a Reformer, the Conservative press had used his revolutionary Irish past against him, and Reform newspapers had defended him from charges that he was an unprincipled and ambitious adventurer. Now the roles were reversed, with the *Globe* in particular taking a hard anti-McGee line. Reprinting his impassioned anti-British poem "The Red-Cross Flag," which McGee had written a decade earlier, the paper contended that Canadians did not need lectures on the meaning of loyalty from a man who had "cursed the 'bloody red flag'" before he came to the country.[42] "As he was unquestionably a traitor when he was a philo-American," the *Globe* commented, "so now he thinks that all who will not follow him to the new extreme he has reached, must be traitors also."[43]

Meanwhile, the *Montreal Gazette*, which had previously "attacked McGee bitterly as an adventurer," became one of his strongest allies and provided a platform for his views.[44] In his letters to the paper, McGee insisted that his Canadian political program should be judged according to its own merits and not by the views he had held as a young man. Point by point, he went through his differences with the *Globe*. The paper continued to view Catholicism as a threat to Canada, while he believed that politics should transcend religious differences. The paper was "hostile to hierarchies," while he tried to "inculcate reverence for religious rank, for old age, for parentage, the magistracy, the legislature, and the Sovereign." The paper advocated a railway to the West, while he supported a railway to the Atlantic as well as the Pacific. And the paper would "disarm and betray this Province into the power of its enemies, by falsely teaching that there is no formidable danger in the distance," while he advised "a wary watchfulness, a wise distrust, and the best possible preparation, against democratic aggression."[45] For years, and in the face of "all discouragements and all dissuasions," McGee had tried to steer the *Globe* towards a "broad and generous" liberalism – all to no avail. "I abandon all hope of making good, liberal-minded men out of the *Globe* people," he wrote.[46]

---

As he made these arguments, attacked the government, gave up on the *Globe*, and won the support of the Conservative press, McGee was still speaking and writing as an independent. But he was voting consistently with the Liberal-Conservatives during the parliamentary session, and it seemed only a matter of time before he and Louis-Victor Sicotte would switch parties. In the case of Sicotte, however, something completely unexpected happened; in September, Sandfield Macdonald bought him off with an appointment to the Superior Court. But whereas Sicotte got out of politics, McGee continued his trajectory towards the Liberal-Conservatives. And at the beginning of October he finally crossed the floor.

The occasion was a heated debate about the Intercolonial Railway, during which McGee accused the government of breaking faith with the British government and of behaving like "a pack of tricksters" towards the Maritime provinces.[47] "The law of your nature is like that of a corkscrew, to go crooked," McGee told Sandfield Macdonald, amid Conservative cheers and laughter. In response, Luther Holton, McGee's former ally, declared that it was "most unfortunate" that McGee "should ever have been a member of the Government of this country" and refused to defend any acts in which McGee had been involved. Later that night, Lucius Seth Huntingdon, the solicitor general for Canada East, joined the attack on McGee, describing him as a man consumed by "great bitterness" over imaginary insults, a man who had turned on his former friends, forgotten his former hostility to the Liberal-Conservatives, and become "another unfortunate gone to his death."[48]

It was always dangerous to challenge McGee in debate. When he stood up to reply, the Reformers tried to shout him down. As the Speaker struggled to regain control of the House, McGee acknowledged that Cartier and John A. Macdonald had said hard things about him and that he had "struck back as hard in return." But they were open enemies, unlike the Reformers who had stabbed him in the back. The best friendships he had made, McGee said, were forged on the field of battle; he hoped that he and Cartier could become friends in the same "frank, outspoken manner" in which they had once been foes. He went on to say that he now viewed John A. Macdonald as "a Conservative statesman of large and liberal views, of great capacity and possessing the power of governing the country in a manner offensive to no religious denomination or no nationality, and in accordance with the principles and traditions of the British constitution, without pandering to Democratic sentiments or principles."

This was in marked contrast with the "leaders of the so-called liberal party, whose religious prejudices and narrow-minded views had

George-Étienne Cartier. During the election of 1863, the former enemies
Cartier and McGee began to support one another. "Mr. Cartier was an open
enemy," McGee subsequently said, adding that "the best friends he ever made
were made on the field of battle," and he hoped to make Cartier his friend "in
the same frank, outspoken manner as he had made him his enemy" (*Canadian
Freeman*, 15 October 1863). (NPA, McCord Museum)


always obstructed its progress and rendered it obnoxious to a large class
of the community – a party whose leaning to and sympathies with the
Democratic theory of Government were so notorious and objection-
able." From now on, McGee said, he would work with "honorable men
and gentlemen, who could inspire the respect and confidence of the
country, and who, in governing the country, could be depended on as a
British party, and not an American party, who could support our char-

acter abroad and give dignity to it at home, and who were determined to maintain and work out our Provincial Legislative system on the principles of the British Constitution, the ripest product of the wisdom and experiences of a thousand years."[49]

It was "one of the most eloquent, witty, and caustic speeches he has ever delivered," commented one journalist. When McGee finished, he received "loud and prolonged cheers" from his new Conservative partners as they welcomed him into their fold.[50] Fifteen years earlier, almost to the day, McGee had proudly described himself as a revolutionary republican whose mission was to destroy landlordism, liberate his country, and blast the British Empire "from cornerstone to cornice."[51] Now he was at the other end of the spectrum – an admirer of the British constitution, an advocate for a Canadian monarchy, and a liberal imperialist who had found a new political home with the Conservatives.

---

The contrast was not lost on radical Irish nationalists, for whom this was yet more proof of McGee's hypocrisy, inconsistency, and unbridled ambition. In Ottawa, John Lawrence Power O'Hanly condemned him for making a "sudden *somersault*" and for supporting the very men whom he had "so often and eloquently characterized and denounced as the enemies of popular institutions – the pillagers of the treasury – the reckless violators of the Constitution – the perjurers of the 'Double Shuffle' – the perpetrators of every species of political crime."[52] One can see his point: McGee had hammered away for years at Liberal-Conservative corruption but was now behaving as if such corruption was irrelevant or non-existent. Two years earlier, McGee had condemned Irish Canadians who switched to the Liberal-Conservatives with the same anger and intensity that was now being directed towards him.[53] Either McGee had never been serious in his attacks on Conservative corruption, his enemies maintained, or he had become corrupted himself. Similar sentiments were voiced in New York, where Irish republicans had long regarded him as an unprincipled political mercenary. "The Democratic tarantella which Mr. McGee used to dance so beautifully," it was argued, "has been entirely cured by the jingling of Treasury silver."[54]

While O'Hanly accused him of treason to his former principles, the *Irish Canadian* contended that McGee had finally found out what other, supposedly less intelligent, Irishmen had been saying for years – that George Brown was an irredeemably anti-Catholic and anti-Irish politician. All in all, the newspaper preferred the McGee who wrote the "Red-Cross Flag" back in 1853; here was a poem that reflected the sentiments of millions of Irishmen and had much more mettle than the "Royal twaddle" that he was currently spouting.[55]

------

With such views, it is not surprising that the *Irish Canadian* reported enthusiastically on the Fenian convention that was held in Chicago at the beginning of November, asserting that physical force was the only option left for Irish nationalists and looking forward to "terrible and sweeping" revenge on Britain. Sharing these sentiments were delegates from Fenian circles in Toronto, Montreal, Quebec, Hamilton, and Goderich; in their honour, one of the toasts at the banquet was to "The True Irishmen of the British Provinces."[56] It was clear that Fenianism was spreading in Canada. It was also clear that McGee was placed in the category of False Irishmen.

As he fought back, McGee found powerful allies among the Catholic bishops who had condemned him four years earlier for allying with George Brown.[57] In September, Bishop Bourget had issued a pastoral letter against secret societies; Father Patrick Dowd, the Sulpician pastor of St Patrick's Church in Montreal and the most influential Irish priest in the city, delivered a powerful sermon endorsing its sentiments. But many of his listeners refused to believe that he was serious. "Oh, FATHER DOWD didn't mean what he said," some apparently asserted; "he only did it for policy-sake!" As the Montreal Fenians continued their strategy of infiltrating the St Patrick's Society, McGee and Dowd insisted that all members of the society must take a loyalty test. After a "hard struggle," they won the day. All prospective members had to declare that they were "not members of any secret society, nor of any society already condemned by the Catholic bishop of this diocese."[58] It was, however, a pyrrhic victory; the Fenians simply feigned loyalty, signed the test, and continued to join the organization – though they were still, at this stage, very much in the minority.

Immediately after the Fenian convention in Chicago, McGee took the fight to Peterborough in Canada West. The choice of location was significant; after the Orange disruption of the town's St Patrick's Day parade earlier in the year, the potential for severe ethnoreligious conflict remained high. In his attempt to calm things down, McGee gave the town's St Patrick's Society the same advice that he had given the Young Men's St Patrick's Association in Toronto – do not hold any more public parades. If Fenianism got a foothold in the area, he said, the principal result would be to divide Irish Catholics and make them even more vulnerable to their enemies. Citing Bourget's pastoral letter, he asserted that Fenianism was contrary to the "voice of God" and told his audience to "avoid, as you would avoid the 'jaws of hell,' the secret brotherhood."[59]

A major reason for McGee's growing concern was the close connection between Canadian and American Fenianism at a time of severe political instability in the United States. In the course of his warnings about the danger of an American invasion, McGee contended that Irish revolutionaries in the United States were awaiting the opportunity to attack the British Empire through Canada. "It is a sad fact, but it should not be concealed from the ministers who have the good of the country at heart," he said, "that the children of the Catholic Celts of Ireland have, in their ignorance, made an enemy of this country, and that it is probable they may be found helping to overthrow our institutions at some future day – and all through that ignorance."[60] McGee was so attuned to Fenian ideology – having been so close to it himself – that he anticipated the Fenian invasion strategy before the Fenians actually adopted it themselves.

It was essential, then, to insulate Irish Catholics from Fenianism and to show that they were second to none in their support for Canada, Britain, and the empire. These goals fitted very well with McGee's new political trajectory: What better way to demonstrate their loyalty than to detach them from the Reform Party and draw them into a new alliance with the Conservatives? To those who argued that his emphasis on authority over liberty was somehow anti-Irish, McGee had his answer ready: "In walking in this path, I am in the right line of succession with all the illustrious Irish statesmen of the past, O'Connell, Plunket, Curran, Grattan and above all, Burke."[61]

In claiming common ground between a patriotic Irish liberal-conservative tradition and Canadian loyalism, McGee could counter criticisms that he had sold out his native country; he could dismiss the Fenians as a revolutionary republican fringe movement and present his compatriots as both good Irishmen and good Canadians. At the same time, he had to ensure that his move from the Reform Party to the Conservatives did not leave him politically isolated. "You know my greatest desire is to bring my friends with me," he wrote to John A. Macdonald, "and I need not say to you, that this can only be done, by time-ing, my movements, whenever possible, to theirs." Working behind the scenes, in private conversations that followed public lectures and in quiet discussions with priests and laymen, McGee set out to disabuse his former Reform allies of "their horror of the Machiavelli of Kingston."[62]

One way of doing this was to move beyond traditional party labels and the old animosities they represented. In December, McGee commented that "the terms *Conservative* and *Reformer*" meant different things to different people and should be replaced by a broad-based "Constitutional Party."[63] "I like the term 'Constitutional,' for its comprehensiveness," he wrote two months later; "it includes the assertion as well as the conservation of great principles. It includes the reform of abuses, as well as the jealous maintenance of all wholesome usage, established precedent, and lawful authority."[64] Here, it seemed, was a way of bringing together Irish Catholics, French Canadians, liberal conservatives, moderate Orangemen, and disillusioned Reformers while placing important and necessary distance between the new political movement and the old Conservative coalition. "I think I am putting a new national basis under this party – at least, I hope so," he told Mary Ann Sadlier.[65]

He had the opportunity to put these ideas into practice in early 1864, during a by-election in South Leeds. The election was occasioned by Sandfield Macdonald's decision to appoint the incumbent, Albert Norton Richards, as the solicitor general for Canada West. If Richards could be defeated, the government would suffer a major political blow, and its majority in Parliament would become even more precarious. Accordingly, John A. Macdonald and D'Arcy McGee joined

John A. Macdonald. Had Macdonald lived in Ireland during the famine, McGee wrote in 1858, "I could, no doubt, have found him among the oppressors of that people – for he is of the very timber for an Irish imitation of Toryism" (*Canadian Freeman*, 13 August 1858). Five years later, McGee described Macdonald as "a Conservative statesman of large and liberal views, of great capacity and possessing the power of governing the country in a manner offensive to no religious denomination or no nationality, and in accordance with the principles and traditions of the British constitution" (Canada, *Debates of the Legislative Assembly*, 2 October 1863). (LAC, C-003811)

forces to turn the Irish vote against Richards – Macdonald appealing to Orangemen, and McGee to Catholics. "Since the day of the nomination," ran one newspaper report, "Mr. John A. Macdonald, a pretended Orangeman, and Mr. D'Arcy McGee, a pretended Roman Catholic, have remained in the riding together, and gone through it hand in hand, holding meetings and canvassing the electors."[66]

In the process, McGee demonstrated that he could more than match Macdonald when it came to Machiavellianism. While McGee was secretly encouraging priests not to support Richards, he was supplying Macdonald with information about Richards's attempts to court the Catholic clergy by dining with them, taking them on excursions, and lending money to their friends – information which, as McGee well knew, Macdonald could then use to turn the Orangemen against Richards. "It would & ought to go far towards his defeat," McGee told Macdonald. In short, McGee was helping Macdonald to attack Richards for doing exactly what McGee himself was doing – currying favour with priests in an attempt to secure the Catholic vote. Anyone who views McGee as a visionary who was above the political fray needs to think again; a visionary he certainly was, but he was also prepared to get dirt under his fingernails when necessary.[67]

The tactics worked. Richards was defeated by the same kind of alliance between Orangemen and Irish Catholics that had defeated George Brown in Toronto in 1861 – when, ironically, McGee had employed equally Machiavellian tactics (in this case, anti-Orange scaremongering) to support the Reform Party. Nor was this the only irony. In 1859 McGee had accused Michael Hayes of "infamous treachery" for advocating an Orange-Irish Catholic alliance in a by-election in North Leeds.[68] All this was forgotten now. "We won," exulted the *Canadian Freeman*; and neither Richards nor anyone else of the "vile anti-Irish, anti-Catholic, and anti-British race shall ever again misrepresent us."[69] McGee's constitutional conservatism had scored its first political victory.

———•———

While McGee was fighting these political battles, he also had a major intellectual triumph – the publication of his long-awaited *Popular History of Ireland* in the early summer of 1863, to great critical acclaim on both sides of the Atlantic.[70] Possibly because it did not fit into the story of McGee's contribution to Confederation, the book has largely been overlooked by his Canadian biographers; and it has generally escaped the attention of Irish historiographers, possibly because it was written in Canada.[71] Yet it was the crowning achievement of McGee's literary career. It deeply influenced subsequent Irish historical writing (most notably, A.M. Sullivan's *Story of Ireland*), it was widely used in late-nineteenth-century Irish classrooms, and it helped to secure his unanimous election to the Royal Irish Academy in 1864.[72] The book was the fulfilment of an ambition that reached back to his boyhood: McGee had long believed that there was no "good *complete* history" of Ireland and intended to supply the deficit.[73] In the meantime, he had written several partial (in both senses of the word) histories, including that of Art Mac Murrough's fourteenth-century campaigns against Richard II, the story of Irish Catholic resistance to the Protestant Reformation, and books on seventeenth-century Irish writers, nineteenth-century Irish politicians, and the Irish in North America.[74]

McGee's historical writing was avowedly utilitarian. At various points in his career, he argued that historical knowledge would break the chains of oppression, elevate the Celtic character, preserve Ireland's national identity, promote religious pride, combat nativist stereotypes, and prepare the way for freedom. His narratives were characterized by melodramatic modes of thought and peopled by heroes, villains, and martyrs. The precise identity of the heroes and villains shifted over time; McGee's historical interpretations generally mirrored the changes and continuities in his ideology. When he challenged "popular fallacies" in Irish history, they always happened to be ones that contradicted his own political position; he was equally good at creating new myths that happened to conform to his current political ideas.[75]

A similar dynamic operated in his treatment of Canadian history, which was pressed into the service of the new northern nationality. The purpose of his oft-delivered lecture on the historical connection between the Irish and the Scots, as we have seen, was to promote harmony between the country's two major English-speaking groups. In his lectures on "The Future of Canada," he argued that history demonstrated the importance of keeping the country within British constitutional traditions.[76]

Yet McGee's historical writing cannot be reduced to an amalgam of utilitarianism and melodrama. The impulse to praise or blame was accompanied by the desire to understand and by an awareness of the dangers of dogmatism; a creative tension between engagement and

Thomas D'Arcy McGee, historian. The fulfilment of a long-standing ambition, and seven years in the making, McGee's *Popular History of Ireland* (1863) was his greatest literary accomplishment. According to Father Michael O'Farrell, it was "confessedly the best that has been yet written, and more wonderful has been written upon a foreign soil, with such scanty material as he could here procure" (*Canadian Freeman*, 16 April 1868). (LAC, PA-042396)

detachment runs through much of his work. "If we go to the oracles of the past in a sincere spirit of enquiry, we shall never fail of instruction," he said. "But we shall find there, precisely what we seek for: if we consult History in a spirit of Hatred we shall find there poisonous and deadly weapons enough; but if, in a sincere desire to know and to hold fast by the truth, we seek that source of political wisdom, we can never come away empty or disappointed."[77]

His *Popular History of Ireland* reflects both a sincere attempt to "know and to hold fast by the truth" and a strong identification with Irish Catholicism and constitutional nationalism. The effect is similar to watching a football match with an intelligent, informed, and agreeable companion who is cheering passionately for one side but who understands the letter and spirit of the game, and recognizes the strengths and weaknesses of both teams. He is clear about who is right and wrong, he treats the star players on his team as heroes, and he is more likely to notice and be outraged by dirty play from the opposition than from his own side, though he will deprecate both. At times, his partisan perspective will cloud his judgment, at times he will shout with rage, and at times he will express admiration for some of his team's opponents. By the end of the match, you will have had a lively commentary on the events, and you will be left in no doubt whatsoever about where he stands.

---

McGee began writing his history in the spring of 1858. For five years, through all the pressures of contemporary political debates and tactical manoeuvring, he became a semi-permanent fixture in the Parliamentary Library, connecting with his homeland through the act of writing. Dedicating the book to his close literary companion, Mary Ann Sadlier, he described the rules that he tried to follow: to "bring out the great events," to "subordinate details to general effects," to "throw the strongest light upon the cardinal characters," and above all to elucidate "the *rationale* of Irish History."[78]

Most historical writing falls into the "full but dull" category, and its chief symptom, as Gwyn A. Williams once remarked, is a permanent dull pain in the head. There are sections of the *Popular History* in which

McGee subordinated general effects to details and where the narrative describes the activities of one damn king after another. But when it is written properly, history is like poetry – and for much of the book, McGee wrote it properly. He was particularly adept at evoking mood and setting scenes, as in his description of Ireland on the eve of the Viking invasions:

> Another era opens before us, and we can already discern the
> longships of the north, their monstrous beaks turned towards
> the holy Isle, their sides hung with glittering shields and their
> benches thronged with fair-haired warriors, chanting as they
> advance the fierce war songs of their race. Instead of the monk's
> familiar voice on the river banks we are to hear the shouts of
> strange warriors from a far-off country; and for matin hymn
> and vesper song, we are to be beset through a long and stormy
> period, with sounds of strife and terror, and deadly conflict.[79]

The immediacy of style corresponds with a strong sense of involvement; McGee's powers of imagination and empathy meant that events in fifth-century Ireland mattered as much to him as events in nineteenth-century Ireland, and he responded accordingly.

Towering over it all was the figure of St Patrick, whose Christian revolution was the pivotal moment in Irish history. The pre-Christian Celtic age was characterized by tribal warfare and the "repulsive repetition of reprisals."[80] But after St Patrick, Christianity gradually softened earlier conflicts and instilled a sense of morality into the chieftains. The power of the church was "always exercised against the oppression of the weak by the strong, to mitigate the horrors of war, and to uphold the right of sanctuary (the *Habeas Corpus* of that rude age), and for the maintenance and spread of sound Christian principles." From the sixth to the eighth centuries, Ireland provided the "intellectual leadership of western Europe" and was renowned for its seats of learning, its skilful teachers, its art, and its music.[81]

This, then, was Ireland's golden age – an age that was shaken to its foundations first by pagan and then by Norman invaders. And this is where a long line of villains enters the picture, from Dermid McMurrough, the archetypal traitor who brought the Normans into Ireland during the twelfth century, to Lord Clare, the scourge of the United Irishmen and architect of the Act of Union that united Britain and Ireland more than six hundred years later. McMurrough, McGee noted with some satisfaction, was buried with the carcass of a dog, and Lord Clare's grave was filled "with every description of garbage."[82] (Ironically, the Fenian Jeremiah O'Donovan Rossa, who regarded McGee as the archetypal traitor, would later write that McGee deserved and received a dog's death.)[83]

Standing up to the enemies of the faith and the fatherland was an equally long line of heroes – men such as the military commanders Owen Roe O'Neill and Patrick Sarsfield, the religious martyrs Oliver Plunkett and Nicholas Sheedy, and the great Daniel O'Connell. McGee admired liberal Protestant "patriots" such as Jonathan Swift and Henry Grattan, but had hard words for Wolfe Tone – partly on the grounds that Tone was an anti-Catholic republican revolutionary and partly because Tone had committed the cardinal sin of suicide.[84] A far better example for the Christian people of Ireland was Father John Murphy, who responded to loyalist violence in 1798 by leading his flock into battle, and who faced his executioners with defiance and courage. "The priest who girded on the sword only when he found his altar overthrown and his flock devoured by wolves," commented McGee, "need not fear to look posterity in the face."[85]

Father Murphy, from this perspective, was defending himself against loyalist atrocities, rather than leading men who were themselves committing atrocities. In this respect, McGee's attitude was symptomatic of wider patterns of thought and feeling. Throughout Irish history – and not just Irish history – there has been a propensity to exaggerate the atrocities of the other side and to understate, extenuate, or deny the atrocities of one's own side. Any combination of the following arguments has been used: the other side started it; they lied about atrocities that we supposedly committed; they provoked us into regrettable but understandable reactions; they employed *agents provocateurs* to blacken our reputation; more generally, they were far worse than we have ever been. The extent to which such arguments are employed is a good gauge of the extent to which communal passions and loyalties take precedence over judgment. On all counts except the *agents provocateurs* line, McGee scores very highly indeed.

The other side started it: A good example is McGee's treatment of the rising of 1641, where he asserted that uncontrolled popular violence began when the Scottish garrison at Carrickfergus slaughtered three thousand Catholics (including some of McGee's ancestors) at Islandmagee; from that point on, he wrote, the war assumed a "ferocity of character" that was foreign to the leaders of the rising.[86]

They lied about atrocities that we supposedly committed: The Protestants were putting it about that the rising of 1641 began with a "wholesale massacre" of Ulster settlers. Such "monstrous fictions," McGee countered, were the product of a pernicious propaganda campaign that was retrospectively used to justify the dispossession of Catholics.[87]

They provoked us into regrettable but understandable reactions: In McGee's view, the risings of 1641 and 1798 were both the product of Protestant provocation. In 1641, Protestant landgrabbers deliberately goaded the Catholic people into insurrection on the grounds that "the more men rebelled, the more estates there would be to confiscate." As for 1798, it was "no longer a matter of assertion merely, but simple matter of fact" that the government provoked a rebellion to pave the way for the Act of Union. "The aggressors, both in time and crime were the yeomanry and military," McGee claimed, "but the popular movement dragged wretches to the surface who delighted in repaying torture with torture, and death with death. The butcheries of Dunlavin and Carnew were repaid by the massacres at Scullabogue and Wexford bridge."[88]

They were far worse than we have ever been: If it was true that a rebel leader such as Phelim O'Neill instigated "acts of cruelty," this was because he had temporarily succumbed to "gusts of stormy passion." Such aberrations paled in comparison with the massacres perpetrated by Protestant soldiers such as Charles Coote, who in 1641 encouraged his men to impale little children on pikes. At the very moment that Coote's men were committing such atrocities, Catholics were protecting their Protestant prisoners from retaliation. The same kind of

thing occurred in 1798: "It would be a pointless task to draw out a parallel of the crimes committed on both sides. Two facts only need to be
recorded: that although from 1798 to 1800, not less than *sixty-five* places
of Catholic worship were demolished in Leinster ... only *one* Protestant church, that of Old Ross, was destroyed in retaliation; and that
although towards men, especially men in arms, the rebels acted on the
fierce Mosaic maxim of 'an eye for an eye and a tooth for a tooth,' no
outrage upon women is laid to their charge, even by their most exasperated enemies."[89]

None of this is close to being impartial, much of it is simply wrong,
and some of it remains highly controversial within Irish historiography. Around fifty Catholics, rather than three thousand, were massacred at Islandmagee – a horrendous event, but not the starting point
for popular violence.[90] The number of Protestants massacred during
the rising was indeed magnified beyond belief later in the decade, but
the probable figure of four thousand cannot be dismissed as a propa-
gandist lie.[91] Far from being a "simple matter of fact," the statement
that Pitt's government deliberately provoked the United Irishmen into
rebellion belongs to the realm of myth; on the other hand, historians
are deeply divided over the extent of Catholic sectarianism during the
rising of 1798.[92] One could go on, but the central point is clear: McGee
was responding and contributing to the prevailing mood of his own
community, to the point where he presented a distorted and partisan
view of the other.

If this was symptomatic of deep religious and political loyalties,
it nevertheless coexisted with a serious effort to write fair-minded
and even-handed history. He respected and admired courage wherever he found it – whether among the Vikings and Normans or in
the "heroic constancy" of the Protestants who withstood the siege of
Derry in 1689.[93] He was aware of the pitfalls of presentism (even if he
often fell into them) and attempted to assess historical figures by the
standards of the time. Although he regarded Dermid McMurrough
as a despicable character, McGee noted that "much of the horror and
odium which has accumulated on his memory is posthumous and
retrospective" and his private life was no worse than that of some of

his contemporaries — "but then they had no part in bringing in the Normans."[94]

Elsewhere, he argued that the attitudes of political leaders should not be judged by the actions of their followers. William of Orange, he pointed out, may have been associated in popular memory with "disaster, proscription and spoliation," but he was "personally averse to persecution for conscience sake." The guilty party was not William but the Protestant Ascendancy (a phrase that he mistakenly attributed to the late seventeenth rather than the late eighteenth century), who violated the Treaty of Limerick, expropriated the property of Catholic landlords, and implemented the Penal Laws.[95]

Such oppression, according to McGee, was part of a recurring pattern of fear, anger, and mutually escalating violence in Irish history. Protestant domination and intransigence had made Irish Catholics despair of constitutional change and pushed them into rebellious or revolutionary movements, which were then used to justify further repression. To break the cycle, it was necessary to attack it from the top and the bottom by opposing Protestant privilege and injustice and the secret societies that such privilege and injustice had spawned. Some of his harshest words were reserved for the "evil genius, whoever he was, that first introduced the system of signs, and passwords, and midnight meetings, among the peasantry of Ireland." And some of his strongest praise went to the Catholic Church for strenuously opposing the "diabolical machinery of secret oath-bound association among the Irish peasantry."[96]

Consistent with this outlook, McGee sympathized and in some senses identified with those politicians who walked the middle path in the quest for religious and political emancipation. He preferred the moderation of the Duke of Ormond to the militancy of Cardinal Rinuccini, just as he preferred the reformism of Henry Grattan to the radicalism of Wolfe Tone. His kindred spirit, though, was Edmund Burke. McGee's interpretation of eighteenth-century Irish history was deeply Burkean, not least in the conviction that full Catholic emancipation would have drawn Ireland and Britain closer together rather than driving them farther apart. There are echoes of Burke in McGee's suggestion that the Act of Union could have worked "had equal civil and religious rights been freely and at once extended" to Ireland's Catholics. But it was not to be: "The Union was never utilized for Ireland; it proved in reality what Samuel Johnson has predicted, when spoken of in his day: 'Do not unite with us, sir,' said the gruff old moralist to an Irish acquaintance; 'it would be the union of the shark with his prey; we should unite with you only to destroy you.'"[97]

But if Ireland's "distinct political nationality" had been lost, its "religious liberties were finally recovered," largely through the efforts of Daniel O'Connell and the Catholic Association. It is no coincidence that McGee's history ends in 1829, with the achievement of Catholic Emancipation – an appropriate conclusion to a grand narrative of a golden age, the fall, suffering, struggle, and redemption. The story of Ireland was the triumph of conscience over coercion, symbolized in the anecdote with which McGee concluded his book:

> A lofty column on the walls of Derry bore the effigy of Bishop
> Walker, who fell at the Boyne, armed with a sword, typical
> of his martial inclinations, rather than of his religious calling.
> Many long years, by day and night, had his sword, sacred to
> liberty or ascendancy, according to the eyes with which the
> spectator regarded it, turned its steadfast point to the broad estu-
> ary of Loch Foyle. Neither wintry storms nor summer rains
> had loosened it in the grasp of the warlike churchman's effigy,
> until, on the 13th day of April, 1829 – the day the royal signature
> was given to the Act of Emancipation – the sword of Walker
> fell with a prophetic crash upon the ramparts of Derry, and was
> shattered to pieces. So, we may now say, without bitterness and
> almost without reproach, so may fall and shiver to pieces, every
> code, in every land beneath the sun, which impiously attempts to
> shackle conscience, or endows an exclusive caste with the rights
> and franchises which belong to an entire People![98]

———•———

The *Popular History of Ireland* not only helped to shape Irish historical consciousness in the mid-nineteenth century; it also provides a valuable map of McGee's mind as he grappled with Canadian and Irish politics between 1858 and 1863. His commitment to Irish Catholicism had the paradoxical effect of simultaneously narrowing and broadening his outlook. On the one hand, it pushed him into partisanship and became the central criterion for his political and moral judgments. On the other hand, it turned him into a defender of minority rights in general who advocated freedom of conscience and attacked religious privilege "in every land beneath the sun." This was accompanied by an empathy and open-mindedness that manifested itself in his admiration for liberal Irish Protestants such as Henry Grattan, and in his willingness to work with liberal Canadian Protestants such as George Brown – as long as they remained liberal, in his eyes.

A fascinating interplay between militant and moderate impulses also runs through the book. His heroes were men who stood up for the weak against the strong, who fought against injustice and the abuse of power, and who defended the Catholic Church against myriad enemies, from outside and within, from above and below. He admired men who took up the sword for faith and fatherland when necessary – soldiers such as Owen Roe O'Neill or guerrilla fighters such as Father John Murphy. He was equally positive about politicians who refused to compromise on key issues – Daniel O'Connell, for example, in rejecting a governmental veto over the appointment of bishops. At the same time, he shared Burke's emphasis on politics as the art of the possible and vehemently denounced secret societies that threatened to trigger a modern version of "the repulsive repetition of reprisals." This fitted closely with his approach to Canadian politics – brokering deals, hammering out compromises, giving ground to gain ground – and with his visceral hostility to the Fenians. The intensity of his language against secret societies in the *Popular History* mirrored the intensity of his hostility to the Fenians in Canada, the United States, and Ireland.

Perhaps the most intriguing aspect of the *Popular History*, however, lies in what it does not say. The story ends with the religious victory of 1829 and not the political failure of 1848. McGee does not treat Catholic Emancipation as a precursor to eventual political emancipation, and he evades the larger question of Ireland's relationship to the Act of Union. If it really was a union between the shark and his prey, then there was much unfinished business at hand. McGee's preferences in the *Popu-*

*lar History* clearly indicate the nature of that business – a Home Rule settlement under the Crown, following the path of O'Connell, Plunket, Curran, and Grattan, with the shadow of Burke in the background.

But this is where the art of the possible came in; however desirable such a settlement was in principle, it was out of the question in practice. "All I have learned for the past fifteen years," McGee told an Irish American journalist around this time, "only helps to convince me that, unless some extraordinary change which I cannot foresee, and, which it would be little short of madness to expect, takes place in the social and political world, there is no possibility that Ireland can ever enjoy self-government. No combination of circumstances, I am satisfied, can, by any chance, take place in our day, by which Ireland would be enabled to take that which England is unwilling to grant. I would, therefore, dissuade my countrymen for wasting their time, and frittering away their energies in trying to accomplish what I honestly believe to be impossible."[99]

To press for an impossible outcome would only feed into the sense of frustration that fuelled the Fenians. Far better, then, to focus on practical changes within the Act of Union, such as tenant rights and the disestablishment of the Church of Ireland, using Canada as a guide and model. If Canada demonstrated that Irish Catholics were loyal when they were treated fairly, what better example could be set for British policy in Ireland? On the other hand, if Fenianism became a significant presence in Canada, the entire premise of McGee's argument would be undermined; a society with religious freedom, economic opportunity, and widespread land ownership would not have reduced revolutionary republicanism and ethnoreligious tensions. The Canadian model would have failed, with dismal consequences for both Canada and Ireland. This, McGee was convinced, must not be allowed to happen.

## CHAPTER EIGHT

# This Extraordinary Armistice
## March 1864 – May 1865

During the spring of 1864, McGee's career moved into a new phase, in which two themes towered over everything else – the campaign for Confederation, and the fight against Fenianism. He had laid the ideological foundations for Confederation in his *New Era* articles of 1857 and had been at war with revolutionary Irish nationalists since the early 1850s. But now external circumstances gave earlier arguments new immediacy. In the context of the American Civil War, growing British disenchantment with the costs of empire, and endemic political instability in Canada, Confederation began to move from the realm of theory to potential practice. Meanwhile, the Fenian Brotherhood was gathering momentum on both sides of the Atlantic. In Ireland, the Fenian leader James Stephens assured his followers that 1865 would be the Year of Revolution; his newspaper, the *Irish People*, was spreading the word, membership was climbing towards the 50,000 mark, and attempts were under way to recruit Irish soldiers in the British army.[1] In the United States, Irish migrants with bitter memories of the famine were joining the movement, the Civil War was providing revolutionary Irish nationalists with military training, and John O'Mahony was promising men, materiel, and money for the struggle back home.[2] In Canada, Fenian circles were emerging within Irish Catholic organizations, and the brotherhood was expanding outwards from its bases in Montreal and Toronto.[3]

From McGee's perspective, there were opportunities and dangers here – the prospect of establishing a new constitution for a new country, and the risk that the growth of Fenianism in Canada could create a massive anti-Irish Catholic backlash. In this sense, the effort to remodel Canada in the image of constitutional conservatism was inseparable from the effort to defeat Fenianism. But the opportunities and the dangers required very different responses. The positive work of Confederation, McGee believed, involved cooperation, compromise, and consensus building; the negative work of demolishing Fenianism involved sledgehammers. If the campaign for Confederation brought out the moderate in McGee, the fight against Fenianism brought out the militant. This chapter assesses his role in the construction of Confederation; the following chapter examines his parallel conflict with revolutionary Irish nationalism.

---

Federalism had been on the backburner since the late 1850s, when Alexander Galt's resolutions on British North American confederation and George Brown's proposals for a federated Province of Canada failed to produce results.[4] Even McGee had relatively little to say on the subject in the period between his "Shield of Achilles" speech in May 1860 and his Maritime tour of 1863; it would, he later remarked, have been "half-daft" to have proposed intercolonial union during the early 1860s.[5] But with endemic sectional divisions and the difficulties of attaining representation by population under the existing arrangement, George Brown decided to try again. In October 1863 he gave notice of his intention to propose an all-party select committee on Canada's constitutional future in the next parliamentary session. Everything would be open for discussion, including the federal union of British North America.[6]

When the politicians returned to Quebec City in February, their mood was anything but conciliatory. With the defeat of Albert Richards in South Leeds and the further reduction of the government's slender majority, the Liberal-Conservatives attempted to move in for the kill, and the Reformers aggressively defended their position. As political debates reached new levels of acrimony, McGee was in the thick of the fight. Barely a week after the session began, the Cork-born Reform MP from Missisquoi, James O'Halloran, pulled out a copy of the New

York *Nation* from 1849, read aloud McGee's editorial on the need for a republican revolution in Canada, and denounced McGee as a man of no principles.

It was, of course, a familiar accusation, and McGee had his familiar answers ready – that these were the views of a young man, driven to revolution by the suffering of the Irish people, and that he had mistakenly believed that Canada was as oppressed as Ireland. But then McGee ratcheted up the rhetoric, charging that O'Halloran had recently uttered the "ferocious and blood-thirsty sentiment" that "it would be well for the country if a few priests were hung." Amid cheers and jeers, three other MPs backed up McGee's claim; a fourth accused him of repeating words that had been spoken in a private conversation, adding that such behaviour was "incomparably below the intrigues of a common informer."[7] Writing to his wife, Brown described it as "an awful scene of abuse," which strengthened his conviction that there "ought to be a shake-up" of the political system, but which also underlined the difficulties of getting Reformers and Conservatives to work together.[8]

Although McGee lashed out when attacked, he was prepared to cooperate with anyone who might advance the cause of Confederation, on the grounds that the issue transcended party politics. The same could not be said of the Liberal-Conservative Party leaders. When Brown introduced his resolution for an all-party select committee, John A. Macdonald and Cartier reacted with a mixture of distrust and derision. In contrast, McGee declared that he would support the proposal, even "if he stood alone among the Opposition."[9]

Before it came to the test, however, Sandfield Macdonald announced that his government was resigning, since it could no longer function effectively with such a narrow majority. "Hear, hear," McGee interjected. "It ought to have been done long ago"; here was the long-sought revenge for the "betrayal" of 1863.[10] By the end of March, the Liberal-Conservatives were back in power, with Étienne Taché as the nominal leader, John A. Macdonald and Cartier as the attorneys general for Canada West and East, and McGee finally in the cabinet position he had always wanted – as minister of agriculture, immigration, and statistics.

In this capacity, he could not only push forward the project of Confederation but also implement the reforms that had been stalled under Sandfield Macdonald's administration – most notably, the comprehensive restructuring of the Board of Statistics to provide accurate information about Canadian economic activity, patterns of immigration, occupation, and ethnicity. Later in the year, McGee appointed the brilliant ultramontane writer and social scientist Joseph-Charles Taché as his deputy minister. Under Taché's leadership, the revamped department laid the groundwork for the first dominion census in 1871, which is still regarded by genealogists and historians as one of the best in the country's history.[11]

The political situation, however, remained volatile and uncertain. The new government turned out to be as precarious as its predecessor; shortly after the House reconvened, McGee privately wrote of "a state of crisis" in Canadian politics.[12] When the debate over Brown's resolution was resumed, it became clear that both the Conservatives and Reformers were internally divided on the issue; McGee may have differed from the leaders of his party, but he did not stand alone among the rank and file.[13] Much to the surprise of John A. Macdonald and Cartier, the resolution received sufficient cross-party support to pass. Immediately afterwards, Brown appointed nineteen committee members, chosen from both parties and reflecting a broad range of constitutional views. At the first meeting, in front of the sixteen members who attended, he locked the door and put the key in his pocket. "Now gentlemen," he said, "you must talk about this matter, as you cannot leave this room without coming to me."[14]

It was a strange scene – seventeen men with disparate political views, some of whom could not stand one another, locked in a room, trying to find a way out of Canada's constitutional problems. John A. Macdonald and Cartier were there, along with the men whom McGee had accused of stabbing him in the back – Sandfield Macdonald, Holton, and Dorion. But they all approached their work, as Brown later put it, "frankly and in a spirit of compromise." Over eight meetings, shrouded in secrecy, they discussed the choices: the status quo, representation by population, the double majority, dissolution of the union, and federalism. On 14 June, Brown reported to the House that the committee had a "strong feeling ... in favour of changes in the direction of a federative system, applied either to Canada alone or to the whole British North American Provinces." The Macdonalds, Sandfield and John A., were among the dissenting minority, but there is no doubt that much of the "strong feeling" in favour had been supplied by McGee.[15]

Later that same day, the government lost a non-confidence motion by two votes. For McGee, as for Brown, the fact that neither party could command a clear majority, that both the Reformers and the Conservatives had been defeated within a three-month period, was symptomatic of the very problem that the select committee had been trying to solve – the political logjam created by the current constitutional arrangement. In these circumstances, Brown did something that shocked many of his fellow Reformers. He broke with Sandfield Macdonald, Holton, and Dorion, and opened up talks with his Conservative enemies, maintaining that this latest manifestation of political instability underlined the importance of "settling the constitutional difficulties between Upper and Lower Canada." If the Conservatives were willing to seize the opportunity, Brown let it be known, he would work with them.[16]

When it became clear that John A. Macdonald had agreed to open negotiations with Brown, there was a sensation in the House – cheers and applause mingled with feelings of bewilderment and betrayal. Many of Brown's followers were nonplussed; Sandfield Macdonald and his supporters were appalled; the *Rouges* were convinced that Cartier had just destroyed his career by forming an alliance with Brown. Meanwhile, the discussions continued behind the scenes, with Brown on one side and John A. Macdonald, Galt, and Cartier on the other. Two issues were at stake: whether a federal solution should apply only to Canada or should encompass British North America in general; and whether Brown and the Reformers should form a coalition with the Conservatives or remain outside the government.

Pragmatic political considerations were at least as important as broader ideological positions. Brown preferred a federal arrangement for Canada alone, partly because any attempt at a wider solution could detract from the urgent task of dealing with the crisis in Canadian politics, but mainly because it would leave the Reformers in immediate control of Canada West. He did not, however, rule out a wider settlement at some stage in the future. In contrast, Macdonald thought primarily in British North American terms, partly to counter the continental expansion of the United States but mainly because the inclusion of the Maritimes would enable him to broaden his Conservative base.[17] As far as a coalition was concerned, Brown had no desire to join a government with his old enemies John A. Macdonald and Cartier, and did not want the Reform Party to get its fingers caught in the Conservative machinery. But the Conservatives wanted him in the ministry, on the grounds that he and his supporters would be easier to control.

After four days of hard bargaining, a compromise was reached. On the first issue, the government agreed to introduce legislation in the next parliamentary session for federalism within Canada; in the meantime, it would explore the possibilities of a more general British North American arrangement. Brown had got what he wanted – a commitment to take immediate action on the Canadian constitution. Cartier also had good reason to be satisfied; he had countered the threat of representation by population with a federal structure that could protect French Canadian religious, legal, and cultural institutions. John A. Macdonald was playing a high-risk game with the worst cards; he had limited support in Canada West, and it seemed unlikely that he could bring in the Maritimes.[18] On the other hand, he had little to lose. The alternative to cooperating with the Reformers, he believed, was electoral defeat followed by a decade of Reform dominance.[19] Macdonald did not buy the "sectional deadlock" argument; his concern was not so much constitutional paralysis as political impotence.

On the issue of coalition, Brown was coming under intense pressure from his own supporters and from the Conservatives to join the government. McGee added his voice to the chorus. "The prospect of the settlement of the Constitutional question now before us, may be most materially affected – either furthered or closed – by your acceptance or refusal of office," McGee told Brown on the morning of 22 June. "How *can* you hope to secure the settlement without your own personal participation in the preliminary and advanced stages of the negotiations?" "Should you conclude to join this government with the view of settling our great and increasing constitutional difficulties," McGee continued, "I can assure you, you will find in me, if not a very able, certainly a very willing coadjutor."[20] That afternoon, Brown made his decision; rather than running the risk of a breakdown in the negotiations, he and his party would form a coalition with the Conservatives. It proved to be a turning point in Canadian history.[21]

<hr />

The key question now was whether federalism could be carried forward from Canada to embrace British North America as a whole – something that could not occur without the approval of Britain and the support of the Maritimes. In the case of Britain, it was very much a matter of pushing at an open door; British politicians generally favoured federal union, provided that the initiative came from British North Americans themselves.[22] In the case of the Maritimes, plans were already underway for a conference on the political union of Nova Scotia, New Brunswick, and Prince Edward Island – a development that McGee had welcomed as an example of expansive thinking and as a possible step towards a broader federal union.[23]

    In early May, before Brown's select committee had been established, McGee had written to the New Brunswick premier Leonard Tilley, assuming that the conference on Maritime union would be held in Charlottetown, asking if he could be invited as an observer, and suggesting that the Maritime meeting should be immediately followed by a general conference on intercolonial union, also in Charlottetown.[24] It was a remarkably prescient letter, which anticipated the broad outline of events in the coming months. On the same day that the coalition government was formed, 22 June, Lord Monck contacted his counterparts in the Maritimes, requesting that a Canadian delegation visit their conference. The following month, the Canadians learned that the conference would take place in Charlottetown at the beginning of September and that they would be welcome to attend in an unofficial capacity. As it turned out, the Canadian delegates would not only attend the conference; they would take it over.

    Meanwhile, McGee set out to promote the cause of Confederation in the Maritimes – which he was singularly well placed to do, given his earlier visits to the region and his advocacy of the Intercolonial Railway. Working through Sandford Fleming, the chief surveyor of the railway line, he asked the boards of trade in Saint John and Halifax to invite some of the "leading men" in Canada on a goodwill tour of their provinces. It was a good example of shrewd public relations; the idea was to dress up a politically motivated Canadian initiative as a non-political visit that had originated in the Maritimes. The boards of trade sent out the invitations, the Canadians duly accepted, and a hundred of them prepared to arrive in August.[25]

Equally shrewd was the decision to include twenty-two journalists among the Canadian visitors. This may well be the first example of embedded journalism in Canadian history. If so, it worked. As the banquets were held, the drink flowed and the music played, newspaper men in the company of prominent politicians and businessmen sent glowing reports to their readers back home. McGee had organized a charm offensive on an impressive scale and was more than willing to sacrifice his constitution for the sake of the Constitution. His tour also tapped into a Maritime desire for external approval, with reporters in Fredericton, Saint John, and Halifax each boasting how much the Canadians liked their respective cities.[26] Timothy Warren Anglin, for one, was not amused. "One of the besetting sins of this people," he wrote, "is vanity, a weak and silly vanity, which attaches immense importance to what others say of us."[27]

Playing on civic pride, dispensing drinks, co-opting journalists, claiming to be nonpolitical, and pretending that they had not invited themselves, McGee and his entourage privately and publicly pressed the case for Confederation and the new nationality.[28] In Halifax, he confronted the main arguments against Confederation – that federal systems were inherently weak, that the Maritimes would be saddled with immense Canadian debts, and that the country was simply too large for one government. On the contrary, he said, the Canadians could learn from American mistakes, combine Old World traditions of authority with New World realities, and construct a strong federal government. Debt would not be a problem; on a per capita basis, Maritimers owed roughly the same as Canadians, and a common market would open up new economic opportunities for all British Americans. Neither was the size of the country an issue, since east-west railway connections would bring people closer together and foster a consciousness of commonality.[29]

At least as important as the content of his speeches was the style in which he delivered them. "His praise is on every lip," commented the Saint John *Daily News*; the Maritime press was full of references to the "brilliant D'Arcy," whose oratory exceeded all expectations, who could give spellbinding extemporaneous speeches, and who had the rare ability to be "joyous and grave, comic and refined, all in the same sentence."[30] "It is not too much to say," commented Charles Tupper's *British Colonist*, "that Mr. McGee has done more to promote the social, commercial and political union of British North America than any other public man in these Provinces."[31]

This was probably true – although, as in 1863, many Maritimers remained unconvinced by his arguments even as they admired his oratory.[32] Some, such as Anglin, were equally critical of the message and the messenger. Following up his attacks from the previous year on McGee's monarchism, Anglin argued that the Maritime tour was based on deception, that McGee was recycling the same tired old speeches, and that all his rhetoric about colonial union was so vague as to be meaningless. The whole thing, Anglin asserted, was merely a smoke-screen to promote the Intercolonial Railway and dissuade New Brunswick from investing in a railway to Maine – even though a connection to Maine made much more sense than running "an Intercolonial Railroad through an unbroken wilderness for hundreds of miles" and saddling New Brunswick with "a crushing weight of debt."[33] Anglin's attitude found echoes in Canada, where McGee's old enemy George Clerk dismissed the tour as "the Big Intercolonial Drink."[34]

Nevertheless, the political momentum was with McGee, and he had good reason to be satisfied with his trip to the Maritimes. During the third week of August, he returned to Quebec City, where his fellow cabinet ministers were preparing their proposals for the Charlottetown Conference. There was a remarkable degree of consensus. Macdonald and Galt had always preferred a centralized federation; Cartier believed that political and economic power should reside with the federal government, provided that Canada East had full control over its legal, religious, educational, and cultural institutions; and both Brown and McGee had moved away from the decentralized system which they had favoured in 1859.[35] It was clear that the Canadians at Charlottetown would emphasize federal power over provincial autonomy.

All this fitted with McGee's view that authority was necessary to prevent liberty from sliding into licentiousness, and with his growing conviction that the American Civil War was not only a conflict over slavery but also the product of weak central institutions – the absence, as he put it, of a fixed and infallible locus of power.[36] This view had been strengthened by his general study of federal systems, ranging from ancient Greece to contemporary New Zealand. The lesson he drew was that decentralized federations either collapsed into chaos or eventually had their powers usurped by the executive. Wise statesmen, then, must anticipate and avert these dangers by constructing a system with strong and clearly defined central powers.[37]

At the beginning of September the Canadians arrived in Charlottetown, disembarked from the *Queen Victoria*, and made their pitch to the politicians who had officially gathered to discuss Maritime union. In a carefully choreographed performance, the major arguments were presented by Macdonald, Cartier, Galt, and Brown, with McGee taking a backseat role. Over four days, in conditions of secrecy, Macdonald and Cartier made the general case for Confederation, while Galt outlined the financial arrangements and Brown discussed the division of powers between the federal and provincial governments.

By the time they had finished, a reasonably coherent picture had emerged. The federal legislature would consist of two houses – an assembly based on representation by population, and an upper house with appointed members drawn equally from the three regions of Canada West, Canada East, and the Maritimes. On the question of finances, the federal government would assume provincial debts and provide revenue to the provinces, based on population. A list of federal and provincial responsibilities was drawn up, with the central government operating the main levers of political and economic power, and the provinces looking after such matters as education, health, roads, and law enforcement.[38] In striking and self-conscious contrast to the

The Charlottetown Conference, 1864. Although he did not play a significant role in the negotiations, McGee's first-hand knowledge of the Maritimes, together with his personal charm, meant that he played a pivotal role in establishing a climate of goodwill among the delegates. (Isabel Skelton, *The Life of Thomas D'Arcy McGee*)

United States, residual powers would lie with the federal government rather than with the "people" or local legislatures.[39]

McGee supported the proposals, resigning himself to the fact that his ideas about a Canadian monarch had been completely ignored. His principal contribution to the Charlottetown Conference lay not in the formal proceedings but in the whirl of social events that surrounded the meetings – the extravagant dinner parties and luncheons, the excursions, and the grand ball at Government House. As historians of Confederation have frequently pointed out, these events were important in creating a climate of camaraderie and allowing new friendships to form.[40] At a long liquid lunch on board the *Queen Victoria*, where "McGee's wit sparkled brightly as the wine," the mood was so euphoric that the delegates good-humouredly proclaimed the banns of matrimony among the provinces.[41] McGee had prepared the way for such good feelings; through his Maritime tour, his personal charm, and his role in introducing Canadian and Maritime politicians to one another, he was, among many other things, the social convener of Confederation.

The mixture of constitutionalism and conviviality proved effective; by the end of the conference, the question of Maritime union had been set aside, and the Maritime delegates supported Confederation in principle, provided that "the terms of union could be made satisfactory" – a crucial qualification.[42] From Charlottetown, the delegates travelled to Halifax, where they agreed to hold another conference in Quebec, with a view to defining the terms of union and making them satisfactory.[43]

———•———

At Quebec the following month, thirty-three delegates from Canada, New Brunswick, Prince Edward Island, Nova Scotia, and Newfoundland met to negotiate the details of a new constitutional arrangement for British North America. As in Charlottetown, McGee did not play a prominent role in the formal discussions, except in the area of education – not surprisingly, given his long battle for improved separate schools legislation and his emphasis on minority rights.[44] In the original resolutions, education was enumerated among the provincial powers. But if education became an exclusively provincial jurisdiction, there was a very real possibility that the Protestants in Canada West would roll back separate schools; the Scott Act, after all, had been passed over and above the objections of the Upper Canadian majority. Similarly, the Protestant minority in Canada East wanted to safeguard its own school system. With this in mind, McGee moved an amendment to guarantee "the rights and privileges which the Protestant or Catholic minority in both Canadas may profess as to their denominational schools, at the time when the Constitutional Act goes into operation."[45] It was carried; minority education had been protected, and a potential deal-breaker had been avoided. The wording of McGee's amendment, it should also be noted, gave Protestants in Canada East and Catholics in Canada West an incentive to demand still better "rights and privileges" before Confederation went into effect – demands that were not long in coming.

Meanwhile, the conference thrashed out the issues of regional representation in the upper house and the federal-provincial allocation of debts, assets, and taxes. Gradually, the delegates from Canada, New Brunswick, and Nova Scotia moved towards a consensus, while dissension emerged within the Prince Edward Island camp. The Newfoundland delegation was on board, but could not count on support back home. Although McGee's precise position during the discussions remains unknown, he endorsed the general plan to strengthen the federal government, construct the Intercolonial Railway, and prepare for the admission of the West.[46] And he reprised his Charlottetown role as the *bon vivant* of the banquets, even though his propensity for excessive drinking sometimes alienated his associates.[47]

As the conference drew to a close and its seventy-two resolutions were formally adopted, the delegates began their campaign to promote the agreement. The first stop was Montreal, where McGee hosted the New Brunswick contingent. Amid extravagant and exuberant celebrations and impassioned public speeches about British North America's future, McGee was in his element. If there were still people who doubted the necessity of Confederation, he said, they need only "look across the border, and they would find reasons as thick as blackberries." In contrast to the United States, the British North American delegates had built new institutions on old foundations, "which would bear the whole force of the democratic winds and waves, and the corroding political atmosphere of the New World, and which they hoped would stand for ages."[48]

When McGee made this speech, it was impossible for Canadians not to "look across the border." Ten days earlier, while the Quebec Conference was meeting, a band of Canadian-based Southern Confederates crossed into Vermont, attacked the town of St Albans, and escaped back into Canada. Their objective was to provoke an Anglo-American war, which would relieve the pressure on the South. They certainly succeeded in heightening Canadian-American tensions, although the fact that the raiders were arrested upon their return to Canada helped to mitigate American anger.

In December, however, the prisoners were released on a legal technicality, with entirely predictable results. Demands for revenge reverberated through the American press, and one United States general called for an invasion of Canada. Not for the last time, the American government attempted to tighten up border security by requiring passports for Canadians entering the United States. And American protectionists, who were already pushing for the cancellation of the Reciprocity Treaty with Canada, now found a clear path before them; free trade between Canada and the United States was another casualty of the raid.[49]

Here was dramatic confirmation of Canada's economic and military vulnerability – and something that the advocates of Confederation could turn to their political advantage. McGee had consistently maintained that a common market and common tariffs would protect British North America if the United States abrogated the Reciprocity Treaty, and had insisted that a new northern nation, backed up by Britain, would have sufficient defensive capacity to deter an American invasion. These arguments now appeared more compelling than ever.

In the immediate aftermath of the Quebec Conference, though, McGee was temporarily out of action. The frenetic pace of the previous months, the constant round of balls and banquets, and the voluminous consumption of hard liquor all took their toll. Shortly after returning to Montreal, McGee went down with a serious illness; according to Lady Monck, he contracted cholera and came close to dying.[50] He was not the only person whose health suffered; the heavy drinking and hard work also caught up with Macdonald, who dropped out of the post-conference celebrations and recuperated in Kingston.[51]

It was not until the end of December that McGee participated in the promotion of the Quebec agreement. He would, he said, have preferred a legislative union, but "where there were so many various existing interests to be ... conciliated and combined – he was quite sure if they had, as a first step, insisted upon the Union taking a legislative form, they would never have taken a second step." As it was, the conference had made the central government as strong as possible and had ensured that minority education rights were "part and parcel of the fundamental law itself" so that "no bigot, east or west, would be permitted to lay his finger on it." Although McGee referred to the St Albans raid and the need to prevent anything like it from recurring, the main message of his speech was one of hope rather than fear. "The present decade – between 1860 and 1870 – was to decide the destiny of all British America," he declared, and no local, temporary, or sectional difficulties should be allowed to stand in the way.[52]

This served as a dress rehearsal for McGee's participation in the parliamentary debate on the Quebec Resolutions. Like the Young Irelanders before them, the supporters of Confederation saved their best orator to the end; the result was a three-hour tour-de-force, one of the greatest speeches of his career, which is still recognized as a classic.[53] As such, it repays close attention.

He began by reviewing the background to the Quebec Conference – the earlier arguments for colonial union, his own writings on the new nationality, and the pamphlets of Peter Stevens Hamilton and Alexander Morris. It was typical of McGee to begin with the intellectual origins of Confederation; it spoke to his deep belief that ideas mattered. From here, he moved to the political developments that turned ideas into actions, singling out Galt's initiative in 1858 and the formation of Brown's constitutional committee in 1864. The ensuing debate about Confederation, McGee continued, was already transforming Canadian politics; fundamental questions about the character of the country were replacing parochial concerns and "mere mercenary struggles for office."[54]

McGee then reiterated his long-standing argument that the status quo was no longer an option. The relationship between Britain and its North American colonies had been transformed since the 1840s; the shift to free trade and responsible government, together with Britain's insistence that its North American colonies must prepare to defend themselves, all pointed towards a new order of things. At the same time, the United States had become increasingly warlike, expanding its army from 10,000 to 600,000 men ("these are frightful figures," he said); in the wake of the St Albans raid, it was also abrogating the Reciprocity Treaty and imposing a "vexatious passport system" on Canadians. All this was combined with Canada's "internal constitutional difficulties," which had resulted in five administrations during the previous two years; it was essential to find a "permanent remedy for such a state of things." "Well!" he said. "We have had our three warnings; one warning from within, and two from without."[55]

Having made the case for change, McGee discussed the kinds of change that had been proposed. Some people believed that a commercial union among the British colonies would answer their needs; the problem with this position, he replied, was that British North America stretched from east to west, while the gravitational pull of trade ran from north to south. A commercial union without "some political power at its back" would be "merely waste paper"; political unity was essential to prevent the British North American colonies from being sucked into the economic empire of the United States. At the other pole, there were those who believed that only full legislative union would keep British North America together; against this, he reminded his listeners that local interests were in "a pretty advanced state of development" and must be accommodated within a centralized federal system. In fact, he said, the growth of provincialism was actually an argument for immediate action; the longer things were postponed, the more powerful local interests would become, until the point was reached when any kind of union, however loose it might be, would never even get a hearing.[56]

This brought McGee to his next major theme – the argument that Confederation could counter the growing military power and the continental ambitions of the United States. Although he had criticized American expansionism before, he had never expressed himself so memorably on the subject:

They coveted Florida, and seized it; they coveted Louisiana, and purchased it; they coveted Texas, and stole it; and then they picked a quarrel with Mexico, which ended by their getting California. They sometimes pretend to despise these colonies as prizes beneath their ambition; but had we not had the strong arm of England over us we should not now have a separate existence. The acquisition of Canada was the first ambition of the American Confederacy, and never ceased to be so, when her troops were a handful and her navy scarce a squadron. Is it likely to be stopped now, when she counts her guns afloat by thousands and her troops by hundreds of thousands?[57]

It was not only a question of resisting an imperialist democracy; it was also necessary to unite against a potential Fenian incursion into Canada. Here, McGee quoted at length from a recent pro-Confederation letter by Archbishop Thomas Connolly of Halifax. Arguing that a Fenian raid could pave the way for a full-scale American invasion, Connolly asserted that only "vigorous and timely preparation" – by which he meant Confederation – would protect British North America from "the horrors of a war such as the world has never seen."[58]

Inserting Archbishop Connolly into the debate was an intelligent rhetorical move that was intended to serve three purposes: to make it appear that the Catholic Church was solidly behind Confederation, to amplify Connolly's message to the laity, and to contrast Irish American Fenianism with Irish Catholic Canadian loyalty. On the other hand, McGee opened himself up to the charge that Catholic bishops and priests controlled the votes of their flock. "No one more deprecates than I do the interference of clergymen in mere party politics," he said, "and I think such is the sentiment also of His Grace of Halifax; but when it is an issue of peace or war, of deliverance or conquest, who has a better, who so good a right to speak as the ministers of the Gospel of peace, and justice, and true freedom?" This was consistent with the position he had taken fifteen years earlier, when he maintained that the clergy had every right to involve themselves in politics if the existence of the nation was at stake.[59] Still, one cannot help feeling that he was trying – and succeeding – to have it both ways.

As well as establishing a bulwark against American imperialism, Confederation would tighten the bonds between Canada and Britain. Those who feared that Canada was cutting itself adrift from the mother country were wrong: "By making the united colonies more valuable as an ally to Great Britain," McGee asserted, "we shall strengthen rather than weaken the Imperial connection." The stronger the imperial connection, the better for both countries; Canada would fulfill its destiny as a great power within the British Empire, and Britain would benefit from its association with Canada.[60]

Everything was falling into place. The formation of the Canadian coalition had coincided with plans for Maritime union; the Canadian tour of New Brunswick and Nova Scotia had encouraged Maritimers to entertain the larger concept of Confederation; the conferences at Charlottetown and Quebec had brought together the best and brightest politicians from all parties and all regions, and resulted in the best possible outcome. In this "Providential concurrence of circumstances," perhaps the most remarkable feature was the cooperation of politicians from different parties. "As our Government included a representation both of the former Opposition, and the former Ministry," McGee commented, "so their [the Maritimes'] delegations were composed in about equal parts of the opposition and ministerial parties of their several provinces." It was, he pointed out, an "extraordinary armistice in party warfare" – and one that was crucial to the success of Confederation.[61]

———

Up to this point, McGee had focused on the ideological, pragmatic, and political origins of Confederation in relation to Canada's internal instability, the perceived threat from the United States, and the changing character of the British Empire. Now he turned his attention to the future, to the kind of society that could be created by Confederation. In keeping with his earlier writings, he envisaged a country that embodied the liberal conservatism of Burke, built on the principle of balance – between minority rights and a common Canadianism, between French- and English-speaking Canadians, between British and American forms of government, between central and local power, and between authority and liberty. Moderation and the middle way would be the chief characteristics of the new nation, along with an equally Burkean ruthlessness towards any religious or political extremists who sought to impose their own agendas on the country.

In considering the mosaic of minorities in a confederated Canada, McGee pointed out that the French communities in New Brunswick and Nova Scotia had once been part of the vast North American empire of New France; through Confederation, these "long-lost compatriots" would be reunited with and protected by the French heart-land in Canada. Other connections would be formed; the Irish who had settled in Newfoundland since the seventeenth century would share a country with more recent Irish immigrants in the rest of British North America, just as the "Highland Scotch" in Prince Edward Island and Cape Breton would find kindred spirits in the Glengarry region of Canada West, and the American loyalists of the Maritimes would be reunited with their counterparts in Canada.[62]

Ethnic groups that had developed over three or four generations retained many of their original religious, linguistic, and cultural char-acteristics, he continued, but had come to regard themselves primar-ily as British Americans; in this sense, they had already marked out the path upon which the new immigrants and their descendants would follow. Referring to his own condition as an immigrant, McGee stated that he combined unqualified allegiance to Canada with "a divided affection between the old country and the new" – something that was perfectly reasonable, provided that it was kept within "just bounds." But it was equally reasonable, he said, to assume that over the follow-ing generations, both allegiance and affection would become Canad-ianized and that people would wonder how anyone could possibly have opposed Confederation.[63]

The other great question concerning minority rights, of course, cen-tred on the relationship between French Canadians and English-speak-ing Canadians. Confederation, in McGee's view, would protect both the French Canadian minority in British North America as a whole and the English-speaking minority in Canada East. As an English-speaking Irish Catholic living in Montreal, McGee declared that he was "not afraid of the French-Canadian majority in the future local Govern-ment doing injustice, except accidentally." He reached this opinion, he said, not because he was "of the same religion as themselves; for origin and language are barriers stronger to divide men in this world than is religion to unite them." But his own experiences and his reading of history had taught him that "the French Canadians have never been an intolerant people; it is not in their temper."[64]

This was particularly evident, he believed, in the area of education, which had once again become a hot topic. After the Quebec Confer-ence had established that the federal government would guarantee existing minority educational "rights and privileges," Protestants in Canada East stepped up their efforts to secure improvements to their educational system. Among other things, they wanted their own department of education, government grants for institutions of higher learning, and separate educational taxation systems. McGee was confident that French Canadians would support changes along these lines, adding, "I, for one, as a Roman Catholic, will cordially second and support any such amendments, properly framed."[65]

But what of the Catholics in Canada West? Like the Protestants in Canada East, they were determined to strengthen their position before becoming locked into an apparently permanent minority status in a new province. It seemed only reasonable that any improvements to the Protestant educational system in Canada East should be matched by improvements to the Catholic educational system in Canada West. Reasonable, perhaps; but Protestants in Canada West were generally under the impression that Catholics had accepted the Scott Act of 1863 as a "finality." Now, only two years later, it appeared that they were breaking what Egerton Ryerson called "an honourable compact" that had been intended to settle the education question once and for all.[66]

Whether or not such a compact actually existed remains a matter of considerable controversy. What is clear, though, is that McGee himself had accepted the Scott Act as a final settlement, as he acknowledged in his speech. "I will be no party to the re-opening of the question," he declared; "but I say this, that if there are to be any special guarantees or grants extended to the Protestant minority of Lower Canada, I think the Catholic minority in Upper Canada ought to be placed in precisely the same position – neither better nor worse." New circumstances had opened up the possibility of educational parity between Catholics in Canada West and Protestants in Canada East – something that McGee had always wanted but had felt was impractical during the debate over the Scott bill; the best would have been the enemy of the good. In 1863 pragmatism had prevailed. But in 1865, the prospect of Confederation appeared to promise the triumph of principle.[67]

Towards the end of his speech, McGee turned to the general concept of confederation or federation (he used the terms interchangeably), re-emphasizing his earlier arguments about the need for a "large infusion of authority" to the dangers of excessive liberty.[68] In eighteenth-century political theory, the British constitution had checked and balanced the competing principles of monarchy, aristocracy, and democracy, represented by king, lords, and commons, and corresponding to different social orders. But in nineteenth-century British North America, everything had become tilted towards democracy:

> We have here no traditions and ancient venerable institutions; here, there are no aristocratic elements hallowed by time or bright deeds; here, every man is the first settler of the land, or removed from the first settler one or two generations at the farthest; here, we have no architectural monuments calling up old associations; here, we have none of those old popular legends and stories which in other countries have exercised a powerful share in the government; here, every man is the son of his own works.

A conservative constitution was needed to redress this imbalance and to protect Canada against tyranny from below; at the same time, the democratic spirit of the age would protect Canada against tyranny from above. "I am not at all afraid this Constitution errs on the side of too great conservatism," he said. "If it be found too conservative now, the downward tendency in political ideas which characterizes this democratic age is a sufficient guarantee for amendment."[69]

But if British North America lacked "aristocratic elements hallowed by time or bright deeds," it had something better – an aristocracy of "virtue and talent, which is the best aristocracy, and is the old and true meaning of the term." It consisted of men who had gained their political experience through responsible government, who had transformed small colonies into great communities, and who were now committed to Confederation. Such men, McGee concluded, were exceptionally well qualified to safeguard their provinces from potential American aggression and to secure British support for the fulfilment of the new nationality.[70]

---

McGee's speech was delivered on 9 February; over the next month, the debate continued in the legislature, where majority opinion supported the Quebec Resolutions. But in Atlantic Canada, a different story was unfolding. In Newfoundland, the government decided to take a wait-and-see approach; in Prince Edward Island, popular opinion was running strongly against Confederation; and in Nova Scotia, opposition to the Quebec Resolutions was cohering around the influential figure of Joseph Howe. Despite, or possibly because of, regional differences, a common set of concerns was emerging; among other things, it was argued, British North American union would mean central Canadian dominance, the loss of local autonomy, and increased taxation.[71]

These developments were difficult but not necessarily disastrous for the confederates; the union could go ahead without Newfoundland and Prince Edward Island, and Tupper's government seemed strong enough to contain the opposition in Nova Scotia. But in New Brunswick the situation was much more serious. Here, an election had been called for early March, and Tilley was in trouble. If New Brunswick rejected Confederation, the entire project would come apart at the seams. The news reached McGee on 4 March: Albert Smith's anti-Confederation coalition had triumphed by thirty seats to eleven. Anglin had played a key role in Smith's victory, and Tilley had lost his own seat. It appeared to be a decisive blow against British North American union and was welcomed as such by anti-confederates, from Newfoundland to Niagara Falls.[72]

For McGee, along with his Liberal-Conservative colleagues, this was deeply disheartening. All his efforts to influence public opinion in the province appeared to be unravelling; as he saw things, the power of parochialism and the influence of "American railway and steamboat interests" had prevailed over British American patriotism. No one should rejoice, he said, at a verdict that was based on "distrust of Canada and a closer connection with her."[73]

There were only two options. One was to abandon British American union and fall back on the federal division of Upper and Lower Canada; this was something with which Brown and his fellow Reformers could live quite comfortably.[74] The second was to stay the course, pass the Quebec Resolutions, take the case to Britain, and hope that Smith's government in New Brunswick would collapse under the weight of its own contradictions; this was the strategy preferred by McGee, Mac-

donald, Cartier, and Galt. It was a long shot, but worth a try. Behind
a common opposition to the Quebec Resolutions, Smith's government
was an unstable compound of diverse interests. Some of its members
supported a stronger union, others favoured a looser union, and still
others wanted no union at all; there were also major divisions over the
degree of government support for a railway line to the United States.
And although Smith had a strong majority, the popular vote was closer
than the division of seats suggested, with many people in New Brunswick still supporting the Quebec Resolutions.[75]

Within a week of the New Brunswick election, the Canadian parliament passed the Quebec Resolutions by a majority of ninety-one to
thirty-three, and arrangements were made for a mission to London. At
a tense meeting, the cabinet agreed that it would proceed with federal
union for Canada alone if significant progress on a wider confederation had not been made by the opening of the parliamentary session
of 1866.[76] Time was tight; much was riding on the discussions with
the British government. Along with Confederation, there were the
issues of renegotiating a Reciprocity Treaty with the United States,
and Britain's contribution to the costs of Canadian defence – a matter
that assumed new urgency in April, when the United States defeated
the South, and was now free to turn its attention to Canada.

Against this background – the check to Confederation in New
Brunswick and the vulnerability of Canada to an American attack –
Galt, Cartier, Brown, and Macdonald left for Britain in April. McGee
crossed the Atlantic separately, although he would join them later in
London. In the meantime, he had important business in Ireland, repre-
senting Canada at the Dublin International Exhibition of Industry,
Science, and Arts, and focusing on the other major issue that preoccu-
pied him during these years – the fight against Fenianism.

# PART THREE

# Fenianism

I said and I say still, that it was necessary the last two years to battle
daily, and nightly almost, against the introduction of this Fenian
pestilence into British America ... Canada and British America have
never known an enemy so subtle, so irrational, so hard to trace,
and, therefore, so difficult to combat.

McGee, "Second Letter to Mr. Geo. Brown,"
*Montreal Gazette*, 14 December 1866

## CHAPTER NINE

# The Goula of Griffintown
## March 1864 – May 1865

In Canadian historiography, the Fenians have generally been studied within the framework of Confederation and have been viewed primarily as an external force. According to the traditional version, they enter Canadian history from the United States in 1866 with a bizarre scheme to liberate Ireland by invading Canada, only to find that the consequences of their actions are the very reverse of their intentions. Far from breaking the British presence in North America, they inadvertently contribute to the "rise of national feeling" in Canada; far from turning the country into a republic, they actually strengthen the cause of Confederation. This view is frequently accompanied by negative stereotypes about Irish Catholics. "Nothing could have been more characteristically 'Irish' in the broadest, most farcical meaning of the word than the conception and execution of this great enterprise," commented Donald Creighton. "With one or two significant exceptions, the leaders of the Fenian movement against British America were a crew of grandiloquent clowns and vainglorious incompetents." Elsewhere in the literature, the phrase "comic opera" occurs repeatedly. Within this historiographical tradition, D'Arcy McGee emerges as the man who single-handedly saved Irish Canadian Catholics from Fenianism and ensured that they followed the path of Canadian loyalty rather than American republicanism.[1]

Along with the patronizing and prejudiced stereotypes, there are several problems with this picture. The plan to trigger revolution in Ireland through the invasion of Canada was not as bizarre as it appears in retrospect, and there was nothing comical about Fenian war preparations and the ensuing battle of Ridgeway in the Niagara peninsula. The argument that Fenianism ironically contributed to Confederation is accurate enough when applied to New Brunswick, where a hastily improvised invasion attempt shattered the colony's anti-Confederate movement. In Canada, however, where the threat was much more serious, the raid in 1866 only reinforced existing support for Confederation.

But the greatest problem with the traditional interpretation is that it misses the most interesting and in some respects the most important part of the story – the presence within British North America of an indigenous and in places influential Fenian movement. Despite McGee's best efforts, a significant minority of Irish Canadian Catholics supported or sympathized with the goal of bringing about an independent Irish republic through revolutionary means, whether or not they believed that an American-based Fenian invasion of Canada should be part of that strategy.

We have already noted the emergence of Fenianism in Toronto and Montreal, where the combined number of sworn Fenians was about 1,000 – 5 per cent of the Irish Catholic population in both cities.[2] In Canada as a whole, it is unlikely that they had more than 3,500 members, in an Irish Catholic ethnic population of around 260,000. This was in marked contrast to the Orange Order, which had 50,000 members in Canada West alone.

These figures, however, can be misleading for at least four reasons. First, they ignore the fact that beyond the number of sworn Fenians there were many fellow travellers who sympathized with physical-force republicanism. Others supported the Fenian objective of a separate Irish republic but rejected the means of violence. Moreover, many constitutional nationalists had ambivalent feelings about the Fenians, believing that their hearts were in the right place even if their actions were misguided. The Fenians in Montreal reckoned that they could draw on the support of a quarter of the city's Irish-born population, and their eventual success in taking over the St Patrick's Society shows that they were an important political force in the city.[3] Similarly, the role of the Fenians in organizing St Patrick's Day parades in places such as Toronto, Ottawa, and Quebec City indicates that they could and did attract wider support.

Second, from 1863 the Fenians were able to reach a large audience through their newspapers. From Toronto, Patrick Boyle's *Irish Canadian* indignantly denied any Fenian connections while disseminating the Fenian message throughout the country. From New York, Patrick Meehan's *Irish American* circulated in Canada. And from Dublin, James Stephens's *Irish People* reached Canadian readers. When the Dublin police raided the offices of the *Irish People* in September 1865, they found a list of subscribers from Quebec City and another from Halifax, Nova Scotia.[4]

Third, although the number of sworn Canadian Fenians was small, they were a pervasive presence throughout Irish Catholic Canada.[5] Fenian circles existed in all the major urban areas, where there was the critical mass for political organization – not only in the cities but also in towns such as St Catharines and Brockville, as well as Guelph, which in 1868 was described as "the central point for Fenian operations in Ontario."[6] There were also Fenians in rural townships, such as Aberfoyle and Adjala. In the township of Aberfoyle, described as "Little Ireland," the activities of energetic individuals, most notably the farmer Peter Mahon, seem to have been an important factor; in Adjala, support for the Fenians reflected and reinforced Irish Protestant-Catholic tensions in the area.[7]

All these Fenian circles were part of a wider North American network. And this brings us to the fourth point: the fact that the Canadian Fenians operated in the context of a much more powerful American organization gave them an influence out of all proportion to their numbers.[8] As a result, there was a large imbalance between the numerical and political significance of the Fenians in Canada during the mid-1860s. This helps to explain why McGee could simultaneously dismiss them as a contemptible minority and treat them as a major source of danger to the Canadian state and to his vision of Canadian nationality.

There were many different strands within the movement. Some Fenians carried their revolutionary republicanism with them from Ireland, while others became radicalized in Canada. People joined from a mixture of motives – a principled political position, an emotional identification with "the cause of Ireland," a means of empowerment in the battle against Orangeism, and a sense of camaraderie, among other reasons.[9] Despite a general commitment to Irish independence, there was no consensus over means and ends. When asked how they intended to help Ireland, the Montreal Fenian Patrick O'Meara recalled that "there had been so many splits between them that it was very hard to say how they intended doing it."[10] Some would probably have settled for a Canadian model for Ireland, with responsible government and significant control over internal affairs; others wanted nothing less than a separate Irish republic. Some combined loyalty to Canada with loyalty to an imagined Irish republic; others looked forward to the day when Canada would become annexed to the United States; still others – a minority within a minority – were prepared to use physical force in Canada to hammer the British Empire, hasten annexation to the United States, and promote the revolutionary movement in Ireland.

When McGee stepped up his attacks on the Fenian Brotherhood in 1863, the public response of revolutionary Irish nationalists in Canada had been relatively muted; the *Irish Canadian*, for example, warned him to be more guarded in his expressions and criticized his monarchism, but that was about it. In the spring of 1864, however, the Fenians fought back with a vengeance, opening up a full-scale, no-holds-barred battle for the hearts and minds of Irish Canadian Catholics.

It began, appropriately enough, on St Patrick's Day. In Toronto, Michael Murphy combined declarations of loyalty to Canada with support for revolution in Ireland, and assured a cheering crowd that "when the time for blood came, the priests would be found to side with the people."[11] Meanwhile, in Montreal, the Hibernian Society organized a dinner at the Exchange Hotel, with speeches that looked forward to the destruction of Britain and the liberation of Ireland. Their festivities included a parody of the British patriotic song "The Red, White and Blue," featuring "Britannia, the curse of the ocean, / The scourge of the brave and the free."[12]

McGee hit back with a blistering public letter which condemned the "orgie of sedition" in Montreal and mocked the Fenian leader John O'Mahony as an "incurably insane" spiritualist who had conceived Fenianism in "a mad-house, near Flatbush, Long Island." The priests would never fight with the people, he said – and he should have known, given his own experiences during the rising of 1848. McGee pointed out that the Catholic Church had condemned the Fenian Brotherhood and that the law had draconian penalties for anyone involved in the organization. The vast majority of Irish Catholics had nothing in common with the "demented ... progeny of a mad-man," he asserted. "Seditious societies are like what the farmers of Ireland used to say of *scotch-grass*; that the only way to destroy it was to cut it up by the roots, burn it to powder, and cast the ashes to the four winds ... The dictate of true prudence is to trample down at once such conspirators." Then came the postscript: "I am sorry to see the disease has broken out violently in Toronto. Those who are responsible for that community should act at once and decidedly."[13]

In early April he took the battle directly to Toronto in a letter to the *Leader*, which was republished in James Moylan's *Canadian Freeman*: "So you have a Fenian newspaper in Toronto. You have a brummagem edition of the *Ami du Peuple* and the *Pere Duchene*. It is called, I am told, the *Irish Canadian*." Unless Irish Catholics unequivocally repudiated Fenianism, the consequences would be catastrophic, he warned. "If this root of suspicion of treason should strike into our ranks, then no good subject of this country, no lover of Canada or her laws, could employ or encourage the settlement of another Irishman among us. No public office which could be withheld – no private employment which could be filled by any one else – no professional patronage, no social recognition, no office of trust, no magisterial duty, could be, or would be, entrusted to one of the suspected denomination. I am, therefore, in the full and faithful discharge of my highest public duty, when I watch over the first symptoms of this disease, which like the cholera or any other pest, may be brought in a bundle of old clothes from the East, yet once let loose, may ravage a whole Province."[14]

It was a declaration of war and was recognized as such. In response, the *Irish Canadian* moved to a full frontal assault, denouncing McGee as "the Goula of Griffintown" ("Goula" was the name of a notorious Irish informer, and Griffintown was at the heart of McGee's Montreal constituency) and more than matching his ad hominem attack on John O'Mahony. McGee was variously described as a "vagabond adventurer," a "pharisaical brawler who misrepresents Montreal West," "the little vulgar arch-hypocrite of Griffintown," and a "truckling traitor" who spat out malice and lies about his fellow countrymen.[15]

This was only the beginning. On 13 April, McGee's thirty-ninth birthday, the paper claimed that during the rising of 1848 he had offered to betray his friends to the British in return for his own safety. It added that in Canada he "struts about like an emancipated negro"; there was no sense here of any revolutionary Irish nationalist identification with non-white victims of colonialism. Further ammunition was provided by the fact that two weeks earlier, on 30 March, McGee had become a cabinet minister in the new Liberal-Conservative government. The most "damning commentary" on his career, ran the editorial, lay in "the simple fact that Mr. McGee has accepted office under Mr. John A. Macdonald, and bartered his tongue and his pen for $6,000 a year, to sustain the political influence of Orangism [sic] in the Government of the country."[16] When Sandfield Macdonald accused McGee in Parliament of inconsistency for having opposed the Orange Order as a secret society but now being "in close alliance with the leading men of that society," the paper jumped on the story – ignoring McGee's response that he was as opposed to the incorporation of the Orange Order as he had ever been.[17]

While the *Irish Canadian* filled its pages with anti-McGee invective, Michael Murphy and John O'Leary of the Hibernian Benevolent Society declared that their organization had nothing to do with the Fenian Brotherhood but that any movement aiming at Ireland's independence would have their "warmest and most heartfelt sympathies." McGee, that "would-be Dictator to Irishmen in Canada," was completely wrong in accusing the Hibernian Benevolent Society of disloyalty, ran one of the society's resolutions; on the contrary, its members would "yield to none in our loyalty to Canada, the free and well-governed land of our adoption."[18] Although this was doubtless true for many members, the declaration was highly and deliberately misleading. It is certainly hard to reconcile with the fact that Murphy was one of the leading Fenians in Canada, that around half the Hibernian Benevolent Society's members were or would become Fenians, that Murphy and other prominent Hibernians later actively supported the attempted

Fenian invasion of New Brunswick, and that many Toronto Hibernians shared the *Irish Canadian*'s subsequent position that Canada should
be annexed to the United States.[19]

---

The vitriolic reaction to McGee's position speaks volumes about the
deepening divisions among Irish Catholics in Canada. On the one
hand, sales of the *Irish Canadian* skyrocketed after its attacks on McGee,
and feelings ran so high that he began to receive death threats in the
spring of 1864.[20] On the other hand, McGee continued to enjoy the
support of prominent Montreal Irish Catholics. In early April, as the
storm broke over Canadian Fenianism, his friends and admirers had
raised sufficient funds to help him buy a new house on St Catherine
Street, to express the "high Sense they entertain of the Sterling worth
of the Honorable Thomas Darcy McGee and their appreciation of his
political career."[21] The fact that he was re-elected by acclamation as
a Conservative cabinet minister that same month testifies to the continuing strength of his base in Montreal West; his enemies among the
city's Irish population clearly lacked the ability to mount an effective
challenge.[22]

Although there were no clear lines of division, younger and working-class Irish Catholics were more likely to gravitate towards the Fenians, while middle-aged and middle-class Irish Catholics were more
likely to support McGee. The Montreal Hibernian Society's dinner
on St Patrick's Day, for example, was attended by "a large number of
young men and some ladies"; similarly, Toronto's Fenian movement
appealed primarily to those lower down in the social scale.[23] In the
male Irish Catholic world of artisans and labourers, centred on taverns, clubs, dances, and sports, there were intense and occasionally violent disputes about whether or not McGee was a traitor to Ireland, and
there was a growing sense that indeed he was.

The most visible sign of this struggle was in the St Patrick's Society
of Montreal, where the radicals were beginning to flex their muscles.
A key issue was whether the society should subscribe to the *Irish Canadian* in the wake of the paper's denunciations of McGee. At a poorly
attended meeting in early May, a majority of twenty-five to eleven

voted in favour of subscription; shortly afterwards, the president, Thomas McKenna (who had helped to organize the fundraising drive for McGee earlier in the year) resigned in protest.[24] The principal supporters of subscription were Patrick O'Meara, one of the founders of the Hibernian Society, and W.B. Linehan, the Montreal correspondent for the *Irish Canadian*. After a protracted controversy, and despite the efforts of the moderates to reach a compromise, the subscription appears to have been sustained. Meanwhile, Linehan and his fellow Fenians, Daniel Lyons and William Mansfield, continued to sign up their supporters. In September and October 1864, eight out of twelve prospective members were proposed by Fenians.[25]

Despite these gains, the Fenians were still a minority within the St Patrick's Society. When, in November 1864, Lyons and Mansfield nominated a fellow Fenian, Felix Callahan, to the Executive Committee, their candidate lost by one vote. Mansfield accused the scrutineers of rigging the result, and resigned rather than "apologize for the insult offered." Efforts to get Mansfield reinstated ran straight into the opposition of Father Dowd, who served as the society's chaplain. Clerical influence proved stronger than republican sentiment, and Mansfield was kept out of the society; two of his allies, including the future Fenian leader, William Conroy, walked out in protest.[26]

Even as a minority, however, the Fenians were changing the character of the St Patrick's Society. In particular, they injected politics into what was theoretically a non-political organization. During the winter of 1864–65, the society conducted a series of debates on Irish nationalism, including one on whether "Moral or Physical force" was "better adopted for the freeing of Ireland." In a debate that was "carried on in a very able & eloquent manner by the speakers on both sides," Patrick O'Meara, along with Henry Murphy, a shoemaker, argued the case for physical force. Shortly afterwards, the society discussed "Whether is a total Separation from English Rule or Independent Parliament under the Protection of Great Britain the most beneficial for Ireland at the present time?" – a question that neatly foreclosed any deliberations about a redress of grievances under the Act of Union, which in McGee's view had become the most practicable option. Linehan and the moral-force republican Peter J. Coyle spoke in favour of total separation.[27] Not only was the society moving beyond its traditional fraternal preoccupations; its members were increasingly occupying the Irish nationalist ground that McGee had vacated a decade earlier.

In the run-up to the St Patrick's Society's annual elections in April 1865, the loyalists, moderates, and republicans vied with one another in signing up supporters. The winner was McGee's old rival, Bernard Devlin, who appealed to a broad base of Irish nationalists and who had severely criticized McGee for his earlier alliance with George Brown and for his efforts to suspend the St Patrick's Day parade in Toronto. Although Devlin was not a Fenian, in style and spirit he was much closer to the Hibernians than he was to the supporters of McGee. During the same election, Fenian candidates for the Executive Committee mustered roughly a third of the vote; the following month, twenty-eight people, including one committee member, left the organization. The committee member was replaced by Felix Callahan – another indication that the Fenians were gaining ground. McGee was beginning to lose his influence over Montreal's most important secular Irish Catholic organization.[28]

Meanwhile, tensions were increasing in Canada West between a resurgent Orangeism and an increasingly assertive Irish Catholic nationalism. In May 1864 an Orange crowd attacked the Corpus Christi procession in Toronto. On Guy Fawkes night, amid rumours that Orangemen were planning to burn effigies of the Pope, Daniel O'Connell, and the Duke of Newcastle, the Hibernians decided to take action. At midnight, four hundred men, many of them carrying guns and pikes, gathered at Queen's Park. From there, they formed two companies, one of which marched east while the other marched west. Two hours later, they saluted each other with rifle fire from either side of the city.[29]

The fact that the Hibernians had temporarily taken control of Toronto must have been empowering for many of the city's Catholics. But it also sent shockwaves throughout Protestant Canada; there were stories that arms were being stocked in Catholic churches and cemeteries, and that plans were afoot to massacre Protestants throughout Canada West.[30] In December, an Orange Hall in Toronto was attacked;

the furniture was destroyed, the banners were cut into pieces, and the Bibles were mutilated.[31] Later in the month, rumours of Fenian atrocities north of the city triggered a social panic, with Protestants abandoning isolated farmhouses and Orangemen taking up arms to defend their villages. Adding more fuel to the fire, there were reports from New York that 50,000 Fenians were planning to invade Canada.[32]

All this tapped into traditional Irish Protestant fears that, as one correspondent to the *Globe* put it, "Papists are masters of the science of secrecy." There were demands (which the *Globe* rejected) for "immediate and vigorous measures," such as forming armed Protestant militia bands.[33] And then, in this highly charged atmosphere, the paper's Montreal correspondent reported that there were 1,500 Fenians in Montreal, that they had infiltrated the militia, and that some of them had been "overheard boasting about what the Fenians would do when they invaded Canada."[34]

When McGee heard the story, he rushed off a note to the *Globe*, lurched to the other extreme, and made the startling assertion that there were no Fenians at all in the city.[35] He followed this up immediately with a speech at a benefit concert for the St Patrick's Society. "I say there could not be 15 such scamps associated and meeting together, not to say 1500, without your knowledge and mine," he declared; "and I repeat absolutely that there is no such body amongst us, and that the contrary statements are deplorably untrue and unjust, and impolitic as well as unjust."[36]

In fact, McGee knew better than anyone that the Fenians were on the move in Montreal, even if the *Globe* report exaggerated their power and influence. What we are seeing here is a tactical denial that was designed to reduce ethnoreligious tensions in Canada West and protect Irish Catholics from a loyalist and Orange backlash. "Any two or more nervous or mischievous magistrates – and with 11,000 men in the commission of the peace there must be some of both these sorts – any two or more of these may subject a neighbourhood to all the rigours of martial law," he told his Montreal audience. "Already indecent and unauthorised searches have been made for concealed arms in the Catholic churches; already, as in some of the townships of Bruce, the magistrates are very improperly, in my opinion, arming one class of

the people against the other." In this way, he continued, "the Protestant million are made to tremble before a fraction of a fraction – for if
there are Fenians in that quarter of the world I venture to say they are
as wholly insignificant in numbers as in every other respect."[37]

But denial was only half the story; it was also imperative that Irish
Catholics demonstrated their own loyalty to Crown and country by
taking strong measures against any manifestations of Fenianism. "If
there is any, the least proof that this foreign disease has seized on any,
the least among you, establish at once, for your own sakes – for the
country's sake – a *cordon sanitaire* around your people," he urged; "establish a Committee which will purge your ranks of this political leprosy;
weed out and cast off those rotten members who, without a single governmental grievance to complain of in Canada, would yet weaken and
divide us in these days of anxiety."[38] The same images occur repeatedly; whenever McGee addressed the issue of Fenianism, the metaphor
of disease – and "foreign disease" at that – came readily to mind; only
through quarantine and inoculation could the contagion be contained.

Yet the Fenian Brotherhood in Canada continued to expand, inspired by the global rise of Irish revolutionary nationalism, drawing on
bitter memories of displacement and dispossession in Ireland, fuelled by
ethnoreligious tensions, and disseminated through the pages of the increasingly millenarian *Irish Canadian*. "The hoarded vengeance for centuries of wrongs, for ages of tyranny" would soon fall on Britain, the
paper prophesied; "there will be storm and tempest and the red blood
shall be poured out like water, before the long wished-for haven."[39]
At the St Patrick's Day celebrations in Toronto, Michael Murphy announced that many new Hibernian lodges had been formed, and he
asserted that he could raise forty thousand men to fight for Ireland's
freedom – doubling the number he had given two years earlier. But the
star speaker in Toronto was the American Fenian organizer, Jim Mc-
Dermott, whom the Hibernian Benevolent Society had invited to the
city. McDermott's speech calling for revolution in Ireland was greeted
with loud cheering, and the demand for copies was so great that the
*Irish Canadian* published it twice. War between the United States and
Britain was imminent, McDermott said; England's difficulty would be
Ireland's opportunity; the people of Canada should organize, "keep

their secrets to themselves," and "take no heed of what the traitorous THOMAS D'ARCY MCGEE should say to them."[40]

In Montreal, things were quieter; the St Patrick's Day speeches were moderate and loyal, prompting the *Montreal Gazette* to remark that Fenianism "does not show its head, which may be accepted as a proof that it has no strength here."[41] Appearances, though, were deceptive, and the city's underground Fenian movement was becoming increasingly influential. Occasionally, one catches a glimpse of its activities and attitudes: sending money to the radical Irish priest Father Lavelle, for example, or publicizing the cause in the columns of the *Irish Canadian*. "What is Fenianism, and who are its members?" asked a Montreal correspondent – possibly John McGrath, one of the city's leading Fenians. His answer: Fenians and Irish nationalists were synonymous; realizing that moral force had failed and that Catholic Emancipation was a sham, they knew that Ireland could be liberated only through physical force. But this did not make them disloyal to Canada, he added, concluding his letter with the slogan "Canada for Canadians – Ireland for the Irish."[42]

Later in the year, the Fenians in Montreal became much more visible and audible, placing themselves at the head of an Irish Canadian nationalist backlash against McGee. To understand how and why this happened, we must follow McGee as he left Montreal in April – cheered by two hundred enthusiastic admirers while a brass band played "St Patrick's Day" and "God Save the Queen" – and crossed the Atlantic for Dublin and his boyhood home of Wexford.[43]

———•———

In Dublin, McGee fulfilled his official functions as one of Canada's three representatives at the International Exhibition of Industry, Science, and Arts, and reconnected with old friends from his Young Ireland days. Among them were Charles Gavan Duffy, now a prominent politician in Victoria, who was visiting from Australia, and Samuel Ferguson, who had supported McGee's election to the Royal Irish Academy the previous year.[44] From Dublin, McGee travelled to Wexford, and in a depressed mood visited the graves of his family in the cemetery at Selskar Abbey.[45] His mother, his brother Laurence, and his sisters Mary and Betsy had all died before he left Ireland in 1848; his father James, whom he had last seen ten years beforehand, had died in 1864.

The following day, 15 May, he rallied his spirits and completed his preparations for the talk that he was giving that night to the Catholic Young Men's Society on "Twenty Years' Experience of Irish Life in America." There, in front of an audience that included many of his old school friends, McGee delivered one of the most important speeches – and certainly the most notorious speech – of his political career. If his speech to the Canadian Parliament the previous February in support of British North American union had been the centrepiece of his campaign for Confederation, the published version of his address in Wexford became the defining moment in his fight against Fenianism.

To anyone who had been following McGee's career, it should not have come as a surprise. Just as his speech on Confederation had gathered together the strands of his earlier statements and presented them with power and eloquence on the most important public stage in Canada, his Wexford speech drew on arguments that he had been making since the early 1850s, and brought them directly to an Irish audience. There was nothing remotely original in what he said at Wexford; all the arguments and even much of the phraseology can be traced to his earlier writings and speeches. Nor was this the first time that Irish audiences had heard his devastating critique of Irish conditions in the United States; ten years earlier, during his previous trip to Ireland, McGee had warned the Catholic Young Men's Societies in Cork and Limerick about the degradation and discrimination that faced Irish immigrants in America.[46]

But much had changed since McGee's last visit to Ireland. In 1855, nationalism in both its constitutional and revolutionary forms had been in the doldrums; now, the Fenian Brotherhood was gathering momentum in the North Atlantic quadrilateral of Ireland, Britain, the United States, and Canada, as well as in Australia and New Zealand. In 1855, McGee had spoken as an influential ultramontane journalist from New York; now, he was in the much more prominent position of minister of agriculture, immigration, and statistics in the Canadian coalition government. This meant that when he challenged Irish nationalist verities at Wexford, his words were amplified and would rapidly reverberate throughout the Irish diaspora. As McGee himself put it, he had "the ear of the Empire."[47]

The text of McGee's speech, which he gave to an editor of the conservative *Dublin Evening Mail*, embraced four main themes. First, McGee touched briefly on his involvement with the Young Ireland movement, and his participation in the rising of 1848. "I am not at all ashamed of Young Ireland – why should I?" he wrote. "Politically, we were a pack of fools; but we were honest in our folly; and no man need blush at forty for the follies of one-and-twenty." He had made the same point in Canada; as we have seen, in 1858 he had defended himself against the attacks of John A. Macdonald by saying that he was only twenty-two when he joined the "rash and ill-guided struggle" for revolution in Ireland, and in 1864 he had taken the same position in his debate with James O'Halloran.[48] But these statements in Parliament had not attracted much attention outside Canada; in Wexford, his assessment of Young Ireland was impossible to ignore.

Having disposed of his revolutionary past, McGee proceeded to challenge dominant nationalist assumptions about Irish Catholics in the United States: "I must set out with the plain statement of this fact – which everyone who knows the United States people knows well to be true – namely, that there is no such thing in existence as a national sentiment of sympathy with Ireland in that country." In Puritan New England, Irish Catholics were despised for their religion and poverty; in the Middle States, they endured intense discrimination, had come into severe competition with "native labour," and had "arrayed themselves insanely and most cruelly against the Negro, while right and justice were plainly on the side of the slave." The Irish were, he claimed, "socially and politically, the weakest community in the Republic – weaker than the negroes themselves, in the free States." They were preyed upon by "Irish-born demagogues," who had done "irrevocable mischief to the Irish character" and who were representatives of a repulsive social system that had ghettoized, impoverished, and degraded their countrymen. To liberate the Irish from urban exploitation, McGee continued, he had participated in plans to resettle Irish immigrants in the Canadian countryside and the American West.

When the project failed, he decided to move to Canada, preferring "an orderly British province in which to live, and a moral city like Montreal in which to bring up my children."

This brought McGee to his third theme, the condition of the Irish in Canada. In British North America, he argued, Irish Catholics experienced a much greater degree of practical freedom and a much higher quality of life than they did in the American republic. Canada occupied a "sort of middle position" between Ireland and the United States: Irish Catholics had equality without American rudeness; they had independence without American impudence, immorality, and blasphemy; they had property without losing their traditional character. In the United States they had to do twice as well to get half the credit. But in Canada they were well represented in politics, religion, law, and business, and received "full and complete justice"; for this reason, they would fight to "uphold the union of Canada with the rest of the Empire." On balance, McGee thought that the Irish would be better off staying at home; but if they had to emigrate, "they might do worse than to direct their course to the British provinces."

Another advantage of Canadian life was that Old Country animosities soon faded in the context of civil and religious equality. Here, McGee turned to his fourth and final theme – a cutting and contemptuous attack on the Fenian movement in North America. He began with the same rhetorical strategy that he had taken in Montreal – ridiculing John O'Mahony as mentally unstable and claiming that there were no Fenians in Canada: "I have never myself seen a specimen of the *genus* Fenian in Canada. I hear there are, and I dare say there may be, some odd ones among our half million, since Solomon says that 'the number of fools is infinite.'"

Even in the United States, he said, the number of Fenians was "grossly and purposely exaggerated." Consumed by a "morbid hatred" of England, they had been easy prey for the recruiting sergeants of the Civil War and had failed to recognize that American public opinion was "not ... one whit more pro-Irish than it is pro-Japanese." "They have deluded each other," he asserted, "and many of them are ready to betray to each other" ... "for as sure as filth produces vermin, it is of the very nature of such conspiracies as this to breed informers." All in all, the Fenians were merely "Punch-and-Judy Jacobins whose sole scheme of action seems to get their heads broken, and then to squeak out in a pitiable treble, 'A doctor! ten pounds for a doctor! Send for a doctor!" He ended with a warning – that the Irish in Ireland were becoming increasingly influenced by the Irish in the United States and must resist the siren call of Fenianism from across the Atlantic.[49]

Such was the written version of McGee's speech as it appeared in the *Dublin Evening Mail*. But the speech that he actually delivered at Wexford differed from the written version in some interesting particulars. Speaking as he was to the Catholic Young Men's Society, McGee said much more at Wexford about the degradation of Catholicism in the United States than appeared in the published text. Irish Catholic immigrants, he told his audience, were falling victim to a "free and easy" approach to religion and were being seduced by the slogan of "every man his own priest." On the other hand, McGee omitted the part about the Irish in Canada being willing to fight for the empire, and said absolutely nothing in Wexford about Fenianism. His opponents argued that his silence on Fenianism stemmed from fear and accused him of moral cowardice. The charge does not ring true; McGee had no shortage of moral courage, and it is more likely that he felt little need to denounce revolutionary nationalism in front of a conservative Catholic audience. His enemies had a point, though, when they noted that the written text included crowd reactions such as "laughter" and "applause" to parts of the speech that he had not actually spoken. "This," remarked one writer, "is a pretty significant specimen of how Mr. McGee gets on, and has got on."[50]

———•———

Taken together, in the written and the oral versions, McGee's speech hit a series of raw nerves as he attempted to demolish what he saw as destructive myths within the Irish nationalist tradition. There was the myth of Young Ireland, whose members had been viewed as flawed heroes, but heroes nonetheless. Other Young Ireland leaders, such as Gavan Duffy and Smith O'Brien, now agreed that they had been mistaken to launch a rising in 1848, but they still maintained that their cause and their actions had been honourable, especially in the context

of the famine and of international revolution. To call the revolutionaries "a pack of fools" was to commit an act of heresy. It was the very
terseness of McGee's remarks that did the damage; he did not hedge his
criticisms with a sense that foolish actions could be extenuated by fidel-
ity to a worthy cause. As an editorial in the *Nation* put it, "Not so much
for what he does say, as for what he does *not* say, while touching on the
subject at all, do we take objection to Mr. McGee's reference to Young
Ireland politics."[51] But by this time, McGee had abandoned the notion
that honourable intentions could justify revolutionary means, and believed that complete Irish self-government was an impossible goal.

Then there was the myth of America as a Land of Liberty where the
Irish could flourish and which could serve as a source of inspiration for
Ireland. Ironically, some of McGee's criticisms of the United States were
shared by many of his fellow exiles of 1848. Thomas Francis Meagher,
writing from New York, told Duffy that he had found "more bigotry
and intolerance in this country, amongst our countrymen, than ever I
was sensible of in Ireland." Michael Doheny believed that liberty in the
United States had lapsed into licentiousness: "If I really thought that
an Irish Republic would result in the degeneracy of the people to the
extent they have been degenerated here," he wrote, "I would prefer
that Ireland should remain as she is" – surprising sentiments for an Irish
republican revolutionary. Similarly, Richard O'Gorman described
American politics as " a filthy pool of shabbiness falsehood and corruption," and John Mitchel complained (well before he set foot in the
country) that the "ardent and devout worship of the Great God Dollar is too exclusive and intolerant."[52] But while they generally whis-
pered their remarks in private correspondence, McGee shouted from
the rooftops. And while they wanted the United States to live up to its
principles, McGee was determined to discredit the idea that America
constituted a revolutionary and republican model for Ireland.

At the same time, McGee's praise for Canada challenged the myth
that Irish Catholics could never prosper or experience equality and justice within the British Empire. Canada conveyed a double message for
Ireland: it showed that reforms such as security of tenure and religious
disestablishment were possible within the empire; and as McGee had
frequently pointed out, it demonstrated that when they were treated

fairly, the Irish were among the empire's most loyal subjects. In this sense, monarchical Canada functioned as a counter-myth to republican and democratic America.

McGee's views of the United States and Canada fitted neatly with his attack on the myth of Fenianism as the authentic voice of Irish thought and feeling. On the contrary, McGee argued, the "true" Irish character was Catholic and conservative, and the Fenians were a dogmatic and anti-clerical sect that aimed to subvert the "faith and the feeling of the people." "This sect," he wrote to James Moylan later in the year, "is altogether novel in Irish history, and it is not to be put down, by half apologetic pleadings of 'good intentions.'"[53] Hence the withering mockery and the caustic tone of his comments on Fenianism. Convinced that he was fighting a nationalist ideology that had acquired the emotive force of a new religion, he believed that Fenianism could not be defeated through reason alone. A full frontal assault, he believed, was the only way to eradicate all vestiges of residual sympathy for Fenianism in Ireland.

———·•·———

All this was music to the ears of Irish loyalists and the British political establishment. "We commend the speech of Mr. Darcy McGee at Wexford to the attention of all intending emigrants to America, – to the attention of all the discontented classes in Ireland, – to the attention of all who believe that there is anything to be gained by plots and conspiracies against the British Government," wrote the *Times*. What gave the speech even more force, the paper continued, was that its author was a former rebel, with direct and immediate experience of revolutionary conspiracies and of the conditions facing Irish immigrants in the United States and Canada. It was the narrative of an "unexceptional witness," the repentant sinner who had seen the light, who stripped away the veil of lies that had been woven by "agitators and demagogues," and who told the truth with "exemplary frankness."[54]

Such praise was hardly likely to win McGee many friends in Irish nationalist circles. He could now be dismissed as "the darling of the *Times*." His talk, remarked one of his opponents, should really have been entitled "How a disappointed politician in the American Republic can get on in the British Colonies."[55] Constitutional and revolutionary nationalists alike condemned his speech, although the constitutionalists were less comprehensive in their denunciations. The *Nation*, whose editors included McGee's literary correspondent Timothy Daniel Sullivan, disagreed with most of McGee's "judgments and conclusions" but nevertheless admired both his style and his nerve: "In these days when mere rhetoric, rhodomontade, buncome, and clap-trap, have so largely flooded the popular platform ... it is absolutely refreshing – though it were only for the effect of a 'cold bath' – to alight upon a man who sets himself so completely as Mr. McGee does in the opposite direction; and who exhibits the moral courage of speaking wholesome, though unpalatable truths to the people."[56] William Kenealy of the *Kilkenny Journal* conceded that McGee's comments on the condition of the Irish in the United States had some validity, but went on to argue that the root cause of the emigrants' difficulties lay in British colonial misrule, and wound up with the comforting conclusion that McGee had become an Orange renegade.[57]

Many revolutionary nationalists responded with visceral hatred. At Wexford, McGee had humorously commented that "the immense vituperative resources of the language are nowhere better understood" than in Ireland; the reaction to his speech certainly bore this out.[58] As sure as God was in heaven, wrote Matthias D. Phelan, the Fenians would "wreak retributive vengeance on the parties who threw obstacles in their way. Remember this Kanuck Darky McGee."[59] An unpublished and anonymous letter to the *Irish People* placed McGee on "what we may farely call a wing of the Devile in this our Country" and asserted that "untill that Rotten limb is severd from the sound trunk of Catholicity our country never never will be pure."[60] "The slime of Mr. D'ARCY MCGEE is upon the Wexford Catholic Young Men's Society," ran an editorial in the same paper, which also noted with satisfaction that McGee's old enemy Michael Doheny had beaten him up on the streets of New York sixteen years earlier.[61]

Beyond such invective, there was a more substantive critique of McGee's arguments. His opponents insisted that he had grossly misrepresented American attitudes to Ireland and that he had traduced the Irish in America. Particularly galling was his statement that the Irish in America were worse off than Afro-Americans; this was nothing less than a "diabolical assertion," a "monstrous outrage," and "humiliating to every right-minded man in the community."[62] "The Irish of this generation inferior to the negroes themselves!" exclaimed the Reverend Beausang. "Sir, in the face of the world, I denounce this as a libel."[63]

On the contrary, it was argued, the Irish had great power and influence at every level of American society. They built the canals and railways, they joined the army, they were responsible for the impressive growth of the Catholic Church, they had been "promoted to high places and honoured by the nation," and they commanded considerable political sympathy among the people – as McGee himself had pointed out in his *Catholic History of North America* ten years earlier.[64] It might be true, conceded the *Dundalk Democrat*, that a tiny minority of Irish Americans – maybe four or five per cent – were "not all we should like to see them." But in generalizing from their experiences, McGee had borne "false witness against the Irish in America" and had exploited the ignorance of his Irish audience about life in the United States; in the process, he had become a different kind of demagogue – the kind who looks down on less "refined" people and who has "taken the gold of England."[65]

McGee's glowing report about the condition of Irish Catholics in Canada was greeted with widespread disbelief. How curious it was, noted his enemies, that he had never once mentioned the Orange Order in his speech to the Catholic Young Men's Association; even more interesting was the fact that McGee was politically allied with the Orange Order through Macdonald's Conservative Party.[66] "Mr. M'Gee may rave as he likes about Canada," declared the *Dundalk Democrat*, "but he will never be able to convince the honest Irish people that the cold and dismal Orangeism of the English provinces is equal to the freedom to be found in the glorious Republic."[67]

Canada, from this perspective, was characterized by an Orange political culture, with everything that this implied: attacks on individual Catholics, church burnings, discrimination, and the contemptuous dismissal of Irish Catholics as poor, ignorant, superstitious "dogans."[68] Had not Bishop Lynch of Toronto written in 1864 to the Irish newspapers about the dangers to faith and morals facing Irish Catholics in both the United States and Canada, recommending that the Irish stay in their own country?[69] In ignoring all this, the argument ran, McGee had deliberately misled his countrymen in a self-serving attempt to boost immigration to Canada and to bolster his own reputation as an imperial politician; it was not simply that his views were untrue, but they were the very reverse of the truth.

"I know that if my opposition to such a movement should fail," McGee once said of Fenianism, "I am sure to make many enemies; but I am ready for that. I know that if the movement be a bad or vicious one (as I believe it is) I shall be able to kill it."[70] In the event, of course, McGee did indeed make many enemies and manifestly failed to kill off Fenianism. It was hubris for him to suppose that he could. Nevertheless, there was also a sense in which McGee's opposition exposed "bad or vicious" elements within the movement – the intolerant, aggressive, racist, and ugly face of Fenianism. This was not the only face of revolutionary nationalism, of course, and the Fenians certainly did not have a monopoly on intolerance and racism. But the vitriolic reaction to McGee's speech revealed far more about Fenianism than about McGee. Ironically, the hate-filled letters and editorials after Wexford are a testimony to much that is admirable in McGee – above all, his moral courage in confronting and combatting revolutionary nationalist atavism and intolerance. But how could you combat such hatred without also feeding it? This was a question that continued to haunt his anti-Fenian endeavours when he returned to Canada, where he faced a hurricane of Irish Canadian nationalist hostility, with his own constituency in Montreal at the centre of the storm.

## CHAPTER TEN

# Uncertainty and Instability
## May – December 1865

McGee left Ireland abruptly a few days after his visit to Wexford – not because of the political fallout from his speech but because he wanted to be in London, where his Canadian colleagues were encountering difficulties in their negotiations with the British government. On the issue of New Brunswick's rejection of Confederation, the discussions had been going well enough; the colonial secretary, Edward Cardwell, agreed to "turn the screw as hard as will be useful, but not harder."[1] The central task was to exert pressure on New Brunswick without generating a backlash against imperial interference in colonial affairs. One approach was to ensure that New Brunswick's lieutenant governor, Arthur Gordon, would abandon his previous opposition to Confederation and toe the imperial line. Another was to hint that without Confederation, Britain might refuse to provide financial support for the Intercolonial Railway.[2] Still, when push came to shove, the extent of British influence was limited, given the realities of responsible government.

Where the negotiations ran into trouble was on the question of Canadian defence. When Galt requested imperial loan guarantees for massive defence expenditures, he hit a stone wall. His plans may have made military sense, but they were a political impossibility for a British government that was deeply divided, had a precarious majority in the House of Commons, and would soon face an election. Besides, there were other reasons for rejecting Canadian demands; it was by no means certain that the Americans were planning to invade now that the Civil War was over, and the militarization of the Great Lakes might provoke the very kind of conflict it was meant to prevent. As the Canadian delegates pressed their case, they found it increasingly difficult to get straight answers from the government.[3]

In this context, McGee arrived in London, staying with Macdonald, Cartier, Brown, and Galt at the Westminster Palace hotel. Although he was not one of the official delegates, he worked closely with them and played an active role in the numerous social events that surrounded the talks. After only three days in the city, he was exasperated by the apparent indifference of British ministers to Canada's future. "The government of this world, at which certain old hands are playing like, as it were, a game of whist, is so wretchedly carried on, that the fate of one third of the American Continent, and a population equal to Scotland, hardly excites an emotion of interest, or surprize," he told Lady Ferguson. "This is simply shocking, and I cannot tell you by what Cartusian [sic] self-denial I am able to keep down my ever-ready tendency to blaspheme against the great men of England, as I am told these people are. If these people would discourage blasphemy, why do they lead such lives, and give such abominable provocations!"[4]

Anyone reading these words – "my ever-ready tendency to blaspheme against the great men of England" – could hardly accept the accusations of his enemies that McGee deferred to aristocrats or was driven by a desire to impress grandees. His Fenian opponents saw the public image of the former Irish revolutionary who was socializing with the British political and social elite, dining with the dignitaries at Oxford University, and attending the races on Derby Day; they did not see the man who shook with repressed rage at British politicians who seemed to care as little about Canada as they did about Ireland. But the radical McGee was still there, invisible to the Fenians and inaudible to imperial statesmen, even as he promoted a conservative form of nationalism in his adopted country.

By early June a compromise was reached. Britain made a general promise to defend Canada in the event of war while deferring specific arrangements until Confederation was in place. The British government also promised to work for a renewed reciprocity treaty between Canada and the United States and to facilitate the transfer of the northwest territories from the Hudson's Bay Company to Canada.[5] Despite his frustrations and despite the failure to secure British contributions to Canadian defence, McGee put the best possible public face on the agreement. The delegates, he later said, had disabused Britain of the notion that many Canadians wanted annexation to the United States and had checked the influence of the "anti-Colonial party" in Britain; as a result, Lord Palmerston's government had adopted a "new colonial policy" that gave Canadian politicians input into reciprocity negotiations, guaranteed the British defence of Canada, and prepared the way for Canadian control of the West – something that could not happen soon enough, given the growth of pro-American feeling on the Red River.[6] Maybe so, but the gap between his public optimism and private frustration about British policy is striking – though hardly surprising, given the political imperative of maintaining the momentum for the cause of Confederation.

When it came to Irish nationalism, in contrast, McGee's public and private arguments were identical – much to the chagrin of almost all his former Young Ireland colleagues. To be seen in public with McGee was now the kiss of death for Irish nationalists, who would be associated with his apostasy unless they denounced him, bell, book, and candle.[7] After McGee was invited to a banquet in London to honour Charles Gavan Duffy, the diners were castigated for rubbing shoulders with such a turncoat, and Duffy was criticized for commenting that McGee, "in whatever else he had changed, had at least remained steadfast in his kindness to him."[8] "Can we believe our eyes, or has Mr. Duffy been misreported?" asked the *Kilkenny Journal*. "We really do not know what to believe, or what to think; but this we shall say that, next to Mr. M'Gee's change of principles, nothing will pain Ireland more than the speech, or rather the silence of Mr. Duffy."[9] The pressure proved effective; constitutional Irish nationalists duly took note and put as much distance as possible between themselves and the views of McGee.

———•———

As the private blasphemer of British politicians and the public blasphemer of revolutionary Irish nationalists, McGee returned in early July to Montreal, where he was welcomed by a group of admirers who endorsed his "plain and truthful" arguments at Wexford.[10] Meanwhile, the city's Fenians had been gearing up to give him a very different kind of reception. They were continuing their efforts to take over the St Patrick's Society and were making tentative plans to start their own newspaper in the city.[11] After Wexford, they saw the opportunity to rally a broad front of Irish Canadian nationalists against the arch-traitor McGee.

"The Irishmen of this city are fully determined that the insult of-fered to their brothers in the United States by their false representa-tive, shall be fully and manfully attoned [sic] for," declared a Montreal correspondent to the Dublin *Irish People*. In the event of an Anglo-American war, he added, "the true Irish people's voice of Montreal shall be heard," and it would be for America and republicanism rather than Britain and the Empire. "Glorious stars and stripes!" exclaimed another Montreal Irishman, writing from "her gracious Majesty's tem-porary dominions of British North America." McGee, he asserted, "dare not here in Montreal repeat his astonishing falsehoods." The au-thors of these letters are unknown, but one of them may have been William Conroy, the *Irish People*'s Montreal agent, who was the centre of the Montreal Circle of Fenians in 1865.[12]

If Conroy was not one of the authors, he certainly agreed with the sentiments they expressed. In June the Montreal Hibernian Soci-ety made one of its rare public pronouncements to denounce McGee as a "Judas" and helped to gather signatures for a public disclaimer of McGee's speech. The organizers claimed six hundred supporters, although several prominent Montreal Irishmen on the list complained that their signatures had been forged, and declared that they agreed with everything that McGee had said.[13] Not all those who genuinely signed were Fenians, but many of the city's active Fenians were on the list. Conroy was there, along with Francis Brennan, whom an informer named "the leading Fenian in Montreal" in 1866. So too were such leaders of the Hibernian Society as W.B. Linehan, Daniel Lyons, William Mansfield, and Patrick O'Meara, as well as the men who played a major role in the city's Fenian movement after 1866 – Henry Murphy, Felix Callahan, and Patrick Doody.[14] McGee had certainly succeeded in polarizing the debate. But it seemed that he and his supporters were the ones becoming isolated, as revolutionary republicans made common cause with moderate nationalists who found his speech deeply offensive.

The attacks were echoed in Canada West, where the *Irish Canadian* provided a forum for anti-McGee letters and articles. How could this man possibly say that Irish immigrants should come to Canada? The first thing that greeted Irish immigrants, wrote the paper's Montreal correspondent, was "a worse than repetition of the pauper's grave; for in Canada – in Montreal, you will find the dust of 6,000 Irish immigrants lying in [an] open, *unconsecrated* field, the victims of English policy." Once in the country, Irish Catholics faced countless examples of Protestant intolerance and bigotry – things that McGee had deliberately ignored, such as the "judicial murder" of the Aylwards in 1862 or the attack on the Corpus Christi procession in Toronto two years later. Far from prospering in Canada, the Irish were at the bottom of the barrel; McGee's own constituents in Griffintown were "the poorest people in Montreal" and "were more despised – the mere Irish over again – than any other people in the city."[15]

Similar arguments were made by Dennis C. Feely, a Fenian based in Cobourg, who had befriended McGee during his first years in Canada but had subsequently "lost faith" with "this disgusting place-beggar."[16] In a letter to the *Irish People*, Feely claimed that in Upper Canada, "to be a Catholic is synonimous [sic] with being disloyal, ignorant, superstitious, treacherous, designing, and unfit to live in any civilized community." "There are whole townships within twenty miles of where I write, in which 'no Catholic dare set his foot' and from which this very Mr. M'Gee once narrowly escaped with his life," Feely wrote. "No Catholic servant will be employed as long as a Protestant can be found. It is almost impossible to get a Catholic into the Commission of the Peace. There is not a Catholic representative elected by any constituency in Canada, where Protestants are in a majority ... Our priests are sneered at, our nuns insulted, and our most sacred rites ridiculed with impunity. The emigrants who come to Canada leave it as soon as they discover the bigotry and fanaticism which prevail."[17]

Particularly revealing are the parts of Feely's letter that the *Irish People* chose not to print: "Better for him that a mill stone were fastened about his neck, and cast into the sea, than he insult the honest hearted, but unsuccessful, patriots of 1848 ... He has committed a national crime, and as certainly as he dined with the Lord Bishop of Oxford, so certain will a national vengeance fall on his head."[18] Feely was to leave Canada immediately after the Fenian invasion attempt of 1866. He settled in Chicago and became one of the architects of the dynamite campaign of the 1880s, which was designed to bomb Britain into leaving Ireland.[19]

McGee had expected such attacks, and he continued to talk and act as if his opponents were an insignificant minority of Irish Catholics; the men who signed the disclaimer against his Wexford speech, he asserted, represented less than 3 per cent of his constituents.[20] But the fact that he felt the need to keep defending himself suggests otherwise. "Perhaps I erred on the side of severity," he conceded about his comments on the Irish in the United States, while insisting that his basic analysis was correct. When it came to the Irish in Canada, he gave no ground at all. "We believe that there is not a freer country under the sun, and we mean to stick up for it, come weal, come woe," he declared. "We are resolved to show the world – from these Provinces – that we are no incurable political hypochondriacs, to whom a grievance is a god-send. Any one, under any garb of Irishism, who purposes to advocate disaffection or disloyalty here, is our enemy, and we shall take every fair means to put him down."[21]

---

Up to this point, McGee had attacked the Fenians on several grounds – that they were an irreligious secret society, their methods were counterproductive and their goals unattainable, they were driven by hatred, they were disloyal to Canada and the British Empire, and they blackened the name of the vast majority of respectable, law-abiding Irish Canadian Catholics. But in the autumn of 1865, a new and even more immediate reason for his opposition arose – the decision of the Fenian congress in Philadelphia to strike at the British Empire through Canada. Henceforth, any Canadian Fenians who supported this strategy constituted a direct and potentially violent threat to the existence of the state.

Pressure to invade Canada had been building since the end of the Civil War, despite the views of the head centre, John O'Mahony, that Ireland should remain the first priority. O'Mahony's principal rival within the movement, William Roberts, had been gathering support over the summer and made his move in Philadelphia. The Fenian Brotherhood was restructured, with a newly established Senate that reduced O'Mahony's power, and plans were set in motion for the invasion of Canada.

From the perspective of Roberts and his supporters, the conditions were not ripe for a republican revolution in Ireland – an argument that was strengthened by the British government's crackdown on the Irish Republican Brotherhood in September, when the *Irish People* was suppressed and leading Fenians were arrested. At the same time, the Civil War had transformed thousands of Irish immigrants into soldiers, many of whom were willing and able to turn their experience against British power. Getting them back to Ireland in large numbers was impossible, given the logistical difficulties and the Royal Navy's dominance of the Atlantic. Getting them into Canada, however, appeared much more feasible.

If the Fenians could take Canada, all things seemed possible. The country could become a base from which to disrupt transatlantic British commerce, or a bargaining chip in negotiations to secure an independent Ireland. And if this seemed too far-fetched, another, more plausible, scenario presented itself. By invading Canada from the United States, defeating the forces of the Crown, and establishing a presence on British American soil, the Fenians could precipitate an Anglo-American war – a prospect that would become more likely if the US government allowed an attack to proceed.[22] Shortly before the Philadelphia Congress, Bernard Doran Killian, the treasurer of the Fenian Brotherhood, broached the subject with US Secretary of State William Seward. According to Killian, Seward informed him that if the Fenians were successful, the United States would "acknowledge accomplished facts."[23] Whether or not Seward actually said this, the Fenians now believed that they were operating with the unofficial blessing of the US government.

Although O'Mahony remained deeply skeptical about a Fenian invasion of Canada, he did not rule it out altogether. "The Canadian raid I look upon as a mere diversion, as far as regards our present action," he told John Mitchel in November. "Unless it drag the United States into war with England it can only end in defeat to those that engage in it. But it is worth trying in the hope that it may lead to such a war."[24] A Fenian victory in Canada would inspire the revolutionary movement in Ireland at the very moment that British troops were being pulled towards British North America. England's difficulty would be Ireland's opportunity, and Ireland would be freed on the plains of Canada.

The invasion plans were drawn up by "fighting Tom Sweeny," the one-armed general who had fought in both the Mexican war and the Civil War. Studying the earlier American invasions of 1775 and 1812, Sweeny concluded that Canada East was the key to victory. Fenian invasion forces from Buffalo and Chicago would compel British and Canadian soldiers to defend Toronto and thus "uncover Montreal." The Fenian army in upstate New York and Vermont would then estab-. lish a firm base in Canada East, isolate the garrisons in Canada West, and force their Orange enemies to "surrender in detail" or be "cut to pieces by our troops."[25]

The success of this strategy hinged not only on American acquiescence but also on the reactions of Irish Catholic and French Canadians. At the Philadelphia Congress, Michael Murphy boasted that he could raise 125,000 Irish Canadians to fight for Ireland – and although Murphy was opposed to an invasion of Canada, his arguments strengthened the conviction of Roberts and Sweeny that the vast majority of Irish Catholic Canadians would not stand in their way and that many would join the struggle.[26] Spending $1,500 on a "secret service corps in Canada," Sweeny planned highly selective operations and local risings, in which small groups of Canadian Fenians would provide strategic information, cut telegraph lines, destroy the railway bridge that connected Canada West and Canada East, infiltrate the Canadian militia, and suborn British soldiers.[27] Meanwhile, Killian informed Mitchel that the Fenians had opened up promising talks with "a representative

General Tom Sweeny. The architect of the Fenian invasion plans in 1866, Sweeny liaised with Canadian Fenians and sent his own agents into the country – with the result that the Fenians who landed in the Niagara peninsula knew the terrain better than the Crown forces sent to oppose them. In McGee's view, Sweeny and his ilk were "the common enemies of all established Governments." "By sea they are pirates, liable to be hung like dogs," he wrote; "by land, mere freebooters, acknowledging no laws, they are entitled to no mercy" (*Nation*, 9 June 1866). (Joseph Denieffe, *A Personal Narrative of the Irish Revolutionary Brotherhood*)

Society of French Canadians" (probably the Sons of Liberty, operating out of Vermont and New York); other Fenian agents assured Sweeny that French Canadians had no love for their British conquerors and would welcome the Fenians as liberators.[28]

While the American Fenians exaggerated the extent of potential Irish Canadian support, the Canadian authorities erred in the opposite direction. According to Sir John Michel, the commander of the British forces in Canada, the Fenian movement "can hardly be said to exist in Lower Canada, whilst in the towns in Upper Canada some traces of it have been discovered though very limited in extent. It is evident that all serious causes of apprehension lie in the United States."[29] His assessment was based on the reports of the newly established Canadian secret police force, under Gilbert McMicken in Canada West and William Ermatinger in Canada East. The force had been formed in the aftermath of the St Albans raid of October 1864 to prevent further Confederate incursions into the United States. When the Civil War ended, it was wound down to five detectives, who reported rumours about Fenianism in Canada but failed to penetrate the movement.[30] Now, after the Philadelphia Congress, the force was reactivated, and its detectives were sent to Canadian border towns and into the United States, where they investigated Fenian activities.

In contrast to his Young Ireland days, when he had associated secret police with despotism and denounced detectives and spies as "fiends, whose element is falsehood and whose trade is perjury," McGee fully endorsed the effort to infiltrate Fenian circles.[31] He ran his own network of informers in Montreal and urged Macdonald to establish "a constant Agency at New York, filled by the very best men we can get, with an understood system of cypher." "The enemy have their head quarters permanently there," he wrote, "and there ought to be no easier place in the world, for a good secret agent to do his work in, than New York."[32]

Rather than following this advice, Macdonald relied on the British consul in New York, the Nova Scotia–born Edward Archibald, whose house became a hub of counter-revolutionary intelligence.[33] Some of McGee's closest allies in Canada conducted their own freelance counter-intelligence missions. Richard Scott tried unsuccessfully to infiltrate the Fenian headquarters in New York; he was followed by the Ottawa businessman James Goodwin, who passed himself off as a Canadian millionaire and potential donor, and managed to meet the upper echelons of the organization.[34] McMicken himself visited

New York in October, staying at the Astor House, where the Fenian Senate was sitting. Among other things, he recommended to Macdonald that the Canadian government should employ "one or two *Clever Women* whose absolute virtue stands questioned by the Censorious," who could "get some of the susceptible members of the 'Senate' into their toils and thus as Delilah with Samson possess themselves of their secrets." There is no record of Macdonald's reply.[35]

---

If one consequence of the Philadelphia Congress was the revamping of the Canadian secret police force, another was a ratcheting up of ethnoreligious tensions in Canada. "The atmosphere of Toronto is, just now, thick with rumours of Fenian raids across our borders and bank robberies to be committed by the unmitigated 'cut-throats' who owe allegiance to that 'worst of men,' John O'Mahoney," commented the *Irish Canadian*.[36] In early November, Ogle Gowan called on the Orangemen to start arming themselves; the unspoken but unmistakable implication was that Catholics could not be trusted and might well turn against loyal Canadian Protestants.[37]

Amid rumours that the government was planning to supply Orangemen with weapons, the St Patrick's Society of Montreal, under the presidency of Bernard Devlin, rushed to the defence of "their Catholic countrymen throughout Canada." Irish Canadian Catholics, the society declared, were second to none in their loyalty and wanted to live in peace and harmony with Protestants; but if the government treated them like second-class subjects and gave preferential treatment to the Orange Order, they would adopt "all legitimate means" to protect themselves. Was it true, the society asked, that the government planned to arm the Orangemen? If not, what means would it take to ensure that guns were kept out of Orange hands? In reply, the provincial secretary, William McDougall, assured the society that the country would be defended solely by the British army, the militia, and the Volunteers.[38]

McGee reacted strongly against the St Patrick's Society's stance, arguing that the correct course of action should have been to calm things down and dismiss the rumours as utterly unfounded. Instead, he wrote, Devlin and his supporters were feeding the flames of sectarianism and playing on Catholic fears to strengthen Fenianism in the city. "If Mr. GOWAN made an unwise speech, in a time of general excitement," McGee asserted, "Mr. DEVLIN, taking up the cudgels on the part of an exclusively Catholic society, was not going to mend the matter, but quite the reverse."[39]

An opportunity to "mend the matter" arose on 15 November when McGee's friends organized a banquet in his honour. Claiming to speak for "999 out of a thousand of all my countrymen in Canada," McGee mocked the American Fenians as a combination of demagogues and dupes, portrayed the Montreal Irish as a loyal, industrious, and religious people, praised England and the empire, and insisted that all Canadians would unite to defend their country. He would continue, he said, to oppose the

> mad and cruel councils of those who teach a misguided portion of the Irish people at home and abroad to cultivate no other politics but "undying hatred to England." Apart from the anti-Christian blindness and guiltiness of such a popular creed, its folly alone ought to condemn it. It is dashing the earthen pot against the pot of iron; it is the weak defying the strong, it is the powerless challenging the powerful. To English reason and justice and policy, I would appeal; and there is no man living more open to reason if you do not first provoke his pride, than the Englishman. But I know full well that a rich empire will not be bullied by a poor people; that from a first rate power even first rate abuse will extort nothing.[40]

McGee also addressed one of the central concerns about his Wexford speech that had been voiced by James Moylan and others – that his attack on Fenianism had not been balanced by "a strenuous statement of Irish grievances, and a loud call for their redress."[41] Implicitly conceding the point, he called for agrarian reform and the disestablishment of the Church of Ireland, and criticized British politicians for their inaction; there were echoes here of his blasphemy against the great men of England. "If any of my friends can devise any national, constitutional effort, by which we can help to impress the necessity of reconstructive and remedial legislation for Ireland on the Ministers or people of the Empire at large, I will go as far as any man amongst them for that object, by those means," he said. "I would willingly be one, for instance, to lay any proper representation on behalf of Ireland, from her Majesty's loyal subjects in British America, at the foot of the throne."[42]

None of this impressed the city's Fenians, for whom petitions to the queen were a waste of time, and talk about Irish loyalty to the Empire was so much nonsense. Shortly after the speech, a letter from one J.J. Sullivan landed on McGee's desk: "I can see through you well, M'Gee, for you are as transparent as glass. The whole object you have in view is, to become popular (which you now are, among the ignorant Irish) and live at your dead ease. Now, in conclusion, I will inform you that I am a fenian, and I give you civil warning that, if you ever again speak of us in public, as you did the other evening, a few fenians, and I at their head, will give you something that you will recollect, and which will not go down with you quite as well as the dinner your received. Hurrah for Fenianism!"[43]

Among constitutional nationalists, the reaction to McGee's proposal was much more positive. Matthew Ryan, one of the Montreal businessmen who had invited McGee to Montreal in 1857, supported the idea of a petition to "abolish the established Church; to secure the tenant against arbitrary ejectment; and to improve the system of national education."[44] In Toronto, Bishop Lynch took up the idea, enlisted the support of Archbishop Connolly in Halifax, and consulted McGee over the wording.[45] McGee insisted that any petition from Canada must include an explicit declaration against Fenianism and that the proper procedure was to address the petition to the Crown rather than the House of Commons.[46] In the event, Lynch sent his Address to a prominent Irish nationalist MP, Daniel O'Donoghue (known as The O'Donoghue), in the hope that it would be forwarded to Parliament. Two years earlier, The O'Donohoe had gathered over 400,000 signatures on a petition for Irish self-government, without any discernible impact on British policy; the Address from "the priests of Toronto and a good many respectable Citizens" never made it to the floor of the House.[47] The Fenians duly took note.

—— ·•· ——

As these events unfolded, the issue of Fenianism in Canada became increasingly caught up with the issue of Confederation; McGee's two great causes were converging, with unforeseen and sometimes deeply uncomfortable results. The supporters of Confederation had been on the defensive for most of the year. In Nova Scotia, Charles Tupper was deploying all his political skills to avoid a vote of confidence on the Quebec Resolutions; Newfoundland was divided, and Prince Edward Island had come out against British American union.

Everything now hinged on New Brunswick, where, in McGee's words, the anti-confederate victory had injected "uncertainty and instability" into British American politics.[48] The longer Smith's government stayed in power, the harder it would be to sustain the Confederation coalition in Canada. Old animosities between Brown and Macdonald were resurfacing, and tensions were growing between Reformers, who were comfortable with a two-Canada settlement, and Conservatives, who were holding out for a wider union. The combination of New Brunswick resistance and Canadian factionalism threatened to derail the entire process.

On the other hand, it was by no means clear that Smith's government could sustain a coherent and united anti-confederation position. "Nobody supposed," said McGee, "that New Brunswick would be able always to go alone in the future, though she might be able to play the poor part of an obstructionist for a season or two."[49] In common with many of his coalition colleagues, he believed that anti-confederation sentiment in New Brunswick was much weaker than it appeared; many of the province's MPs who opposed the Quebec Resolutions, McGee argued, would support modified proposals for British American union.[50] There was much truth in this: two of Smith's cabinet ministers, Robert Wilmot and John Campbell Allen, supported British American union in principle, and Smith himself was open to a revised version of the Quebec Resolutions. In contrast, Anglin remained strongly opposed to any form of confederation.[51] At the same time, there were deep divisions in the New Brunswick cabinet over railway policy; Anglin wanted the government to provide financial support for a Western Extension railway connecting Saint John with Maine, while Smith was unwilling or unable to cover the costs.[52]

The first major crack came in September, when Wilmot visited Quebec to discuss the prospects of a renewed reciprocity agreement with the United States. During the talks, he came to the conclusion that legislative union was impossible, that renewed reciprocity was probably unattainable, and that federalism was the only way forward.[53] Shortly afterwards, he joined a group of about fifty Maritime politicians and journalists on a tour of Canada that McGee had arranged as a reciprocal gesture of goodwill after the Canadian visit to the Maritimes the previous year. In Toronto, Wilmot shed his earlier inhibitions and announced that there were "vast numbers" in New Brunswick who supported British American union and who would eventually embrace the Quebec Resolutions.[54] When Anglin read the speech, he privately wrote that Wilmot should be fired from the cabinet.[55]

In other respects, though, McGee's tour was not a success; it actually threatened to backfire on the cause of Confederation. The organizing committee was late in issuing the invitations, the number of delegates was smaller than expected, and McGee was ill in Montreal while the visitors were travelling through Canada West.[56] Even more seriously, it was proving very difficult to raise the necessary funds. In Canada West, the hosts were just about able to hold things together. But in Montreal, where the tour was to end, a public relations disaster was looming; the visitors were about to arrive, there was not enough money to look after them, and members of the organizing committee were squabbling with one another. In desperation, McGee sent two telegrams and an urgent letter to Galt, the minister of finance. Unless someone came up with the money quickly, McGee wrote, Confederation would receive "an irreparable blow."[57] In New Brunswick, Anglin had seized on the divisions within the committee to vilify the Canadians as being tight-fisted and mean-spirited – not at all the kind of people with whom Maritimers should form an alliance.[58] After considering McGee's request, Galt subscribed $5,000 to the fund, while expressing his disappointment at the lack of Canadian support for the tour.[59] But it had been a very close call.

Looking back on the tour two months later, McGee glossed over the problems and focused on the positives – particularly the number of Irishmen among the Maritime visitors. Their presence, he claimed, demonstrated that Irish Catholics in the region continued to support British American union, despite anti-confederate scaremongering tactics. "The Orangeism of Western Canada has been held up to them as a bugbear," McGee said; "the crimes and errors of the Irish Union had been artfully placed before them, as a sample of what they might expect of a Union with Canada. If ... those inflammatory and unfounded appeals to their hereditary prejudices, had taken root, the Irish of the Maritime Provinces would at this moment have been as hostile to their fellow-countrymen in Canada, as the demented Fenians of New York."[60] In fact, such appeals had been more successful than McGee admitted. Although Archbishop Connolly was exaggerating when he wrote that in New Brunswick "nearly the whole Catholic population needlessly flung themselves on the side of Anticonfederation," a substantial section of the colony's Irish Catholics was opposed to British American union in any shape or form.[61]

The question of Irish Catholic attitudes towards Confederation and the relationship between Irish Catholics and Fenians became a major issue in New Brunswick politics towards the end of the year. In November, a key by-election was fought in York County, where Charles Fisher – whom the Duke of Newcastle had described as "the worst public man in British America" – ran against Smith's government.[62] Knowing that a victory for Fisher would weaken the anti-confederate position, Tilley asked Macdonald for "eight or ten thousand dollars" to influence the outcome.[63]

During the election campaign, Fisher and his supporters opened up a generalized attack on Irish Catholics, Fenians, annexationists, and anti-confederates. By "innuendos and hints and other such crafty means, as well as by more open assertions," noted Anglin, the confederates strove "to create the impression that Fenianism has sympathizers in this Province, and that the only way to save the Province from being gobbled up by them is to elect Mr. Fisher and the other nominees of the Canadian party."[64] If you scratched an Irish Catholic, ran the message, you would find a Fenian; and wherever you found a Fenian, you found an enemy to British Protestant liberty and a supporter of annexation to the United States. The conflict over Confederation, from this perspective, became a stand-up fight between loyalty and Fenianism.[65] The tactics worked; Fisher was elected by a comfortable majority.

It was, along with the defection of Wilmot in September, a significant psychological boost for the confederates. When he heard the news, McGee described Fisher's victory as a "cheering omen." "Surely," he added, "if ever, now is a time, when all British subjects in these Provinces should resolve to draw closer the bonds of Colonial Union, so as to defeat the machinations of conspirators against us, and to demonstrate the hopelessness of attempting to force us into Annexation, either by commercial coercion, or by more violent means."[66] Annexation, for McGee, meant absorption into democratic uniformity; colonial union meant minority rights. "So long as we respect in Canada the rights of minorities, told either by tongue or creed, we are safe," he said three weeks later; "but when we cease to respect these rights, we will be in the full tide towards that madness which the ancients considered the gods sent to those whom they wished to destroy."[67]

Yet the means that Fisher had employed to win the York by-election and further the cause of Confederation – making coded appeals to anti-Catholic sentiment and tarring Irish Catholic opponents of Confederation with the brush of Fenianism – contradicted the ends of McGee's new nationality, with its emphasis on minority rights and ethnoreligious harmony. McGee repeatedly attempted to shatter the perception that Irish Catholics were coterminous with Fenians; but Fisher won in part by playing on precisely such perceptions. "The diverse elements of our population, in language and creed, in Canada, make it a difficult country to govern," McGee commented shortly afterwards; his observation was equally applicable to the Maritimes.[68]

Hard on the heels of Fisher's victory, Smith's government received another blow with the resignation of Anglin from the cabinet – not as a result of the by-election but over the government's failure to start work on the Western Extension railway.[69] Although Anglin continued to fight against Confederation in the *Morning Freeman* and in the legislative assembly, the fact remained that, as Gordon put it, "the most determined isolationist ... is no longer a member of the Government."[70] Immediately after the by-election, the Canadian coalition sent George Brown to the Maritimes to explore the possibilities opened by Fisher's election and Anglin's resignation; in Fredericton, Brown and Gordon spent three days discussing the best strategy for Confederation.[71] Now that Anglin was out of the way, pressure would be exerted on Smith to support a modified form of Confederation. If Smith refused, the lieutenant governor would call on Wilmot to form a pro-union government; should such a government fail to command a majority, there would be an election. And this time, buoyed by the success of Fisher, the confederates expected to win.

It seemed that McGee was right: New Brunswick could not hold out indefinitely. But while political factionalism in the colony was encouraging for the supporters of Confederation, events in Canada remained a cause for concern. When Brown returned from his trip to the Maritimes, he became embroiled in a controversy with Galt over the best way to conduct negotiations on reciprocity with the United States.[72] Finding himself isolated in the cabinet, Brown resigned in December, leaving the coalition that he had reluctantly joined eighteen months earlier. His fellow Reform cabinet ministers remained in the coalition, and Brown still undertook to support British North American union until the agreed deadline of the next parliamentary session, after which plans would proceed for a two-Canada federation. But his resignation did nothing to reduce the sense of uncertainty and instability in British North American politics.[73]

As the year drew to a close, George Clerk jotted down some notes in his diary that captured the mood: "All is troubled in political horizon. George Brown has left the Ministry. Confederation remains in *status quo*. The Yankees are bitter, the Fenians menacing, and it will be lucky indeed if peace on borders be preserved."[74] For McGee, as for his colleagues, major challenges lay ahead.

## CHAPTER ELEVEN

# The Brethren of Sedition
## December 1865 – May 1866

By the end of 1865 the divisions within the Fenian Brotherhood between John O'Mahony and William Roberts reached breaking point and drove the organization apart. Ostensibly about whether O'Mahony or the Senate had the authority to issue Fenian bonds, the split was actually over the Canadian invasion strategy and was sharpened by personality conflicts. "The traitors are about throwing us over-board and giving up Ireland for Canada," wrote O'Mahony, claiming that Roberts was conspiring with informers to destroy the brotherhood.[1] Such accusations of duplicity occurred repeatedly in the history of Irish revolutionary nationalism; the same anger that was directed against British rule was frequently turned inwards and applied to rivals within the movement.[2]

The split had major repercussions for revolutionary Irish nationalists in Canada, where the news "cast a gloom" over the Fenians and their sympathizers.[3] In Toronto, Michael Murphy and the *Irish Canadian* supported the O'Mahony wing and denounced the "mad and traitorous" idea of liberating Ireland through an attack on the "unoffending people" of Canada.[4] In Montreal, the Fenians tried to carry on as usual but eventually divided along American lines, with a significant section backing the Senate wing's invasion plans.[5]

Bad news for the Fenians was apparently good news for the authorities in Canada and Britain. "The Fenian cause has been much injured by the dissensions among its leaders & by the charges of treachery & corruption they make against each other," wrote Frederick Bruce, the British minister to the United States. Such "evidences of incapacity and bad faith," he remarked, only strengthened the American Anglo-

Saxon "spirit of antagonism" towards Catholic Celts – a "far deeper & more enduring sentiment than the superficial sympathy which has been evoked by irritation against England."[6] In Canada, the "spirit of antagonism" was intensified by the continuing possibility of a Fenian invasion; bullets were fired into the Loretto Convent in Toronto, and "well dressed youths" hurled abuse at priests and nuns on the city's streets.[7]

Facing the prospect of a full-scale loyalist Protestant backlash and torn by internal divisions, Canadian Fenians were also confronted with conservative opposition within Irish Catholic communities. As the temperature rose, verbal violence was sometimes accompanied by physical assault. In Montreal, Francis Bernard McNamee, the founder of Fenianism in the city, beat up McGee's close friend Lawrence Devany, much to the delight of McNamee's fellow Fenians.[8] But the principal Fenian hate figure remained McGee himself. When he appeared at a St Patrick's Society concert in Montreal in January, a small but vocal minority greeted him with whistles and hisses, while his enemies commented caustically on the "tramp tramp tramp" of the police bodyguards who came to the podium for his protection.[9] A week later, he was in Toronto, speaking to the Mechanics' Institute about his visit to Oxford – a city which he saw as balancing tradition and innovation, and an example for the people and institutions of Canada. During his lecture, a group of "suspicious looking men," less impressed with the virtues of Oxford, were waiting for him outside the building; once again, he needed a police escort to ensure his safety.[10]

---

Against all expectations, the Fenian split did not weaken the movement in the United States; on the contrary, the rival factions became increasingly energized as they tried to outbid each other for popular support.[11] Roberts and Sweeny announced that they had bought large quantities of arms and war materiel, promised that Canada would be invaded before the summer, and declared that Canadian hostages would be held for "our brave patriots at home." "For every man they hang of ours," said Roberts, "we will suspend in a row five of theirs."[12] Among the hostages would be Lord Monck, "other government officers," and – no surprise here – D'Arcy McGee.[13] Not to be outdone, O'Mahony claimed that plans were underway to fit out forty privateers and to send twenty thousand armed men to Ireland.[14]

American Fenianism received a further boost when news reached the United States that the British government had suspended habeas corpus in Ireland – an event that Killian described as "our salvation here."[15] In early March, thousands of Irish Americans gathered at Jones Wood in New York to hear O'Mahony call for arms and ammunition to support the revolutionary movement in Ireland.[16] While O'Mahony continued to focus on Ireland, stories were circulating that the Senate wing was on the point of invading Canada. "The time for action has come," reported Edward Archibald in New York, "and it is certain, I believe, that a movement will be made on Canada by Roberts and Sweeny before this month expires – probably very shortly after St. Patrick's day. Sweeny professes to have obtained the fullest and most accurate information of the defences of Canada and other Provinces."[17]

Within Canada, McMicken's detectives reported that supporters of Roberts and Sweeny were storing revolvers and pikes in safe houses in Toronto, that Fenians in Fort Erie were planning to bring in arms from Buffalo, and that revolutionary Irish nationalists in Port Huron were boasting that Canada could be taken in a day.[18] Information from Malone near the Canadian border, from Buffalo, and from the Senate wing's Pittsburgh Convention all pointed in the same direction – that the Fenian invasion of Canada would be launched on St Patrick's Day.[19] With rumours of imminent invasion and internal subversion, there was a run on the banks, and something approaching a Great Fear gripped much of Canada.[20] On 7 March, Macdonald called out ten thousand Volunteers for active duty; the response was so enthusiastic that three times that number could easily have been raised.[21]

McGee's response to these developments was both ideological and tactical. At the beginning of March, he published "The Irish Position in British and Republican North America," which challenged the American Fenian assumption that the Irish in Canada were an oppressed people who needed to be liberated from the yoke of British colonialism. In taking this position, he acknowledged that he was part of a minority tradition among the Irish in North America – although he also maintained that this minority was larger than most people realized, encompassing all the bishops, most of the priests, a majority of successful farmers, businessmen, and professional men, and "all the influential and wealthy Irish Protestant population."

Three-quarters of Irish Americans, he wrote, lived in towns and cities, where they supplied the demand for unskilled labour and fell under the influence of unscrupulous ward bosses who kept them pinned down in poverty: "Hence this strangely contradictory result: that a people who hungered and thirsted for land in Ireland, who struggled for conacre or cabin even to the shedding of blood, that this same people when they reached a new world, in which a day's wages saved would purchase an acre of wild land in fee, wilfully concurred under the lead of bad advisers, to sink into the miserable condition of a miserable town tenantry, to whose moral squalor, even European seaports can hardly present a parallel." An impoverished, ghettoized, and alienated Irish American population produced the perfect breeding ground for Fenianism: "This very Fenian organization in the United States," McGee asked, "what does it really prove, but that the Irish are still an alien population, camped but not settled in America, with foreign hopes and aspirations neither shared in nor respected, by the people among whom they live?"

The contrast with Canada could not have been more striking. "Our rural numbers are almost in the inverse ratio to the urban to what the same classes are to each other in the United States … If not quite three-fourths, certainly the large majority of our emigrants here, live by land, and own land." In British America, the Irish were dispersed throughout the countryside, rather than being crammed into cities; they enjoyed freedom of religion and their own separate schools; and their leaders were generally gentlemen rather than ward bosses. In this environment, there was little or no room for Fenianism. The one exception was Toronto, where "Orangeism has been made the pretext of Fenianism, and Fenianism is doing its best to justify and magnify Orangeism." But even there, "the brethren of sedition are a handful, and their head centre a nobody. Meantime the great healthful mass of the Irish farmers of Canada, men breathing pure air and living pure lives, are untouched by the infection, thanks to their own sound sense, to the conservatism which springs from property; and thanks, too, whenever it is required, to the timely warnings of their parish clergy." "And these are the people," he commented, "their own flesh and blood (though not of the same spirit) the New York 'bloody sixth ward boys,' are coming here to invade, or they call it, 'to liberate.'"[22]

McGee's analysis reached back to his Wexford speech and antici-pated much subsequent research on the Irish in North America. He was right that most Irish American immigrants lived in urban areas, and his argument that urban alienation intensified revolutionary Irish Amer-ican nationalism has been echoed by modern historians.[23] In Canada, Gordon Darroch and Michael Ornstein have demonstrated that ethnic Irish patterns of residency and occupation matched those of the popu-lation as a whole, and that farming was the single most important occupation of Irish Protestants and Catholics alike – findings that have been used to explain the supposedly weaker position of Fenianism in British North America.[24] McGee's point that the minority tradition to which he belonged was stronger than it appeared in the United States (and, by implication, was a majority tradition in Irish Canada) has not been taken up by modern historians but is well worth pursuing. On the other hand, his reduction of Canadian Fenianism to a radical rump in Toronto significantly underestimated the depth and breadth of revo-lutionary Irish Canadian nationalism, another minority tradition that was stronger than it seemed.[25]

This was almost certainly a deliberate underestimation on McGee's part, stemming from his strategy of marginalizing Canadian Fenian-ism and stressing Irish Catholic loyalty. On a tactical level, his immedi-ate preoccupation in the spring of 1866 was to pre-empt any concerted action between the Fenians in the United States and Canada – and particularly to isolate the "brethren of sedition" in Toronto. Having received intelligence reports that Canada would be attacked from St Albans and Buffalo on 17 March, and that the Hibernian Benevolent Society in Toronto contained around six hundred and fifty Fenians, McGee feared that the city's St Patrick's Day parade would become linked with the anticipated invasion.[26] "It cannot be tolerated," he told George Brown, "that a seditious society should, at one and the same time, be parading our own streets – distracting or pre-occupying, the attention of the authorities." "I believe we are likely, indeed I would say to *you* certain," he wrote, "to have trouble from these rascal Fenians. I have fought them, against every menace, – even personally delivered to myself – and I will fight them to the end. But we need all our Union and all our strength."[27]

To this end, he wrote an impassioned letter to Bishop Lynch ("though he is no great friend of mine"), informing him that the American Fenians intended "to signalize (God help them!) St Patrick's day – by blood and rapine, and the invasion of a country that has done them no shade of wrong," and imploring him to withdraw the church's support for the parade. "If they set your authority at defiance," McGee added, "I have reason to fear the Mayor [Francis Medcalf] will, as he can, on the affidavit of two or more householders, proclaim the procession, and of course both the Volunteer and regular forces, must be subject to his order, within his bailiwick. It is a question for Murphy and his gang whether they will voluntarily obey their own Bishop, or be *put down* – by Mr Medcalf, and the troops."[28] "The position of our Church & race, for the next 25 years, will be determined by the stand taken, during these six weeks, next ensuing," he told Lynch in a follow-up letter.[29]

McGee's arguments, together with the threat of military force, proved effective. After receiving the letters, Lynch issued two circulars reminding his flock of their duties as "pious Catholics and loyal subjects," and instructing the Hibernian Benevolent Society not to have a procession to the cathedral. "There is a society that has learned too well the Protestant lesson of despising the authority of the Church," Lynch wrote, referring to the Fenians. "Let the members of the Hibernian Society show themselves better men and better christians, as well as loyal subjects."[30]

As it transpired, St Patrick's Day passed off peacefully; the reports about an impending Fenian invasion turned out to be false, and in any case the leading Fenians in Toronto were associated with O'Mahony rather than Roberts and Sweeny. Just before the parade, McMicken met with Michael Murphy, received assurances that the parade would not be provocative, and persuaded Mayor Medcalf not to adopt a confrontational strategy. As a result, McMicken reported, over five hundred Hibernians marched in "peace and quietness." After the march,

Murphy claimed once again that forty thousand Irish Canadians were prepared to fight in Ireland, declared that annexation to the United States was preferable to Confederation, and condemned "that thing, McGee." But he also denounced those who would "bring war and its attendant horrors" into Canada.[31] Meanwhile, in Montreal, McGee gave what his supporters described as a "spirit-stirring oration" to the St Patrick's Society, which proclaimed its loyalty to Canada – although his detractors claimed that the audience mocked his words, cheered loudly for Bernard Devlin, and did not sing "God Save the Queen."[32]

Despite the anti-climax of St Patrick's Day, ethnoreligious tensions in Canada remained high. While Sweeny continued his preparations for the invasion, the *Irish Canadian* accused loyalist politicians of fomenting hysteria about an attack that would never happen, and claimed that Orangemen were spreading rumours about Fenian plans to subvert the Canadian militia.[33] There may, in fact, have been some substance to the Orange rumours. In late March, McNamee wrote a confidential letter to one of Sweeny's aides in New York, suggesting that the Fenians in Montreal could use "a little deceit" against their enemies. The priests, McNamee noted with disgust, were preaching loyalty, while McGee was trying to raise Catholic militia companies to defend Canada. But the situation could be turned to the Fenians' advantage. They could profess their loyalty to the Crown, form their own militia company, and offer their services to the government. If the offer was accepted, they would acquire guns and experience in drilling, and then could turn against the government when the invasion occurred. If the offer was rejected, they would "raise a hue and cry against the Govt for doubting our loyalty, after we obeyed the holy Church, &c &c." It was a win-win proposition: "In either case we will have the Govt. in a fix, as also the loyal dogs who are yelping at our heels."[34]

McNamee's scheme has to be placed in the immediate context of fear and suspicions about Irish Catholic loyalty in Montreal. Shortly after St Patrick's Day, Thomas McCready, apparently drawing on information received from McGee, reported that many Irish Catholics in Bernard Devlin's Prince of Wales Regiment were refusing to fight their fellow countrymen – a charge that Devlin vociferously denied. At the same time, the *Irish Canadian*'s Montreal correspondent claimed that Irish Catholics were being excluded from the city's newly established Home Guard, on the grounds that they could not be trusted. "This insult has been offered to the entire Catholic population," he commented, "and not one man has yet protested against it. Mr. McGee has not a word in condemnation of it."[35]

Given this dynamic, it is not hard to see how and why McNamee developed his conspiratorial plans. But what makes the story even more intriguing – and the word is used advisedly – is that one of his friends and fellow Fenians, William Mansfield, believed that McNamee was actually an informer. In early April, Mansfield told Sweeny's aide that McNamee was secretly working for Cartier and McGee, and was pretending to support the invasion in order to infiltrate the Fenian headquarters in New York. "Dont [sic] have a spy in the camp," he warned.[36]

If there actually was a connection between McGee and McNamee, both men were very good at covering their tracks; McNamee would have taken his part to extreme lengths by beating up McGee's close friend Lawrence Devany, and McGee would have kept everyone out of the loop, including John A. Macdonald, whose private correspondence about McNamee contains no hint that he may have been an informer. It is clear, though, that someone was supplying McGee with reliable inside information about the Fenian Brotherhood in Montreal and that many Irish Canadians in Montreal pointed the finger at McNamee.[37] In the present state of the evidence, however, their accusations remain unsubstantiated.

An equally contentious issue concerned McGee's relationship with another leading Fenian – none other than Bernard Doran Killian, O'Mahony's right-hand man in New York. Over a decade earlier, when McGee was editing the *American Celt*, he and Killian had been personally and professionally close; Killian was the associate editor of the newspaper, and he took it over during McGee's frequent lecture tours.[38] Since then, Killian had moved towards revolutionary Irish nationalism – or, from McGee's perspective, had "prostituted his talents" to the Fenians.[39] Yet rumours persisted that there was more to this than met the eye and that the two men were still secretly working with each other.

Initially, this took the form of insinuations that McGee was actually a closet Fenian, hiding beneath the mantle of loyalist respectability. In February, the New York *Herald* published a letter purportedly written from McGee to Killian, in which McGee referred to "my friend O'Mahony" and praised his "wise and statesmanlike policy" of supporting Irish colonization projects in the American West. When it was reprinted in the *Globe*, McGee rushed off a note to Brown, saying that he was "deeply grieved and wounded" by the editorial decision to run the story, and publicly denouncing the letter as a forgery – as did Killian himself. If even McGee was suspected of sympathizing with the Fenian Brotherhood, who among the Irish Catholics in Canada would be immune? "*Do* teach your lieutenants that their duty *now* is to excite confidence, not suspicion, of all Irishmen resolved to do their duty," he told Brown.[40] Before long, though, the suspicion that McGee and Killian were clandestine allies would assume a very different form, as Killian persuaded the O'Mahony wing to move in a new and unexpected direction.

On St Patrick's Day, while the Canadian Volunteers were on full alert and McGee was making his loyalist speech in Montreal, O'Mahony called a meeting of the Fenian Brotherhood in New York. Here, Killian pushed hard for a change in strategy. To avoid losing more ground to the Senate wing, he argued, they should seize the initiative and move from talk to action. His idea was to capture the island of Campobello, which he mistakenly believed was disputed territory between Britain and the United States. From this base, the Fenians could send out privateers to attack British ships, organize an expedition to Ireland, and plunge Anglo-American relations into crisis; had not Seward said that he would recognize "accomplished facts"?

After much discussion, O'Mahony agreed; the prospect of provoking an Anglo-American war was probably the decisive factor.[41] At any rate, it seemed worth trying and was certainly taken seriously by British diplomats in the United States, whose immediate reaction was one of concern rather than derision. "If any such plan were to succeed," wrote Frederick Bruce, "great pressure would be brought to bear on this Govt. to recognize these adventurers as belligerents as a means of

John O'Mahony. A veteran of the rising of 1848, O'Mahony founded the American branch of the Irish Republican Brotherhood, which he renamed the Fenian Brotherhood. Although he believed that the movement should focus on an Irish revolution rather than an invasion of Canada, O'Mahony reluctantly agreed to organize an attack on Campobello Island in the hope that it would provoke an Anglo-American war. In McGee's mocking words, O'Mahony "turned spirit rapper, and rapped at the door of the Flatbush insane asylum, where was first conceived this crazy conspiracy" (*Montreal Gazette*, 23 March 1864). (Michael Doheny, *The Felon's Track*)

inflicting damage on British commerce in retaliation for the losses the Confederate Cruizers inflicted on American Shipowners during the Civil War."[42]

Killian immediately began organizing the movement of men and materiel to Eastport, Maine, which would be the staging area for the attack. Included in the call were O'Mahony's supporters in Toronto. On 21 March, Killian sent a coded telegram to Philip Cullen, a member of the Hibernian Benevolent Society, instructing him to select men with military experience, prepare them for action, and await further orders. In early April, Cullen, Murphy, and five other Toronto Fenians, armed with revolvers and knives, set out for Eastport. But the Canadian authorities had been tipped off about the telegram and were monitoring Cullen's movements. After Murphy and his companions boarded the eastbound train, they were intercepted and arrested in Cornwall. Three leading Hibernians in Toronto also were arrested, amid reports that other Canadian Fenians had slipped across the border to the United States and were continuing their journey to Eastport.[43]

By the second week of April, several hundred Fenians had gathered in northeast Maine, where they waited for the arms and ammunition that were being shipped from New York. While they waited, the imperial authorities in New Brunswick strengthened their defences. A British naval squadron arrived off the coast, regular troops and artillery were brought to the border, and the provincial militia prepared for action.[44] When the arms shipment arrived, the American government was forced to take action it would rather have avoided. Closing down Fenian operations would alienate much-needed Irish American voters, but allowing the Fenians to proceed would produce a major conflict with Britain. There was no doubt about the way the US government would jump. After some initial attempts at buck-passing, the cabinet endorsed the actions of the American general on the ground who had already detained the Fenian ship and confiscated the arms. Far from recognizing accomplished facts, the government prevented the facts from being accomplished in the first place. In the face of American intervention and the defensive measures in New Brunswick, the Fenian cause was hopeless, and Killian's strategy lay in ruins. The result: total failure, a price tag of nearly $40,000, and widespread ridicule. Contemporaries and historians alike dismissed the entire endeavour as a "fiasco" and a "farce."[45]

Nevertheless, as contemporaries and historians also pointed out, there was another side to this altogether – the impact of the Fenian threat on the Confederation debate in New Brunswick. As we have seen, the anti-confederates had been running into difficulties over the previous six months. Robert Wilmot's conversion to Confederation, the by-election victory of Charles Fisher, the resignation of Timothy Warren Anglin, and the pro-Confederation pressure exerted by Lieutenant Governor Arthur Gordon had all weakened Albert Smith's government. At the same time, the alternative to Confederation – the constitutional status quo, with a railway line connecting Saint John to Maine, and a reciprocity agreement with the United States – had clearly failed. "The political news from New Brunswick is cheering," McGee told Brown in early March.[46] When New Brunswick's House of Assembly reconvened that month, Gordon set out to implement the strategy he had discussed earlier with George Brown: to persuade Smith's government to accept British North American union or force it to resign.

New Brunswick politics were reaching the crisis point at the very moment when the Fenians were gathering in northeast Maine. During the second week of April, Smith's government resigned and was replaced by a pro-Confederation administration that included Wilmot and McGee's old ally Peter Mitchell.[47] Shortly afterwards, at a Fenian convention in Calais, Killian declared that the Fenians would not stand idly by while Britain coerced New Brunswick into Confederation and said that they would assist any rebellion in the province.[48] Meanwhile, a proclamation from the "Republican Committee of St. John" denounced Confederation as a British plot and urged New Brunswick to become an independent republic; this was almost certainly the work of the "small circle" of Fenians in Saint John who supported the invasion of British North America.[49]

Here, it seemed, was clear evidence that opposition to Confederation in New Brunswick corresponded with the republican agenda of the Fenians on the frontier. For the confederates, it was almost too good to be true; they played the loyalty card, caricatured their opponents as aiding and abetting the invaders, argued that British North American union was necessary for defence, and reaped the political dividends. When the election was held in June, Tilley had a landslide victory; the Fenians (along with liberal quantities of Canadian cash) played a crucial role in breaking the principal barrier in the way of Confederation.[50]

Trapped by events beyond their control and outmanoeuvred by their enemies, many anti-confederates became convinced that they were victims of a vast conspiracy, orchestrated by the Canadians and conducted by McGee. All the pieces seemed to fit. McGee and Killian had been editorial partners in the *American Celt*, which denounced revolutionary republicanism and supported British American union. Since then, McGee had moved to Canada, where he became the leading North American opponent of Fenianism and the chief publicist of Confederation. In the meantime, Killian had joined the Fenian Brotherhood and persuaded O'Mahony to endorse a course of action that simultaneously undermined revolutionary Irish American nationalism and promoted the cause of Confederation. Was it not self-evident that McGee and Killian were still working together and had concocted the whole affair to serve their predetermined ends?

Anglin certainly thought so. "If Mr. Killian were in the pay of the Canadians and Mr. D'Arcy McGee himself wrote his speech for him, he could not have said anything better suited to the purposes of the Canadian party," he wrote. The following year, Anglin asserted that "the movement on the New Brunswick frontier was the result of some common purpose of these two men."[51] Many Fenians felt the same way. According to one report, O'Mahony believed that Killian was "secretly in league with Mr. D'Arcy McGee" – a connection that had long been suspected by Senate wing Fenians.[52] Even Edward Archibald, the British consul in New York, commented that it seemed "difficult not to believe that Killian deliberately played the part of a traitor in order to break up the organization" – although he went on to explain that Killian's real motive was "jealousy of Roberts & Sweeny, and fear lest their earlier & more energetic action might lessen the power and importance of the leaders of the O'Mahony faction."[53]

While such suspicions among the anti-confederates and the Fenians are understandable, they exist entirely in the realm of supposition; they cannot be supported by evidence and are too far-fetched to be taken seriously. Not, of course, that this would deter any good conspiracy theorist worth his or her salt, for whom the very lack of evidence only testifies to the success of the conspiracy. As might be expected, McGee strenuously denied the allegations and challenged Anglin to prove his insinuation that he and Killian were working together: "Stand forth, then, Mr. Anglin, and make good your words, or eat them, or else stand convicted of slandering an absent man, for the sake of promoting your anti-union ends and purposes."[54] Unable to provide any proof, Anglin made the unconvincing reply that since Killian's words and actions "rendered great service to Confederation" and since McGee supported Confederation, "whether by previous arrangement or not, they worked together."[55]

———

On two key fronts, then, things were going McGee's way in the spring of 1866: the O'Mahony wing of the Fenian Brotherhood had been clipped at Eastport, and the confederates were reaping the benefits in New Brunswick. But the third front of the Senate wing remained active and was actually strengthened by the influx of disgruntled O'Mahony men after the failure of Killian's strategy.[56] Not only that, but there were indications that Roberts and Sweeny had significant support among nationalists in Ireland. While reading the Irish American press, McGee encountered excerpts from the *Nation* – the constitutional nationalist newspaper for which he had written during his Young Ireland days    suggesting that "the Irish people" would sanction the invasion of Canada. There was no way that he could let this pass. On 25 May he penned a long public letter to the *Nation*'s editor, Alexander Martin Sullivan, registering his "extreme regret" about the excerpts. "This," he wrote, "is the disturbing cause which compels me, like an apparition of the past, to present myself in Lower Abbey-street, scroll in hand."[57]

"The Irish people" would support the invasion of Canada? "From the fact of their being confidently quoted on all sides," McGee commented, "one hardly knows what to believe, at present, as to the whereabouts of 'the Irish people.' Never was *Figaro* in the Opera more badgered and bewildered by the array of voices invoking his presence." But of this much he was sure: Irish Canadians had every right to protest against "any such encouragement and sanction being given to the desolation of our homes and the destruction of our people, in the (we believe) grossly abused name of the Irish people."

There should be no confusion, he added, between the "ethics of national insurrection" and the "immorality of private war." Although he did not spell it out in his letter, McGee held a clear and consistent position on the ethics of revolution. "I know there was a time when I would have encouraged every open manifestation of disloyalty in Ireland, and when I would have rebelled myself against the landlord oligarchy of Ireland," he told an Irish American journalist earlier in the decade. "I would have encouraged Irishmen to fight, and would have fought myself for the recovery of our Irish Parliament; and I will ask you to believe me when I say that I would do the same to-morrow if I thought there was any chance of success. But I do not think there is."[58] A national insurrection may have been justifiable in theory, but it was impractical and therefore immoral in practice; the earthen pot could not break the pot of iron.

But when it came to filibustering, there was no justification whatsoever, whether in theory or practice. "The immorality of private war," he declared, "has been asserted long ago by all the great tribunals of Christendom – by General Councils formerly, the Congresses of statesmen and writers on international law, more recently." Sweeny was on a par with men such Aaron Burr, Narciso López, and William Walker, who had organized expeditions against Mexico, Cuba, and Nicaragua, respectively. Burr had been driven in disgrace from public life; López had been garrotted by the Spanish; Walker had been executed for his troubles; and Sweeny "richly deserved" the same fate. "These breeders and fomenters of private wars are the common enemies of all established Governments," wrote McGee. "By sea they are pirates, liable to be hung like dogs; by land, mere freebooters, acknowledging no laws, they are entitled to no mercy."

And yet here was the *Nation* encouraging a Fenian filibuster on Canada – and this despite the fact that Canada had good relations with Ireland, as evinced by the warm welcome given to William Smith O'Brien in 1859, by Canadian support for the establishment of a Catholic university in Ireland, and by the money that Canadians sent for famine relief in the west of Ireland. "We strove to save her from one scourge – famine," McGee wrote; "you repay us by knotting for us even a worse scourge – private war!" What made this worse still was that the *Nation* knew full well that Canada was a self-governing country where the Catholic Church enjoyed a status far above that in the

United States and where Irish Catholics were prosperous, popular, and influential. "You know all this," he told Sullivan, "yet simply from a rash, unreasoning hatred to the mere name of '*British* Province,' you would strike down *our* liberties, beggar our institutions and our people, your own countrymen included, under the pretended authority of 'the Irish people.'"

In any case, McGee continued, the Fenian invasion was as impractical as it was immoral. Canadians would unite against "any marauding invasion," and the force of three million people backed up by British power meant that the Fenians could never succeed: "They may, it is true, get up border raids; they may keep up a sort of Tweedale terrorism, they may destroy many fruits of peaceful industry; they may obstruct the channels of trade; they may rob a bank; they may and will throw thousands of your countrymen and mine out of their daily bread; they may take many a good man's life; they may earn many a widow's curse. All this I admit they may do, quoting you as their justifier. But conquer Canada 'as a base of operations against England'! They conquer Canada! Psha!"

"Sir, I write warmly, and so would you, if you were within fifty miles of the still peaceful frontier over which these people are urged by you to pour, in the name of the cause of Ireland," McGee explained. His anger was also connected to his belief that the *Nation* was dragging down Ireland's reputation. While he himself was arguing that the Fenians did not represent "the Irish people" or the "cause of Ireland," Sullivan was apparently suggesting that in some sense they did. "Never, never before, did 'the cause of Ireland' present itself in the guise of mere brigandage and spoliation," McGee wrote. "Oh, shame! shame ineffable!"

In this respect, McGee's letter reprised an important but often overlooked aspect of his Wexford speech the previous year – that American Fenianism was undermining the Irish character. "Formerly," he said at Wexford, "the Irish in America were a sort of social colony of the Irish at home; they used still to take many of their ideas from this country, after they had left; but, whereas Ireland then influenced her emigrants, they now – such is their numerical attraction – influence her; and it does appear to me that this influence is not decreasing at present ...

Have a care; you are giving away hands and brains to a system destined to combat your system of government, sooner or later."[59] The change in attitude that McGee detected in the *Nation* – from admiring Canadian institutions to equating a prospective Fenian invasion with "the cause of Ireland" – only appeared to confirm his judgment. The diaspora was rebounding on the homeland, and the same kind of political, social, and moral values that McGee had denounced in the United States were now creeping into Ireland. "I do not look on these men – these American Fenians – as enemies of England, for in that light they are contemptible," he informed Sullivan, "but as enemies of Ireland, and in that light they *are* formidable."[60]

---

While McGee was writing his letter, the American Fenians were moving to the Canadian border. After the failure of Killian's plan to seize Campobello, the Senate wing decided that it had to act quickly; if more time was allowed to pass without action in Canada, the Fenian Brotherhood would lose credibility, and its members would drift away. But Sweeny did not have enough men and materiel for a successful invasion, and he knew it. The choices facing the Fenians were bleak: postpone the invasion and risk the disintegration of the movement or launch the invasion and go down to defeat. In the event, Sweeny decided to go ahead, on the grounds that a defeat with honour was preferable to doing nothing at all. It was 1848 all over again; the Fenians, like the Young Irelanders before them, had gone so far that they could not turn back, and a grand revolutionary gesture, a glorious failure, was better than the ignominy of inaction.[61]

And so Sweeny prepared strikes from Buffalo into the Niagara peninsula, from upstate New York into Canada East, and from Chicago into Goderich, while his secret service agents coordinated plans with sympathetic Fenians in Canada.[62] McMicken's detectives were reporting the buildup of Fenian arms in upstate New York and Illinois.[63] But it was not clear to the Canadian authorities whether all this was a gigantic charade to keep up Fenian morale or a serious attempt to begin the Irish revolution in Canada. After the previous false alarms in Canada and the events in New Brunswick, the general consensus

was that the colony was not in any immediate danger. "I cannot conceive it within the bounds of a reasonable possibility that Sweeney will
attempt any demonstration upon Canada now," reported McMicken in
the middle of May.[64]

McGee fully concurred. On 25 May, the same day that he wrote to
Alexander Sullivan of the *Nation*, he sent a letter to Lord Wodehouse,
the Lord Lieutenant of Ireland, assessing the current situation. "The
prospect of a Fenian invasion of Canada," he wrote, "has worn away to
almost nothing. The promptitude of our Volunteers – the report that
a few gunboats were coming out to patrol our inland waters – and the
virulence of the schism among the New York ringleaders – saved us.
The absurd fiasco at Eastport was a real gain to us, inasmuch as it first
established the fact, and made it evident all over the Fenian circles, that
the U.S. government would *not* connive, at any breach of the neutrality
laws."[65] His logic was impeccable.

Six days later the invasion began.

## CHAPTER TWELVE

# Those Men Deserve Death

## June 1866 – January 1867

"All is confusion and wild excitement," wrote George Clerk in his diary on 1 June 1866 on hearing the "startling news" that a Fenian army had captured Fort Erie and that Fenian regiments were gathering on the border of Canada East.[1] Earlier that morning, around a thousand men under the command of Colonel John O'Neill had crossed the Niagara River – a self-styled "Irish army of liberation," urging Irish Canadians to remember "seven centuries of British iniquity and Irish misery" and to "smite the tyrant where we can."[2] The following day, O'Neill's army intercepted and defeated a Canadian Volunteer force at the Battle of Limestone Ridge, near Ridgeway; among the dead were several students from the University of Toronto. But Fenian reinforcements from Buffalo were cut off by the American authorities, and some five thousand British and Canadian soldiers were pushing into the Niagara peninsula. O'Neill's men had little choice but to retreat. As they returned to the United States, they were immediately arrested for violating the country's neutrality laws.[3]

Some three hundred miles to the east, the Fenians in upstate New York and Vermont were running into similar problems; the number of recruits fell far short of Sweeny's expectations, and the US army was confiscating their arms. On 6 June, President Johnson issued a Neutrality Proclamation, condemning the Fenians for breaking American laws; that same day, Sweeny was arrested in St Albans. In a gesture of defiance, a thousand poorly armed men crossed the border into Canada and occupied several villages before retreating in the face of overwhelming British and Canadian forces. The Fenian raids, it appeared, had been an unmitigated failure; the Canadians had reacted with a rush of patriotism, the Americans had disrupted Fenian operations, and the Senate wing had apparently met the same dismal fate as the O'Mahony men at Eastport.[4]

Yet the situation for the Senate wing was not as bad as it seemed. The very fact that Fenian soldiers, fighting under the name of the Irish Republican Army, had entered Canada and beaten the forces of the Crown was a source of pride and inspiration for many Irish nationalists – and not just for the Fenians. In Ireland, Alexander Martin Sullivan's *Nation* was ecstatic at the news. Only the week before, Sullivan had indignantly denied McGee's charge that the paper was encouraging Sweeny and Roberts; now, it exulted that "for the first time in well nigh seventy years the red flag of England has gone down before the Irish green." Such news, it declared, "fills our people with tumultuous emotions impossible to describe, impossible to conceal." If these were the views of Ireland's leading constitutional nationalist newspaper, the reaction of revolutionary nationalists in the country must have been off the scale.[5]

In New York, Edward Archibald reported that "the excitement among the Irish caused by the news of a collision and bloodshed was everywhere manifest."[6] The "treachery" of the US government provided a useful scapegoat for failure, as did the defection of the O'Mahony wing. The "if only" syndrome kicked in: if only the US government had been true to its word and if only O'Mahony had supported the cause, there would now be two hundred thousand Fenians in Canada, O'Neill claimed.[7] "The great design has not been abandoned," Roberts told a large and enthusiastic crowd in New York; there was unfinished business at hand.[8]

———

McGee, along with the entire Canadian political and military establishment, had been taken completely by surprise. The effect was akin to being punched in the nose by someone who had always boasted that he would punch you in the nose. All McGee's familiar reactions were triggered: the Fenians were the "turbulent and the dissolute floating population" of American cities, deluded and ignorant men who had been "crammed full of falsehoods" about the oppression of Irish and

French Catholics in Canada, and who in no way represented Ireland. "A more wanton, immoral, unjustifiable assault never was made upon a peaceful people," he declared, "and the fate of pirates and freebooters is the only fate they can expect."

In the face of such aggression, Irish Canadian Catholics had a special obligation to take "a determined and conspicuous stand in the defence of this country," he wrote. "There must be no half-way work – there must be no milk-and-water lukewarmness on our part. All Canadians have their duties; but we have a duty additional to the duty of others. We are belied as a class, we are compromised as a class, by these scoundrels; and as a class we must vindicate our loyalty to the freest country left to Irishmen on the face of the globe." To fulfill this duty, his countrymen must enlist in the Volunteer corps, inform the authorities about Fenians in their midst, and support the suspension of habeas corpus.[9] Just as McGee himself had done, they must overcome "the hereditary Irish fear of the nickname 'informer'" and recognize that the suspension of habeas corpus was a regrettable but necessary response to the Fenian threat.[10] His message was amplified in the *Canadian Freeman*, where Moylan supported a petition for the suspension of habeas corpus while assuring his readers that the political influence of McGee and Macdonald would safeguard innocent Catholics against any abuses of power by hardline Protestants.[11]

In the immediate aftermath of Ridgeway, there was a real danger that simmering Protestant fears about Irish Catholic loyalty would boil over and that all Irish Catholics would be regarded as Fenians or Fenian sympathizers unless proved otherwise. Stories began to trickle into the press about instances of injustice – Irish Catholics being excluded from the militia, being imprisoned on suspicion of Fenianism, and being subjected to insults and discrimination. It is difficult to assess the extent to which this was happening; but by the end of June, George Clerk could write of a "social persecution of Catholics commencing in U. Canada," which he blamed entirely on the *Irish Canadian* and the Hibernian Benevolent Society.[12] Many years later, Bishop Lynch made the wildly exaggerated and wholly improbable claim that between 1866 and 1868, seven thousand Irish Catholics had been driven out of Toronto as a result of "Orange taunts" and job discrimination.[13]

Both McGee and Macdonald worked hard to prevent an anti-Catholic backlash. After habeas corpus was suspended on 8 June, Macdonald ensured that the Canadian government could veto the decisions of local magistrates and he issued a circular urging them to avoid "hasty and ill-judged arrests."[14] As well as endorsing these actions, McGee criticized "the absurd and mischievous attempts ... in some parts of Upper Canada ... to exclude Roman Catholics from the Volunteer and drill associations," and he insisted that the vast majority of loyal Irish Catholics should not be held accountable "for the sins of a few miserable individuals" who supported the invasions. "The man who would divide us by sectarian or sectional lines," he wrote, "– by creed or race or speech, – in the presence of the enemy is worse than the worst Fenian."[15]

Above all, and in keeping with his earlier writings, McGee drew a clear line between the loyal and the disloyal, the innocent and the guilty. The guilty were to be given no quarter. Fenianism was founded on the "diabolical principles" of hatred and revenge, cloaked in the language of liberty, equality, and fraternity. No compromise, no equivocation, and no rest were possible in the face of such a movement. "I have thought it a duty I owe to Canada, and I may add my duty to Ireland, and to Irishmen at home and abroad, wherever a channel of access to them was open to me, to exhibit the folly, the falsehood and the criminality of this organization," he declared. "I have diagnosed it as epidemic disease ... I had rather err, for my part, on the side of activity, than on the side of sluggishness and inaction."[16]

One manifestation of this was his attitude to the Fenians who had been taken prisoner after the raids – sixty-five of them in Toronto and another sixteen in Canada East.[17] "Some examples must be made here," he told Lord Wodehouse, "but our intention is to inflict only the *minimum* of capital punishment, sentencing the rank and file to hard labor, probably upon those permanent earthworks, opposite Montreal, so strongly recommended by Colonel Jervois, in his reports on the defence of this country."[18] Such views – which were shared by the cabinet – immediately set off alarm bells in British government circles;

McGee's minimum went well beyond their maximum. In Washington, Frederick Bruce informed Lord Clarendon, the foreign secretary, that any executions would produce a massive Fenian reaction and would give new power to Irish American republicanism. It was far better, in his opinion, to play the "misguided dupes" card and adopt a policy of leniency – and this was the policy that eventually prevailed.[19]

Although McGee came to accept this position on pragmatic grounds, he never deviated from his belief that capital punishment was a just response to the Fenian invasion. In what George Brown privately described as "a very fine speech" in Parliament, McGee described the Fenian Brotherhood as "an aggregate of individual murderers banded together for wholesale murder," and declared that they could be "put to death as common enemies of all mankind."[20] When a Catholic priest asked him to intercede on behalf of one of the Fenian prisoners, Terence McDonald, McGee refused point blank. "The person for whom you ask my intercession was one of those who sought out our people, on our soil, and maimed and slew as many as they could," he wrote; "and those who sent them have exulted in the exploit." Men such as McDonald must face the consequences of their actions; they would receive a fair trial in Canada, "but to whatever punishment the law hands him over, no word of mine can ever be spoken in mitigation; not even, under these circumstances, if he were my own brother. I grieve that I must deny you; but so it is."[21] In the event, McDonald did receive a fair trial – and was acquitted.[22]

After the first round of trials had been completed that autumn, seven men were found guilty and sentenced to death. Among them was a Catholic priest, Father John McMahon; in contrast, a Protestant minister, David Lumsden, was among those who were acquitted – a decision which, as McGee put it, "gave a great handle" to the Fenians.[23] For many Irish Catholics in Canada, far beyond Fenian circles, this was a clear-cut example of Protestant bigotry at work.[24] Privately, McGee had very good information that McMahon had "openly aided and abetted Fenianism."[25] But he thought that the evidence against Lumsden was equally strong and that justice had not been served. This remains an open question. In his study of the Fenian trials, R. Blake Brown concluded that it was Lumsden's more impressive defence rather than religious prejudice that was the crucial factor.[26] Still, the optics were bad, and it is not surprising that McGee subsequently called on the government to reconsider McMahon's case.[27]

From New York, the Fenian leadership viewed the trials with public indignation and private opportunism. According to one well-placed informer, William Roberts wanted the death sentences to be carried out on the grounds that the executions would breathe new life into the brotherhood.[28] If this was indeed Roberts's view, he would be disappointed; immediately after the sentences, the Canadian government, including McGee, agreed that the sentences should be commuted.[29]

Still, McGee felt that the guilty parties had got off lightly. "Those men deserve death," he declared at an Irish concert in Montreal, amid hisses from a section of the audience. "I repeat deliberately those men deserve death," he said, walking towards the footlights; "but, I will add, that the spirit of our times is opposed to the infliction of capital punishment where any other punishment can reach the case, and in these cases I hope it may be possible to temper justice with mercy. As to that handful who hissed just now in the far corner, if I had not stood between them and the machinations of these men and their emissaries; if I had not stood between them and the consequences of their criminal sympathies, some of them would be sharing to-day the fate of these fairly tried and justly condemned men." As the shock waves pulsed through the audience, McGee held up his right hand: 'Yes! I have held in that hand the evidences of your criminal folly, and I could put some of you where you could not hiss or hear much; but you were not worth prosecuting; you may be worth watching, and there are those among yourselves, I can tell you, as there were among the Toronto Fenians, who are keeping a good account of all your ingoings and outcomings."[30]

Such words only intensified Fenian anger and hostility – which were at a high enough pitch before Ridgeway. Feelings were particularly strong in Montreal, where McGee had been denounced as a "prostituted pile of human flesh"; there were also reports that some members of the brotherhood had been planning to assassinate him during the invasion.[31] In New York, the *Irish American* condemned McGee's "blood-thirsty spirit in reference to the Fenian prisoners" and threatened retaliation. "The Irish people," it declared (that phrase again), would "wreak upon the murderers of their brothers a vengeance that, in deeper terror, will blot out the horror of their fate."[32]

---

While the Fenian reaction was entirely predictable, McGee's speech at the Montreal Irish concert drew fire from a totally unexpected quarter – George Brown's *Globe*. On 23 November the paper published a letter from "An Englishman" that twisted McGee's words into a pro-Fenian statement – quite a feat, in the circumstances. According to the letter, McGee had said that "his blood ran cold in his veins" upon learning that his fellow Irishmen were to be hanged. These words, contended "An Englishman," left "a false, injurious, and most erroneous impression on his countrymen – as tending to make them question the justice of our laws." The letter also seized on McGee's comment that he had evidence that could put his hecklers behind bars; if that was the case, why had not McGee taken that evidence to the authorities? By the time he had finished, "An Englishman" had presented McGee as sympathizing with the men who received the death sentence, as encouraging Irish disrespect for Canadian laws, and as sheltering the Fenians by withholding information against them.[33]

The charge was utterly bizarre; but what made it even worse was the fact that Brown had published it in his newspaper. McGee had been fighting Fenianism with all his power in the face of death threats and intimidation from "a secret enemy who never sleeps" – and now, thrown in his face by a man he had long considered a friend and colleague, was this accusation that he was "untrue to Canada on the subject of Fenianism." His earlier alliance with Brown, their continuing good relations and mutual respect after the parting of their political ways, their cooperation in the cause of Confederation – all this now counted for nothing. While McGee was leading the battle against Fenianism, Brown had attacked him from behind. "Having done so – having sought me out as an opponent – having cancelled all past obligations by your own act – I now, take you up as an undisguised enemy," McGee wrote. "In the presence of the people of Canada, especially the people of Upper Canada, whose name you so often invoke and abuse, I say and I shall maintain, that your conduct of which I complain is not that of an honest man."[34]

From this point, there was no turning back; the two men never exchanged a civil word again. McGee pointed out that the comments of "An Englishman" were "exactly the opposite of the truth," and demanded that Brown reveal the name of the writer.[35] Brown stood by the letter, adding that McGee's threats against his hecklers were unbecoming of a cabinet minister, and mocking McGee for presenting himself as an anti-Fenian martyr. Nor would Brown divulge the identity of "An Englishman" – although, as it turned out, the writer had given him a false name and address. McGee reckoned that the letter actually emanated from the Fenians in Montreal, and he was probably right. A possible candidate was W.B. Linehan, one of the founders of Montreal's Hibernian Society, a correspondent for the *Irish Canadian*, and an officer in the St Patrick's Society. He was definitely not English.[36]

Why did Brown take such a hostile position towards McGee? In truth, it had little to do with McGee's attack on Fenianism; after all, Brown had privately praised McGee's speech in Parliament describing the Fenians as a gang of murderers. The answer lay in Canadian politics, and specifically in Brown's growing estrangement from the Liberal-Conservative members of the coalition government. As we have seen, Brown had resigned from the coalition the previous December. During the parliamentary session following the Fenian raids, the partisan spirit that he had kept under restraint in the cause of Confederation returned in full force.

Macdonald, not McGee, was the principal target. This was partly because Macdonald had not fulfilled his promise to retract his earlier attacks on Brown and partly because Macdonald spent much of the parliamentary session in an alcoholic stupour. In Brown's view, the captain of the ship was drunk in charge, with the result that the militia was in a state of disarray and the government had missed the opportunity to obtain final British approval for Confederation. The longer the government waited before sending a delegation to London, the greater the danger that the whole deal would unravel – especially in the context of anti-confederation sentiment in Nova Scotia, where Charles Tupper could not postpone an election indefinitely. When the delegates were finally selected, Brown was not among them. According to McGee, Brown's "fury" and "savagery" towards Macdonald stemmed from a sense of thwarted ambition.[37]

Whether or not this was the case, Brown viewed McGee as being guilty by association with Macdonald – not least because McGee was aiding and abetting Macdonald in the relentless consumption of alcohol. "The last Session of the last Parliament of Canada," McGee told Moylan, "was such a scene of re-Union and general jollification, that I was nearly *hors d'combats*" ("jollification" being a nineteenth-century euphemism for serious drinking).[38] Not only that, but McGee was publicly defending Macdonald against Brown's criticisms. At a banquet in Kingston, McGee praised Macdonald's work as minister of militia, arguing that his "activity, sagacity and firmness" had prevented a Fenian raid in March and had contributed towards the failure of the raid in June; and he commended Macdonald for playing the leading role at the Quebec Conference on Confederation "while some of those who are now crying out so loudly as to his inattention to public business never enriched our conference with an idea, a suggestion or a proposition" – a clear hit at Brown.[39] In response, the *Globe* contended that McGee was so drunk himself that he was probably under the table during most of the Quebec Conference and was therefore in no position to make any comments on who drew up the resolutions.[40]

---

One of the resolutions for which McGee was definitely above the table was that on education – an issue that resurfaced during the parliamentary session of 1866 and did nothing to improve relations between McGee and Brown. Here, it is necessary to recall three things: in 1863, McGee had accepted the Scott Act as a final settlement of the schools question; the following year, at the Quebec Conference, he ensured that the federal government would protect pre-Confederation educational rights; shortly afterwards, Protestants in Canada East campaigned for greater control over their school system, with the result that Catholics in Canada West were pressing for educational parity. Now, in Parliament, the new demands came up for debate. On 31 July, Hector Langevin, the solicitor general, brought in a government-supported bill to improve Protestant school rights in Canada East; hard on its heels, Robert Bell, a Presbyterian politician from Canada West, moved to introduce a private member's bill that would provide equal treatment for the Catholic minority in his part of the province.

For McGee, as for Bell, this was a basic question of equity and fair play; sauce for the goose was sauce for the gander. For Brown and the vast majority of Canada West politicians, however, there was no equivalence between the sectarian schools of the Catholic Church and the non-denominational schools throughout the province; in their view, Bell's bill was an attempt to undermine the non-sectarian state system in Canada West under the guise of religious tolerance. "We will fight this Bill in every possible way that Parliamentary rules will permit," declared Brown. McGee countered that the bill should be accepted or rejected on its own merits; to defeat it through parliamentary technicalities, as Brown proposed, would only add insult to injury and inflame religious tensions in the province. Either way, Canada West would not accept any changes to the existing educational arrangements – arrangements which, Brown noted, McGee had previously accepted as "a final settlement."[41] As the debate became increasingly heated, one thing was clear: If the majority in Canada West rejected Bell's bill, the majority in Canada East would withdraw their support for Langevin's bill. The result would be a return to the status quo, the frustration of rising expectations, and a heightened sense of insecurity among religious minorities on the eve of Confederation.

To defuse the situation, the government decided to drop Langevin's bill and bring the parliamentary session to a close. "The minority in both Upper and Lower Canada," Macdonald said, "will be obliged to throw themselves on the justice and generosity of the majority." Alexander Galt, who had promised that Protestant educational rights in Canada East would be strengthened before Confederation, resigned from the cabinet. McGee was left to make the best of a bad situation. "I will frankly tell you that I greatly feared the ignorant and despotic tone taken by the Upper Canada Majority on the late Separate School discussion in the House of Assembly would have had a very bad effect," he said a few weeks later; but the educational rights of Catholics in Canada West were still much better than those in Massachusetts or

New York, and Catholics could take some consolation from the fact that Macdonald had supported Bell's bill.[42] Left unspoken was another possibility – that the forthcoming conference in London on the British North America Act might be able to improve minority educational rights before Confederation went into effect.

---

McGee fully expected to be part of that conference. At the end of August, he told Moylan that he had been invited to participate in the proceedings.[43] A month later, though, he learned that he had been excluded from the delegation – a decision that took him completely by surprise and left him in a state of shock. Many years later, reflecting on McGee's career, Moylan identified "two mysteries" that had never been satisfactorily explained; one concerned the circumstances of his assassination, and the other was his exclusion from the London Conference – a decision that left Irish Canadian Catholics without any representation and that "amazed" the Catholic bishops, clergy, and laity.[44]

One possible answer for his exclusion was that McGee was the victim of personal payback for privately attempting to have Macdonald replaced as minister of militia. At Caledonia Springs, recovering from the alcoholic excesses of the parliamentary session, McGee had begun a sober assessment of the state of Canadian defences. Contrary to his public praise for Macdonald's role in the defence of Canada, he believed that the militia was badly organized and excessively expensive, and he had come to the conclusion that Galt could provide more effective leadership than Macdonald. After putting his proposal to Governor General Monck, to Narcisse Belleau – who had become leader of the government on Taché's death – and to Galt himself, McGee informed Macdonald about his concerns; it was not his style to stab people in the back.[45]

Although Macdonald's reaction is unknown, it is safe to assume that he was not amused. At the very time that the *Globe* was hammering Macdonald for being too drunk to defend the country, here was McGee, his drinking companion, joining in the criticism and trying to have him ousted from his job.[46] The possibility that McGee's concern may have been valid was beside the point; indeed, it probably sharpened the point. Before Macdonald learned about this, McGee was part of the delegation; afterwards, McGee was shut out from the delegation. It seemed both a punishment and a warning: If ever you cross me, you will suffer the consequences.

On the other hand, Macdonald was the consummate Machiavellian politician, who would make a deal with just about anyone who would advance his party. It is unlikely that he would risk alienating McGee, the Catholic Church, and the loyal Irish Catholic laity simply for the sake of a personal grudge – although if any such grudge operated in conjunction with other political considerations, it might assume more significance. This takes us to a second explanation, which gained some currency towards the end of the year – the possibility that the British government did not want McGee in the delegation owing to his remarks at the Provincial Exhibition in Toronto in September.[47] During his speech, McGee had compared Canadian Confederation with the American Revolution; the Americans, he said, had broken with the British Empire in a just cause, and now the Canadians were following in their footsteps.[48] One can see why this would have irritated many (but by no means all) British politicians. Yet McGee's comments drew no press reactions at the time, and there is no paper trail connecting the British government with McGee's exclusion.[49]

A third possibility is that McGee's position on educational parity for religious minorities was too hot to handle; rather than risking a renewed flare-up of sectional and religious tensions, Macdonald preferred to remove McGee from the scene. In the view of Charles Murphy, the early-twentieth-century Liberal cabinet minister, Macdonald and Galt "conspired to deprive the Roman Catholics of denominational schools" by altering the wording of McGee's Quebec Resolution on education.[50] Although McGee's resolution guaranteed existing minority educational rights and privileges in Canada, it did not apply to the Maritimes. As the delegates grappled with the issue, they concluded that only educational rights and privileges that had already been established "by law" would be protected under Confederation. This did not change the situation in Canada, where the educational system had indeed been established by law. But it was a different matter in Nova Scotia, where existing minority educational rights and privileges were established by custom and usage, rather than by law. It would also be a different matter in new provinces, such as Manitoba, where no existing laws applied.[51]

In effect, denominational schools outside much of Canada had been cut adrift. There is no evidence that Macdonald and Galt conspired to reach this result before they left Canada, and the new educational resolution may well have been the product of extensive negotiations at the London Conference. But McGee would have fought strenuously against any such alteration to his original resolution – and Macdonald must have been acutely aware of the fact. If McGee was likely to get in the way of a compromise resolution, it made sense to get him out of the way.

This is the most likely answer to Moylan's "mystery" – although Macdonald's anger at McGee's attempt to have him replaced as minister of militia may well have played a subordinate role. Nevertheless, there is another more general explanation for McGee's exclusion – the fact that his political stock was falling within Irish Catholic Canada. "If you want Irish Catholic support," Joseph-Élie Thibaudeau had told George Brown eight years earlier, "appoint McGee."[52] Now it was no longer clear how much Irish Catholic support McGee could command. Irish Catholics were divided between Fenians and their sympathizers, at one pole, and clerically supported loyalists at the other, with a large number of ambivalent moderates in the middle. McGee's ferocious attacks on the Fenians went down very well with unequivocal Catholic loyalists and their Protestant counterparts. But they had alienated many of his compatriots, for whom McGee spent far too much time exhorting the Catholic victims of Protestant prejudice to remain loyal, and not nearly enough time admonishing their Protestant victimizers.[53] The more that McGee lost Irish Catholic support, the less was his value to the government – something that his principal ally in Toronto, James Moylan, also experienced.[54] In this respect, McGee's efforts to save Canada from Fenianism wound up weakening his political power and influence within the country.

The official reason for McGee's exclusion was that he was needed at home to ensure that the cabinet had a quorum in the event of an emergency. He was told that at the end of the year, one of the Canadian delegates would return to Ottawa, and McGee could take his place in the negotiations.[55] There was only one kind of emergency that was likely to arise: a renewed Fenian invasion attempt. In July and August, intelligence reports from McMicken's detectives indicated that the Fenians were regrouping, and there were signs that another invasion was being prepared.[56] George Brown was sufficiently worried that he advised his wife to hasten her plans to spend the summer in Scotland, and McGee sounded out his old friend James Sadlier in New York about the probability of another Fenian raid.[57]

These concerns were heightened by the fact that many American politicians were giving new encouragement to the Fenians.[58] With elections coming up in the autumn, and with Radical Republicans and Democrats fighting for control of Congress, both parties began a bidding war for the Irish vote – and, rightly or wrongly, the "Irish vote" was associated with the Fenian Brotherhood. Only three weeks after Ridgeway, William Roberts was feted in Washington and invited to the floor of the House of Representatives. In July, the prominent Radical Republican and former nativist Nathaniel P. Banks, who supported the annexation of Canada to the United States, introduced a bill to revise America's neutrality laws. It was, in the view of a British government spy, "virtually a Bill to permit the Fenians to attack Canada and to make war on Great Britain."[59] And it was passed unanimously in the House of Representatives – though, as Goldwin Smith pointed out, its supporters knew that it would fail in the Senate. Beneath the public attempt to win the "Irish vote" lay the private understanding that the neutrality laws would remained unchanged.[60] Nevertheless, the Fenians took heart from these developments. "Their leaders are set free without any charge against them," reported the *Irishman*. "They visit Congress and are received with as much courtesy and state as if they were illustrious foreigners from Russia and Japan ... Altogether the picture has been reversed from the dark side to the bright; and the Fenians are jubilant again."[61]

Surveying all this, McGee wrote of the "desperate struggle now going on between the remaining elements of Conservatism in the Federal Government and the leading demagogues, native and naturalized" – the same kind of struggle that he had fought and lost during his years in the United States.[62] Over the summer, he believed, "a formidable American Irish combination" of annexationists and Fenians had been getting the upper hand. Their strategy was to sustain pressure on the border, creating a climate of fear and uncertainty, and driving up the costs of defence beyond the country's capacity to pay. In these circumstances, a combination of insecurity, high taxes, and bankruptcy would produce an annexationist party within Canada and pave the way for union with the United States. With congressional elections coming up in October and November, he added, the Fenians might well seize the opportunity to launch a "second and more serious invasion of Canada." The best way to counter this was for Britain to take a more active and energetic role in defending the country – a move that was entirely justifiable, given that Canada was paying the price for an imperial issue not of its own making.[63]

Meanwhile, the American Fenians continued to assert their presence near the Canadian border. In Rochester they organized a dramatic re-enactment of the Battle of Ridgeway, in which the Queen's Own Rifles fought bravely and briefly before being comprehensively clobbered by the Irish Republican Army; afterwards, the "downcast and sorrowing 'Queen's Own' betook themselves to the consolation of drowning their grief ... in friendly potations with their late adversaries."[64] The Fenians received a further boost in September, when President Johnson returned all the arms that had been seized after Ridgeway. Yet for all this, the Senate wing lacked the money and materiel to synchronize a second invasion attempt with the congressional elections. As it turned out, the Republicans did so well in those elections that they no longer needed Irish support; without an American bidding war, the Fenians began to lose their political leverage in the United States – at least for the time being.[65] By the end of the year, when McGee was supposed to leave Canada for England, the immediate threat had passed.

———·———

Within Canada, the Fenian movement proved remarkably resilient in the aftermath of Ridgeway. Some local leaders, such as Denis C. Feely, escaped to the United States; most, however, dug in their heels, and many became radicalized by the events of the summer. The invasion attempt demonstrated that ideas had been translated into action, that American Fenians were serious about liberating Canada, and that the forces of the Crown could be beaten; the task ahead was to recruit more members and prepare for the next invasion, which surely would come. Those who had supported the O'Mahony wing took heart from the fact that Michael Murphy and five of his fellow Fenians broke out of Cornwall jail in September and made it safely across the border.[66] Fenians from both factions, along with many other Irish Catholics, were incensed by the contrasting fates of the Catholic priest John McMahon and the Protestant minister David Lumsden during the Toronto trials. More generally, heightened ethnoreligious tensions could make Murphy's language of defiance more attractive than McGee's language of loyalty.

In Montreal, the Fenians continued their efforts to recruit more members into the St Patrick's Society, which was increasingly becoming a focus of anti-McGee sentiment. McGee's Wexford speech, his earlier criticisms of Devlin, and his hard line on the prisoners had angered many of his countrymen, including large numbers who were not Fenians. During the late summer and autumn, much of this anger found a new focus in the form of the Felix Prior case. After a night of drinking, Prior had climbed through the window of the wrong house, where he was mistaken for a burglar and shot dead. Prior was an Irishman; the man who shot him was English. After the coroner's jury returned a verdict of justifiable homicide, there was a sense of outrage among many of the city's Irish Catholics, who felt that this was yet another example of Protestant prejudice. Prior's funeral procession was a mile long; the St Patrick's Society made him a posthumous member and demanded a full public inquiry.[67]

McGee would have none of it. In two anonymous letters in the *Montreal Gazette*, he insisted that "national societies" had no business interfering in the administration of justice; once that precedent was established, there was no telling where it might end.[68] Not surprisingly, the St Patrick's Society insisted that it had every right to seek justice for Irish Canadians, and it resolved that the "statements made in those letters were false and groundless and of a character calculated to injure this society most seriously."[69] Patrick O'Meara, the Fenian

St Patrick's Hall, Montreal. An impressive symbol of the Irish Catholic presence in Montreal, St Patrick's Hall was modelled on Cormac's Chapel in
Cashel. In August 1866, McGee was a member of the association that successfully petitioned the legislature to incorporate the hall. The following month,
his enemies in the St Patrick's Society were strong enough to exclude him
from the board of directors. The cornerstone was laid in 1867; five years later,
in 1872, the building was destroyed by fire. (NPA, McCord Museum)


leader who was now the society's recording secretary, demanded to
know the identity of the author; it is a safe bet that everyone realized
it was McGee.[70] Revenge was not long in coming. At a meeting of the
stockholders of the proposed St Patrick's Hall, there were hisses when
McGee's name was mentioned. After a "long and acrimonious" debate
that involved some four hundred people and stretched into the early
hours of the morning, McGee was removed from the list of directors; it
was, as the *Irish American* reported, "a bad omen for his re-election for
Montreal."[71]

Characteristically, McGee stood his ground. "It is not always an easy task, nor always a pleasant position, to stand against the exaggerated pretensions of classes and creeds, in our mixed population," he said during a public dinner the following month. "To do so, indeed, is the statesman's duty – is what best distinguishes the statesman from the demagogue – but it is not always either an easy or a pleasant duty to perform. I had thought we had got the demon of class discord pretty well laid in our own city, till I saw a crazed attempt to make a national question out of a late deplorable homicide, to coin the blood of a slaughtered country-man into the small currency of political intrigue."[72] When O'Meara and W.B. Linehan demanded that McGee appear before the society to explain himself, he refused on a point of principle; the society, he replied, had no right to call its members to account for comments they had made outside its meetings.[73] In response, a majority of members voted to censure McGee for his "unfounded and unjust remarks." Later in the meeting, thirty more people were proposed for membership in the society, including Patrick Doody, James Kinsella, and Michael Enright. All three were part of a group of Fenians centred at Scanlan's tavern and were good friends with a man who was developing an obsessive hatred towards McGee – a tailor by the name of Patrick James Whelan.[74]

While McGee was fighting these battles at home, his colleagues were en route to London for the conference on Confederation, which began in early December. His sense of frustration grew with every week. According to his fellow cabinet minister Alexander Campbell, McGee was "disgusted" by his exclusion from the delegation and tried to cover himself by spreading false stories about the reasons why he had to remain in Canada.[75] "I am only anxious to reach London before the Bill is introduced," McGee told Macdonald on 19 December, "in order to save my promises to my friends."[76] His anxiety increased as December stretched into January without any word from London; the longer the delay, the greater the damage to his political reputation. Unless he heard something soon, the only reasonable conclusion would be that his colleagues now regarded him as being superfluous to requirements.[77]

He was thrown a lifeline towards the end of January and arrived in London just as the final draft of the Confederation bill was being completed. McGee had missed everything – the negotiations over education, over federal and provincial powers, and over the character of the Senate. His presence when the bill moved through the House of Commons and House of Lords enabled him to save some face, but his exclusion from the London Conference indicated that he was no longer an indispensable ally of the Conservatives, just as his ejection from the directors of St Patrick's Hall indicated that he was alienating many of his constituents. The arc of his career was changing in 1866, and the curve was beginning to turn downwards.

Shortly before he left for London, McGee was invited to speak to the Irish Protestant Benevolent Society in Montreal. The fact that that a Protestant Irish society would invite a Catholic to speak should serve as a model and example for Ireland, he said. "No doubt I would be severely handled by the demagogues and by some newspapers, but I am getting used to that sort of thing now, although in my early days such attacks made me feel uneasy in my seat. It reminds me of the story of the Englishman and Irishman who were going to execution ... The Englishman was expressing his fear of the prospect of the gallows, when the Irishman said what did it matter, it would soon be over. 'Ah,' said the Englishman, 'that's very well, I will only be hung once, but you Irishmen are accustomed to be hanged.' I am getting accustomed to all these attacks."[78] Accustomed to the attacks he may have been, but that did not lessen their impact.

## CHAPTER THIRTEEN

# Moral Courage
## February – September 1867

When McGee finally arrived in London, the Irish Republican Brotherhood was finalizing its plans for the much-anticipated and much-postponed rising in Ireland. The Fenian movement, commented the Dublin spymaster Robert Anderson, had "sunk to a very low ebb" in America but was becoming a serious "cause of alarm" at home; as a result, Irish detectives in the United States were being called back for duties in Ireland.[1] In New York, the O'Mahony wing had lurched through a series of leadership crises; James Stephens, on the run from Ireland, had replaced O'Mahony after the Eastport fiasco but was himself deposed by a more militant faction led by Tom Kelly. According to Frank Millen, a Fenian general who doubled as a British informer, Kelly was "a much more dangerous man than Stephens, & had expressed his determination, if rebellion failed, to have leading men who opposed it assassinated."[2] Kelly's correspondence confirms this assessment. Dismissing Stephens as "Little Baldy," he demanded total allegiance from his countrymen: "It is better for the Irishman who does not now throw in all he has got, or himself, that he never was born," Kelly wrote. "He is a renegade, – an imposter, – a traitor. Show him no quarter."[3]

While McGee crossed the Atlantic to support Confederation in Canada, Kelly and about fifty leading Fenians were sailing from New York to launch a revolution in Ireland. The insurrection was planned for mid-February; the main action was to take place in and around Dublin, with multiple risings elsewhere in Ireland and diversionary attacks in Britain to tie down the troops. After arriving in England, though, Kelly decided to wait until early March – only to run into the opposition of a rival faction led by John McCafferty, who insisted upon immediate action. Taking the initiative, McCafferty brought hundreds of Fenians to Chester Castle in the northwest of England, with plans to seize arms and ammunition, get to Ireland, and trigger the revolution. Any remote chance that this might have worked was destroyed when an informer, John Corydon, alerted the authorities. Troops were rushed into the region, the revolutionaries abandoned the operation, and McCafferty was captured shortly afterwards. Meanwhile, in County Kerry, some two hundred Fenians launched their own rising in the mistaken belief that Kelly's original timetable was still in place; acting in isolation and confronted by superior forces, they quickly melted back into the general population.[4] One of their leaders was the Toronto Fenian and founding member of the Hibernian Benevolent Society, Murtagh Moriarty, who had been arrested the previous year en route to join the Fenians in Eastport and who, along with Michael Murphy, had broken out of prison and escaped to New York.[5]

When Kelly's insurrection did take place, on 5 March, it fared no better. Corydon supplied the government with detailed information about the plans, which were hardly likely to succeed in any case, given the power imbalance between the forces of the Crown and the revolutionaries. But there was significant working-class support in Dublin for the Fenians, and about a thousand men marched through blinding sleet and snow to the rallying point in Tallaght, southwest of the city.[6] One of marchers was Joseph Whelan, whose public house in Marlborough Street was a well-known Fenian meeting place; he was a man of strong views who entertained his customers with revolutionary songs and swore soldiers into the Irish Republican Brotherhood. After the rising collapsed, he reportedly said that "the Fenians should have murdered every one who did not assist them particularly the magistrates and others in authority."[7] Arrested and found guilty of "complicity in the Fenian Conspiracy," Whelan spent close to a year in jail before being released on condition that he leave for America.[8] Instead, he travelled to Canada, the home of his brother Patrick James.

Against this background, but before the rising of March, McGee penned a long letter about transatlantic Fenianism to Benjamin Disraeli, the chancellor of the exchequer and leader of the House of Commons in Lord Derby's minority Conservative government. Most Irish

Americans, McGee wrote, were "passionate and prejudiced ... against everything English," and their "immense mass of votes" gave them considerable political power. In the event of an Anglo-American conflict, up to two hundred thousand Irishmen would enlist in the United States army; this number would become even higher as Irish immigration increased. "Their deep-rooted and dangerous, hostility to England, and her Provinces in North America," he argued, "can only be mitigated, or extinguished, by measures to be taken, by the Imperial Government, in Ireland." Far-reaching reform in Ireland would not only be beneficial for its own sake; it would also undermine support for international revolutionary republicanism.

The root of the problem, then, lay in Ireland, not the United States. "What is first wanted among the Irish at home," McGee asserted, "is *confidence in the good intentions of Imperial Statesmen*. If this confidence could be established even by slow degrees, it would almost immediately infect the Irish in England's foreign possessions, in the English and Scotch cities where they are not without force, and it would gradually disarm, if not convert Irish-American hostility, in the U. States." The best way to create this confidence would be to establish a royal commission consisting of "seven or nine Irishmen, of the first character; men resident all their lives in the country; all whose interests were and are there; men of local popularity, so that the confidence felt in the men, might be, by a natural effect, transformed to the Imperial Government." By doing this, and by ensuring that "none but Irishmen should be connected with the Commission," the government would be demonstrating its goodwill and laying the foundation for enlightened imperial legislation and harmonious Anglo-Irish relations.[9]

There is no record of Disraeli's reply, but there is some evidence that the government was willing to consider a royal commission on the state of Ireland, although not necessarily along McGee's all-Irish lines.[10] Such a strategy could, however, have created more difficulties than it resolved. When it came to the key issues of land reform, the disestablishment of the Church of Ireland, and a state-funded Catholic university, there were limits beyond which Derby's government would not move. On land reform, its proposed bill to give tenants compensation for improvement to their farms fell far short of long-standing

demands for fixity of tenure and fair rents.[11] Instead of supporting disestablishment, the government floated the idea of concurrent endow-
ment for both the Catholic and Protestant churches – a position that
the hierarchy unequivocally rejected. And there was no way that a
government committed to mixed education would support a Catholic
university.[12] All this meant that McGee's proposed royal commission
could result in the frustration of rising expectations and make the political situation worse rather than better. In the end, the government did
not act on his advice.

During his time in London, McGee attended the parliamentary discussions that culminated in the British North America Act, which
was passed in early March.[13] It was twenty-one years since he had
been the parliamentary reporter for the O'Connellite *Freeman's Journal*, writing acerbic, insightful, humorous, and sometimes sympathetic
articles about the debates and making scathing comments about the
city of London and its inhabitants.[14] Now, as a cabinet minister in the
Canadian government, he observed the routine, matter-of-fact way
in which the bill moved through its final stages. There was an air of
anticlimax about it all; British North America appeared as a sideshow
while the Derby government's controversial Reform Bill occupied the
centre stage. The Canadian delegates had indeed triumphed, but they
were left with a slightly bad taste in their mouths. Macdonald later remarked that the British North America Act was treated as "a private
bill uniting two or three English parishes," and Galt was left with the
strong feeling that British politicians "want to get rid of us." There was
nothing here to change McGee's view that the great men of England
treated British North America as a low card in a game of whist.[15]

Nevertheless, it must have been a great moment after all the complex
negotiations, fierce debates, backroom deals, electoral manipulations,
and extensive speeches, setbacks, and victories over the previous three
years, and McGee had good reason to feel deeply satisfied. Canada, he
believed, had shaken off its colonial status and could now move forward as an ally rather than a dependency of Britain. "Theoretically,

it is true, the work is done," he told Macdonald; "but, practically, it is only beginning."[16]

Now that the foundations had been laid, the construction must begin. The Pacific West should be incorporated into Confederation as soon as possible to counter the American attempt to "out-flank our fellow-countrymen" following the purchase of Alaska from Russia. McGee then set out four major tasks that lay ahead, all of which were rooted in his original vision of Canadian nationalism. More immigrants must be attracted to Canada – a measure that could be achieved by establishing public works and a protective tariff. The entire population must be armed, as a deterrent against potential American aggression. Provincial majorities must respect minority religious educational rights, and religious minorities should only exert their right of appeal to the federal government when fundamental matters of justice were at stake. Above all, Canadians must become a united people, at one in their rejection of Fenianism and the *"sectarian animosity"* that McGee associated with Brown and the Reformers. All these issues, he pledged, would be his priorities in the Dominion of Canada's first Parliament.[17]

---

Before returning to Canada, though, McGee had pressing business at hand in Rome and Paris. His journey to Rome was occasioned by a major religious conflict that had broken out in Montreal the previous year. In November, Bishop Bourget had announced his intention to reorganize the city's parishes; if his plans were implemented, St Patrick's Church would no longer be an exclusively Irish centre of worship, and Irish Canadians would become minorities in all the city's parishes. Within Irish Catholic Montreal, there was total communal resistance. Father Dowd organized a petition of protest against his own bishop and quickly gathered six thousand signatures. Bourget was unmoved; the protest, he said, was "insufficient," and Irish fears that they would be swamped by the French were completely irrational and unreasonable. Had not French priests and nuns sacrificed themselves to help the Irish – those "unfortunate people" – during the famine? Given this history, how could anyone argue that the French were anti-

Irish? Enough was enough; the Irish should remember their duty to be "humbly submissive" to their bishop and should accept the fact that the reorganization was going ahead.[18]

Nothing could have been better calculated to inflame the situation; employing the famine as an argument against the protestors was deeply offensive to Irish sensibilities. McGee had consistently rejected stereotypes of the Irish as victims, and had long regarded Bourget as a French Canadian nativist.[19] Now, in conjunction with a committee of the St Patrick's congregation, he wrote a defiant reply to Bourget's arguments: "Your Lordship will not allow us to forget our sad destiny," he wrote. "The memory of all past afflictions must be kept fresh; and all the charities of which we have been the sad recipients, must be turned into an argument to force us to surrender, in silence, all the advantages of our present altered condition." If Bourget proceeded with his plans, McGee argued, they would "likely lead to bloodshed, and consequently, to a domestic war between Irish and Canadian Catholics throughout the city." "We state this deliberately," he told the bishop, "not as a menace but as a dutiful warning. We know pretty well how far the influence of our priests may go. In this matter it would be powerless."[20]

There was, of course, a thin line between a warning and a menace. But Bourget stood his ground and demanded that the parishioners respect his authority. In response, McGee and his fellow committee members took Father Dowd's petition to Archbishop Baillargeon of Quebec, who agreed to send the document to the papal authorities.[21] Since McGee was already going to Europe, he decided to visit the Vatican and raise the matter directly with Pope Pius IX. After the British North America bill had made its way through Parliament, he set out for Rome.

He arrived on 16 March, which must have been one of the greatest days of his life: visiting St Peter's, hearing mass at the Irish college, dining with cardinals, and driving out to San Pietro in Montorio, where he "knelt on the graves of the O'Neills and O'Donnells."[22] That evening, in a contemplative mood, he wrote his poem "Sunset on the Corso, at Rome," contrasting the promise, strife, and sorrow of this world with the prospect of eternal life embodied in the Eternal City.[23]

The following week, he and his fellow Montreal politician Thomas Ryan had an audience with the Pope and presented their case against Bourget's plans.[24] "We, of course, got no positive assurance as to the decision likely to be reached at Rome," he told Bishop Horan, "but, personally, we had great reason to be satisfied, and gratified, with our reception."[25] Although their visit had no immediate effect, it did keep the issue alive. To resolve the problem, the Vatican subsequently appointed the new archbishop of Quebec, Elzéar-Alexandre Taschereau, as a mediator, with the result that Bourget's plans were overturned in 1873. It was a victory for McGee, albeit a posthumous one.[26]

From Rome, McGee travelled to Paris for the Universal Exposition that opened in April – the largest and most spectacular international exhibition ever held, which attracted some fifty thousand exhibitors and more than nine million visitors over the next seven months. Here was a glorious opportunity for Canada, on the cusp of Confederation, to win international recognition and respect. The previous October, McGee's department had been allocated $50,000 for the Canadian display, with most of the practical work being done by Joseph-Charles Taché as deputy minister. The Canadian exhibit showcased the natural environment (including, without any sense of irony, five hundred stuffed birds), natural resources, agricultural implements, arts and crafts, the paintings of Cornelius Krieghoff and photographs of William Notman, and state-of-the-art technology, from the latest industrial tools to a Grand Trunk sleeping car.

In line with McGee's wishes, the display associated Canada with modernity, progress, creativity, and dynamism; the emphasis was on future possibilities rather than traditional ways of life. Two years earlier, during the Dublin exhibition, McGee had banished the display of a Native chief's headdress, on the grounds that it showed what the inhabitants of Canada had been like in the seventeenth rather than nineteenth century. After some initial problems – the collection for the display was temporarily lost in transit and was late in arriving in Paris – the Canadian exhibit was a resounding success. And McGee must have been particularly pleased when the rowing crew that he had entered from New Brunswick won the international regatta, earning the kind of prestige that is today associated with an Olympic gold medal. All in all, Canada's performance at the exposition was a real boost for McGee's new nationality.[27]

Still, McGee was keen to get home, especially after Macdonald informed him in early April that his political future hinged on his rapid return.[28] "News of electioneering and cabinet-making intrigues from Canada, induced me to hasten my return three or four weeks," he told Mary Ann Sadlier. "As you may suppose, passing out of one state of political existence into another there is no end of intrigue, and compromises, and re-arrangement."[29] Leaving Paris as soon as possible, he was back in Montreal on 24 May, and headed for Ottawa four days later. Ahead lay the most tumultuous summer of his Canadian career.

————

McGee's immediate task was to ensure that he would be included in the new federal cabinet.[30] Now that he was back at the centre of Canadian politics, he was confident that he could hold his place as minister of agriculture, immigration, and statistics. "About my own position I have no anxiety," he wrote "– I feel that I shall get just what I am able to command, as is usually the case in politics: and the man is a fool who looks for more."[31] As it turned out, he was able to command much less than he expected.

The art of Canadian cabinet making proved to be as complex as playing multidimensional chess. Macdonald's task was to select twelve cabinet ministers who reflected the political, religious, linguistic, and regional character of the country – four each from Ontario and Quebec, and two each from New Brunswick and Nova Scotia. At first, everything seemed to be going smoothly. The Maritime ministers would include Charles Tupper from Nova Scotia and Leonard Tilley from New Brunswick. In Quebec, Cartier and Langevin would represent French Canadian interests, Galt would represent English-speaking Protestants, and McGee would represent Irish Catholics. Ontario would be divided equally between the existing political parties – Macdonald and Alexander Campbell for the Conservatives, and William Howland and William McDougall for the Liberals.

But in early June, Howland and McDougall demanded that Ontario must have five cabinet ministers – three Liberals and two Conservatives – on the grounds that Ontario was more populous and prosperous than Quebec and that the Liberals were a majority in the province. In response, Cartier insisted that Quebec must have a minimum of three French Canadian ministers, leaving only one minister to represent English-speaking interests. This meant that either McGee or Galt would have to back down and that the stage was set for a showdown between Irish Catholics and British Protestants. "I will, if in Parliament, give way neither to Galt, nor to a third Frenchman, 'nor any other man,'" McGee had told Macdonald that spring; for his part, Galt was equally adamant that he would not give way to McGee.[32] With no solution in sight, Macdonald threatened to resign; it appeared that the launching of Confederation would be characterized by the very kind of political instability it was intended to stop.

With the 1 July deadline rapidly approaching, Charles Tupper offered McGee a choice that could avert the potential crisis. If McGee would yield to Galt, Tupper would relinquish his own cabinet seat for Edward Kenny, an Irish Catholic from Halifax. Tupper's proposal guaranteed Irish Catholic representation in the cabinet, which was of fundamental importance to McGee. If McGee continued to insist on a cabinet post for himself, the existing political arrangement would unravel, Macdonald would resign, and George Brown would reap the political benefits. On the grounds of principle and prudence, and in the interests of national unity and religious equality, McGee decided to accept the offer. But the political price was high. Not only had his personal ambitions received a severe blow, but he went into the next election as a politician who had been excluded from both the London Conference and the first federal cabinet, and whose career was in decline.[33]

———•———

As the politicians geared up for the first federal and provincial elections, McGee was active on three fronts: supporting the Conservatives in and around Toronto, running for a provincial seat in Prescott, and working for his re-election in Montreal West. The campaign for the Catholic vote in Ontario opened up in July, when Frank Smith, a politician and businessman from London, organized the Catholic Convention in Toronto with the aim of bringing Irish Catholics into the

Reform Party. Smith's supporters included not only some of McGee's former Reform allies in the city but also radical Irish nationalists such as Patrick Boyle and John Lawrence Power O'Hanly, who had come to the conclusion that Irish Catholics could gain more from Brown's Reformers than from a Liberal-Conservative coalition containing McGee and prominent Orangemen.[34]

To counter this, Macdonald, Moylan, and McGee threw their combined weight against the convention, with significant support from the Catholic Church.[35] "I know that as a general rule, your Lordship does not interfere in politics," Macdonald wrote to Bishop Lynch; "but in the present great crisis I feel quite justified in seeking the aid of your great power and influence in support of the present Government."[36] The Reformers, Macdonald reminded the bishops, had a long history of anti-Catholic prejudice and would nominate Irish Catholic candidates only in constituencies where they were bound to fail. In contrast, the Conservatives had supported separate schools and had a long track record of appointing Irish Catholics to high office, despite the opposition of Brown and his "Scotch fanatics."[37]

While Lynch obligingly directed his priests to work for "their old friends" the Conservatives, Moylan's *Canadian Freeman* criticized the convention, and McGee attacked what he called the "Grit-Fenian clique" in Toronto.[38] What, McGee asked, could be said of George Brown? He was nothing more than a hypocritical agitator who had boasted in the legislature about his opposition to minority rights, who had repeatedly resisted all attempts to strengthen Catholic educational rights, and who now had the temerity to court the very people whom he contemptuously dismissed as Dogans.[39] The pressure was effective; despite the convention's efforts to mobilize the Catholic vote behind Brown, the Conservatives were triumphant in Toronto.[40] In Prescott and Montreal, though, McGee had a far rougher ride.

McGee's decision to run in Prescott stemmed from his conviction that Irish Catholics in Ontario needed effective representation in the provincial legislature to protect them from the Protestant majority.[41] His opponent was an Irish-born Methodist preacher turned lumber merchant, James Boyd, who had been working the constituency long before the election. Boyd had "no end of brothers-in-law, and small debtors," McGee remarked, and had become "a very hard man to beat."[42] As an outsider, albeit a well-known one, McGee was at a natural disadvantage, which he attempted to offset by enlisting clerical support.[43]

Setting up his campaign headquarters in Caledonia Springs and going out on the stump, McGee quickly realized that he was facing an uphill battle.[44] Winning the seat, he wrote, would require "a great deal of labor, and about $1500"; he could supply plenty of the former but little of the latter. But to his intense frustration, and despite his threats to withdraw from the campaign, Ontario's Catholic bishops ignored his requests to secure the financial backing that he needed.[45] The reasons for their refusal were probably related to long-standing doubts about his personal character. Bishop Horan, for example, cannot have been impressed by reports he was getting about McGee's "low drunken habits" and may have shared George Clerk's view that "to acknowledge such a man as a champion or guardian of Catholic interests would be most degrading to the Church."[46]

Along with appeals to the bishops, McGee also sought help from Macdonald. A potential complication was the fact that John A. Macdonald had cut a deal with McGee's old enemy, Sandfield Macdonald: John A. had agreed to support Sandfield in the provincial election in return for Sandfield's backing in the federal election. The trouble was that McGee had already pledged himself to support Sandfield's opponent in the Cornwall constituency and would rather quit the Prescott election than renege on his commitment.[47] Macdonald smoothed over the situation in characteristic fashion. Writing to McGee, he promised not to interfere in the Cornwall election and agreed that the pledge must be honoured. Explaining to Sandfield why McGee would be supporting his opponent, Macdonald lied through his teeth and wrote that McGee had threatened to "come out strongly against us and to run on opposition principles for Montreal West" rather than betray his ally. Macdonald then happily ignored his non-interference promise to McGee by providing Sandfield with tactical advice to help him in the election.[48] The man was not called the Machiavelli of Kingston for nothing.

Struggling in the campaign against Boyd and feeling cut adrift by the bishops, McGee urged Macdonald to encourage potential campaign donors, and asked him to schedule the federal election in Montreal before its provincial counterpart in Prescott; in this way, the momentum from his anticipated victory in Montreal would carry over to Prescott.[49] Macdonald was sympathetic, believing that McGee was facing not only the open opposition of Boyd but also the closet operations of the Fenians: "Money is spent freely against him, and it is more than suspected that the Fenian Treasury contributes something towards his defeat," he told one correspondent.[50] Ultimately, however, McGee had to rely entirely on local funding. And with his prospects of success receding, it transpired that the voting in Prescott would take place immediately before the ballots were cast in Montreal.

———•—•———

Since his first election ten years earlier, McGee had not faced any serious challenges in his own constituency; he had been re-elected by acclamation three times and had easily fought off his Reform opponent, John Young, in 1863. With this track record, with the support of the Grand Trunk Railway and other business interests, and with what seemed like a secure base in the Irish population, McGee was confident that his seat was "safe against all comers."[51] Indeed, this was a major reason why he entered the provincial election in Ontario; he felt that he could "throw the burden of protecting Montreal West on my friends" and could concentrate on the campaign in Prescott.[52] As he soon found out, this was a major miscalculation; repeated success had produced a false sense of security, and the opposition in Montreal proved much more formidable than he imagined.

Standing against him was Bernard Devlin, president of the St Patrick's Society, commander of the Volunteer regiment the Prince of Wales Rifles, and a prominent lawyer. As we have seen, Devlin had initially welcomed McGee to Canada, praising him as "an accomplished scholar and gentleman."[53] Within a year, though, relations between the two men had soured. In Devlin's view, McGee was more interested in advancing his political career by kowtowing to Protestants rather than standing up for Irish Catholics: How else could one explain McGee's pusillanimous stance on St Patrick's Day parades in Toronto, his refusal to spare the lives of the Aylwards after their conviction for the murder of William Munro, and his constant attempts to placate the Orange

Bernard Devlin. McGee and Devlin first met in 1856, at the Buffalo Convention to promote Irish Catholic colonization in Canada and the American West. Initially among those who encouraged McGee to move to Montreal, Devlin came to believe that McGee was willing to sacrifice Irish Catholic interests to advance his own political ambitions. Although Devlin was not a Fenian, his strong Irish nationalist sympathies and deep dislike of McGee impelled him towards an alliance with Fenians during the election campaign of 1867. The two men disliked each other intensely; after the election, Devlin spat on McGee in the street. (NPA, McCord Museum)

Order? Instead of travelling all round the country speechifying about Canada's destiny and pontificating about the Fenians, McGee should have been dealing with practical and immediate issues affecting the people of Montreal. And instead of backing down in the face of Orange bigotry, McGee should have been taking an assertive, confrontational approach to the enemies of his countrymen.

Devlin was not a Fenian, but his message certainly appealed to revolutionary Irish nationalists in the city. "I do not say that every man on

Mr. Devlin's side is a dangerous disloyal man, far from it," commented a correspondent to the *Montreal Gazette*; "but I do say that every man who was last year an object of distrust on account of his Fenian sympathies is ranged on that side, and making the most frantic efforts to secure the defeat of Mr. McGee."[54] This assessment was substantially correct. Francis Bernard McNamee organized Devlin's first election meeting; prominent Montreal Fenians such as W.B. Linehan, Daniel Lyons, and Henry Murphy played an important role in his campaign; and lesser-known figures were active at the grassroots level.[55]

Welcoming this support, Devlin combined overt declarations of loyalty with coded appeals to the city's Fenians. On the one hand, he finished his meetings with loud cheers for the dominion and the Crown; on the other, he presented himself as a radical Irish nationalist.[56] "There is nothing in my past conduct, after twenty four years residence among you, which I feel myself compelled to apologise for, and to attribute to the errors of my youth," he said, in an obvious swipe at McGee's Wexford speech. "I am the same in 1867 as I was in 1847 ... If a man must be proclaimed a rebel because he loves his country, then I am a rebel."[57] Unspoken, but fully understood by all his Irish nationalist listeners, was the fact that in 1848 Devlin had advocated an Irish American invasion of Canada, claimed that the Irish in Lower Canada were ready to rise, and boasted that Irish Canadian revolutionaries had spiked cannons in Quebec.[58] Since the Fenians among Devlin's campaign workers supported the current invasion plans for Canada, his declaration of consistency was exactly what they wanted to hear.[59]

"I find the feeling in Montreal more unsettled than I could imagine," McGee commented as the contest began, though he still expected to win by a thousand votes.[60] His opening speech emphasized his support for minority rights, his "policy of conciliation," and his stature as a national figure. "Halifax and St. John, so far as I understand their wants," he said, "shall be as near to me, politically, as Montreal or Toronto." Devlin, in contrast, was portrayed as a dangerous and divisive man who was trying to "inspire with hatred against me, a portion of my fellow-countrymen." That hatred had nothing to do with his

# THE BARNEY-KILL

OR,

## WEST WARD WARBLER.

A COMPLETE COLLECTION OF
NEW AND POPULAR SONGS, DUETTS, OPERAS, &c., &c.
(Original, and for the first time printed.)

No. 1.

## BARNEY LET McGEE ALONE.

Set to the popular Air—" Barney Let the Girls Alone."

(*Chorus*)—*Barney let McGee alone,*
*Barney let McGee alone,*
*Barney let McGee alone,*
    *You never can come in.*

**I.**

Barney take advice from me—
You have my counsel without fee,
Don't be fooled by McNamee,
    You never can come in.
      (*Chorus.*)

**II.**

Listen well my man of law
Samson with just such a jaw,
What was he but a poor cat's paw,
    That never could come in!
      (*Chorus.*)

**III.**

Sheridan and Howley, too,
May get their balance, over due,
And make a mortar-man like you,
    But still you can't come in!
      (*Chorus.*)

**IV.**

Lawyer Cassidy may prate,
Rouge is written on his pate,
He tried Montcalm, but found too late
    He never could come in!
      (*Chorus.*)

**V.**

Little Donavan may growl,
'T is he that is the generous *soul*,
A mighty mouser is your owl—
    But he could not come in!
      (*Chorus.*)

**VI.**

So take advice my shining blade,
Stick to Coursol's—that's your trade,
For backing burglars you were made—
    You never can come in!
      (*Chorus* )

**VII.**

Take advice—make up your mind,
Before the action let us find
The Colonel has again resigned
    And never can come in!
      (*Chorus.*)

The Barney-Kill. A pro-McGee handbill from the election campaign, based on the popular song "Barney Let the Girls Alone" (to the same tune as "Polly Put the Kettle On"). (Brown Chamberlin Fonds, LAC, MG24-B19, f. 34) work as a Canadian legislator, McGee continued, and everything to do with his attacks on Fenianism. If the Irish in Montreal transferred their allegiance to Devlin, he declared, they would "fall under evil influences."[61]

Meanwhile, the anti-McGee forces were gathering momentum. John Carroll, one of the city's leading Fenians, supplied Devlin's supporters with questions to ask McGee. What was he doing when the Aylward case came before the Executive Council in 1862? Why was he kicked out of the Russell House in the winter of 1866? The answers were contained in the questions: McGee was a drunkard and a disgrace to Ireland who put the bottle and his career above the lives of innocent people.[62] His character became a major campaign issue. "Darcy's personal conduct which is as bad as ever is disgusting every body," remarked Holton – by no means a disinterested observer, of course.[63] In an interesting twist on the argument, the Montreal Herald used McGee's talents against him; McGee was doubtless a great poet and orator, but Montreal needed a man of action and not a man of words.[64]

As part of his counterattack, McGee sought public endorsements from the Catholic hierarchy, with mixed success.[65] Bourget, of course, was out of the question, given the split over St Patrick's Parish; in Ontario, Bishops Farrell and Horan were no more willing to help McGee in Montreal than they had been in Prescott. The one exception was McGee's friend and admirer in Halifax, Archbishop Connolly, who declared in an open letter that McGee had "done more for the real honour and advantage of Catholics and Irishmen, here and elsewhere, than any other I know of since the days of the immortal O'Connell." Connolly then sent two thousand copies of his letter to McGee for distribution among the Irish in Montreal. Devlin's supporters initially denounced it as a forgery and then complained about external clerical interference in the election campaign. Before long, they were to have internal clerical interference to deal with as well, in the figure of Father Dowd.[66]

As the campaign continued, Devlin's supporters relied heavily on widespread intimidation to win the election. When McGee challenged Devlin to a series of nightly debates, Devlin refused, on the grounds that such debates would "arouse a spirit of disorder." The debates

Father Patrick Dowd. The Sulpician pastor of St Patrick's Church in Mont-real, Father Dowd shared McGee's uncompromising hostility to Fenian-ism. After an anti-McGee riot during the 1867 election campaign, he told his parishioners that if such scenes were repeated he would "shoulder a musket and shoot down those who dare to intimidate and keep back from the polls peaceable citizens" (*Montreal Gazette*, 7 August 1867). (Courtesy of St Patrick's Basilica, Montreal)

never took place, but the spirit of disorder was aroused anyway. At a public meeting on 2 August, McGee and Alexander Ogilvie (running as McGee's ally for the provincial election) were pelted with stones and prevented from speaking; they had to leave under police protec-tion.[67] Two days later, at High Mass in St Patrick's Church, Father Dowd issued a stern warning to his parishioners. "I myself ... if needed will shoulder a musket," he said, "and shoot down those who dare to intimidate and keep back from the polls peaceable citizens."[68]

At his next meeting, with the police well in attendance (but pre-sumably without Father Dowd and his musket), McGee criticized his opponents for denying free speech and delivered an all-out attack on Devlin and the Fenians. "As for Fenianism," he said, "I strangled it when it first attempted to concentrate in Canada, and I am not now going to be annoyed by the odour of the carcase." What kind of representative did Montreal need? McGee asked. A man who unequivocally confronted Fenianism or a man who would "temporize with the introduction of firebrands and foreign schemes for the destruction of the Government"? He recalled the advice that Devlin had once given him: if you leave the Fenians alone, they will leave you alone. On the contrary, McGee said, he was going to expose the conspiracy and name the ringleaders by publishing "documents which would put in their proper position the Fenians of Montreal."[69]

Almost immediately, the death threats came in. If McGee revealed information about the Fenians in Montreal, ran one anonymous letter, he would be assassinated. Another letter, wrapped in a copy of the Buffalo *Fenian Volunteer*, featured a sketch of a gallows and coffin, with the words, "You arch-traitor, if you oppose Devlin, by God, such will be your fate!" ("I beg you to keep these papers for me," McGee told his election committee; "my collection would be incomplete without them.")[70]

Among those who wanted to see McGee dead was Patrick James Whelan, who had taken time off work to participate in Devlin's campaign and had been enlisted by a man named O'Meara – possibly Patrick O'Meara, the recording secretary of the St Patrick's Society and a leading Fenian.[71] After reading McGee's speech on Fenianism, recalled a lodger in Whelan's house, Whelan flew into a rage, put his revolver in his pocket, and declared that he would "go up & blow McGee's bloody brains out." He joined two of his friends, Thomas Murphy and Michael Enright, to stake out McGee's house and did not return until the morning. McGee, he said, had betrayed the Fenians and "turned over to the Protestants."[72]

Against this background, McGee sent one of his campaign workers, Richard Wright, to spy on the Devlin camp. Attending numerous meetings and spending long hours in Irish taverns, Wright described

Griffintown as "a hot-bed of Fenianism," where any mention of McGee evoked intense feelings of "bitterness and Deadly hate." After a drinking session with Bernard's younger brother Owen, Wright concluded that Owen was "a most Dangerous man" who was "violently disposed" towards McGee. After listening to Wright's information and heeding his warnings, McGee "took the precaution of having Several Policemen, come privately to guard his House every night for Some time."[73]

In the press and in public meetings, his opponents rode the wave of anger. If McGee had secret information about a dangerous Fenian conspiracy, asked the Montreal Herald, why was he waiting until now before revealing it? All this talk of Fenianism in Canada was nothing more than an election ploy, and McGee's bloated image of Canadian Fenianism would only encourage American Fenians to launch another invasion.[74] Luther Holton added his voice to the anti-McGee chorus. "We are not identifying ourselves very closely with Devlin's candidature," he had told Brown in July, "but at the proper time we shall give him all the assistance we can."[75] Now the proper time had come. During a meeting in Victoria Square, Holton pointed out that McGee had been dropped from the cabinet, and criticized him for preaching against the Fenians instead of focusing on practical ways to pursue Montreal's economic interests.[76] Devlin was up next, delivering a blistering attack on McGee's promise to expose the Fenian conspiracy and denouncing McGee as "a foul informer, a corrupt witness, a knave and hypocrite." As he did so, a cry of "He's dead" came up from the crowd – not surprisingly, given the traditional punishment meted out to real or suspected informers.[77]

All this was far from the relatively smooth ride that McGee had anticipated. The Fenians, the Reformers, and even some of Cartier's supporters were determined to defeat him; the Catholic bishops, except for Thomas Connolly, were ignoring his requests for help; and he was fighting two campaigns, with an uphill battle in Prescott and a major fight on his hands in Montreal. He had been in poor health in Paris and had been working flat out since his return. "I never was so busy in my life," he told Bishop Horan – and that was saying something.[78] Shortly after his anti-Fenian speech, the stress finally got to him; he

was suffering so much from an ulcerated leg that he had to stop campaigning.[79] For a full week, the field was wide open for his enemies,
who were only too happy to occupy it. From his bed, he prepared his
exposé of the Fenians in Montreal, writing to Macdonald for copies
of Fenian correspondence that the post office had intercepted and
opened.[80] By the third week of August, he was ready. His "Account of
the Attempts to Establish Fenianism in Montreal," published in three
issues of the *Montreal Gazette*, ratcheted the campaign up to an even
higher level of intensity.[81]

Contrary to his earlier promise, McGee did not publish the damning
documents that he had promised to disclose, subsequently explaining
that "he could not make the whole of them public without the consent
of the Government."[82] Instead, he based his argument on a wide range
of sources, such as correspondence from friends in the United States,
intercepted Fenian letters, and reports from informers. Although he
did not produce any specific evidence, he did name names – including
McNamee, Owen Devlin, Daniel Lyons, W.B. Linehan, J.J. [sic: P.J.]
O'Meara, John McGrath, Felix Callahan, and John Carroll.[83]

These men, he argued, had developed a twin-track strategy of forming their own Fenian circles and infiltrating the St Patrick's Society.
To this end, they had established the Hibernian Society, which held
its first meetings in Owen Devlin's office. But largely thanks to the
opposition of Father Dowd, the Hibernian Society had made little
headway – at which point, they had focused their attention on the St
Patrick's Society. In 1863, McNamee had invited John O'Mahony to
speak to the society, and a "surprise majority" had approved of cooperation between the society and the Fenian Brotherhood in New York.
After the Fenian raids in 1866, McGee asserted, Fenians in the society
had destroyed all evidence of the Fenian correspondence by starting
a fire at its meeting place in Nordheimer's Hall and burning the record books.[84]

Initially, there had been only seventeen members of the Hibernian
Society. But within two years, the numbers had increased dramatic-
ally. Using published Fenian sources about remittances from Canada,
McGee estimated that in 1865 there were around 800 Fenians in To-

ronto, 200 in Quebec City, and 355 in Montreal. One of the reasons why the Fenians had gained ground, he wrote, was that loyal Irish Catholics feared the consequences of challenging them – being branded as informers and subjected to a barrage of personal attacks. But as the only Irish Catholic cabinet minister in the government, he had a special duty to face them down: "If I do not set an example of determination and vigour," he asked himself "– of moral courage – in this case – how can I expect my friends, A, B, or C, – who have no especial responsibility in the public as I have, to fight the incoming evil, in their private walks of life?"[85]

Such an example had become all the more important, given the close connections between the Senate wing and the Montreal Fenians, and the growing evidence of a conjunction between external invasion and internal subversion. Shortly after Ridgeway, wrote McGee, he had seen a letter from "a former citizen of Montreal, now residing in New York," urging a run on the banks, and this had actually been attempted. Other sources had revealed "a deliberate plan to fire our towns and cities in order to distract the movements of our troops, and to occupy our people in various places simultaneously." The Fenians in Canada were making serious efforts to "corrupt the regular and volunteer forces," enlist policemen into the brotherhood, and enrol workers in the strategically vital Grand Trunk Railway.[86] An American Fenian emissary named John Lennon had come to Canada the previous autumn to lay the groundwork for an attack on Ottawa; he had also travelled to Montreal, where he discussed his plans with McNamee and John Carroll. An informer had leaked an account of Lennon's tour, which McGee said was now in his personal possession.[87]

The men at the heart of this "criminal complicity," he continued, were Devlin's strongest supporters; they had "emerged from their covers" and were attempting "to take the destinies of the city, under their control, by force and violence."[88] Devlin's own role in all this was "suspicious in the extreme"; after Ridgeway, Devlin had "refused to exert himself to recruit the ranks of his own regiment," had "talked of 'the hardship of fighting against his own countrymen' – that is, the American city rabble" – and had taken "the very first opportunity he could seize to cast up his commission." Under Devlin's presidency, members of the St Patrick's Society were putting up pictures of leading Fenians and singing revolutionary songs. It was no surprise, then, that Devlin and the Fenians were working so closely together during the election campaign.

"The narrative which I have thus hastily thrown together, while ill in body, and pre-occupied in mind, between two contested elections, in constituencies nearly a hundred miles apart, I present to the public – especially to my fellow-citizens with all its imperfections on its head!" McGee concluded. "For every fact stated, I am personally politically, morally, and legally responsible. I can safely say that I have overstated nothing for any case whatever, against any person whatever ... Instead of overstating, I have rather understated my case."[89]

How accurate were McGee's accusations? T.P. Slattery, in his generally sympathetic biography of McGee, noted that many of his revelations were "unprovable or unfounded," and concluded that "the threats, the violence and the fever of the campaign ... had pushed McGee off balance."[90] This was mild compared to the reaction of McGee's contemporary political enemies. The *Montreal Herald* described his allegations as "the veriest rubbish ... entirely unsupported by the slightest evidence."[91] According to Devlin, they were a "disconnected, disjointed, and incoherent and stupid hash, of distorted trash and of falsehood, but with a small ingredient of true veracity." Devlin opened his next public meeting by saying that he would not pollute the atmosphere by mentioning his opponent's name, referring to McGee instead as a "poisonous serpent" who had become "the chief detective and informer against his countrymen."[92] Such statements were so inflammatory, wrote the *Montreal Gazette*, that they were an incitement to violence – a view that was strengthened by the shouts of "We'll hang him!" and "We'll cut his ears off!" that came from the crowd.[93]

Among those whom McGee had named, Owen Devlin categorically denied that the Hibernian Society had ever met in his office, while McNamee insisted that he was the innocent victim of McGee's lies. He did indeed meet O'Mahony, he said, but told him that "we in Canada were blessed with prosperity and peace under the shadow of a Government than which no better can be formed by human devices." A few years earlier he also met McGee, who had recited one of his revolutionary poems and advised him that "deception was the only weapon with which to fight our common enemy." Supposedly shocked by these sentiments, McNamee claimed that he resolved to have nothing further to do with the man – and there was not a shred of truth in the charge that he had any connections with American Fenians who wanted to invade Canada.[94]

Yet McGee's accusations are not so easily dismissed. We know from the papers of General Tom Sweeny that McNamee presented himself as a strong supporter of an American invasion and that Lyons, McGrath, and Callahan would follow suit.[95] We know from a court case in Montreal fifteen years later that McNamee had established a Fenian circle in the city after meeting O'Mahony in New York and that McGee's revelations about the Hibernian Society were correct.[96] We know from the records of the St Patrick's Society that W.B. Linehan was a republican separatist.[97] And we know that McGee was correct in arguing that the Fenians had set out to take over the St Patrick's Society.[98]

The case of Owen Devlin is more difficult to discern. In the spring of 1864 he had contributed towards the testimonial that raised funds for McGee's new house, and McGee had proposed him for vice-president of the St Patrick's Society. In 1866 McGee had also recommended him for a job with the Mechanics' Bank of Montreal.[99] All of this strengthened Owen Devlin's claim that McGee "never doubted my loyalty and respectability before I dared to use my right as a citizen to oppose him as a candidate for Montreal West."[100] On the other hand, there is evidence that McGee had only recently become aware of Owen Devlin's Fenian connections. Before recommending Owen Devlin for the job with the Mechanics' Bank, McGee had asked him if there was any truth to the rumours that he was a Fenian; Owen Devlin had assured him that the rumours were false.[101] During the election, though, McGee had received information that Owen was channelling Irish American Fenian funds into his brother's campaign – information that turned out to be wrong.[102]

Equally contentious was McGee's charge that the Fenians in the St Patrick's Society had set the fire at Nordheimer's Hall to destroy records of their correspondence with John O'Mahony. To exonerate the society, Bernard Devlin demanded a public inquiry into the fire and publicly produced the "books of record," explaining that they had actually been kept at the home of Patrick O'Meara, the recording secretary. "I challenge the vile slanderer of our creed and race," Devlin said, to "tremendous cheers"; "I dare him to hazard his just punishment for perjury by repeating *under oath* his imputations before such judicial authority."[103] Several months later, the society presented the books of record to the mayor, confirming that they went back to 1856.[104] It seemed clear that McGee had been lying to discredit his enemies. Yet he stuck to his story, and it may be significant that there is no record of the O'Mahony correspondence among the extant St Patrick's Society's papers – or, indeed, of any minutes and proceedings before April 1864.

Leaving aside the case of Owen Devlin and the fire at Nordheimer's Hall, McGee's exposé of Fenianism in Montreal was generally well founded. In fact, there were some important names that he missed – that of Henry Murphy, for example, who was an active member of Devlin's campaign and "one of the principal Fenians in Montreal."[105] The accuracy of his allegations only intensified the anger of his enemies. When McGee appeared on the hustings at the end of August, he was shouted down by a hostile crowd and had to leave without speaking.[106] And the pattern of intimidation was widening; McGee's friends began to receive "threatening letters, menacing them with the destruction of their houses and places of business, threatening them with burning and the loss of personal property."[107]

Then, two days before the polls opened in Montreal, news of the Prescott election results came into the city: McGee, for the first time in his life, had gone down to electoral defeat.[108] Now there was the very real possibility that defeat in the provincial election could carry over into the federal campaign. McGee could be presented as a triple loser – shut out from the London Conference, excluded from the cabinet, and spurned as a "vile informer" in Prescott. The same fate, his enemies hoped, awaited him in Montreal.[109]

The polling took place on Thursday, 5 September, and Friday, 6 September. At the end of a relatively quiet first day, McGee was well ahead in the largely English-speaking Protestant ward of St Lawrence and the predominantly French-speaking ward of St Antoine, with a combined majority of more than five hundred votes. But in St Anne's ward, the city's Irish heartland, Devlin had a narrow lead of sixteen votes. On Friday, Devlin's supporters went all out to increase their lead in St Anne's and to break McGee's hold on the other wards – and this time, things started to get rough. During the afternoon, two of McGee's scrutineers were assaulted at a polling station and a policeman was beaten up so badly that he was almost killed. Shortly afterwards, a crowd of Devlin's supporters attacked McGee's campaign headquarters at the Mechanics' Hall. In the course of the riot, shots were fired on both sides, and two of Devlin's men were wounded – one apparently by McGee's longtime supporter, Thomas McCready. Seeking revenge, the crowd turned its attention to McCready's house, smashing its windows before the police arrived.[110]

Devlin outpolled McGee in all three wards on Friday. McGee held on to his majorities in St Lawrence and St Antoine, but Devlin increased his lead in St Anne's. Only 266 people from St Anne's voted for McGee on the second day, while Devlin received 435 votes – giving Devlin a total majority in St Anne's of 185, with 2,041 ballots cast. It was almost enough to give Devlin the seat – almost, but not quite. When the dust had settled and the votes from all three wards were counted, McGee had won by 262 votes.[111]

Later that night, Devlin thanked his supporters and blamed his defeat on the combined influence of the Grand Trunk, "the Government and all its departments," and the press. The Mechanics' Hall riot, he said, had been deliberately provoked by McGee's supporters, who had then fired on the crowd; "I deny," he said, "that there is any excuse for using fire-arms to quell a mere squabble in a public street." McGee may have been returning to Parliament, Devlin continued, but he had lost the support of the Irish; the result in St Anne's convinced Devlin that he himself "was really, the representative of the Irish Catholics in Montreal."[112] The *Montreal Herald* concurred, arguing that McGee's "comparatively small majority" signalled "the moral repudiation of that candidate by the great constituency whose votes he solicited."[113]

Most historians have followed this verdict, and there is indeed much truth to it. Nevertheless, the notion that McGee "lost the support of the Irish" is much too simple and needs to be qualified in four main ways. First, sheer physical intimidation was a large part of the story. On the second day of polling, when Devlin's men were flexing their muscles on the streets, many of McGee's supporters decided to stay at home. In the view of one of McGee's campaigners, his Fenian exposé had been a major tactical error, not only because he had put his own life in even greater danger but also because many Conservatives of "weak nerve" became afraid to vote.[114] Second, the fact that McGee was running two campaigns at once worked against him: "In this double fight he was going with his hands tied, as every time he left Montreal, he left behind him an able, bitter and industrious opponent."[115] Third, his illness did not help; as well as his absences in Prescott, McGee had been laid up in bed for a week during the campaign. And fourth, it is worth noting that McGee still commanded the allegiance of 45 per cent of the voters of St Anne's ward – though his percentage of the Irish votes in St Anne's may well have been significantly lower.

All this suggests that while the depth of Irish Catholic hostility towards McGee cannot be overstated, its breadth may have been much less than is often supposed. Having said this, however, the point remains that he had been overconfident, that his attacks on Fenianism had alienated a substantial section of the city's Irish Catholics, and that his political position had been further weakened as a result.

## CHAPTER FOURTEEN

# The Most Critical Period
## October 1867 – April 1868

In McGee's assessment, the violence during the election cost him a thousand votes, and the attack on his headquarters "demonstrated beyond doubt or denial that there was a dangerous element in our midst struggling for power" – an element that had taken over the St Patrick's Society, infiltrated the Grand Trunk, the army, and the city police, and "entertained a project for firing this city, in conjunction with a foreign invasion of our soil." This element, he argued, had been aided and abetted by the editors of the *Montreal Herald* for the crass purpose of increasing their sales, and by Bernard Devlin for the selfish objective of getting into Parliament – the same people who would actually be among the first victims of an Irish revolution in Canada, destroyed by the very forces that they had helped to create. All this underlined the need for the "respectable classes" of the city to take a strong stand against subversion and to assert the rule of law over the rule of the mob.[1]

Among those who had been defeated, the air was thick with bitter recriminations. "Although McGee is elected the bloody old pig won't reign long," Patrick James Whelan was reported to have said, "and I will blow his bloody old brains out before the session is over."[2] Facing a relentless barrage of accusations by Devlin that he was an informer, a Canadian Titus Oates, and a traitor to his people, McGee finally snapped. "Under extreme provocation during all the late election contest," he wrote, "I have endeavoured, on my side, to keep the issues above personality. I had only to go as far as the Court House for facts, which would have blasted my opponent for ever, not only politically but professionally."[3] When Devlin read these words, he was apoplectic;

to have his professional reputation impugned through such insinuations was insulting and infuriating – as, indeed, it was meant to be. Later that day, he accosted McGee on the street and demanded an explanation. When McGee said that he meant every word, Devlin called him a "damned scoundrel" and spat in his face; McGee hit him on the shoulder with his cane, and the two men had to be separated before matters got even worse.[4]

McGee was not seen again on the streets for several weeks after the spitting incident; the health problems that had been dogging him during the election campaign returned with a vengeance, and he was forced back to bed with the combined effects of his "lame foot" and "a previously disordered state of the blood." Although he was physically incapacitated, his mind was as active as ever. "Three weeks – almost – of unbroken meditation, and mental foddering, have left me brimming over, with thoughts, or what seem to be such," he told Macdonald in mid-October. He was reading ten hours a day and floating through his illness on "cold water," rather than his customary consumption of whisky.[5] Not for the first time in his life, McGee had decided to stop drinking. On previous occasions, his resolve had not lasted long. But now, confined to his home and being looked after by Mary, there were fewer temptations to revert to the old ways; this time, he finally kicked the habit.

By the beginning of November, his "unbroken meditation" found public expression in a speech he gave to the Montreal Literary Club on "The Mental Outfit of the New Dominion." Although he was still in pain – he had to be carried to his chair and spoke from a seated position – McGee presented a clear and comprehensive analysis of the relationship between literature and nationalism. Central to his argument was the assumption that reading had the power to shape values and ideas, and thus the character of the nation. With this in mind, he raised a "warning voice" against the cumulative consequences of reading gutter journalism, trashy novels, and foreign books.

To counter the prejudices and partisanship of the press, he called for "a higher style of newspaper" in Canada, noting that this was the responsibility both of editors and of the reading public. The recently formed Press Association was an important step in the right direction;

it could professionalize journalism, cut out "scoundrelism," and foster a culture of "personal courtesy and good manners." When it came to fiction, McGee was scathing in his criticism of "sensational and sensual books, many of them written by women, who are the disgrace of their sex" – another indication of his belief that women had a special responsibility to embody the highest moral virtues. Instead, young people should be encouraged to read "books which enlarge our sympathies; and do not pervert them; which excite our curiosity, and satisfy it, but not at the expense of morals": travel literature, for example, or novels that promoted the values of truth, justice, honesty, and courage.

"Who reads a Canadian book?" he asked. Hardly anyone, he replied, for such books were "exceedingly scarce." To establish their own literature, Canadians had to create a positive, warm, and welcoming atmosphere for aspiring writers. Such a development was critically important to the future of the country, since "our mental independence is an essential condition of our political independence." At the same time, McGee insisted that Canadian literature should avoid the pitfalls of "intolerant nationalism." "When nationalism stunts the growth, and embitters the generous spirit which alone can produce generous and enduring fruits of literature," he said, "then it becomes a curse rather than a gain to the people among whom it may find favour, and to every other people who may have relations with such a bigoted, one-sided nationality." Rather than succumbing to destructive and chauvinist forms of nationalism, Canadians should develop a broad-minded approach that combined the best of their own traditions with the best of other countries. This was a vision that owed much to his Young Ireland background and also fitted closely with his critique of Fenianism. After the Montreal election, the dangers of what he viewed as a "bigoted, one-sided nationality" were very much on his mind.[6]

Despite his illness, McGee attended the opening of the new dominion's Parliament in Ottawa – an event that he was determined not to miss. His speech on the Address to the Throne was one of the highlights of the session. "That speech," wrote one correspondent, "we do not hesitate to say *will live*."[7] A synthesis of his earlier writings on the new nationality, it contrasted the rationalism and majority rule of American republicanism with the "faith and reverence" and minority rights that underpinned the Canadian form of government.[8] Turning to Fenianism in Canada, McGee pointed out that a recent meeting of the St Patrick's Society in Montreal had displayed the names of prominent Fenians on its walls, and argued that the continuing suspension of habeas corpus would prevent revolutionary violence from breaking out in Canadian cities.[9]

Two weeks later, Macdonald announced that his government would indeed renew the suspension of habeas corpus. While McGee focused on the internal threat of Fenianism, arguing that "one Fenian in Canada, was worse than ten outside," Macdonald emphasized the external danger.[10] The government, Macdonald told the House of Commons, had "distinct evidence of increasing activity" on the border; Fenian arms were being stockpiled near the frontier, and the possibility of another invasion remained very real. It was thus essential that renewed steps be taken for the apprehension and trial of "foreign aggressors." "The object of the bill," Macdonald declared, "was to prevent parties from making undue raids upon our territory."[11]

McGee and Macdonald were basing their position on common sources of counter-intelligence. While McGee was fighting for his political survival in Montreal, the Senate wing had been meeting in Cleveland, to regroup after the failure of 1866. Its convention was a contentious affair, with major divisions over a resolution for an oath of secrecy (which was passed) and over a resolution to include women in Fenian circles (which, in one of the great ironies of an organization riddled with male informers, was "answered in the negative, because of their inability to keep a secret"). But on one thing all were agreed: money and arms must be raised for a new invasion attempt, which was scheduled for March 1868.[12] According to an informer, "20,000 dollars has been voted by the Cleveland Convention for the purpose of drawing the Irish soldiers of the Queen's Service in Canada from their allegiance, and inducing them to join the organization. A number of trustworthy Agents have already been sent to Canada for this purpose, and I have myself read letters from non commissioned officers of the Army serving in Canada who are actually engaged in spreading disaffection among their comrades." As McGee had said, the Fenians planned to spike the guns and artillery of loyal soldiers. Meanwhile, arms and ammunition were being smuggled into Canada from four different border points, to escape the attention of American authorities.[13]

Although this evidence was withheld from members of Parliament on the grounds of national security, they took Macdonald at his word. Even Anglin, despite considerable skepticism, acquiesced in the renewed suspension of habeas corpus. If there really was an immediate external Fenian threat, he said, then the measure could be justified.[14] But Anglin took great exception to McGee's critical comments about the St Patrick's Society in Montreal. As someone who was attempting to replace McGee as the most important Irish Catholic voice in Canadian politics and who had been a guest of honour at the very meeting which had been attacked in Parliament, he denounced McGee's "atrocious and disgraceful" attempt to "cast a burning stigma on the Irishmen of Montreal for the sake of building himself up."[15]

Outside Parliament, the reaction of Irish Canadian nationalists to McGee's remarks was equally hostile. All this talk about Irish Catholics conspiring to burn down Canadian cities was the product of McGee's paranoia, wrote John Lawrence Power O'Hanly. The fact of the matter was that there were no Fenians in Canada. Had not Sir James Cockburn, the solicitor general of Canada West, said so himself the previous March? McGee was resurrecting old myths that Irish Catholics were ready to massacre their enemies, and his "charges of disloyalty must aggravate and intensify prejudices, which in their normal condition are unhappily too active." Such scaremongering could only subject a defenceless minority to "the irresistible fury of a panic-stricken, armed, organized majority." "If reprisals, retaliation, violence, blood shed and loss of life should grow out of it," O'Hanly asked, "who is to blame?"

There was a personal dimension to this. "The effect of your wholesale denunciations is but too apparent in the following incident, which tho' in itself trifling, reveals a sad spectacle," O'Hanly told McGee. "My little boy on his return from school one evening with great earnestness asked me 'are all Catholics, "Fenians"'? I said 'why do you ask.' 'Because I hear the scholars say so; and they call the Bowes and me' (only Catholic children attending school) 'Fenians.' 'And why do they

call you a Fenian?' 'Because they say I'm a Catholic; and they say Catholics are bad people, and will all go to h–ll. Are they, Pa?' This was my
son's first lesson in religious discords – thus did he acquire the alphabet
of sectarian nomenclature – thus did he learn to distinguish between
creeds. From my lips he never heard an invidious distinction between
Catholic and Protestant ... The boys at school only repeated the saying
of their parents at home; and this was a select school of whose teachers
I cannot speak too highly, and whose patrons would be supposed above
the frailties too common to the mass."[16]

McGee was not in Ottawa for the debate, such as it was, over the
renewed suspension of habeas corpus; shortly after his opening speech,
the pain in his foot had become so severe that he was forced back home
to Montreal. While he was struggling with his illness, the political
temperature in Ireland and the diaspora was rising rapidly as a result of
events in the northwest of England. On 11 September, the Fenian leaders Tom Kelly and Timothy Deasy had been arrested in Manchester; a
week later, their fellow revolutionaries set out to rescue them as they
were being transferred from the magistrate's court to the prison.

The operation was coordinated by Edward O'Meagher Condon,
one of the founders of the Toronto Hibernian Benevolent Society, and
was based on his earlier plan to spring Michael Murphy and his fellow
Fenians from Cornwall jail after they had been intercepted en route to
Campobello. In Cornwall, the plan was never put into practice, since
Murphy engineered his own escape; in Manchester, it succeeded in freeing Kelly and Deasy, at the cost of killing their guard, Sergeant Charles
Brett. Several of the rescuers were caught and arrested, including William Allen, whom witnesses identified as the man who killed Sergeant
Brett, and Michael Larkin, who had apparently been seen shooting at
another policeman. Also rounded up were Thomas Maguire, Michael
O'Brien, who gave his name as "Gould," and Condon himself, who
went under the pseudonym of "Shore."[17]

At the subsequent trial, all five men were found guilty of murder.
After delivering a speech that impressed even many of his enemies,
Condon closed with the words "God Save Ireland!" – which T.D. Sul-
livan turned into Ireland's unofficial national anthem, to the melody

of a Civil War song, and which also inspired *Speeches from the Dock*, one of the sacred texts of Irish nationalism, and became a rallying cry for Irish nationalists throughout the world. In the event, neither Maguire nor Condon was hanged – Maguire because the evidence against him was very weak, Condon because he had not carried a weapon. But the death sentences against Allen, Larkin, and O'Brien were carried out. On 23 November, before a small crowd and in the midst of massive security, the three men went to the scaffold – the first Irish political revolutionaries to be hanged in the United Kingdom of Great Britain and Ireland since the execution of Robert Emmet in 1803.[18]

In Britain, there was a widespread sense that the murderers had been punished and justice had been served; in Ireland and the diaspora, Irish nationalists regarded Allen, Larkin, and O'Brien as martyrs who had been convicted on erroneous evidence and sacrificed on the altar of anti-Irish Catholic prejudice. From the cities of England to the gold-fields of New Zealand, among Irish Catholic communities throughout the world, there were mass protests, mock funerals, and impassioned speeches against the "legal murder" of the "Manchester Martyrs."[19] And nowhere was the anger felt more keenly than among Fenian circles in the United States and Canada.

The trials in Manchester were occurring at the very time that Macdonald was preparing to renew the suspension of habeas corpus; indeed, he justified the measure partly on the grounds that "the Fenian body were now pursuing a course of outrage in England" and constituted a "widely extended organization" that could strike again in Canada.[20] On the eve of the sentences, border communities in Canada went on the alert amid rumours that "Fenian marauders" would seek vengeance "by shooting down a few unoffending Canadian farmers."[21]

After the executions, Irish Canadian nationalist outrage found public expression in the *Irish Canadian* and private expression in taverns and on the streets.[22] In Toronto on New Year's Day, a man by the name of Christian Norman got into a conversation with two soldiers who were walking along Queen Street, invited them into his house, and sent his wife out for whisky. ("I did not drink any of the whiskey," one of the soldiers explained; "– I am a Welshman.") Upon finding out that the other soldier was Irish, Norman described himself as a "true Fenian" and started talking about "the men being hung in Manchester."

"He said he wished he had his throat cut the morning they were hung," reported the Irish soldier. "He then asked me if I would assist him to blow up the barracks – the old fort – that he could find plenty of men to assist me to burn the barracks down if I would show them how to go about it, and that they would then send me to the States."[23]

In this increasingly tense atmosphere, McGee used support and sympathy for the Manchester Martyrs as further evidence of the malign influence of Fenianism. Noting that the St Patrick's Society of Montreal had passed a resolution thanking Anglin for his "very able, eloquent and generous defence of our body," McGee asserted that "the very same persons would have passed a still higher eulogium, if they dared, on Messieurs Gould [sic], Allen and Larkin, 'for their able, eloquent and generous' murder of Sergeant Brett, of the Manchester police, in the discharge of his duty to his country."[24]

Shortly afterwards, during a brief return to Parliament, he referred to the Manchester murderers (as he would have put it) while supporting a bill to prevent "the unlawful training of persons to the use of arms, and the practice of military evolutions or exercises." Many Irish Americans, he said, had been "worked up to a reckless pitch of excitement by the course of recent events in England," and the Fenian press in the United States was urging its readers to emulate "the devoted men, who in their own phrase, were not afraid on the other side of the ocean to take their lives in their hands and die in the heart of the enemy's country." With another presidential election coming up – it was, McGee remarked, "one of the leap years of Democracy" – and with the renewed competition for Irish American votes, "the next six months would prove the most critical period that Canada had ever experienced."[25]

Nothing could have been better calculated to provoke the Fenians and their fellow travellers into paroxysms of fury. McGee was pilloried as "a veritable Corydon," a paid informer with "blood-money which shrieks in your pocket," a traducer of heroes. Allen, Larkin, and O'Brien were "now a nation's property," the *Irish Canadian* declared; "– a legacy bequeathed to the Irish race; and he who wantonly steps forth and pours the essence of his black heart over their new-made graves incurs the deadly hate of the guardians of their pure and irreproachable memories."[26] "I might also be content to treat with merited contempt," added McNamee, "… a man who had been kicked by Devin Reilly, cow-hided by Doheny in New York, ignominiously hurled down stairs by McKing in Quebec, and spit upon by Devlin in Montreal."[27]

Within the St Patrick's Society of Montreal, revenge was not long in coming. McGee's Wexford speech, his criticisms of the society during the controversy about arming Orangemen in 1865 and the Felix Prior case of 1866, his hard line against Fenian prisoners, his attacks on Devlin, his accusations that Fenians had taken over the society and burned its record books, and now his vilification of the Manchester Martyrs – all this demonstrated that he was indeed deserving of "deadly hate." A committee that included W.B. Linehan denounced him for "endeavouring to brand as incendiaries and conspirators the Representative Irish National Body of this city." When the committee presented its report, a motion to expel McGee from the society was carried overwhelmingly. Only one person voted against.[28]

---

Against this background, the authorities in Montreal received reports about Fenian plans to burn down stores, the fire stations, and the Grand Trunk buildings on Christmas Eve. In response, the Montreal Water Police (which had been formed specifically to counter the Fenian threat) was called out onto the streets. The government had initially intended to disband the police force in the middle of January. But with the heightened state of tension and the "present state of excitement in numerous circles on the frontier," it was decided to keep the force intact for at least another month.[29] "Here, in the City where some of our most esteemed citizens have received letters of a most threatening character," wrote Charles Coursol, the head of the Water Police, "they act as a secret body guard, thereby protecting life and property in case of danger."[30]

But the Water Police were nowhere to be seen on New Year's Night 1868, when two men came to McGee's house on St Catherine Street – Patrick James Whelan and his friend Thomas Murphy. Whelan had moved from Montreal to Ottawa the previous November (shortly before McGee had gone to Ottawa for the opening of Parliament) and had returned to the city on Christmas Eve.[31] Around 1:30 in the morning, he knocked on McGee's door, while Murphy hung back in the shadows. When John Joseph McGee, Thomas D'Arcy's half-brother, opened the door, Whelan told him that he had a message for McGee and must see him personally. Locking the door behind him, John Joseph escorted Whelan to McGee's library, where Whelan introduced himself as "Smith of the Grand Trunk" and told McGee that his house was going to be burned down at four o'clock that morning. McGee dashed off a note to the superintendant of the Water Police and asked Whelan to deliver it – which Whelan did, at a quarter to five, well after the time of the supposed attack.[32]

Possibly with this incident in mind, McGee subsequently informed Macdonald that there were "many suspicious strangers" in Montreal, and called for a special report on the situation.[33] Meanwhile, Macdonald's own sources indicated that McGee's life was in danger. "Many thanks for your hint about my personal safety," McGee wrote to Macdonald in February. "I shall not forget it."[34]

———•·•———

But anyone who wanted to assassinate McGee in the early weeks of 1868 – and there could have been a long list – would have to wait. From late December to early March, he was confined to his house, still suffering from his illness. Although alcohol may have dulled the pain, he continued to resist the temptation to resume drinking. The previous November, at the beginning of Parliament, one of his first (and successful) endeavours had been to get the bar removed from the House of Commons – something that would have been distinctly out of character only a year earlier.[35] In December, he told the Lachute Sons of Temperance that he had "resolved, with the aid all men need, to give total abstinence, as we say of the Ministry here, a 'full and fair trial,'" adding that he would like to give himself sufficient time ("a year or two at least") before speaking publicly on the subject – another indication that he was determined not to repeat his previous pattern of backsliding.[36]

Now that he had stopped drinking, he told his old friend Charles Meehan, it would no longer be possible for his enemies "to slander my private life in order to injure my public usefulness." "Though I was

not, until last year, a teetotaler," he added, "I never could have done
the things I have done, or surmounted the obstacles I did overcome
in this country, if I had been the wretched thing these unscrupulous
gentlemen stigmatize me of being. Of course with my temperament
I must have enemies, but I feel that I should outlive the malice if not
the men."[37]

As his illness dragged on, McGee struggled with "physical exhaustion" and probably with depression as well. "The keen cares and an-
noyances were always with me," he wrote to Macdonald in February, "and very uncomforting companions they were."[38] Among the
"keen cares" was his increasingly difficult financial situation. Now that
McGee was no longer a cabinet minister, he lost the salary that went
with the position. In the past, he had made money on the lecture circuit, but the state of his health prevented him from accepting speaking
engagements.[39] He had incurred heavy election expenses during his
campaigns in Montreal and Prescott, and his creditors were pressing
in on him. "I am pestered and penniless," he told Macdonald in a letter marked Strictly Confidential, "and want about $1000, to gain time,
and save my credit. Could you let me have half, 'payable on Demand,'
which I hope would mean, during this present year."[40]

In these circumstances, he began to take stock of his life and to look
for new directions – yet another turn in his variegated career. In February, Macdonald suggested that he take up an appointment as the commissioner of patents, a position that was a significant step down from
his previous status as a cabinet minister. At first, McGee demurred. "I
shall not feel, that either a hampered or subordinate office, is a sphere
into which I ought to go, or any friends to ask me," he replied. "I
have never asserted my personal pretensions very much; but I cannot
consent to write myself down, as without any."[41] But the only viable
alternative was to resume his work as a journalist, and he had lost all
desire to devote himself "to those infernal gods – the Publishers, for
daily drudgery."[42] Before long, a combination of financial desperation
and a potentially substantial salary made him change his mind. "This
is my last Session in actual legislative harness," he told James Sadlier.
"That arrangement which I mentioned to you and Mrs Sadlier as on
the tapis, of a life office, worth $4,000 a year, will be completed, please

God, before June. It will be right welcome and sore is it needed. It will enable me, too, to return to literature, which was my first, and at all times my favorite, line of exertion."[43]

It was a momentous decision. Now that Confederation had been accomplished, now that his political career was in trouble, it was through literature that he would "do something yet, not discreditable to my Country."[44] He had consistently argued that literature was the lifeblood of the nation and had moved from prescription to practice with his Canadian ballads. While he was laid up in bed, he occupied himself with writing a 650-page semi-autobiographical "Irish-American tale" (no copy of which seems to survive) and continued his poetic compositions.[45] In the years to come, he planned to contribute to a new literature for the new nationality – although, McGee being McGee, he would have remained as politically engaged as ever. Had he lived, McGee would have set out to become for Canada what Thomas Davis had been for Ireland.

---

Had he lived ... There was no other Irish Catholic politician anywhere in the world who was detested as much by the Fenians and their sympathizers as McGee. The death threats continued to come in, at the very time when the most militant Fenians in Montreal were renewing their efforts to support the next invasion attempt, which appeared imminent.

After John O'Neill replaced William Roberts in January as the leader of the Senate wing, preparations for a spring invasion acquired a new urgency.[46] Then, in February, a new source of information reached British and Canadian authorities from an informer in New York, who went under the pseudonym of James Rooney.[47] At the beginning of March, the Fenian leadership sent Rooney to the frontier to distribute arms and ammunition at Rouse's Point and Malone.[48] In St Albans, he met a delegation of four men from Montreal – John Ward, Patrick Cashen, a Mr Connelly, and a Mr Hughs – and gave them boxes of arms.[49] They were apparently coordinating their activities with a grocer named Nicholas Hart, who along with two men named Jackson was "head of a gang" that would support O'Neill's invading army.[50] The attack on Montreal was planned for the night of St Patrick's Day, when there would be an assault on the military barracks and the officers' quarters in the centre of the city; while this was going on, the main force would capture the arsenal on St Helen's Island. "There is a man – living of the Island of the name of O'Brien," Rooney reported, "and I believe he keeps the keys of the Magazine and they tell me he is 'all right.'" "The Canadian men have great hopes," reported Rooney, "and Ward said it will not be lost like the Papineau War."[51]

The city's authorities went on full alert. A close watch was kept on the men whom Rooney had named. Charles Coursol reported that Hart sold illegal liquor to soldiers, "which looks rather suspicious"; the chief constable, John McLoughlin, described Ward and Connelly as "wild characters."[52] From the frontier, one of Ermatinger's detectives reported that "arms are coming to St. Albans daily," and Ermatinger himself reckoned that Rooney's information about an arms build-up on the frontier was "quite probable."[53]

As it transpired, everything was quiet on St Patrick's Day; the parade passed off peacefully, and the St Patrick's Society held an evening concert featuring Anglin as the guest of honour.[54] On the streets, the military and police were out in force, guarding key installations and seeking any signs of Fenian activity. Nothing happened. Either the counter-measures had deterred the Fenians or Rooney was retailing rumours. Rooney, of course, preferred the former explanation and attempted to restore his reputation by supplying British authorities with the Fenian cypher for secret messages. Ermatinger, for his part, believed that this was yet another example of exaggeration, while McMicken dismissed the reports as "entirely baseless."[55] But the situation on the frontier remained volatile, and the Montreal Fenians who were working with the prospective invaders continued to regard McGee as their greatest public enemy.

---

McGee was not in Montreal on St Patrick's Day; nor would he have been welcomed there by many of the Irish organizations in the city, with the principal exception of the Irish Protestant Benevolent Society. He was in Ottawa, speaking at a banquet in his honour, before a mixed audience of Irish Protestants and Catholics, and accompanied among others by Cartier and Macdonald. The central theme of his talk was the need for justice in Ireland. Rather than "keeping a pot boiling in Ireland to scald us out here in the colonies," he said, British politicians should learn from the example of Canada. "The best argument we here can make for Ireland is to enable friendly observers at home to say, 'See how well Irishmen get on together in Canada. There they have equal civil and religious rights; there they cheerfully obey just laws, and are ready to die for the rights they enjoy, and the country that is so governed.' Let us put that weapon into the hands of the friends of Ireland at home, and it will be worth all the revolvers that ever were stolen from a Cork gunshop, and all the Republican chemicals that ever were smuggled out of New York." Then, with a rendition of "The Red, White and Blue," a toast to "The Land We Left," and an address of thanks for McGee's "god-like work of making peace among all classes of the community," he left what would be his last St Patrick's Day celebration.[56]

Ireland's future, he believed, would lie in practical reforms rather than unattainable revolution; it was the tradition of Burke, Grattan, O'Connell, and Duffy that had to prevail, rather than that of Paine, Tone, Mitchel, and Stephens. McGee saw his own future as lying more in literature than politics, although he would never view them as entirely separate entities, and he would write for Ireland and Irish America as well as for Canada. "I hope this fall to issue a volume of ballads at New York," he told Charles Meehan on 6 April. "What do you say to this title: 'Celtic Ballads and Funeral Songs'? You know I am an old keener, and half my lays are lamentations. It could not well be otherwise in this age with an Irish bard, if I am worthy to be called a Bard of Erin."[57]

Death was on his mind. His old friend Lawrence Devany had died only a month earlier; McGee had been one of the pallbearers, and composed "Requiem Aeternam" in his honour.[58] The warnings about threats on his own life were taking their toll; the day before he wrote his letter to Meehan, McGee had a disturbing dream in which he fell into Niagara Falls while trying to save others from going under – a powerful metaphor for his relationship with Irish Canadian Catholics.[59]

But life was on his mind as well. His health had improved during March, he was still off the drink, he had secure economic prospects as commissioner of patents, and he had shaken off the depression that had dogged him during the winter. He was turning forty-three on Easter Monday, 13 April, and his friends and admirers in Montreal were planning to present him with a "life-size portrait in oil," painted by Bell-Smith.[60] In anticipation of his return home, he wrote a letter to his daughter Peggy, then ten years old: "Mamma sent me all your kind messages and kisses, which I have counted up, and find you owe me in all 220. Remember that. Frasa wrote me, since I came here two very nice letters, and I hope next year, to be able to have a few lines from you. I sent 'Frasa a little locket because it was her birthday; and as Easter Monday (April 13th) is mine, I propose to give you some little memorial of the day. What it is to be, I can't tell till I consult Mamma. I hope Alley and Katy and you enjoy this beautiful weather, and that Fido and the dolls are all well, and dutiful as usual. Don't forget your lessons, dear old woman, is the special request of Papa."[61]

And then there was the future of Canada. "Our friends in the Cabinet seem to be getting on very well together," he wrote to Charles Tupper on 6 April. "The breakers ahead have gone down, and all is plain sailing at present ... The temper of our House – except an odd mauvais subjet, like Parker, is extremely good."[62] "Parker" was Doctor Thomas Parker, the MP for Wellington Centre in Ontario, who maintained that the government's tariff policy discriminated against the Maritimes and who criticized the government for sending Tupper to London, where he was countering the activities of a separatist Nova Scotia delegation.

Later that night, in the House of Commons, McGee took Parker on directly. Rather than approaching the issue in a fair and reasonable manner, McGee said, Parker was "seeking for subjects of irritation" – strange behaviour for a doctor, he added. And rather than openly opposing the principles of the union, Parker was striking below the belt by attacking Tupper when he was not there to defend himself.[63] As McGee said these words, a messenger in the House of Commons, Edward Storr, saw two men in the east gallery respond with anger. One of them clenched his teeth, shook his fist, and "put his right hand towards his breast, as if feeling for something, and nodded to a companion, who did the same."[64]

Either ignoring the men or unaware of their gestures, McGee continued with his speech. Tupper may have been unpopular in Nova Scotia, but "mere temporary or local popularity" should never be the test "by which to measure the worth or efficiency of a public servant … He who builds upon popularity builds upon a shifting sand." A true leader, said McGee, is someone who is "ready to meet and stem the tide of temporary unpopularity, who is prepared, if needs be, to sacrifice himself in defence of the principles which he has adopted as those of truth – who shows us that he is ready not only to triumph with his principles, but even to suffer for his principles."[65] Every word could also have been applied to McGee himself in his battle with Fenianism; in a sense, he was writing his own epitaph.

Privately, McGee was convinced that the opponents of Confederation in Nova Scotia were closet annexationists. A few weeks earlier, he had suggested to Macdonald that "both Masonic and Orange influences of the right kind, might be brought to combat these republican tendencies" – another indication of how far he had travelled from his earlier blanket condemnations of the Orange Order.[66] Publicly, McGee tried to distinguish between what he saw as genuine grounds for complaint and those which he thought were being manufactured or exaggerated to further a secret annexationist agenda. If Nova Scotians presented a reasonable case for reform, in a spirit of goodwill, specific issues such as tariff impositions could be settled with fairness and justice.[67]

Continuing his speech, McGee said he had "great reliance on the mellowing effects of time." Time would show that the union was in the interests of all, that there was no threat to Nova Scotia, and that Confederation would operate in a spirit of benevolence. "Its single aim from the beginning," he concluded, "has been to consolidate the extent of British North America with the utmost regard to the independent powers and privileges of each Province, and I, Sir, who have been, and still am, its warm and earnest advocate, speak here not as the representative of any Province, but as thoroughly and emphatically a Canadian, ready and bound to recognize the claims, if any, of my Canadian fellow subjects, from the farthest east to the farthest west, equally as those of my nearest neighbour, or of the friend who proposed me on the hustings."[68] And with these, the last words of his last speech, he sat down. This, too, would be a kind of epitaph.

# PART FOUR

# Assassination

My mother remembered being at her grandfather Mulvihill's when
he came in with the paper announcing Thos. D'arcy McGee's death –
Grandma raised her hands to heaven saying "May the Lord have mercy
on his soul" – while Grandpa did a step, waving the paper over his
head, saying "Hell's flames to your soul, Thomas D'arcy McGee."

Nora Daly, "Sketches of Our Ancestors:
The Thomas Daly Family," private manuscript, 1968, 2–3

## CHAPTER FIFTEEN

# A Chain of
# Circumstantial Evidence

He was in a good mood when the House adjourned shortly after two o'clock in the morning. He had completed his letter to the Earl of Mayo about the Canadian example for Irish reform; he had written to Charles Meehan and Charles Tupper about his literary pursuits; and he had spoken to "great applause" in the House about the spirit of Confederation. By way of celebration, he bought himself three cigars, lit one of them, and left the House with his fellow MP Robert MacFarlane. It was a surprisingly mild night for early April, and the moon was full. A few yards behind them was a group of four men, employees of the House of Commons. One of them, John Buckley, called out, "Goodnight, Mr. McGee." "Good morning," he replied. "It is morning now." He turned off by himself at Sparks Street, walking slowly with the help of his cane; his lodgings, in Mrs Trotter's boarding house, were a hundred yards away.

Mrs Trotter was still up, waiting for her thirteen-year-old son Willie to come home from the House, where he was working as a page. Suddenly, she heard "quick steps passing the dining room window," followed by "a noise as of some one rattling at the hall door." As she opened the door, she thought someone had set off a firecracker; then she saw a figure slumped against the right-hand side of the doorway. She rushed back into the hall, reached for a lamp, and realized that her doorway was spattered with blood; she saw the slumped figure fall to the ground and knew immediately that he was dead. His face was unrecognizable.

Detective Edward O'Neill was awoken sometime before three o'clock in the morning. He was well known within Ottawa's Irish Catholic community and was well placed to ask the right people the right questions. Among other people, he questioned Patrick Buckley (John's brother), who had been chief marshal at the recent St Patrick's Day parade and was a doorkeeper at the House of Commons and a sometime coachman for both George Brown and John A. Macdonald. At first, Buckley refused to talk. "My God, do you want to ruin me, and have my house burned over me?" he asked when O'Neill started questioning him. As O'Neill kept pressing him for information, Buckley told him to "go to Eagleson's and arrest the sandy whiskered tailor there."[1] Eagleson's was a tailor's shop on Sussex Street; its owner, Peter Eagleson, was one of the leading Fenians in the city, and he had visited the scene of the assassination between four and five o'clock in the morning, when very few people knew about it. All this made him an early object of suspicion; he was the first person arrested in connection with the murder.[2]

But who was the "sandy whiskered tailor" whom Buckley mentioned but refused to name? After further investigations, O'Neill identified him as Patrick James Whelan, generally known as Jim Whelan, who was lodging at Michael Starrs's hotel and had been in the parliamentary gallery the previous night. Around nine thirty in the evening, O'Neill and four other policemen followed Whelan into Starrs's hotel and searched his room.[3] They found "a number of papers called *Irish American*, published in New York, dated 7th March 1868," along with a badge of the Toronto Hibernian Benevolent Society, a membership card of the Montreal St Patrick's Society, and a ball ticket for the Ottawa St Patrick's Literary Society. They also found a drawing of a man hanging on a log, with the verse, "This is the shadow of what really should be / Of all unworthy beings such as thee. / A log of wood and a bit of twine / Will suit you better than me for a valentine."[4]

The *Irish American* supported the invasion of Canada; the fact that Whelan possessed several copies of the same issue suggested that he was one of the paper's Ottawa distributors. As we have seen, the Toronto Hibernian Benevolent Society, contained a large number of Fenians; its badge contained the Fenian symbols of the sunburst and the phoe-

Patrick James Whelan. When he was arrested the day after McGee's assassination, the police found copies of the *Irish American*, a Fenian newspaper, along with membership cards to Irish nationalist organizations, a threatening note, and a gun that had apparently been fired within the previous two days. Whelen always denied that he shot McGee, although he said just before his execution that he knew who did so and that he had been present when McGee was killed. (LAC, C-017572)

nix. We have also seen that the St Patrick's Society in Montreal had been taken over by the Fenians; in Ottawa, the St Patrick's Literary Society was the home of the city's most radical Irish nationalists.[5] It seemed clear that Whelan moved in a Fenian milieu, that he was either a Fenian or a Fenian sympathizer. It also seemed clear that the drawing and the verse had been intended to threaten someone – McGee himself, perhaps, on Valentine's Day? But if so, why had it not been sent?

If Whelan was indeed a Fenian, this did not of course make him the murderer. But O'Neill and his detectives found something that was much more incriminating – Whelan's Smith & Wesson revolver. Five of the cartridges had been in the gun for a long time, O'Neill reported, but the sixth "had every appearance of having been recently put in." Not only that, but Whelan had pressed fresh grease on top of each ball. "It appeared to have been done," O'Neill said, "to avoid suspicion of the revolver being just lately discharged." Whelan had also cleaned the inside of the barrel, but "the muzzle showed fresh powder, as if it had been recently fired off." When asked how long such a powder mark would remain in the muzzle, O'Neill replied that it would "last perhaps two days after the discharge" – and he had examined the gun less than twenty-four hours after the murder.[6]

Everything appeared to fit. Whelan was a Fenian or at the very least a Fenian sympathizer; his gun had been fired within the previous two days; he had left the House of Commons at the same time as McGee; and he had no alibi for his whereabouts between ten past and half past two on the morning of the murder. He had the motivation, the means, and the opportunity; it seemed an open-and-shut case. Whelan was arrested, charged with murder, and incarcerated in the Ottawa jail.

———

The Police Magistrate's Inquiry into the assassination began two days later, with Martin O'Gara presiding. Although no one in power knew it, O'Gara was actually playing a double game; outwardly loyal, he was feeding information to leading Irish nationalists about counter-intelligence operations against the Fenians.[7] But he handled the inquiry with consummate professionalism – and its evidence did not look good for the prisoner. Mrs Trotter testified that Whelan had made two late-night visits to her boarding house shortly before the murder; William Graham, a doorkeeper at the House of Commons, reported that Whelan had been restless, nervous, and anxious on the night of the murder. Had he been staking out the scene of the crime and steeling himself for the assassination?[8]

It also transpired that three years earlier, Whelan had been arrested in Quebec for attempting to swear a soldier into the Fenian Brotherhood while using the pseudonym of James Sullivan – Sullivan being his mother's maiden name. Although he had been acquitted, a cloud of suspicion hung over his head; it was notoriously difficult to convict anyone for suborning soldiers, since two witnesses were required. Knowing this, Fenians usually approached potential recruits in the army one at a time. In the Quebec case, only one soldier testified against Whelan, and that was not enough.[9]

After the first day's proceedings, the Crown's counsel, James O'Reilly, asked for an eight-day recess so that he could gather more evidence; O'Gara agreed. In the meantime, under the suspension of the Habeas Corpus Act, the police were making more arrests. Peter Eagleson, Whelan's employer, was already in jail; now he was joined by Michael Starrs, Whelan's landlord, and by some of Whelan's friends and acquaintances in Ottawa. On the night of the murder, Whelan had spoken in the House to Patrick Buckley and had spent some time with his old friend John Doyle; both men were arrested, along with an Ottawa schoolteacher whom Whelan knew, Ralph Slattery.[10] Before long, the net widened to include Whelan's former drinking companions at Kate Scanlan's tavern in Montreal – Michael Enright, Thomas Murphy, and James Kinsella.[11] Whelan's wife Bridget was kept in custody while her house was searched; nothing was found, and she was released the following day.[12]

The government also moved against the Fenian leadership in Montreal – men who had frequently appeared in the reports of spies and informers, and who may or may not have known Whelan. One of them was Henry Murphy, who had spent the weekend before the assassination in the Fenian headquarters in New York, where he had held a five-hour secret meeting with John O'Neill. Another was Patrick Doody, who was thought to have been the head centre of the Canadian Fenians.[13] Others included the radical printer Felix Callahan and the pork dealer John Curran, both of whom had been involved in McNamee's plot to raise a Fenian regiment in Montreal.[14] McNamee himself was conspicuously absent among those who were arrested – thus strengthening rumours that he was a government spy.

James O'Reilly. An Irish Catholic Queen's Counsel from Kingston, O'Reilly played a leading role in investigating Fenianism in Canada, and he was the prosecuting attorney at Whelan's trial. One of his first acts was to exclude his co-religionists from the jury to counter the "well-known sympathy on the part of many Roman Catholics in this neighbourhood with Whelan" (*Globe*, 8 September 1868). (NPA, McCord Museum)

A major reason for the arrests was the belief that Whelan had not acted alone. Macdonald was initially convinced that the assassination was "a deliberate decision of the Fenian Organization," with orders coming from the top.[15] Such a view was not beyond the bounds of possibility; the Fenians in Ireland, under the leadership of Tom Kelly, had their own assassination circle, and it seemed reasonable to assume that American Fenians felt the same way.[16] But the reports from spies and informers in the United States told a different story; John O'Neill not only publicly condemned "the dastardly, cowardly assassination of McGee" but privately repudiated it as well.[17]

Yet the possibility remained that the assassination had been planned and carried out by a group of Canadian Fenians, acting on their own initiative. After making more inquiries, Detective Edward O'Neill certainly thought so. "I believe the conspiracy was hatched by Whelan Murphy Enright and others at Scanlans," he told Macdonald on 13 April, the day of McGee's funeral.[18] Macdonald concurred; McGee's murder, he wrote some three weeks later, was "not the act of one individual only, but the result of a conspiracy, and it is to be more than feared that many of the conspirators are now at large."[19]

At the same time, the arrests served two other purposes. The greater the number of Fenians who were rounded up, the more likely it became that one of them could be pressured into providing evidence for the Crown.[20] Beyond this, the assassination provided the government with the opportunity to disrupt the Fenian movement in Canada. In May, the government arrested the editor and the proprietor of the *Irish Canadian*, along with leading figures in Toronto's Hibernian Benevolent Society; shortly afterwards, real or suspected Fenians in Guelph also were imprisoned.[21] The arrests in Toronto and Guelph had no discernible connection with McGee's murder; their intention was to muzzle the Irish Canadian nationalist press and decapitate Canadian Fenianism.

———•·•———

When the Police Magistrate's Inquiry resumed on 16 April, more evidence against Whelan began to accumulate. Alec Turner, who had lodged in Whelan's house during the previous summer, testified that Whelan was a Fenian, had repeatedly threatened to kill McGee, and had gone to McGee's house with that purpose in mind. John Joseph McGee related the story of the suspicious nocturnal visit on New Year's night and identified Whelan as the man who had called himself "Smith of the Grand Trunk." Another witness, Louis Roy Desjardins, recounted that on 1 April, the Wednesday before the murder, Whelan sat next to him in the parliamentary gallery, behaved in an agitated manner, and carried a revolver in his breast pocket.[22]

Later that same Wednesday night, someone had fired a shot into the windowsill of Mrs Trotter's boarding house.[23] On the Saturday after the murder, a crier for the Court of Queen's Bench, Edward Armstrong, decided to do a little freelance investigation. Entering an unlocked and abandoned house directly opposite Mrs Trotter's, he found "a piece of paper, soiled with powder stains" on the second floor, indicating that a gun had been fired from the upstairs window. Could this have been the work of Whelan? The week before the murder, he had not only visited Mrs Trotter's boarding house twice but spent three consecutive nights in Mrs McKenna's tavern, next door to the abandoned house – including Wednesday night.[24] Even more suspicious were the boot prints in the snow that Armstrong found at the rear verandah of the abandoned house. Detective O'Neill came round with a pair of Whelan's boots and found that there was a perfect fit, right down to the nail marks in the heel.[25] It would have taken someone less than a minute to get from the Parliament Buildings to the verandah.[26]

According to the governor of the jail, Alexander Powell, Whelan "seemed agitated" when his boots were taken away and insisted that he was not wearing them on the night of the murder.[27] But the pieces could easily be put together to make a plausible picture – that of Whelan stalking McGee with malicious intent, using the abandoned house as his base, returning on the night of the murder, waiting to see if the coast was clear, and then seizing the opportunity to assassinate the man whom he regarded as a traitor to Ireland.

James Moylan of the *Canadian Freeman* summed it up. "Link by link the chain of circumstances which serves to connect the man Whelan with the murder of Mr. McGee is completed," he wrote after the inquiry had completed its work:

> His complicity hardly admits of the possibility of a doubt. – The evidence, thus far, though barely circumstantial, is so well knit, so convincing, and so minute in all its details, that it is exceedingly difficult to divest the mind of the impression that Whelan has been connected with the perpetration of the dreadful crime.

The threats so distinctly sworn to by the witness Turner; the change of residence from Montreal – where Whelan had been in the receipt of ten dollars a week from his trade – to Ottawa, at the opening of the session in November; his attendance at the galleries of Parliament, where on one occasion he was most positively identified by an intelligent witness with a pistol in his pocket; his frequent visits to the gallery on the fatal night; his dodging about the lobby after the adjournment and just when the Hon. T.D. McGee was leaving the building; the foot prints in the snow in the rear of the building opposite Trotter's; his subsequent identification at the Russell House immediately after the murder; his pretended ignorance of the fatal occurrence after he had been more than once informed of it; and the pistol found on him after his arrest with such evident marks of one chamber having been discharged but recently – all these present a chain of circumstantial evidence of appalling weight, which in the absence of any exculpatory testimony, cannot but produce a deep impression on the public mind.[28]

Then, just when it seemed that things could not get any worse for Whelan, three developments occurred that appeared to shatter any remaining possibility that he might be innocent. The first came when the police picked up rumours that a French Canadian lumberjack, Jean-Baptiste Lacroix, had been walking along Sparks Street early in the morning of 7 April and had witnessed the murder. Instead of rushing to help the victim, Lacroix had kept on walking and on the following day told his neighbours what he had seen. Not wanting to get involved in the case, he had left for the Lachine Rapids, some nine miles out of town. On Wednesday, 21 April, two weeks later, the police tracked him down and brought him in for questioning. He said that he had seen a man trying to open the door of a house when someone came up from behind, circled into the street, and shot the man in the back of the head.

Lacroix had not got a good view of the killer's face but caught a glimpse of some side whiskers and remembered that the killer was wearing light pants, a dark coat and a hat – all of which fitted with other descriptions of Whelan.[29] When the sheriff, William Powell, made Whelan and his friend James Kinsella dress in the clothes they had been wearing on 6–7 April and put them in an identity parade with several others, Lacroix picked out Whelan, saying that he "recognized him by his size and way of acting." But he also said that he "would not like to swear for certain that he is the person."[30]

Lacroix's story was thoroughly checked. His aunt and uncle confirmed that he had been walking home from their house late that night. Some of the details seemed telling. Lacroix had said that immediately after the murder, the killer started running back, struck his leg on a post and cried out "Jesus." There was indeed a post near Mrs Trotter's door. Ironically, the fact that Lacroix had tried to keep out of trouble by not coming forward as a witness actually strengthened his credibility. So too did the stereotypical image that emerged of Lacroix as a "simple" French Canadian; it seemed that he had neither the incentive nor the ability to manufacture a story for the reward money. Up to this point, all the evidence against Whelan had been circumstantial; now, the Crown had, or thought it had, an eyewitness.[31]

The second development came as a direct result of Alec Turner's testimony at the Police Magistrate's Inquiry on 16 April. Earlier that week, Governor Powell and a prisoner, Robert Hess, had overheard Whelan and his fellow prisoners talking and singing in their cells. According to Powell, Whelan explained why he had stayed in Ottawa immediately after the murder: "I would have been off only Peter [Eagleson] was arrested. If I had the least suspicion, they would never have got hold of the pistol – I would have made away with it." Whelan also struck up a song with the words: "It was with the greatest of glee, I heard of the death of the bloody traitor, D'Arcy McGee, D'Arcy McGee."[32]

But some of the other songs were in Irish, which Powell did not know.[33] So he arranged a meeting with Detective Andrew Cullen, who had come from Montreal on 7 April to assist the investigation and had accompanied Detective O'Neill when Whelan was arrested. Cullen was originally from the Irish-speaking area of County Clare. His surname was actually Cullinan; he had been a member of the Irish Constabulary before moving to Montreal in 1865 and would later be promoted to chief detective in the city.[34] At the governor's request, Cullen and Hess hid themselves near the cells when Whelan returned from the inquiry on 16 April. What they heard, or thought they heard, or said they heard was explosive.

"I was nailed bloody tight to-day," Whelan apparently told Doyle, who was in the opposite cell. "You don't know who's the informer? ... Alick Turner ... I would not give sixpence for his carcass. There was boys there to-day that spot him. I saw a great deal of them here from the country – from Gloucester and all around." Among the "boys" was the brother of his fellow prisoner Ralph Slattery – possibly Richard Slattery, who had organized Fenian circles in Quebec City in support of the invasion. After the brother's name came up in the conversation, Whelan urged everyone to "keep as mute as a mouse here"; he then pro- ceeded to ignore his own warning, and kept on talking. When Doyle said, "I wish you'd never done it, and I wish you never came near me that night," Whelan replied "I would not have come near you only I was drunk." "Jim, I'm sorry for you," Doyle said shortly afterwards; "the whole world will know it." "Yes, I'm a great fellow," Whelan replied. "I shot that fellow ... I shot him like a dog. You're here; I'm here. I'm a great fellow; my name will go down to posterity."[35]

Whelan then began to talk about his mother and his brothers. "What a fine family my mother had – what a fine lot of boys," he said. "One thing, they were fond of Ireland. One was shot at the firing of the police barrack [at Tallaght, during the rising of 1867], one is in prison for the same, and I am in here." Whelan also said that he himself had served eighteen months in the west of England for Fenianism. After saying all this, he then returned to the theme of not saying anything at all. "John," he said to Doyle, "you and me must quit telling about what you know. You understand these buggers might be listening around."[36]

According to the *Globe*'s special correspondent in Ottawa, this was conclusive evidence against Whelan, and the prosecution viewed it "as ample to go to a jury with."[37] Much of the conversation rang true. As Whelan predicted, Turner was indeed targeted as an informer; six weeks after his testimony at the inquiry, he was attacked at an Ottawa dance, and only saved himself by pulling out a revolver.[38] Whelan's brother Joseph had been imprisoned for "complicity in the affray" at

Tallaght during the rising of 1867; although Whelan did not know it, Joseph had already been released and was on his way to Canada.[39] But other parts of the conversation cannot easily be verified; if Whelan had been imprisoned as a Fenian in the "west of England," the record remains elusive.

The third development got underway some two weeks after the press broke the story of the jailhouse conversation. On 7 May, a former English policeman and Great Western Railway detective named Reuben Wade sought a meeting with James O'Reilly.[40] He told O'Reilly that the previous December he had been staying in a Montreal "grocery and groggery" run by Michael Duggan and his wife Mary, and that Whelan had been a regular visitor. On the night of 21 December, Wade reported, he caught snatches of a conversation among Whelan, Duggan, and two other men about the McGee-Devlin election contest. For most of the time, the men were on their guard; but as the whisky flowed, Whelan became increasingly animated, saying that McGee had betrayed his friends and would not live past the New Year. At this point, one of the other men clapped Whelan on the back, saying "Smith, here's our man, he is sound on the goose, and a better man could not be had for the job" – Smith, of course, being the name that Whelan would use when he went round to McGee's house.[41]

The following night, the men met again – and parts of their conversation seemed to be about the best way to assassinate McGee. According to Wade, Michael Duggan said, "My brother John thinks two could go in and two or three outside would be sufficient"; John Duggan was a lawyer who had trained with Bernard Devlin.[42] It sounded as if John Duggan was talking about a four- or five-man hit squad that would kill McGee at his house. One of the others exclaimed, "D'Arcy the poor devil! If he only knew the fate that awaits him he would fly and it would not be the first time either" – a reference to the myth that McGee had run away from danger during the rising of 1848. Wade went on to report that during a conversation on Christmas Eve, one of the men referred to Whelan as "Sullivan." Michael Duggan asked why he was known as Smith and Sullivan instead of his real name. "At the head or under the foot of the stairs," was Whelan's enigmatic reply.[43]

The case for the prosecution was formidable; a guilty verdict appeared to be a foregone conclusion. As well as Whelan's threats, his association with Fenianism, his late-night visit to McGee's house, his behaviour before the assassination, and the police evidence that his gun had been fired within two days before his arrest, O'Reilly now had the eyewitness testimony of Lacroix, the jailhouse confession overheard by Cullen and Hess, and the evidence from Wade that Whelan was the hit man in a Montreal Fenian plot to kill McGee.

There was also evidence against Whelan that the government chose not to introduce at the trial – the reports of two different informers that Whelan was a significant figure in the Fenian Brotherhood. Information reached the British consulate in New York that he had been "the Delegate from Canada to the Cleveland Convention" in September 1867, when the Fenians discussed their invasion plans.[44] It is impossible to assess the accuracy of this report, but its *ex post facto* character means that great skepticism is in order. More intriguing, though, is the report from "James Rooney," the informer from upstate New York who was in contact with Francis Lousada, the British consul in Boston. "I know and had seen this man Whelan several times in New York," wrote Rooney, "and had herd [sic] him express his wish to dispatch some of her Majesty's Subjects and friends in Canada. You remember I mentioned his name sometimes long before the murder."[45] It is unlikely that Rooney would have reminded Lousada of something that he had not previously said, although it is also possible that he had confused Whelan with another Patrick James Whelan, an Irish American journalist.[46]

One thing, though, was abundantly clear: If Whelan was to have any chance of being found not guilty, he would need the best lawyer in the country.

———·———

And that is exactly what he got. We have met John Hillyard Cameron before in these pages – the grand master of the Orange Order, who had presented the Orangemen's petition to Queen Victoria against the treatment of the order during the Prince of Wales's visit to Canada.[47]

John Hillyard Cameron. A former grand master of the Orange Order, with a reputation as the finest lawyer in Canada, Cameron agreed to defend Whelan, partly as a matter of principle and partly because he needed the money. His cross-examination of the Crown's witnesses was brilliant, and his closing address to the jury was described as "one of the most eloquent speeches ever made in Canada" (*Montreal Gazette*, 15 September 1868). (NPA, McCord Museum)

One reason why he took the case was a matter of principle – that of due process and the duty of advocates to defend the accused, even or especially in the face of severe popular prejudice.[48] Another reason was more prosaic; Cameron had lost a fortune in the stock market and needed the money.[49] How much he received for defending Whelan remains unknown; according to one newspaper report, he demanded the staggering sum of $10,000.[50] Whatever money he actually received was raised largely from Irish Catholic Canadians who believed that Whelan was the victim of a rush to judgment, a convenient scapegoat who was being sacrificed to appease the loyalist "thirst for blood."[51] Many, but by no means all, of the subscribers to Whelan's defence fund would have been Fenians and Fenian sympathizers; it is also reasonable to assume that American Fenians contributed to the cause.

When the trial began at the fall assizes in Ottawa on Monday, 7 September, Whelan found himself in the unusual position of being defended by an Orangeman and prosecuted by an Irish Catholic – and James O'Reilly's first act was to challenge and exclude his co-religionists in the process of jury selection. "A Catholic Queen's counsel, and, moreover, an Irishman," complained the *Irish Canadian*, "has enrolled himself amongst the ranks of our worst and most rancorous enemies."[52] According to the *Globe*'s reporter at the trial, O'Reilly justified himself by referring to the "well-known sympathy on the part of many Roman Catholics in this neighbourhood with Whelan."[53]

During the week that followed, Cameron was assisted by Matthew Crooks Cameron and Kenneth McKenzie, with unofficial but energetic support from the Quebec lawyer and politician John O'Farrell. Before the trial, O'Farrell was best known for his defence of Ribbonmen in Saint-Sylvestre who had been accused in 1855 of murdering Robert Corrigan, a Catholic who had converted to Protestantism; O'Farrell had probably been a Ribbonman himself.[54] During the trial, there were reports that O'Farrell had bribed people to become witnesses for the defence; he was also observed signalling to the defence witnesses as they were being cross-examined.[55]

Afterwards, rumours circulated that O'Farrell was actually behind the assassination; both O'Reilly and Macdonald suspected as much, and McGee's close friend James Goodwin felt the same way.[56] According to one story, Goodwin regularly invited McGee back to his house after the parliamentary sessions and had arranged to meet him on the night of the murder. But he was prevented from doing so by an unexpected visit from a man whom he hardly knew and who "detained him with a long, rambling talk" – none other than John O'Farrell, who, it seemed, wanted to ensure that the coast was clear for the assassin.[57]

———•———

And so the former grand master of the Orange Order and the probable ex-Ribbonman joined forces to defend the suspected Fenian and apparent assassin. One of their immediate objectives was to discredit the testimony of Lacroix. In his cross-examination, Cameron established that Lacroix had not been able to pick out Whelan in an identity parade; only when Whelan was brought back wearing the clothes he had worn on the night of the murder could Lacroix make the identification. When Cameron asked Lacroix to describe the man who was shot, Lacroix said that the victim was wearing a black beaver hat; in fact, McGee had been wearing a white hat.[58]

Cross-examining the two policemen who had initially interviewed Lacroix, Matthew Crooks Cameron found further evidence that undermined Lacroix's testimony. Both policemen testified that Lacroix spoke of a small man following and shooting a taller man. But Whelan was taller than McGee; Lacroix got both the height and the hat wrong.[59] Meanwhile, O'Farrell rounded up seven witnesses who testified that Lacroix was a congenital liar, a thief, and a boaster. Most observers of the trial put little stock in these witnesses, and O'Reilly elicited that O'Farrell had paid at least one of them to testify against Lacroix. The defence, O'Reilly remarked, attempted to undermine Lacroix "by bringing men here with a five dollar bill in one hand and the holy gospel in the other."[60] According to the *Globe*'s reporter, O'Farrell's witnesses were unable to substantiate their arguments, and the result was "beyond question as decided a collapse as I have ever seen in a Court of Justice."[61]

Nevertheless, the defence had found enough inconsistencies in Lacroix's story to make his evidence untrustworthy, to say the least. The fact that he had not been able to recognize Whelan in the initial identity parade, that he described Whelan as a short man and McGee as a tall man, and that he said McGee was wearing a black beaver hat when he was actually wearing a white hat, all indicated that Lacroix was either hopelessly confused or lying for the reward money. The defence had scored a clear victory here, as O'Reilly implicitly conceded during the trial. Even without Lacroix's testimony, he said, the "chain of circumstantial evidence" and the condition of Whelan's gun would be enough to secure a conviction.[62]

―――――

Having effectively discredited Lacroix's testimony, the defence set out to undermine another key witness for the Crown, Reuben Wade. According to the prosecution, Wade's testimony demonstrated that Whelan was the designated hit man in a conspiracy to assassinate McGee – that when he had knocked on McGee's door on New Year's night, a week after the overheard conversation, it was with precisely that purpose in mind.[63] Behind this was the implication that Whelan was a Fenian – an issue that never came up at the trial, since whenever the prosecution attempted to introduce evidence about Whelan's political beliefs, the defence objected and the judge sustained the objection.

Wade had told O'Reilly that the conspiratorial conversations at Duggan's tavern in Montreal occurred between 21 and 24 December. But O'Farrell found five witnesses who swore that Whelan was actually in Ottawa until Christmas Eve, when he took the afternoon train to Montreal, arriving at midnight. Duggan himself testified that Whelan had not visited his house at any time over Christmas; this was backed up by his wife Mary and also by a boarder and a family friend.[64]

O'Reilly countered by questioning the motivations of these witnesses and established that one of them, John Lyon, was an Ottawa agent for the *Irish Canadian*.[65] (In fact, the government had information that Lyon's grocery store in Ottawa was a Fenian meeting place, but this was not introduced at the trial.)[66] Another witness, Patrick Kelly, came up with the unlikely story that Whelan admired and liked McGee.[67] Nor did Michael and Mary Duggan appear as sympathetic figures; Michael answered questions reluctantly, and Mary contradicted herself so blatantly that people in court started to laugh at her replies.[68] If O'Reilly wanted to plant the idea that these witnesses were lying to protect a fellow Fenian, he may have met with some success.

But the defence had succeeded in casting considerable doubt on Wade's evidence. If Wade's testimony "fails in one particular," John

Hillyard Cameron reasoned, "you will not think it safe to believe him in any." Not only had several witnesses sworn that Whelan was actually in Ottawa on the nights that Wade supposedly heard him in Montreal; Cameron also pointed out that Wade's story was inherently implausible. "Do you think that men engaged in a conspiracy – men engaged in an act of so daring a character as taking away the life of the foremost man in the land, would meet together in a room 16 by 18 and speak about the plot in the presence of a stranger who had nothing to do with them? whom they never saw before? and speak too so that he should overhear every word they said?" he asked. The answer was obvious: "On the testimony of Reuben Wade not a particle of reliance can be placed."[69]

------

Another crucial task for the defence was to challenge the evidence that Whelan had repeatedly threatened to kill McGee. Here, the main target was Alec Turner, with his stories that Whelan had been enraged with McGee during the Montreal election, had promised to kill him before the parliamentary session was over, and had twice gone to his house with the intention of assassinating him – first during the election campaign and again on New Year's night. After the first visit, Turner had told McGee that there were people in Montreal who meant to kill him; McGee replied that it was probably "only the excitement of the election, and will probably die away," but he asked Turner to keep him posted. After the second visit, Turner testified that while working as a waiter at the Russell House in Ottawa, he overheard Whelan tell John Doyle that had McGee opened the door, he would have "shot the bugger like a dog."[70]

Under a rigorous cross-examination from Matthew Crooks Cameron, Turner stood his ground "remarkably well and came out very creditably," according to the Globe's reporter.[71] In fact, Turner introduced more testimony against Whelan, describing an incident that had happened just before the Montreal election. Under the influence of liquor, Whelan had gone to see Dion Boucicault's play Arrah-na-Pogue, featuring the song "The Wearing of the Green," with its words "they're hanging men in Ireland / For the wearing of the green." This produced an impassioned response from Whelan; when someone in the audience told him to be quiet, he turned round and started choking the man. Afterwards, at a tavern, Whelan produced a photograph of a "young lady" from Quebec he loved, and started crying. All in all, Turner's description of Whelan was that of an intense and volatile Irish nationalist with a hair-trigger personality, a man with a grudge and a gun who hated McGee, stalked him, threatened to kill him, and was likely to make good on those threats when intoxicated.[72] This fitted with Whelan's apparent admission in prison that he had been drinking on the night of the murder.[73]

Having failed to shake Turner's testimony, the defence took two lines of attack. First, as with Lacroix, it tried to show that he was lying for the reward money. Six witnesses, who had been with Turner at Eagleson's shop after Whelan had been arrested, came forward. When Turner learned of the arrest, they testified, Turner had said that Whelan was the "last man he would suspect of the murder" and that he was a decent man who would not hurt "the child unborn." And when Turner heard that the government was offering John Doyle $16,000 for information against Whelan, the witnesses agreed that Turner had said he would swear his own grandfather's life away for half that amount.[74]

O'Reilly responded by highlighting small discrepancies in the witnesses' accounts and by claiming that no reward had actually been offered on the day that the conversation took place. (In fact, the Canadian government, along with the governments of Ontario and Quebec and the city of Ottawa, had all proclaimed a reward on 7 April.)[75] He also made an oblique reference to the reputation of Eagleson's shop as a hangout for Fenians, asking "how it was that Eagleson's was headquarters for news about the murder." As with the witnesses who testified against Wade, O'Reilly implied that they were concocting a story to protect one of their own.[76]

The defence's second line of attack was to hit Turner's testimony at its weakest point, applying the principle that if one part of his story did not hold up, the rest must fall. Hillyard Cameron noted that when Turner was examined at the Police Magistrate's Inquiry in April, he had said nothing about any conversation in the Russell House between Whelan and Doyle after the New Year's night visit to McGee's house.[77]

The explanation for this apparently inconceivable omission, Cameron said, was that Turner appeared at the inquiry before John Joseph McGee had told the police magistrate about Whelan's visit. "It was then, and only then," asserted Cameron, "only after he had listened to this new feature of the case, that we find Turner coming in with a tale of which he had given no hint heretofore, a tale which was more damning than any that had been told before." Turner, he concluded, in keeping with a man who would swear his grandfather's life away for half the reward money, was obligingly manufacturing a link in the Crown's broken chain of evidence.[78]

Not only that, the defence argued; the link itself was badly flawed. Turner had said that he overheard the conversation during the lunch-time shift at the Russell House. But the place was busy, Turner was in a glass pantry washing his hands, and Whelan and Doyle were talking in low tones in an adjacent passageway. How, then, with all that noise, could Turner possibly have heard what they were saying, if indeed they were saying anything at all?[79]

In response, the prosecution arranged a re-enactment of the Russell House conversation. Two men (one of whom was Detective Cullen) in the passageway repeated Whelan's words "in a low tone," while two others in the glass pantry turned on the water and washed their hands. The conversation, they reported, could be heard quite distinctly.[80] If this lent credence to Turner's story, the fact that he had omitted it from the Police Magistrate's Inquiry still left a large question about his evidence. Turner himself offered two explanations – first that he had only been asked about events in Montreal, and second that he was too frightened to volunteer the information.[81] Neither one was credible; Hillyard Cameron had punched a large hole through Turner's testimony.

But the rest of Turner's evidence – the repeated threats that Whelan had made towards McGee during the election contest – could not be so easily dismissed. Two other witnesses, Joseph Faulkner and James Inglis, corroborated Turner's testimony that Whelan had threatened to kill McGee. Faulkner, a tailor who worked with Whelan in Montreal, stated that Whelan had told him that McGee "was a traitor and deserved to be shot." Inglis, who had been a lodger in Whelan's house, remembered Whelan saying that if McGee won his seat, he would not keep it for long. "Who would do anything to him?" Inglis had asked. "I would, if nobody else," Whelan replied. Inglis also testified that Whelan had paid a nocturnal visit to McGee's house after the election.[82]

The defence had no answer to this. Hillyard Cameron was forced to fall back on the argument that any such threats arose merely from the ephemeral excitement of a hotly contested election campaign and should not be taken seriously. After all, he claimed, neither Faulkner nor Inglis had "attached any weight" to Whelan's words when they heard them, and neither should the jury.[83] Yet it was not clear that Faulkner and Inglis had in fact taken Whelan's words lightly, and there is no doubt that those words carried greater retrospective weight after the assassination.

Nor did the defence have a good explanation for Whelan's New Year's night visit to McGee's house. If Whelan had indeed threatened McGee in the heat of the election campaign, it was hardly likely that he would go on a goodwill mission to McGee's house to warn him about an impending attempt to burn it down. And if Whelan really had gone on such a goodwill mission, why did he delay telling the police until well after the supposed threat had passed? It seemed more likely, in the circumstances, that Whelan had indeed set out to assassinate McGee but had been frustrated by the presence of McGee's brother.

On the question of threats, then, the prosecution's case had been dented but not broken. Even if Turner's testimony is dismissed in its entirety, the unchallenged evidence of Faulkner and Inglis, along with the suspicious circumstances of the New Year's night visit, remained important links in the Crown's chain of circumstantial evidence.

———————

Another link in that chain was Whelan's behaviour shortly before the murder. At the trial, Louis Roy Desjardins reiterated his earlier testimony that a "nervous and excited" Whelan had brought a gun into the parliamentary gallery five days before McGee was shot. Still more strikingly, Edward Storr, a messenger in the House of Commons, testified that Whelan was behaving aggressively towards McGee on the night of the assassination itself.[84] "I noticed the prisoner leaning, with his fingers pointed threateningly at McGee," Storr told the court. "I noticed his face, and that his teeth seemed to close, and his features seemed to wear a sort of grin; his hand was over the rails and closed, and the forefinger opened pointing and shaking at McGee ... There was a small, light-compexioned man, dressed in light clothes, on his right hand side. A few minutes after he placed his hand on his breast, and seemed to be feeling for something; he then put his left hand inside his breast pocket, on the right side, and nodded to the other man; he seemed to motion to the party sitting; he nodded his head and moved his hand like a signal; the other man nodded in the same way, and also put his hand on his coat in just the same way." Storr was so disturbed by the behaviour that he wrote about it later that night in his diary: "Noticed four men in the gallery next the Speaker's, very restless, one young man fair compexioned, the worst."[85]

This description corresponded with William Graham's testimony at the Police Magistrate's Inquiry that Whelan had been agitated on the night of the assassination – testimony that had resulted in a death threat against Graham a few weeks later, but which he repeated at the trial.[86] Graham also told O'Reilly that Whelan visited the House only when McGee was speaking. Taken in conjunction with Mrs Trotter's and Mrs McKenna's accounts of Whelan's repeated visits to their establishments just before the murder, this suggested a pattern of stalking.[87] Another witness, John Downes, said that when the parliamentary session finished on 7 April, he saw Whelan walking alone down the centre walk from the House, rather than eastwards in the direction of the Russell House or Michael Starrs's hotel. And the centre walk would have taken him towards Sparks Street and the scene of the murder.[88]

How could the defence counter this body of evidence? Again, Hillyard Cameron went for the weakest link – William Graham. In his initial deposition to the police, Graham had said that Whelan was wearing a light-coloured coat and cap on the night of the murder, and could not remember the pants. But in court, Graham recalled that Whelan wore "a dark frock coat, light trowsers, cravat with a piece of green in it, and a cap." Graham had changed his testimony to make it fit with the description that Lacroix had given of the killer – a man wearing a dark coat and light pants. This being the case, nothing that Graham said could be believed.[89]

When it came to the evidence of Desjardins, Storr, and Downes, however, the defence hit a stone wall — and their testimony was deeply damaging to Whelan. Cameron's only recourse was to downplay the significance of their stories. Whelan might have been carrying a gun five nights before the assassination, but no one saw him with a gun on the night itself. There was nothing in McGee's final speech that would have incensed an impassioned Irish nationalist, as Whelan was said to be. If Whelan was pointing his finger, what did that prove? He could have been pointing it at anyone. If Whelan was "restless," it was probably because he had to make frequent trips to the toilet. And if he was walking towards Sparks Street, so what? "It showed simply that he was one out of many men who were then abroad, and one out of many men *might* have committed the crime."[90] It was the best defence that could have been mounted in the circumstances. How effective it was, though, is another matter.

Even more challenging for the defence was the evidence of Andrew Cullen and Robert Hess about Whelan's jailhouse confession on 16 April. Here, Cameron faced a particularly difficult problem: although it would be relatively easy to cast doubt on the character of Hess, who had been a prisoner at the time, it would have been neither wise nor politic to suggest that Detective Cullen was lying to secure a conviction. Probably for this reason, O'Reilly made sure that Cullen's testimony preceded that of Hess during the trial.

During his cross-examination, Cameron questioned the accuracy of Cullen's memory and the notes of Whelan's conversation and confession. But Cullen was an impressive witness, and the defence failed to cast doubt on his story. Then Hess came to the stand, where he repeated Cullen's testimony "in a slow sing-song, as though learned by heart."[91] Cameron's colleague Kenneth McKenzie conducted a full-press examination. What were you in jail for? Assault. Was it not true that you were allowed to go outside the jail on occasions? Yes, but this was because of good conduct. Were you not given a new suit of clothes by the Sheriff in exchange for your testimony? True, but they were provided for the trial and on condition of subsequent repayment. Did you not tell three fellow prisoners that you would be rewarded if you helped to stretch Whelan's neck? No, there was no truth in that at all.[92]

According to one observer, Hess "gave his evidence firmly and decisively, and without variation throughout." Nevertheless, had he been the only witness to testify about the confession, the defence would have raised enough questions to induce skepticism about his evidence in particular and the value of jailhouse testimony in general. As it was, though, the presence of Cullen stood in the way. So too did the testimony of John Little, a turnkey in the jail, who reported that three days later, on 19 April, he heard Whelan tell Doyle: "It is true that there were three of us, but I was alone when he was murdered." Doyle asked what happened to the others. "They skedaddled home," Whelan reportedly replied, "and if I had not been drunk I would have gone home too."[93]

The only chance that the defence had to break Cullen's testimony was to bring in one of Whelan's fellow prisoners and ask him about the conversation. William Mitchell, a cabinet maker from Toronto, seemed the best bet; he had moved into Starrs's hotel on the night of the murder, had been arrested under the suspension of habeas corpus (probably because of his sudden appearance in Ottawa and because he had refused to take the oath of allegiance as a Grand Trunk worker immediately after the Ridgeway raid) and had been kept in jail for two weeks. After his release, Mitchell had moved to Cincinnati; now he came back to Ottawa as the final witness for the defence. At first, everything went well. Mitchell said he had overheard Whelan talk about Turner's testimony but "did not at any time hear him say anything about his share in the murder of Mr. McGee, or that he had shot him like a dog."

Then, halfway through the examination, O'Reilly paused to confer with Detective Cullen, after which the questions took a new turn. What time, asked O'Reilly, were you in the corridor, listening to the conversation? Between five thirty and six o'clock came the reply. Immediately afterwards, O'Reilly called Governor Powell to the stand. Mitchell could not have been in the corridor during that time, Powell testified, since he had been locked in his cell before five thirty so that Cullen and Hess could position themselves to overhear the conversation. "I swear most positively," Powell said, "both to the fact and the hour." The prosecution then called the turnkey of the jail, who corroborated Powell's account. Mitchell, it seemed, had been caught in a lie; and because his cell was at the opposite end of the corridor from Whelan, he would not have been in a good position to hear what was said.[94] Cullen's story stood, and Mitchell's testimony had backfired on the defence.

———•·•———

Along with the alleged confession, the other piece of critical evidence against Whelan was the condition of his gun. Here, the testimony of Detective O'Neill was of central significance, and it is not surprising that he received a threatening letter ("O'Neill, mind your words; you are being watched") two days before his appearance in court.[95] As at the Police Magistrate's Inquiry, O'Neill said that five cartridges in the gun had been in the cylinders "for some days" and that the sixth "appeared to have been recently put in." All the cartridge balls had been carefully greased, he explained, but the grease on the new cartridge was much brighter than the others and was easily distinguishable. The inside of the barrel also had been "newly and recently cleaned and greased," but it "showed signs of having recently been fired off, bearing marks of powder." The bullet that killed McGee, O'Neill continued, was "the same size as those in the cartridges" – bullets made by C.D. Leet, which were generally used with Smith & Wesson revolvers. Under questioning from Hillyard Cameron, O'Neill confirmed that the mark of powder in the muzzle would last two days; this being the case, Whelan's gun must have been fired between 5 and 7 April.[96]

In his cross-examination of O'Neill, Cameron established that the fatal bullet was consistent with any Smith & Wesson revolver of Whelan's calibre – and such bullets and such guns were commonplace in post–Civil War North America. This did not, of course, challenge O'Neill's conclusion that the gun had been fired around the time of the assassination. Here, Cameron took a new tack, bringing in two witnesses whose testimony provided a completely different explanation for the condition of Whelan's gun.

The first was Euphemie Lafrance, a serving girl at Starrs's hotel. On 19 February, more than six weeks before the assassination, she was cleaning Whelan's room and found his gun "between the mattress and

DETECTIVE O'NEILL.

Detective Edward O'Neill. He played a crucial role in the conviction of Whelan. It was his information that led to Whelan's arrest, and it was his forensic evidence about the gun and the fatal bullet that convinced the jury of Whelan's guilt. (*Montreal Gazette*, 11 September 1868)

the feather bed"; as she set it aside, it went off in her hand, leaving a powder burn on her arm. There was no doubt that she was telling the truth; a doctor at the hospital confirmed that he had treated her that morning.

The second witness was William Goulden, a clerk at Eagleson's shop. Like others who worked in the shop, Goulden challenged the testimony of Wade and Turner, and claimed that Whelan spoke positively about McGee. But Goulden also said that he had inspected Whelan's gun only a week before the assassination, and one of the chambers was empty. The reason he inspected the gun, Goulden added, was that Whelan wanted to sell it – hardly the behaviour of a would-be assassin.

Here, then, was a perfectly innocent explanation for the condition of the cartridges in the cylinder; five of them had indeed been in there for a long time, while the sixth had been put in just before the assassination to replace the bullet that Euphemie Lafrance had accidentally fired. O'Neill had mistaken the powder in the muzzle as coming from a recent firing when in fact it came from Euphemie Lafrance's accident some six weeks earlier. Just as Detective Cullen had heard what he wanted to hear, O'Neill had seen what he wanted to see.[97]

O'Reilly countered with a line of questions that were designed to raise doubts about Goulden's impartiality as a witness: Were you a member of the St Patrick's Society, along with Eagleson, Buckley, Starr, and Whelan? Yes. Were you and Whelan both in the Shamrock Quadrille Club? Yes again. Did you subscribe to the Whelan defence fund? No. Were you at the dance hall on the night that Turner was assaulted? No again. The questions, however, may have made as much an impression on the jury as the answers.[98]

In any case, the prosecution had established that Whelan, unlike the vast majority of people in Ottawa at the time, possessed a loaded gun, which he kept in his bed, took to work, and brought into the House of Commons. And the powder in the barrel of the gun, according to Detective O'Neill, indicated that it had been fired not only by Euphemie Lafrance on 19 February but also by Whelan himself around the time of the murder. If O'Neill had got it wrong, there was no one with the knowledge or ability to contradict him. And if O'Neill had got it right, there was forensic evidence that Cameron and his team simply could not get around.

As Cameron and O'Reilly prepared their final speeches, the key question faced the jury: Was the Crown's chain of circumstantial evidence strong enough to convict Whelan beyond a reasonable doubt?

## CHAPTER SIXTEEN

# The Grip of Suspicion

After six days of testimony and a day of rest on Sunday, the closing addresses took place on 14 September. Hillyard Cameron gave one of the greatest speeches of his career, lasting over two and a half hours, in which he pulled together all the threads of the defence's case. "The law demanded justice, not vengeance," he told the jury; "– the life of a criminal, not the death of a victim."[1] Circumstantial evidence, he said, was insufficient and untrustworthy; to make his point, he cited two cases in which men hanged on such evidence were subsequently proven innocent. Turning from the general to the particular, he argued that there was nothing in Whelan's behaviour on the night of the murder to prove that he was the assassin. He was one of many people who were out late; no one saw him with a gun that night; he could have been pointing his finger at anyone when McGee gave his speech; he was restless because he had to make repeated visits to the toilet. All these circumstances were "consistent equally with innocence as with guilt," and the jury must assume innocence when guilt could not be proved.[2]

True, he said, Faulkner and Inglis reported threats in the summer, but feelings always ran high during elections, and neither man took the threats seriously. Reuben Wade's testimony was worthless and had been contradicted by numerous witnesses; the conspiracy was a figment of his imagination, and no man's life should hinge on such implausible and tainted evidence. Turner's testimony was no better; he was out for the reward money, and he had changed his story after he learned about Whelan's New Year's night visit to McGee's house. Nor should the jury read anything into the fact that Whelan owned a pistol.

There was nothing illegal about that, and he had never tried to conceal its existence; in any case, the evidence of Euphemie Lafrance and William Goulden showed that it had last been fired over six weeks before · the murder.[3] As for Lacroix, there were so many contradictions in his testimony that no jury could take it seriously. Most importantly, Lacroix had failed to recognize Whelan in the identity parade; if Lacroix had been the only witness for the prosecution, the judge would have thrown the case out immediately.[4]

When it came to Whelan's supposed confession, Cameron pointed out that jailhouse evidence, while technically admissible, was notoriously unreliable. If anything, he continued, it actually revealed the weakness of the prosecution's case; lacking hard evidence to convict Whelan, the Crown had decided to surround his cell with "turnkeys, penal-serving prisoners, and detectives" who were eager to pick up any scraps that might strengthen its case. As things stood, the modus operandi seemed to be "find the accused guilty first, and proceed to search for evidence against him after!" And how strange it was that no one heard Whelan confess to the murder until a detective just happened to be listening outside his cell. Whelan was actually repeating Turner's testimony, Cameron explained, and "had thus said, not 'that he had shot McGee like a dog,' but that Turner had sworn that he had said 'he had shot or was ready to shoot McGee like a dog.'" Whelan's words had been twisted ("through misadventure alone," Cameron hoped) into a confession that never actually occurred. There was no basis for a conviction here.[5]

Cameron then repeated his initial point: The jury "must remember that it was upon nothing but the most convincing evidence that they could find a verdict, and that, however abhorrent the crime might be to them or to himself, still Justice was not Vengeance, and that here it was Guilt that was to be punished, and not a Victim to be immolated because the nation had demanded a victim."[6]

The reporters at the trial were deeply impressed. Cameron's "magnificent oratory had carried every listener with him from the beginning," commented one observer, and there was spontaneous applause as he sat down.[7] The *Globe*'s correspondent described the speech as "a masterly effort," and the *Montreal Gazette* called it "one of the most eloquent speeches ever made in Canada."[8]

---

As the applause died down, O'Reilly stood up to present the case for the Crown. Cameron's speech, he began, was "one of the most eloquent ever delivered at this or any other bar." But the jury must not allow itself to be carried away by such eloquence; no reasonable person could hesitate in finding Whelan guilty. The circumstantial evidence was overwhelming, starting with Whelan's threats on McGee's life during the election campaign – threats that went far beyond the usual heated rhetoric of such contests. The evidence of Faulkner and Inglis alone was proof of that – and the defence had raised no questions about its veracity. Their evidence only strengthened the credibility of Turner's testimony – and especially Turner's account of Whelan's violent reaction to McGee's anti-Fenian speeches. "Why should the prisoner at the bar feel indignant with McGee for having denounced Fenianism?" O'Reilly asked. "Was he the special guardian or protector of Fenianism, that he should undertake to destroy McGee's life for having denounced it?"[9]

It was a shrewd opening. O'Reilly not only turned Cameron's eloquence against him but also connected Whelan with Fenianism. This connection, O'Reilly continued, lent weight to Wade's account of the clandestine conversation in Duggan's tavern; and if Wade's sworn testimony could be relied upon, there was "evidence of the most damning character" that Whelan was part of a conspiracy to assassinate McGee. This, in turn, explained Whelan's nocturnal visit to McGee's house only a week later. During that visit, McGee himself had sensed danger; why else would he have asked his brother to stand by him when Whelan came into the house? The fact that Whelan refused to give his real name and had delivered McGee's letter to the police well after the supposed threat had passed meant that McGee's instincts had been correct. All this fitted perfectly with Turner's testimony about Whelan's "shot the bugger like a dog" conversation with Doyle at the Russell House a few days later.[10]

Throughout all the time that Whelan was making these threats, he was carrying a gun, O'Reilly reminded the jury. Contrary to what Cameron said, this was highly unusual; people in Ottawa did not normally go around with loaded revolvers, let alone take them into the House of Commons. To this should be added the clear evidence that Whelan had gestured menacingly at McGee on the very night that he was shot, as well as the fact that he was seen leaving towards Sparks Street rather in the direction of his own home. And why had Whelan been hovering around Mrs Trotter's and Mrs McKenna's on the days before the murder? After previous attempts to assassinate McGee in Montreal, Whelan had been preparing to accomplish the task in Ottawa.[11]

So much for the circumstantial evidence. But there was also direct evidence – specifically, the testimony of Lacroix and the confession overheard by Cullen and Hess. Lacroix was "a simple-minded French Canadian, incapable of concocting the narrative he had told before the jury," a man who had been "afraid of appearing in court"; there was thus no reason to suppose he was lying, despite the testimony of defence witnesses who had been bribed to testify against him. But, O'Reilly added, even if the jury dismissed Lacroix's testimony, the case against Whelan remained overwhelming – not least because of the condition of the gun: "His pistol [was] found to have one chamber just freshly loaded; and the bullet which had been found in Mrs. Trotter's door, was found to correspond exactly with the other balls in the prisoner's revolver."[12]

The final piece in the picture was supplied by the testimony of Cullen and Hess. "Did they think that Andrew Cullen was a perjured witness?" O'Reilly asked the jury. "They could not believe anything of the kind; it was impossible to suppose that he could be so." If Whelan was found guilty on their evidence, and if in fact they had been lying, O'Reilly added, "the blood of the prisoner would be upon their heads, not upon the jury." But why should Cullen and Hess lie? What was in it for them? And what about the testimony of John Little, who was "a respectable farmer from Nepean" and who also had heard Whelan say that he killed McGee? Any jury that had "minds like a sheet of clean white paper" could only find Whelan guilty of murdering D'Arcy McGee.[13]

It was, in its own way, as brilliant as Cameron's speech. Rather than trying to match Cameron's eloquence, O'Reilly had taken a restrained and reasoned approach, delivering what one reporter described as "a very clever, calm, dispassionate address."[14]

When the speeches were over, Judge William Buell Richards picked up his trial notes and delivered his charge to the jury. He was suffering from asthma, which could not have been helped by the crowded court-room, and he had not been looking well during the trial.[15] Neverthe-less, he read and reviewed the testimony for almost six hours, impress-ing upon the jury "the importance of divesting their minds of all foregone conclusions," and insisting that they reach a verdict based on a fair-minded assessment of the evidence.[16] By the time he had finished, the jury had heard close to ten hours of speeches.[17] Shortly before nine o'clock that night, they retired to consider their verdict.

We will never know precisely what went on in the jury room, but we do have a rough idea. In 1934, Chief Justice Robert Latchford, who as a young boy had seen McGee's blood on Sparks Street, recalled over-hearing a conversation between his father and one of the jurors imme-diately after the trial. The man told Latchford's father that the jury believed Lacroix was committing perjury and dismissed his testimony; the "simple-minded French Canadian" argument of the prosecution clearly cut no ice. What did impress the jury, though, was the combina-tion of circumstantial evidence and the forensic evidence about the gun and the bullet.[18]

Whether or not they believed the testimony of Wade and Turner, the jurors must have been impressed with the uncontested evidence of Faulkner and Inglis, with John Joseph McGee's account of Whelan's New Years' night visit, and with the reports of Storr and others about Whelan's behaviour on the night of the murder. Their assessment of the evidence about the confession remains unknown, but it is virtually certain that they took the word of Detective Cullen, backed up as it was by Hess and strengthened by Little, over the testimony of William

Mitchell. And as Judge Richards pointed out, if they believed Cullen's evidence, it was "almost conclusive against the prisoner."[19]

When all of this was put together with the condition of Whelan's gun, any remaining reasonable doubt disappeared. There was apparently incontrovertible evidence that the gun had been fired within two days of Whelan's arrest and that the fatal bullet matched those in Whelan's possession. Sometime during the night of 14 September, the jurors reached their verdict. The next morning, they announced that Patrick James Whelan was guilty of the murder of Thomas D'Arcy McGee.

That same night, Whelan sat in his prison cell and penned a letter to John A. Macdonald. "I have Been Moast Foully and ungustley persecuted," he wrote; the evidence had been manufactured against him by the sheriff and by the governor of the jail – the brothers William and Alexander Powell. They were determined to get him hanged, they had paid witnesses to testify against him, and they had rigged the identity parade to ensure that he was picked out as the murderer. "That will show you sir," he wrote, "The Trechery and The Conspirrissy To Take my Life." Sheriff Powell "said to my fase that hee would Beet Fenians like mee I told him I was no Fenian that my Fatter was English and I was born in Eddinbourgh … Sir I have served my Queen and my Country for 9 years and 8 months in a Caverley Redgment I was 5 years in Indya and Sir if that noble little woman wanted my servis as my Contry i would sacrafies the last Drop of Blod In her Defense To morrow that is the Fenianism I profess."

As further evidence of his loyalty, Whelan stated that he had been a sergeant of the Canadian Hussars in Quebec during the Fenian raid, and claimed that he had been forced to leave Montreal after informing McGee about the plan to burn down his house. "I dont mind in the least if i am found guilty in The way that the Evadans was produced against mee," he wrote, "But Sir It does not make mee guilty in the site of god." "I Remain," he concluded his letter, "your most Respectful an Innosent persecuted Brittis subject."[20]

When the guilty verdict was delivered, Whelan struck exactly the same note. "I am here standing on the brink of my grave," he told the court, "and I wish to declare to you and to my God that I am innocent, that I never committed this deed, and that, I know in my heart and soul."[21] He had never been a Fenian, he said, although he was a member of the Ottawa St Patrick's Society. He had not participated in the Montreal election, although he had been asked to serve as a scrutineer – a word, he added, that he had never heard before. He held McGee in high regard. On New Year's night he had overheard a conversation at Kate Scanlan's tavern in Montreal about a plot to burn McGee's house and went round with a friend to warn McGee; it was his friend, and not himself, who used the name Smith. In Ottawa, he had visited Mrs Trotter's boarding house but had no idea that McGee was staying there. On the night of the murder, he had been in the House of Commons but had not made any threatening gestures and had not left on the centre walk towards Sparks Street. After his arrest, he had been beaten up in his cell ("they got all they could out of me – you know what I mean")[22] and was generally ill-treated by the sheriff.

And why had all this happened? Because he was a Roman Catholic, the victim of prejudice. "I never took that man's blood," he said. "I never owed him spite. I knew that he was talented and clever, and the pride of his country. This is my impression, that we Roman Catholics are looked upon as traitors; and why, because there is a feeling in this country and it is a curse to any country – party. I stand here a victim to it in all its shapes. I may be accused; I may be found guilty, but I know I am innocent. If I had been in the same place as the jury, getting the same evidence, I would very likely bring in the same verdict. I exonerate them from all blame, but if they knew the way the evidence for the Crown was manufactured they would form a different opinion. I am accused of being a Fenian. Every Irish Roman Catholic has to stand just the same imputation. Any man is welcome in England to say what he likes, but if a poor starved Irishman dares to lift his voice in favor of Irish liberty, he is seized, charged with assassination, hanged, drawn and quartered, or sent in chains to an English gaol, to a terrestrial hell, one of the living damned."

At this point, Judge Richards cut him off, reminding Whelan that "we are not in England" and asserting that the Canadian justice system treated all men equally, regardless of religion or origins. "In the evidence as to your crime," he told Whelan, "there are some facts entirely uncontradicted, and from these the jury have drawn the judgment of your guilt." Whelan had been given a fair trial and had been found guilty of murder, he said; it only remained to pronounce the sentence – to be taken "to the place of execution, and there be hanged by the neck until your body be dead, and may God have mercy on your soul."[23]

Whelan stood there without any sign of emotion. A few minutes later, as he was being led out of the court, he stopped, brushed his hat with his coat sleeve, and turned to the judge. "All that sentence, My Lord," he said, "cannot make me guilty."[24]

---

If Whelan was telling the truth, then almost every witness for the Crown was either lying or, at best, unconsciously misrepresenting reality – Turner, Inglis, and Faulkner, with their cooked-up reports of Whelan's spite and malice towards McGee; Lacroix, with his fabricated story about witnessing the murder; Wade, with his fantastical tale about overhearing the assassination plot; Storr, Downes, and Graham, with their false accounts of Whelan's behaviour and movements on the night of the murder; Cullen, Hess, and Little, with their concocted confession; O'Neill, with his insistence that the gun had been fired within two days of Whelan's arrest; and Alexander and William Powell, with their rigged identity parade and perjured testimony.

How could such a conspiracy be explained? Some of the witnesses may have been vying with each other in a ruthless pursuit of the reward money, while others may have been caught up in the quest for a convenient scapegoat. Still others may have been convinced by O'Neill's forensic evidence; once it seemed clear that McGee had been killed by Whelan's gun, they may have decided to help things along by inventing or manipulating more evidence to ensure that the guilty man got what he deserved. It certainly would not have been the only time that such things have happened.[25]

Then there was the question of Whelan's speech from the dock. If he really was a Fenian, why would he proclaim his loyalty to the Queen, disavow Fenianism, and profess his admiration for McGee? His speech astounded everyone in the room; the only explanation that the *Globe*'s correspondent could think of was that Whelan "aimed at making himself famous by his address." If so, the reporter continued, the result was a complete failure, since Whelan "startled and disgusted" his friends without convincing any of his enemies.[26]

Other possibilities present themselves. Whelan knew that Cameron was going to appeal for a retrial and could have been positioning himself accordingly. He may have realized that to have publicly identified Fenianism with assassination would have played into the hands of its enemies, and decided instead to present himself as an innocent victim of British, Canadian, and Protestant oppression and injustice. Or he may have been an innocent victim of British, Canadian, and Protestant oppression and injustice.

---

Further questions arise from these speculations – most notably, whether or not the bullet that killed McGee was actually fired from Whelan's gun and whether or not Whelan received a fair trial. In 1970, T.P. Slattery attempted to discover whether modern forensic science could determine if the bullet that killed McGee was compatible with Whelan's gun, and asked Roy Jinks of Smith & Wesson to conduct the relevant tests. Slattery had located the fatal bullet (in a metal case marked JA MACD, together with one of McGee's teeth), but at the time of his inquiry Whelan's gun had gone missing. After running tests with a similar gun, Jinks concluded that the fatal bullet was consistent with two models of Smith & Wesson revolvers, one of which was the No. 2 .32 calibre model that Whelan owned.

Slattery then asked three experts to analyze the fatal bullet itself to see if it was compatible with the C.D. Leet bullets that were found in Whelan's possession on the night of his arrest. The results were far from definitive, but two of the experts reached tentative conclusions to the effect that, in Slattery's words, "the fatal bullet could have been fired by either a Smith & Wesson model No. 1½ or a model No. 2, but *it was not made by C.D. Leet or in America, and probably came from England or Germany.*"[27] On balance, then, Slattery's forensic investigations pointed towards Whelan's innocence.

That was in 1970. Three years later, though, Whelan's gun was found. Douglas Lucas and Robert Nichols at the Ontario Centre of Forensic Sciences conducted new tests and reached very different conclusions from those of Slattery's experts. Their test bullet, fired from Whelan's gun, "bore a remarkable resemblance to the McGee bullet," and the "likelihood of it being a Leet bullet was emphasized by the identical spacing of the cannelures." This did not prove that Whelan shot McGee; the lead on the fatal bullet had oxidized, and it was impossible to delineate striations that could be linked specifically to Whelan's revolver. But the tests did indicate that McGee had been killed by the kind of gun that Whelan owned and by the kind of bullet that Whelan used. It must be remembered that there were thousands of such guns in North America and that their owners generally used Leet bullets; Whelan's gun was part of a lot of fifty that had been shipped to a Montreal dealer in 1866. Nevertheless, the argument that the fatal bullet could not have been fired from Whelan's gun had been undermined.[28] As Slattery himself noted, "the latest tests of the Centre of Forensic Sciences have tightened the grip of suspicion on Whelan."[29]

Slattery had also called into question Detective O'Neill's testimony about the fresh discharge of black powder in the barrel of Whelan's gun – testimony that meant the gun had been fired around the time that McGee was shot. According to Slattery, O'Neill's account of the gun was garbled and could be taken to mean that the powder in the barrel was "white as snow." Had the gun been fired within the previous two days of Whelan's arrest, Slattery wrote, the powder would have been black; but over the course of time, he contended, it would have changed colour, turning light grey or "practically white." "If, therefore," he concluded, "Detective O'Neill saw a residue of powder at the muzzle that was 'white as snow' on the very day of the murder, it could not indicate that Whelan's revolver was discharged that same day. If anything, it could have been the residue from the accidental discharge by Euphemie Lafrance *seven weeks before the murder*."[30]

None of this is convincing. O'Neill's testimony was actually quite clear on the point: he was describing the grease on the cartridges, not the powder in the barrel, as being "white as snow."[31] And in any case,

Slattery was wrong to suppose that the powder residue would have eventually turned white; in the view of the forensic scientist Douglas Lucas, such a development was unimaginable, and it contradicted all his own experience in the field.[32] There is nothing here to loosen the grip of suspicion on Whelan.

Suspicion is one thing; justice is quite another. Which leads to the next question: Did Whelan get a fair trial? By present-day standards, the answer clearly is no. During the proceedings, in a crowded courtroom, John A. Macdonald was given a seat next to Judge Richards – and as Slattery and others have pointed out, his presence on the bench could easily have been interpreted by the jury as a sign of Whelan's guilt.[33]

Equally problematic was the issue of the jury selection. At the beginning of the trial, Judge Richards ruled that the defence could not challenge jurors for cause until it had used up its allotted share of twenty peremptory challenges. After Whelan was found guilty, Cameron appealed the decision. By this time, Judge Richards had been appointed chief justice of the Court of Queen's Bench, which meant that he would rule on his own decision. The two other judges in the court disagreed with one another, leaving Richards with the casting vote – concluding that he had indeed made an error in law but that because the prisoner had not been harmed by the error, there were no grounds for a retrial. Cameron then took his appeal to the High Court of Error and Appeal, where ten judges, including Richards, considered the matter. Again, the judges were evenly split. And again, Richards tipped the balance and rejected the appeal. By modern standards, of course, this is a clear case of conflict of interest, and a judge in Richards' place should have recused himself from the appeal process.[34]

Yet it can be misleading to project modern standards onto the past. Although these issues would now be enough to invalidate the trial, they were not considered contentious at the time. Macdonald's presence on the bench received only passing mention in the press and did not elicit any outrage. Even the editorials and letters in the *Irish Canadian* ignored the issue. Particularly striking was the response of John Lawrence Power O'Hanly, whose radical Irish nationalist credentials were impeccable. In the middle of a furious outburst against the way

in which Irish nationalists were treated after McGee's murder, after
asserting that "the life of an Irish Nationalist in Ottawa was not worth
24 hours' purchase," O'Hanly argued that Macdonald was a powerful force against conservative extremism. "The Minister for Justice
[Macdonald] attended the trial," wrote O'Hanly; "he saw how the cat
jumped, he humanely shut down and muzzled the thirst for blood."[35]
There was no sense here or anywhere else that Macdonald's presence
on the bench prejudiced the jury against Whelan; that argument would
only be made in retrospect.

The same applies to Judge Richards's pivotal role in the appeal process against his own ruling on jury challenges during the trial. His
position was not seen as unusual, abnormal, or prejudicial at the time
and was not an issue in the press coverage – not even in the *Irish Canadian*, where one would have most expected a hostile response.[36] The
*Irish Canadian* did, of course, attack O'Reilly for challenging and rejecting all Irish Catholics on the jury panel. But O'Reilly was operating within the bounds of the law, and one does not expect lawyers for
the prosecution or the defence to accept any jurors who might conceiv-
ably turn the case against them.

In general, the Canadian press regarded the trial as a model of justice; the prisoner had been defended by the best lawyers in the country, the judge had summed up the evidence in a fair, reasonable, and
impartial manner, and the jury had based its verdict on what seemed a
compelling combination of circumstantial and forensic evidence. Had
not Whelan himself said that he would have reached the same verdict
had he been on the jury? Whelan, of course, asserted that the evidence
had been manufactured against him, and was particularly incensed by
Sheriff Powell's role in the identity parade. In fact, as we now know,
the jury did not believe that Lacroix had witnessed the murder, so the
issue of the identity parade was not a factor in its verdict. Whether or
not the Crown had manufactured more evidence against him remains
an open question.

———•·•———

Where does this leave us? We have a prime minister who sat next to
the judge during the trial, a judge who made an error of law in the jury

selection and then had the casting vote in two appeals, and a jury that consisted entirely of Protestants. We have prosecution witnesses who were lying. Nothing that Lacroix and Wade said can be believed; some (but not all) of Alec Turner's testimony is dubious; William Graham changed some of his evidence to correspond with the prosecution's case. We have the sheriff helping Lacroix to identify Whelan. And we have the further possibility that Cullen and Hess either mistook Whelan's tone of voice or simply invented Whelan's confession.

On the other hand, we have John O'Farrell for the defence paying or treating witnesses to assail Lacroix's character. We have very strong evidence that Whelan was either a Fenian or a Fenian sympathizer; that he hated McGee and made threatening visits to his house (as reported not only by Turner but by the more reliable witnesses Inglis and Faulkner); that he behaved in a highly suspicious manner on New Year's night 1868 (as recalled by John Joseph McGee); and that he made threatening gestures immediately before the assassination (from the testimony of Edward Storr). We know that Whelan had the means to kill McGee – the Smith & Wesson that he routinely carried in his breast pocket. According to Detective O'Neil, the gun had been fired shortly before Whelan's arrest, and according to modern forensic evidence it was consistent with the fatal bullet. And we know that Whelan had the opportunity to commit the murder – that he was waiting for McGee to leave the House of Commons (from the testimony of Edward Storr and Patrick Buckley) and that he was seen by John Downes walking in the direction of Sparks Street just before the assassination. And we know that he had no alibi.

There are no easy answers. Upon weighing the evidence, different people will reach different conclusions; it could hardly be otherwise. Some will maintain that Whelan was guilty beyond a reasonable doubt; some will believe that he was probably or possibly guilty; others will argue that he was an innocent man who was stitched up and scapegoated by the police.

———•··•———

Let us turn to the words of Whelan himself after all of his appeals were exhausted, two days before his execution on 11 February 1869.

"I know the man who shot McGee," he told Martin O'Gara and the crown attorney Robert Lees; he also said that he was present when McGee was shot, although he continued to insist that he did not pull the trigger.[37] Whelan also told his wife when she visited him in prison that he knew the identity of the killer but would rather be hanged than be called an informer.[38] This fits with a rumour that was circulating several months earlier. After his arrest, when he was alone with Detective O'Neill, Whelan supposedly struck his breast and said, "I have it here; they can't take it from me; I will never be a Corydon, a Massey, or a Nagle, let them do as they will."[39]

What are the implications of this? If his statements just before the execution were truthful, several things follow. First, he was lying in his letter to Macdonald and in his speech from the dock, when he presented himself as a loyal Canadian who respected McGee.[40] If the John Hillyard Cameron principle is applied to Whelan – that if the testimony of a witness fails in one particular, it is not safe to believe him in any – then nothing Whelan wrote or said can be trusted. It is no wonder that Macdonald summarily dismissed Whelan's statement that he did not shoot McGee.[41] Second, all the defence witnesses who swore that Whelan liked McGee were engaged in a joint lie to save him from the gallows; they would have included Richard Quinn, William Goulden, Patrick Kelly, John Lyon, William White, and James Kinsella. Third, and conversely, the prosecution witnesses who testified that Whelan had repeatedly threatened McGee were telling the truth. Fourth, Lacroix, aided and abetted by the Powell brothers, was lying about witnessing the murder. Fifth, Cullen, Hess, and Little had invented or mistaken Whelan's jailhouse confession. Sixth, O'Neill's forensic evidence was either wilfully or inadvertently wrong – unless, of course, someone else shot McGee with Whelan's gun. And seventh, Whelan would still have been found guilty of murder, not as the actual assassin but as a principal participant in the crime.

Something else follows as well. Once the Crown had bought into Lacroix's eyewitness testimony that Whelan, acting alone, had shot McGee, the possibility that Whelan was part of a hit squad was immediately foreclosed, and any evidence to that effect was either ignored or not pursued. Reports that a buggy had sped from the scene were forgotten. And a key suspect – the man whom Edward Storr saw with Whelan in the parliamentary gallery on the night of the murder, patting his breast pocket in a menacing gesture – was left on the sidelines.

Storr had said that three "very restless" men were with Whelan that night.[42] One of them was Reuben Lawrence, a member of the Ottawa St Patrick's Society who had been a parade marshal with Whelan on St Patrick's Day; another was Richard Quinn, who also was a member of the St Patrick's Society and who was a defence witness at the trial. Quinn had testified that he and Whelan left the House of Commons together on the night of the murder and that Whelan had left on the east walk, away from Sparks Street and towards his hotel; none of this was true.

Who was the third man? Six months later, during the trial of Patrick Buckley as an accessory to the murder, Storr identified him as James Kinsella, Whelan's drinking companion at Kate Scanlan's tavern in Montreal.[43] Kinsella had moved to Ottawa around the same time as Whelan, and worked with John Doyle as a waiter at the Russell House. He had been arrested after the assassination and charged with "treasonable practices" on the grounds that he was a member of the Fenian Brotherhood and was working with American Fenians for the invasion of Canada.[44] During Whelan's trial, Kinsella said that on the night of the murder he had worked at the Russell House until eleven o'clock and then gone straight home.[45] His father assured John A. Macdonald that three witnesses could testify that James was asleep in bed when the murder took place.[46] In the end, the case against Kinsella, like that against Buckley and Doyle, was thrown out for lack of evidence.[47]

Kinsella's story did not add up. If Storr was right, why was Kinsella lying about his whereabouts on the night of the murder? And why had Quinn said nothing about Kinsella's presence with Whelan in the gallery? Kinsella's testimony at Whelan's trial was vague and unconvincing; under cross-examination, he suffered from severe memory loss, prompting one reporter to remark that he was "very much confused."[48] If Whelan was indeed covering up for someone, Kinsella is a possible candidate.

Possible; but that is all. It is equally possible that Whelan had arranged to meet someone else entirely and that his role was to alert the assassin when McGee would be returning to Mrs Trotter's boarding house. Various names have been suggested: a "low down contempt-ible thug" named Giroux, who was "paid to do the dirty work"; John O'Farrell, either pulling the strings in the background or present at the scene, urging Whelan on and escaping in the mysterious buggy; or Francis Bernard McNamee, either because he hated McGee or because he was an informer who feared that McGee would blow his cover.[49] Or it could have been someone else entirely, or no one else. Ultimately, we will never know.

But there is persuasive evidence that Whelan was a Fenian, in the generic sense of the term, and that he hated McGee. Taking the trial alone and using the criminal law criterion of reasonable doubt, he should have been acquitted. Taking all the available evidence and using the civil law criterion of the balance of probabilities, he was involved in the murder of Thomas D'Arcy McGee, either as the assassin himself or as an accomplice of the assassin, and he should have been found guilty.

## CHAPTER SEVENTEEN

# Mutations

Sometime on the morning of Tuesday, 7 April, Father Dowd, accompanied by two Grey Nuns, broke the news of her husband's death to Mary McGee. Her distress, they said, was uncontrollable. Also in the house was ten-year-old Peggy, her father's letter promising a present still on her desk. Frasa, seventeen years old, was brought home from the Woodlands Convent where she attended school.[1] Their private grief was accompanied by an outpouring of public sympathy. In Parliament that afternoon, Macdonald addressed the House with "feelings of pain amounting to anguish" as he extolled McGee as a "martyr to the cause of his country." "It would be a long time," he said, "before we should see his like again." Other politicians spoke of McGee's charm, his eloquence, and his courage, and the importance of providing for his family. The following morning, Macdonald, Cartier, and Tilley were among the pallbearers who carried McGee's body from Mrs Trotter's boarding house to the Catholic cathedral, in preparation for the train journey to Montreal. By the time the train arrived at five o'clock that afternoon, thousands of people had come to meet it. They stood in silence as the hearse was carried to McGee's house at 1074 St Catherine Street. Over the next four days, somewhere between forty and fifty thousand people came round to pay their respects.[2]

The funeral took place on Monday, 13 April, the day that would have been McGee's forty-third birthday, the day that his friends had planned to present him with Bell-Smith's portrait. It was the largest funeral that British North America had ever seen. In bitterly cold weather, 15,000 people, from all walks of life, participated in the funeral parade, while 80,000 more lined the streets – this in a city with a population of around 105,000.[3] According to McGee's old enemy George Clerk, it was "a most inspiring ceremony."[4] At St Patrick's Church, Father Michael O'Farrell was frequently overcome with emotion as he delivered the oration, taking as his text 1 Maccabees, chapter 9, verse 21: "How is the mighty man fallen that saved the people of Israel." Speaking to a congregation consisting largely of Protestants, O'Farrell emphasized McGee's great love for Ireland, his writings (with pride of place to the *History of Ireland*), and the "honest, outspoken indignation" with which he attacked the Fenians. "There must be no sympathy for such a dastardly crime," he said; "the man or woman who could feel any joy at such a diabolical deed, would be as horrible to my soul as the assassin himself" – words that were greeted with spontaneous applause. "This is the House of God," O'Farrell immediately reminded his audience.[5]

Nearly eight hundred miles away, in Halifax, McGee's old friend Archbishop Connolly was so distraught that he cancelled all his Easter Week appointments. It was a full two weeks before he was able to speak publicly about McGee. In his oration, he spoke of McGee's efforts to reduce religious tensions in Canada. When McGee arrived in the country, he said, Orangeism was rampant, and Catholics were being harried, persecuted, and driven off their farms. "By Herculean labor," Connolly continued, "he succeeded to a large extent in tearing up, root and branch, senseless and inveterate prejudices, and blending all hearts in one common effort for one common weal … And this, I confess, is the secret why I myself esteemed, loved and admired him, as *the* Catholic Irishman, with all his failings, of whom I felt most proud."[6]

McGee's political enemies in Canada also were shaken by the assassination and bent over backwards to dissociate themselves from the act. In the House of Commons, Anglin expressed his "horror and detestation" of the murder and attempted to absolve Irish Catholics from any charges of collective guilt. "Because we are all one people," he feared, "the crimes of any portion of that people will redound upon us all."[7] At the St Patrick's Society in Montreal, Devlin described the assassination as an "atrocious crime," while McNamee helped to draft a resolution declaring the society's "profound sorrow and indignation" at the murder and conveying its "heartfelt sympathy" to McGee's family — words that rang rather hollow after McNamee's earlier celebration of

The Funeral of Thomas D'Arcy McGee. On 13 April 1868 – what would have been his forty-third birthday – some eighty thousand people thronged the streets of Montreal, and fifteen thousand participated in the funeral parade. It was the largest funeral that British North America had ever seen. (LAC, C-083423)

physical violence inflicted on McGee by Devin Reilly and Michael Doheny.[8]

The *Irish Canadian* struck a similar note. "The atrocity of this horrible murder has shocked beyond description the feelings of the entire community," wrote Patrick Boyle, "and nothing is heard but heartfelt sorrow for the terrible end of the ill-starred victim."[9] True, Boyle added, in opposing McGee the paper "may have used language which the heat of argument alone could excuse" – a slight understatement for the stream of personal invective portraying McGee as a pile of prostituted flesh, Ireland's most degenerate outcast, and a traitor of the darkest dye.[10] While it is probable that Anglin, Devlin, and Boyle were genuinely appalled at McGee's fate, they must have known that the assassination had severely damaged their own ambitions to become leaders of Irish Catholics in Canada. And they had no sense whatsoever that by whipping up a gale of hatred towards McGee, they might in any way have encouraged or influenced the man or men who killed him.

Beneath the official condemnation of the assassination by the *Irish Canadian* and the Montreal St Patrick's Society, there were many who felt that McGee had got exactly what he deserved. Although spies who had infiltrated the Fenian Brotherhood reported that the leadership condemned the killing, they also registered significant grassroots approval of the assassination – Irishmen who rejoiced over McGee's death, who felt that his assassination was the "Judgement of Heaven," who drank toasts to the "*Man* that shot *Darcy McGee*," who wished hell's flames to his soul.[11] Something of this mood surfaced in the Fenian press. Reviewing editorials about McGee in the *Irish People* from Dublin, the *Irish American* from New York, and the *Fenian Volunteer* from Buffalo, James Moylan asserted that they "assail cruelly and recklessly the memory of the lamented deceased" and "basely and treacherously plunge the moral stiletto into the bosom of his bereaved widow."[12]

Mary McGee never recovered. D'Arcy McGee's Aunt Bella – his surrogate mother, who had looked after him when he first arrived in America twenty-six years earlier – rushed to Montreal to offer comfort and support. "Since your departure," Mary wrote after Bella's return to Rhode Island, "I only could realize my sad, sad loss and my mind has been in such a state of Chaos, that I could not compose myself to write even to you." McGee's brother James and his wife had also come to Montreal, but their presence only added to her stress. Each day they stayed gave her "more anxiety & trouble & disgrace to his Brothers memory," wrote Mary. "... I hope it will be the last visit they will ever pay here." She occupied her time "collecting darling Thomas's Poems for Mrs. Sadlier to arrange also collecting his Speeches and Lectures, which are to be published here" – the volume that came out in 1869.[13]

Two years before the assassination, Mary's mother, Martha Caffrey, had died. Mother and daughter had been close, with Martha providing much-needed companionship during McGee's frequent absences; after Martha's death, Mary suffered from "occasional fits of depression."[14] During the 1850s, Mary had lost three of her children – Martha, Thomas Patrick, and Rose. Now she felt terribly alone. More than a year after the assassination, she wrote of her "desolation and loneliness," and of the split with James. "I never hear from him, or of him," she wrote; "his nonentity of a wife has never written to me & neither of them came to see me when I was at Mrs. Sadlier's. John [McGee's half-brother] I often hear from, he has more affection for me & my children than the rest of the Family."

The trial of Whelan ("that wretched man," she called him) kept the wound open; she was "perfectly disgusted with the manner which the whole trial was conducted, as they [the defence] used every stratagem to get him acquitted." The acquittal and release of Buckley and Doyle in April 1869 only made things worse; she was convinced that Whelan's accomplices had been allowed to go free.[15] Consumed with grief and oscillating between depression and anger – two sides of the same coin – she died three years after her husband, in 1871.

Frasa and Peggy, the two surviving children, were deeply scarred by their father's sudden death. Frasa went on to marry Francis Alphonse Quinn, a lawyer, and moved to California. She reacted strongly against the public world of politics. When in 1902 Henry James Morgan requested her photograph and autograph for his McGee collection, she politely declined. "I have always lived a very retired life," she wrote, "never in any way gone before the public, either thro' literature, art or philanthropy; were my father still alive it might be different." Her

(*left*) Euphrasia (Frasa) McGee. Born in 1851, Euphrasia was the second of five children and the oldest one to survive childhood. Valuing her privacy, she turned her back on the public world of politics. "Were my father alive," she told Henry James Morgan, "it might be different" (Euphrasia McGee Quinn to Morgan, 7 October 1902, LAC, Morgan Fonds, vol. 14, ff. 5299–300). (Isabel Skelton, *The Life of Thomas D'Arcy McGee*)

(*right*) Agnes Clara (Peggy) McGee. The youngest daughter, Peggy stayed in Montreal, where she became a nun. In the words of her sister, she had a "very retiring disposition." (Euphrasia McGee Quinn to Morgan, 7 October 1902, LAC, Morgan Fonds, vol. 14, ff. 5299–300). (Isabel Skelton, *The Life of Thomas D'Arcy McGee*)

sister, she added, also had a "very retiring disposition."[16] Peggy became a nun and remained in Montreal; she died on 6 January 1941, the day on which Franklin Roosevelt delivered his famous "four freedoms" speech to Congress.[17]

Among McGee's greatest admirers were five men who met in Ottawa shortly after his funeral: William Foster, a barrister and writer from Toronto; Charles Mair, Canada's "warrior bard," a schoolteacher and poet from the Ottawa Valley; Robert Grant Haliburton, a lawyer, pamphleteer, and coal-mining promoter from Nova Scotia; Henry James Morgan, an Orangeman, civil servant, and writer working in Ottawa; and Father Aeneas Dawson, the Catholic chaplain to British troops in Ottawa and an advocate of Canadian expansion into the Northwest. Intensely patriotic, and envisaging a powerful British North American nation at the centre of an "Empire of Equals," they founded the Canada First movement. It was in some respects a Canadian version of Young Ireland in its pre-revolutionary incarnation – a group of poets, intellectuals, writers who set out to replace a colonial mentality with a sense of pride and self-worth, who employed history and literature for the cultivation of national sentiment, and who stood for self-government within the empire. And as Carl Berger pointed out, "McGee became their patron martyr and his speeches saluting the rising northern nation became their litany."[18]

Nowhere was this more evident than in the movement's manifesto, William Foster's *Canada First: or, Our New Nationality*, where McGee was presented as "one who breathed into our new Dominion the spirit of a proud self-reliance, and first taught Canadians to respect themselves." Foster took as his motto McGee's statement during the Confederation debates in Parliament: "When I can hear our young men say as proudly, *our* federation, or *our* country, or *our* kingdom, as the young men of other countries speak of their own, I shall have then less apprehension for the result of whatever trials the future may have in store for us." The very circumstances of McGee's death, Foster argued, had helped to hasten that day; united in the agony of grief, Canadians had come to realize how much they had in common. The task now was to complete the journey – "to attain the fruition of our cherished hopes, and give our beloved country a proud position among the nations of the earth."[19]

Similar sentiments were voiced by Charles Mair, who wrote a sixteen-stanza poem, "In Memory of Thomas D'Arcy McGee," four days after the assassination, a poem written through tears and clenched

fists, expressing anger at those who had killed McGee, and admiration
for his dreams:

> And in his songs was light,
> And in his words was might
> To lift our hopes unto the wished-for end
> When jealousies of creed
> Shall, like a loathsome weed,
> Be cast away, and man with man be friend,
> Nor any think the souls unpriced
> That linger sadly at the feet of Christ.
>
> And in his vision true
> There came high forms anew –
> Dim outlines of a nation yet to stand,
> Knit to the Empires fate,
> In power and virtue great,
> The lords and reapers of a virgin land –
> A mighty realm where Liberty
> Shall roof the northern climes from sea to sea.[20]

In attempting to realize this vision, Foster and his colleagues drew
heavily on McGee's view that Canadians were "a Northern people"
and that "the climate of the North is favorable to the highest efforts of
human genius."[21] "We are the northern men of the New World," wrote
Robert Grant Haliburton. Canada was the home of northern races
of Celts, Saxons, and Normans, displaying the characteristic northern virtues of strength, chivalry, courage, and independence. Here, it
seemed, was a unifying myth around which English and French speakers could cohere, as well as a compensatory myth for living in one of
the coldest places on the planet.[22]

Equally concerned with transmitting McGee's ideas to the next generation was Henry James Morgan, who as a younger man had once
invited McGee to speak at an Orange Lodge celebration of the Apprentice Boys of Derry. (McGee prudently declined, on the grounds
that there was no place for such "partizan" activities in Canada.)[23] In

1865, Morgan edited McGee's *Speeches and Addresses* on British North American union; thirty years later, after his retirement, he began contacting McGee's friends, colleagues, and family members with a view to writing a biography. The project was never completed, although the material he gathered became an invaluable resource for McGee's historians.[24]

As Carl Berger has shown, these men stood for a strong and united Canada in a strong and united British Empire – an imperial alliance, characterized by a common heritage, complementary interests, and shared affections. Through their writings, McGee became incorporated into a form of Canadian nationalism that reached back to loyalist traditions and anticipated the imperial federalist movement of the late nineteenth century. This was the McGee whom the Earl of Mayo described as "one of the most eloquent advocates of British rule and British institutions … on the face of the globe."[25]

In the process, McGee's devout Catholicism became filtered out of the picture. Foster, Mair, Haliburton, and Morgan were all Protestants, for whom McGee's political writings were much more important than his religious beliefs; in fact, Mair and Haliburton held stereotypical views about Catholic backwardness and superstition that McGee would have found deeply offensive.[26] The fifth person at the Canada First meeting, Father Aeneas Dawson, naturally saw things rather differently. While Dawson shared the prevailing Canada First view that McGee was a genius whose greatest service to Canada was "his advocacy of and devotion to the cause of Confederation," he also emphasized McGee's Catholic upbringing and "divine faith," and argued that "the principles of Christianity which he had imbibed in earliest youth, were the principles of his maturer manhood." As such, McGee served as an example and inspiration to the coming generations – and especially to the coming generations of Catholics.[27]

This theme persisted in the Canadian Catholic press, where the coverage of McGee was overwhelmingly positive. The only exception concerned his attitude to the hanging of the Aylwards in 1862. His "callousness" in the matter, commented E.J. Duggan in the midst of an otherwise adulatory biographical sketch, was the "one stain on his memory." "When an unnatural death closed his own life," Duggan added, "there were those who said 'He had followed swiftly on his track, the Alwyards [sic] were revenged.'"[28] Apart from this, McGee was idealized as a deeply religious man who loved both the country of his birth and the country of his adoption, and who possessed "the soul of a poet, the brain of a statesman, and the heart of a patriot."[29] To keep his memory alive, the *Catholic Register* began a campaign for a McGee statue in Toronto. "Catholics, and particularly Irish Catholics," the newspaper asserted, "should not longer allow the example of this great one of their own race and religion to be lost upon their children and their children's children."[30]

Although the campaign attracted the support of the Toronto Irish Catholic middle class, it got nowhere – perhaps not surprisingly in the most Orange city in Canada.[31] But there had also been wider calls for a McGee monument in Ottawa, and these began to gather momentum in 1908, with the fortieth anniversary of his death.[32] The following year, Parliament approved in principle the erection of statues to both McGee and George Brown. But while everything went smoothly with Brown, McGee's statue soon ran into difficulties.

The original idea was to place the statue of McGee in the centre of the city (where the war memorial now stands) so that it would be "the first thing which will strike the eye of the visitor," in the words of Prime Minister Wilfrid Laurier. But local Orangemen objected on the grounds that McGee "had been a Fenian." When the Conservatives defeated Laurier two years later, the issue had still not been resolved, and the sculptor, George William Hill, had still not been paid. After some equivocation, the new government decided that the statue should be placed in the rear of the Parliament grounds, out of sight and out of mind. By this time, further problems had arisen. When friends and family saw the original model of McGee's head, they objected that it was not a good likeness and needed to be remodelled. Having done this, George Hill sent the statue in the summer of 1914 to the Bronze Company in Brussels for casting.[33]

The timing could not have been worse. War was declared that August, German troops marched into Belgium, and the company buried the statue to protect it from the invaders. When it was eventually returned to Canada, the Irish War of Independence had begun, and

The Thomas D'Arcy McGee statue. Despite opposition from the Orange
Order, initial design flaws, the German invasion of Belgium, and the delaying
tactics of some Conservative MPs, the statue was eventually erected in 1923 –
not in the centre of Ottawa as had been originally planned, but at the back of
the Parliament Buildings. (Courtesy of Bruce Walton)

Conservative Orange MPs were in no mood to honour the memory of a man who had once been a rebel and who had supported separate schools. And so, having been hidden from Germans, the statue was "buried away" once again, this time thanks to Orangemen. There it remained until 1921, when Mackenzie King's Liberals came to power and decided that the statue could win Irish Catholic votes. The original city centre site was no longer available; after extensive consultations with the McGee family, the statue was finally erected in 1923, behind Parliament and facing the library. It is usually depicted in heroic terms – the great orator of Confederation, a muse at this feet and a book in his hand, silhouetted against the Laurentian Hills. Completely forgotten is the fact that its location was regarded by many Irish Catholics as a victory for "anti-Irish and anti-Catholic bigots."[34]

The man who pushed hardest for the statue was Charles Murphy, the Liberal MP for Russell, who had served as Laurier's secretary of state and became postmaster general under Mackenzie King. Born in Ottawa in 1862 of Irish parents, Murphy had long regarded McGee as an iconic figure whose career exemplified the Irish contribution to Canada. That contribution, he believed, had never been given the recognition it deserved; the Irish had been written out of Canadian history, and McGee had not even been mentioned in George Wrong's school textbook, *Canada: A Short History*, published in 1924. "Whether it is due to the usual conspiracy of silence, or the fashionable habit of drawing the pall of oblivion over the achievements of Irishmen," wrote Murphy, "we are going to have a change made."[35] And the best way to make this change was through a highly visible public celebration of the centenary of McGee's birth.

The preparations went on for months. Five hundred people, comprising successful and respectable Irish Canadians along with members of the country's political and social elite, were invited to a banquet at Ottawa's Chateau Laurier hotel on 13 April 1925. As the plans got underway, Murphy was inundated with letters from Irish Canadians who remembered and idealized McGee in much the same way that a future generation would remember and idealize John Fitzgerald Kennedy. Most people who wrote to Murphy about the banquet were middle-class men of Irish Catholic ethnicity; lawyers' letterhead featured prominently in the correspondence. There were people who recalled his speeches, people who remembered what they were doing when McGee was shot, people who had attended his funeral, people who had attended Whelan's trial. The letters came from all over Canada – Vancouver, Calgary, Saskatoon, Regina, Winnipeg, Toronto, Montreal, Fredericton, Charlottetown, Halifax.

Murphy intended to make the banquet a glorious affair worthy of McGee's memory. One of the invitees was William Butler Yeats, who had won the Nobel Prize for literature two years earlier and was asked to compose a poem for the occasion. But Yeats was in Rome and had prior engagements in April; no poem was forthcoming.[36] Also invited was John McCormack, singer of "It's a Long Way to Tipperary," one of the first recording superstars, who had become an American citizen in 1917. The invitation proved highly controversial; there were reports in the press that McCormack had criticized Britain during the war, and some Irish Canadians were horrified at the prospect of having him at the banquet. "To make such 'a player to the gallery' disloyalist a prominent person in doing honour to the memory of one who – if my memory is not at fault – was killed because of his loyal[t]y would be the height of incongruity and indeed an insult to the loyal man's memory," one correspondent told Murphy. "It would be impossible for me to even in the most distant way connected with it."[37] The controversy was avoided when it turned out that McCormack, like Yeats, would not be able to attend; he wanted to come and was "quite interested in D'Arcy McGee," his manager explained, but he was already committed to an engagement in Omaha.[38]

If prominent Irishmen were unavailable, there were always prominent Canadians – and they were, after all, the real target audience. Mackenzie King, as prime minister, was an obvious choice. But King declined the invitation on the grounds that it had been a long parliamentary session and he needed a holiday over Easter, when the banquet was taking place. In his reply, Murphy pointed out that the banquet's speeches would be broadcast coast-to-coast on CNRO radio, with an anticipated audience of "at least 10,000,000 people" – a rather optimistic estimate, given that it was greater than the entire population of Canada.[39] (In the event, the actual listenership was around 100,000, which was impressive enough.)[40] Murphy's powers of persuasion proved effective; King showed up and delivered a speech about McGee that was actually written by O.D. Skelton – one of his first assignments in what turned out to be a long and illustrious career in the civil service. Perhaps not entirely coincidentally, the speech included a plug for a new 550-page biography of McGee, which happened to be written by O.D. Skelton's wife, Isabel.[41]

Sitting at the same table with King was Viscount Julian Hedworth George Byng, the governor general. In a brief speech, Lord Byng compared McGee to Giuseppi Garibaldi, Alexander Hamilton, John Pym, and John Hampden, strange bedfellows indeed; one wonders who might have been added to the list had he been given more time.[42] (King and Byng would be the principal characters in a rather different affair the following year, which paved the way for Arthur Meighen and the Conservatives to return briefly to power.) Meighen was also at the head table and spoke for a full hour, while King probably wished he had taken that vacation. "If Macdonald and Cartier were the architects of Confederation, McGee was its prophet," Meighen said. "He was the triumphant missionary of union."[43] His view reflected contemporary historiographical and hagiographical orthodoxy about McGee. The same argument, in much the same language, had been made by Professor D.C. Harvey in his *Thomas D'Arcy McGee: Prophet of Canadian Nationality*, published two years earlier, and it also characterized the centenary biographies written by Isabel Skelton and Alexander Brady.[44] Along with Meighen was R.B. Bennett, who would succeed him as leader of the Conservative Party. Although Bennett was not among the speakers, he was a deep and genuine admirer of McGee. No soldier on the battlefield who won a Victoria Cross, he wrote, displayed more courage than McGee did in his battle against the Fenians.[45]

By all accounts, the banquet was a great success; there was a lot of talk about McGee's vision of Canada's future greatness, his love of the country, his support for unity in diversity, and his inspirational oratory.[46] Conspicuously absent were any references to the circumstances of McGee's assassination; to have highlighted intra-Irish violence would have defeated Murphy's purpose. Because the anniversary of McGee's murder was only a week before the anniversary of his birthday, the memory of the assassination threatened to cloud the celebration of his achievements. To prevent this from happening, Murphy wrote to Canadian newspaper editors asking them not to mention the assassination; he also suppressed rumours about who killed McGee and generally attempted to "choke off" anyone who raised the subject.[47] In this way, he could keep the focus on McGee as a constructive statesman and could deflect attention from the stereotype of the Irish as quarrelsome, violent, and disloyal people. This was particularly important in 1925. During the previous decade, Irish Catholic Canadians had faced a barrage of criticism from the Orange press on the grounds that they had backed the Home Rule movement, had sharply criticized Britain's Irish policies, and supported or sympathized with Sinn Féin.

There was some foundation to this. Although Catholic newspapers in English-speaking Canada condemned the Easter Rising, they had been equally critical of Britain for refusing to face down the Unionists and for executing the leaders of the rising. The Catholic press had strongly opposed conscription in Ireland and began to view Sinn Féin as the authentic voice of Irish nationalism after its electoral victory in December 1918. During the Troubles of 1919–21, the leading Catholic papers expressed outrage about British atrocities in Ireland while saying little or nothing about IRA violence; the *Catholic Register* argued that most stories about IRA violence were products of British propaganda, while the *Catholic Record* took the view that the killing of policemen was "the result of the example set by the military and police themselves."[48] Members of Catholic organizations such as the Ancient Order of Hibernians and the Knights of Columbus sympathized with Sinn Féin, while the Self-Determination for Ireland League of Canada attracted around 25,000 members and was particularly strong in Montreal and Quebec City.[49]

Irish Catholic Canadian supporters of Sinn Féin argued that the Great War had been fought for the rights of small nations and for the right of "civilized peoples" to decide their own system of government."[50] Approaching Sinn Féin demands in terms of Canadian precedents, they argued that Ireland simply wanted the freedom that Canada already possessed. It was up to the Irish to decide what form of government they wanted, but the best way to save the British Empire was to recognize that it was "a great commonwealth held together by the strongest of ties – that of mutual good will," rather than blind obedience to Britain.[51] In this way, many Irish Catholic Canadians were able to combine support for Sinn Féin with participation in the Great War, loyalty to Canada, and the idea of imperial equality.

Canadian Orangemen were not impressed. In their view, the Great War had been fought to preserve "the unity and integrity of the Empire" and not to break it "into independent Sinn Fein Republics." "The boys who died in France," averred the Orange *Sentinel*, "were not Sinn Feiners."[52] An attack on the British hub of Empire, from this perspective, was an attack on the whole. And it seemed clear that it was a religious attack, deeply rooted in Catholic hostility to an empire that was Protestant as well as British. Irish Catholic Sinn Féiners were held to be cowardly murderers of the brave policemen and soldiers who were defending the empire. In a mirror image of the Catholic press, Orangemen argued that stories about British atrocities were products of Sinn Féin propaganda. And all this talk about Ireland participating in an "Empire of Equals" was simply a smokescreen. According to the Orange press, the signatories of the Easter Proclamation had viewed the Germans as their "gallant allies," and Sinn Féin wanted Ireland to become an independent republic; its aim was to smash the empire, not redefine it. The same applied to Sinn Féin supporters in Canada, whose real goal was to make Canada a completely independent nation, wrote the *Sentinel*; they reserved "all their love and loyalty for Canada alone at the expense of the Empire as a whole."[53]

It is against this background that the McGee Centenary is best understood. "The object," wrote John Evans Adamson, "was not mere glorification of McGee but to counteract some misapprehension & some deliberate misrepresentation which the last few hectic years in Ireland have made possible" – the "misapprehension" being the view that Irish Catholics were closet republicans; the "deliberate misrepresentation" being the view that they were conspiring to establish papal rule on the ruins of the British Empire; and the "last few hectic years" being the revolution and civil war from 1916 to 1923.[54] "You have brought honor to our race and our religion and written a bright page of Canadian history," Jonathan Barrett told Murphy a week after the celebration.

"I am proud of you. You have given the Orange Tory Bigots something to think about. It would be amusing to get a copy of the Orange Sentinel!"[55]

Bringing honour to the "race and religion" and giving the "Orange Tory Bigots something to think about" was precisely the point. Still, Barrett would have been disappointed had he seen a copy of the *Sentinel*. The paper said little about the centenary except that McGee had helped to lay the foundations of Canada, that he was a man of whom all Canadians could be proud, and that his contribution to Confederation had been exaggerated by his admirers.[56] Nevertheless, there was a sense in which McGee had become an ethnic weapon in a conflict between Irish Catholic Canadians and Canadian Orangemen over the meaning of empire. Murphy's McGee would not only put Irish Catholic Canadians back on the historical map but would also liberate Canadians in general from "the prevailing Imperialistic idea that the inhabitants of this country owe a duty, first, to some other country, and, after that, some duty of some kind to Canada – if they have any to spare." "That is what I object to; that is what I have never subscribed to, and never will subscribe to," wrote Murphy.[57]

The same impetus lay behind Murphy's subsequent initiatives, building on the success of the centennial celebrations. As postmaster general, he used his influence to include McGee in a "historic series" of Canadian stamps. Like the McGee statue, the choice proved controversial – although this time the opposition came not from the Orange Order but from French Canadians who wanted to honour someone from their own community. In the event, a five-cent McGee stamp was issued in 1927 – making McGee the first Irishman in the English-speaking world to appear on a postage stamp.[58] That same year, with the support of Bishop Michael Francis Fallon in London and the Montreal tycoon Sir Herbert Holt ("the richest man in Canada, who happens to be an Irishman"), Murphy helped to establish D'Arcy McGee Scholarships for the study of Canadian history. "By this means," he told Bishop Fallon, "we would make certain that, for centuries to come, there will be young men and young women engaged in the work of making known to our people, as well as to the people of other countries, not only Canadian history, but also the part that the Irish people have played in the

The Thomas D'Arcy McGee stamp. Largely thanks to the efforts of Postmaster General Charles Murphy, McGee was featured in a "historical series" of Canadian stamps – making him the first Irishman in the English-speaking world to appear on a postage stamp. (Courtesy of John Talman)

making of that history."[59] Murphy also welcomed the establishment in 1928 of the Thomas D'Arcy McGee Memorial Camp for Boys, based in Montreal, with its motto "Save a man and you save a life – Save a boy and you save a nation" – although he threatened to withdraw his support on learning that the boys were saluting the British rather than Canadian ensign.[60]

Outside Canada, the centennial of McGee's birth received relatively little attention, although there was a brief encomium in the *Irish Times*, praising his poetry and his political realism, and condemning the "ignorant and illiberal genius of negation" that lay behind his assassination.[61] Some of his writings retained considerable traction – most notably his *History of the Irish in North America* (the first book of its kind), his *Popular History of Ireland* (which really was popular), and poems such as his "Salutation to the Celts." But neither his historical writings nor his poems have appealed to modern audiences. His histories are no longer read, and his poetry, which once earned high praise, appears increasingly anachronistic. When Patrick Crotty edited the recent *Penguin Book of Irish Verse*, he decided not to include any of McGee's poems on the grounds that they were simply not good enough.[62]

Politically, McGee did not fit into the Irish national narrative, except for a cameo appearance as a traitor to "the cause." Nationalists did not want him, and unionists did not need him. In the story of Young Ireland, he was eclipsed by such romantic figures as "Meagher of the Sword" and John Mitchel. After the Wexford speech of 1865, McGee's Irish reputation never recovered; from being treated as the villain of the piece, he was almost completely written out of the story.

Despite McGee's hopes to the contrary, the Canadian example had little or no impact on Irish politics during the twentieth century. When, during the Home Rule crisis of 1912–14, some Canadian writers and politicians turned to McGee's writings for answers to the Irish question, they were ignored. In 1912 the Montreal journalist and novelist Watson Griffin wrote a pamphlet, *The Irish Evolution*, pointing out that McGee had opposed the idea of a separate Irish republic, had emphasized national unity, and had supported federal systems of government. Such insights, Griffin believed, could be applied to Ireland. Steering between separatism and unionism, why not have a federal United Kingdom, with provincial legislatures for England, Wales, Scotland, Ulster, and Southern Ireland?[63]

The following year, Charles Murphy suggested a variant of this plan to the constitutional nationalist politician T.P. O'Connor. "It ought to be possible," wrote Murphy, "to have a Federal Parliament with subordinate Legislatures for each of the Provinces, as we have in Canada and if some such arrangement as that were made, each of the Irish Provinces – including Ulster – would have the management of its own local affairs. That ought surely to meet the views of any person who is honestly desirous of putting an end to the evils of centuries."[64] But it was not at all possible. Such a plan fell far short of nationalist demands and went much too far for unionists – the same problem that McGee himself had faced during the 1840s when he sought a federal alternative to the Act of Union between Britain and Ireland.[65]

Back in Canada, the momentum generated by the centennial celebrations proved impossible to sustain, and McGee gradually receded from public consciousness during the Great Depression and the Second World War – as indeed did the Irish Catholic population in general. There was a brief revival in the early 1950s, with the publication of Josephine Phelan's ultraromantic and award-winning biography, *The Ardent Exile*. Meanwhile, in diplomatic circles, McGee functioned – and still functions – as a symbol of Irish and Canadian friendship.

In much the same way that North America's First Nations exchanged wampum beads before conducting negotiations, Irish and Canadian politicians exchanged tokens of McGee on visits to each other's country. In 1959 an Irish delegation in Canada presented their hosts with a McGee plaque, which was placed near the site of his assassination. Two years later, when John Diefenbaker visited Dublin, he gave the taoiseach, Seán Lemass, plaques in English and Irish honouring McGee. Still, it was not quite the same McGee whom the prime minister and the taoiseach honoured. Diefenbaker's McGee was primarily the one who contributed to Canadian Confederation, rather than the Irish rebel of 1848; Lemass's McGee was primarily the one whose "love of Ireland showed itself in the leading part he played in the militant Young Ireland movement of the 1840s."[66]

Like the McGee statue, the plaques in Dublin were buried away – this time, for thirty years. But they were pulled out of storage for the visit of another Canadian prime minister, Brian Mulroney, in 1991. Mulroney had long been an admirer of McGee, and he particularly enjoyed quoting McGee's poem "Am I Remember'd in Erin?" – which he subsequently recited at the funeral of Ronald Reagan.[67] During his visit, Mulroney joined the taoiseach, Charles Haughey, for the unveiling of a McGee monument, consisting of a bust and the two plaques, at Carlingford, McGee's birthplace. It was not universally popular; later in the decade, someone spray-painted the words "Police Spy" beneath the bust – a good indication that the Fenian image of McGee was also being remembered.

By this time, McGee had experienced something of a revival in Canada, beginning with the publication of two books by the Montreal lawyer T.P. Slattery – one on McGee's life and the other on the trial of Patrick James Whelan. But there were deeper and wider reasons for the increased interest in McGee's career. During the 1960s and 1970s, the rise of Quebec nationalism triggered a crisis of confidence in English Canada, in which McGee's writings on national unity acquired a new relevance. Here was a broad, tolerant, and inclusive pan-Canadian vision that could strengthen the federalist case against separatism. Not altogether surprisingly, a Bloc Québécois MP recently told me that, like Seán Lemass before him, he preferred the revolutionary McGee of 1848 to the Liberal Conservative Father of Confederation.

At the same time, the renewed Troubles in Northern Ireland, and particularly the war of the Provisional IRA, brought McGee's anti-Fenian writings into sharper focus. McGee's arguments against the Fenians during the 1860s were strikingly similar to the arguments of Eoghan Harris, Kevin Myers, and Conor Cruise O'Brien against the Provisional IRA during the 1970s and 1980s. It was no coincidence that O'Brien in 1978 described McGee as the greatest Irishman in Canadian history; nor is it a coincidence that revolutionary republican attacks on O'Brien (right down to the "hell's flames to your soul" syndrome) were identical to Fenian attacks on McGee.[68]

Over the years, then, McGee's career was pressed into the service of complementary and contradictory traditions as different figures from different generations remade him after their own image, employed him for their own purposes, and created multiple McGees. For Canada First, McGee was both a conservative nationalist and an advocate for empire, whose writings became an inspiration for imperial federation. For Charles Murphy, who regarded "Imperial Federation as the negation of Canada's right to self-government," McGee was a liberal nationalist who exemplified the Irish Catholic contribution to Canada.[69] For Father Dawson and the English-speaking Catholic press, McGee was the ideal Irish Catholic, a model of faith and loyalty for future generations. During the later twentieth century, McGee was resurrected as a symbol of good relations between Ireland and Canada, a spokesman for national unity, and a scourge of revolutionary republicanism. And support for all these positions can be found within McGee's Canadian writings.

How will McGee be remembered as we move towards the bicentenary of his birth in 2025? As Canada has become a multicultural society, McGee's attempt to balance core values with minority rights will probably assume increased importance, as will his insistence that immigrants and ethnic groups should not inject old hatreds into their new environment. In this respect, the legacy of 11 September, the rise of radical Islam, and the persistence of revolutionary elements in some of Canada's ethnic groups is likely to call forth the McGee who took an uncompromising stand against militants within his own ethnoreligious community, who challenged self-righteous political and religious certainties, and who argued for a broad, tolerant, decent, open-minded, and compassionate society in which people did not push others off the path. This is the McGee who belongs in the company of people such as Tarek Fatah, the founder of the Canadian Muslim congress, and the Liberal politician Ujjal Dosanjh, who challenged extremists within the Sikh community and who bore the brunt of verbal attacks, physical assaults, and death threats. It took great courage. In McGee's case, it cost him his life.

# Notes

## ABBREVIATIONS

ARCAT  Archives of the Roman Catholic Archdiocese of Toronto
BAnQ  Bibliothèque et Archives nationales du Québec
CUA  Concordia University Archives
LAC  Library and Archives Canada
NAI  National Archives of Ireland
NLI  National Library of Ireland
TNA  The National Archives [United Kingdom]

## INTRODUCTION

1 McGee, "The Policy of Conciliation," *Speeches and Addresses*, 6–7.
2 *Patriot* [Toronto], 2 November 1864.
3 *Halifax Evening Reporter*, 25 April 1868.
4 Wilson, *Thomas D'Arcy McGee*, vol. 1: *Passion, Reason, and Politics*, 222–3, 230–7.
5 Mary McGee to Thomas Devine, 20 August 1863, CUA, PO30, HA254, folder 7.
6 *Montreal Gazette*, 3 April 1866.
7 *Montreal Gazette*, 11 November 1867.
8 Kate Simpson-Hayes, "D'Arcy McGee as I Saw Him," *Saturday Night*, 25 June 1927.
9 Hugh MacMahon to Henry Morgan, 21 February 1901, Henry J. Morgan Fonds, LAC, MG29-D61 [Morgan Fonds], vol. 14, ff. 5287–8.
10 Taylor, *Thomas D'Arcy McGee*, 18–19.
11 See, for example, *Wexford Independent*, 22 January, 2 July 1842; *Irish Canadian*, 20 April 1864; "McGee's Speech against Divorce," J.J. O'Gorman Fonds, LAC, MG30-D20 [O'Gorman Fonds], folder 5.

12 *American Celt*, 5 April 1851.

13 *Catholic Register*, 25 April 1895.

14 J.M. Kilbourn to Hugh MacMahon, 6 August 1894, Morgan Fonds, vol. 14, ff. 5267–8.

15 Ged Martin to author, personal communication, 9 January 2009 (used with permission).

16 *Canadian Freeman*, 4 July 1867.

17 *Canadian Freeman*, 6 May 1859; Canada, *Debates of the Legislative Assembly*, 28 April 1859; *Globe*, 21 May 1859.

18 Duffy, *Young Ireland*, 2:216.

19 Victor Rabinovitch, "The Golden-Tongued Martyr," *Literary Review of Canada* 16 (May 2008): 24.

20 Curtis, *Politics of Population*, 22.

21 *Saint John Morning News*, 21 August 1863.

22 Canada, House of Commons, *Debates*, 6 April 1868, 469–71.

23 Ibid., 14 November 1867, 72.

24 Canada, *Debates of the Legislative Assembly*, 12 March 1863.

## CHAPTER ONE

1 For a slightly fuller account, see Wilson, *Thomas D'Arcy McGee*, vol. 1: *Passion, Reason, and Politics*.

2 McGee to de Charbonnel, 10 July 1856, ARCAT, CAH01.01.

3 McGee, "Consolation," *Canadian Ballads*, 71–2.

4 Canada, Department of Agriculture, *Censuses of Canada, 1665–1871*.

5 Akenson, *Irish in Ontario*, 3–47; Houston and Smyth, *Irish Emigration and Canadian Settlement*, 43–78.

6 The best general treatment remains Careless, *Union of the Canadas*; on the educational controversy, see 176–7, 197–8.

7 See, for example, *Globe*, 9 July 1850; Careless, *Brown of the Globe*, 1:120; Walker, *Catholic Education and Politics*, 76–113. For the controversy in Britain and Ireland on the Ecclesiastical Titles Bill, see Kerr, *Nation of Beggars*, 241–81.

8 This figure is extrapolated from the 1851 census, using Donald Harman Akenson's estimate that Catholics constituted one-third of Canada West's Irish population (Akenson, *Irish in Ontario*, 24–6). Because his estimate deals with ethnicity rather than immigration, and because the percentage of Irish Catholic immigrants was rising in the late 1830s and 1840s, the figure for Irish-born Catholics in 1851 errs on the side of caution. For an excellent survey of Irish Catholics in Canada, see McGowan, "Irish Catholics," 1–30.

9  Careless, *Union of the Canadas*, 165.

10  For McGee's vision, see "Canada – Its Future Destiny," in *New Era*, 22 October 1857.

11  *New Era*, 25 May 1857.

12  *New Era*, 29 May 1857. For McGee's earlier views that Ireland should have its own militia, see *Boston Pilot*, 1 March 1845, and *American Celt*, 22 April, 3 June 1854.

13  *New Era*, 1 June 1857.

14  Wilson, *Thomas D'Arcy McGee*, 1:170–4.

15  *American Celt*, 21 April 1855; *New Era*, 25 May 1857.

16  *New Era*, 1 June 1857, 8 April 1858.

17  *New Era*, 19 January 1858; see also 16 February 1858.

18  *New Era*, 16 February 1858.

19  *New Era*, 4 August 1857. The classic critique of laissez-faire policies during the famine is Woodham-Smith, *The Great Hunger*. For more recent analyses, see Donnelly, *The Great Irish Potato Famine*; Kinealy, *This Great Calamity*; Gray, *Famine, Land, and Politics*; Ó Gráda, *Black '47 and Beyond*; and Haines, *Charles Trevelyan and the Great Irish Famine*.

20  *New Era*, 1 April 1858; for McGee's Young Ireland "buy Irish" campaign, see *Nation*[Dublin], 24 April, 15 May, 26 June, 16 October 1847.

21  *New Era*, 1 April 1858.

22  *New Era*, 4 August 1857.

23  *American Celt*, 26 October 1850.

24  *New Era*, 4 August 1857.

25  Wilson, *Thomas D'Arcy McGee*, 1:272–3.

26  *New Era*, 25 May, 18 August 1857.

27  *New Era*, 17 June 1857. For a general discussion of McGee's literary nationalism in Ireland and Canada, see Holmgren, "Native Muses and National Poetry," 139–209.

28  *New Era*, 24 April 1858.

29  *New Era*, 25 July 1857.

30  McGee, "Arm and Rise!" *Canadian Ballads*, vii, 45

31  *New Era*, 24 April 1858.

32  *American Celt*, 25 October 1856. "Our Ladye of the Snow!" was not McGee's first Canadian poem; ironically, that honour belongs to "The Red-Cross Flag" of 1853, in which he cursed the Union Jack that flew on Canadian soil. The poem was republished in the *Globe*, 28 August 1863.

33  McGee, *Canadian Ballads*, vii.

34  McGee, "The Arctic Indian's Faith," *Canadian Ballads*, 29.

35  McGee, *Canadian Ballads*, vii–viii.

36  "Apostrophe to the Boyne" and "To a Friend in Australia," *Canadian Ballads*, 53–7

37  McGee to Mary Ann Sadlier, 8 January 1864, James Sadlier Fonds, Library and Archives Canada [LAC], MG24-C16 [Sadlier Fonds].

38  *Nation* [Dublin], 19 September, 28 November 1846, 9 January 1847.

39  *Nation* [New York], 28 April, 19 May 1849.

40  *New Era*, 29 May 1857.

41  *New Era*, 26 January 1858.

42  *New Era*, 26 September 1857.

43  *New Era*, 4 March 1858.

44  *New Era*, 12 September 1857.

45  Stewart, *Shape of Irish History*, 186.

46  On Tumblety's experiences in Montreal, see McCulloch, "'Dr. Tumblety,'" 49–66; McGee's satirical "Memoir of Francis Tumblety" appeared in *New Era*, 31 October and 3 November 1857; see also Tumblety, "Be Wise Before It Is Too Late," and *New Era*, 17 October, 17 November 1857.

47  Tumblety, *Sketch of an Eventful Career*, 14; see also Tumblety, *Narrative of Dr. Tumblety*, 6–7.

48  Evans and Gainey, *The Lodger*; Begg, *Jack the Ripper*, 278–81.

49  *New Era*, 28 November 1857; James Meagher, "Separate and Common Schools: A Fair Parallel," in *New Era*, 13 February 1858. For a comprehensive analysis of the separate schools debate during the mid-1850s, see Walker, *Catholic Education and Politics*, 140–218.

50  *New Era*, 22 October 1857. For a broader comparative analysis of Quebec and Ireland, see Stevenson, *Parallel Paths*.

51  *New Era*, 7, 9 January 1858; see also *New Era*, 7 November 1857.

52  *New Era*, 15 September 1857.

53  Hughes, "Reflections and Suggestions," 653.

54  Houston and Smyth, *The Sash Canada Wore*, 24.

55  *New Era*, 19 September, 27, 29 October, 19 November 1857.

56  *New Era*, 15 September 1857.

57  *New Era*, 3 April 1858.

58  *New Era*, 15 September 1857.

59  *New Era*, 12 June 1857. See also *New Era*, 14, 16 July 1857.

60  *New Era*, 14 July 1857.

61  *New Era*, 13 October 1857.

62  *New Era*, 21 July 1857.

63  *New Era*, 14 November 1857.

64 *New Era*, 29 September 1857. See also *New Era*, 15 September, 10, 13, and 27 October 1857.

65 *New Era*, 29 October 1857.

66 *Patriot* [Toronto], 6 May 1857. For a rollicking, semi-fictional biography of Gowan, see Akenson, *The Orangeman*.

67 *True Witness*, 18 June 1858.

68 *New Era*, 10 October 1857.

69 Ibid. See also *New Era*, 13 October 1857.

70 *New Era*, 14 July 1857. See also *New Era*, 16, 21 July 1857, 25 March 1858.

71 See, for example, *New Era*, 19 January 1858.

72 *New Era*, 8 August 1857.

73 *New Era*, 22 October 1857.

74 See, for example, McGee, *Memoir of Charles Gavan Duffy*, 3; *American Celt*, 17 November 1855.

75 *Boston Pilot*, 26 April, 10 May 1845.

76 *Nation* [New York], 17 March 1849; *American Celt*, 10 May, 20 December 1856.

77 *New Era*, 1 August 1857. See also *New Era*, 25 May 1857.

78 *New Era*, 27 May 1857. See also *New Era*, 3, 8 June 1857.

79 The three European ports in which McGee wanted Canadian immigration agents were Hamburg, Bremen, and Le Havre; see *New Era*, 27 May 1857.

80 *New Era*, 22 October 1857. For a general discussion of the place of the Northern Myth in the formation of Canadian nationalism, see Berger, *Sense of Power*, 128–33.

81 *New Era*, 8 December 1857.

82 *American Celt*, 9 July 1853.

83 *Quebec Morning Chronicle*, 10 February 1865. See also Cuthbertson, *The Old Attorney General*, 106–13; Sewell and Robinson, *Plan for a General Legislative Union*; Durham, *Lord Durham's Report*, 160–74.

84 Haliburton, *Address on the Present Condition*; *New Era*, 10 June 1857. See also *New Era*, 24 April 1858.

85 Hamilton to Macdonald, 13 January 1868, John A. Macdonald Fonds, LAC, MG26-A [Macdonald Fonds], vol. 116, ff. 47057–60; *Quebec Morning Chronicle*, 10 February 1865; Morris, *Nova Britannia*. Published in 1858, Morris's work cannot be considered as an influence on McGee's "new northern nationality," although it was very much in the same tradition.

86 *American Celt*, 16 August 1856. Hamilton, for his part, attended McGee's lectures in Halifax and described them as a "rich intellectual treat." See *Acadian Recorder*, 26 July 1856.

87  Hamilton, *Observations*, 4, 9, 12–14, 50–1.
88  Ibid., 17, 51.


CHAPTER TWO

1  McGee to de Charbonnel, 10 July 1856, Archives of the RC Archdiocese of Toronto [ARCAT], CAH01.01; *New Era*, 22 October 1857.
2  For McGee's thoughts on Burke and the "possible best," see *Montreal Herald*, 16 March 1861; for his desire to win "honest fame," see McGee to Urquhart, 12 October 1847, Oxford University, Balliol College, Urquhart Papers, 1/J6
3  Walker, *Catholic Education and Politics*, passim and 113; *New Era*, 17 April, 2 July 1858; *Canadian Freeman*, 12 March 1863.
4  Houston and Smyth, *The Sash Canada Wore*, 148; see Wilson, *Thomas D'Arcy McGee*, 1:347–8, and *Globe*, 11 February 1856.
5  *Globe*, 21 February 1857; Walker, *Catholic Education and Politics*, 188, 213.
6  *New Era*, 28 November 1857.
7  Ibid.
8  *New Era*, 25 May 1857.
9  *New Era*, 1, 19 September 1857.
10  *True Witness*, 9 October, 13 November 1857; *New Era*, 7 November 1857.
11  Keep, "Irish Migration to Montreal," 47–50.
12  *New Era*, 1 December 1857.
13  *New Era*, 28 November, 8 December 1857.
14  Charles Alleyn, letter to *Montreal Gazette*, 15 December 1857. See also *Montreal Gazette*, 12, 18 December 1857; *Montreal Daily Transcript*, 9, 17, and 19 December 1857.
15  See, for example, *New Era*, 10, 17 December 1857.
16  *New Era*, 26, 28 December 1857.
17  Canada, *Journals of the Legislative Assembly*, vol. 16, part 1, 94–8.
18  *New Era*, 15, 19, and 22 December 1857.
19  *Montreal Pilot*, 12 January 1858.
20  *New Era*, 14 January 1858.
21  *True Witness*, 18 December 1857.
22  *True Witness*, 24 June, 1 and 15 July 1859.
23  *New Era*, 4 January 1858.
24  Walker, *Catholic Education and Politics*, 181–2, 200–2.
25  *New Era*, 6 March 1858.
26  Newspaper clipping, n.d. [c. 4 March 1858]; Canada, *Debates of the Legislative Assembly*, 1858.

27  *Globe*, 4 March 1858.

28  *True Witness*, 12 March 1858.

29  *New Era*, 11 March, 1 April 1858.

30  Clarke, *Piety and Nationalism*, 158–60; Taylor, "A Fatal Affray in Toronto"; *Globe*, 23 March 1858.

31  *Leader* [Toronto], 22 March 1858.

32  *Leader* [Toronto], 18 March 1858.

33  *New Era*, 25 March 1858.

34  Ibid.

35  *Mirror*, 14 May 1858.

36  *New Era*, 3, 10 April 1858.

37  *New Era*, 12 January 1858.

38  *New Era*, 1 April 1858.

39  *New Era*, 27 March 1858.

40  *Mirror*, 16 April 1858. It is sometimes suggested that Charles Donlevy, the proprietor of the *Mirror*, was behind the petition. However, Donlevy was in poor health, and the *Mirror* was "altogether in the hands" of O'Neill, according to McGee; see *Canadian Freeman*, 23 July 1858.

41  *Mirror*, 2, 23 April 1858.

42  For an early example of the recreational activities of the Hibernian Benevolent Society, see *Patriot* [Toronto], 17 November 1858, which describes a rowing match between the Hibernians (with Michael Murphy at the oars) and the Shakespeare Club. The Hibernians won.

43  *Irish Canadian*, 11 March 1863; Toner, "Rise of Irish Nationalism in Canada," 27–9; Clarke, *Piety and Nationalism*, 169–70.

44  *Globe*, 22 April 1858.

45  *New Era*, 3 April 1858; *True Witness*, 14 May 1858.

46  *True Witness*, 14 May 1858; *Mirror*, 9, 23 April 1858.

47  *New Era*, 3 April 1858. For Cotter's fight with Lennox, see *New Era*, 8 April 1858.

48  See, for example, *Boston Pilot*, 1 March 1845; *Nation* [New York], 9 March 1850.

49  Cottrell, "St. Patrick's Day Parades," 63–5; *Globe*, 18 March 1859; *True Witness*, 25 March 1859.

50  These included not only Michael Murphy but also Edward O'Meagher Condon, Murtagh Moriarty, and Patrick Boyle, who would become the editor of the pro-Fenian *Irish Canadian*. See *Mirror*, 11 June 1858.

51  Walker, *Catholic Education and Politics*, 188, 195.

52  *New Era*, 23 February, 27 April 1858.

53 *Mirror*, 30 April 1858.

54 *New Era*, 11 February, 15 April 1858.

55 *Globe*, 26 May 1858.

56 Diary of George Clerk, Bibliothèque et Archives nationales du Québec [BAnQ], 28 May, 1 June 1858.

57 *Mirror*, 11, 18 June 1858.

58 Walker, *Catholic Education and Politics*, 203–6.

59 *Mirror*, 30 April 1858.

60 *Brockville Recorder*, 27 May 1858.

61 McGee to O'Donohoe, n.d. [29 May 1858], Library and Archives Canada [LAC], Charles Murphy Fonds, MG27–IIIB8 [Murphy Fonds], f. 14284; *Catholic Citizen*, 10 June 1858; *Mirror*, 11 June 1858.

62 *Mirror*, 11 June 1858.

63 *Mirror*, 18 June 1858.

64 Diary of George Clerk, BAnQ, 12 June 1858; *Catholic Citizen*, 3 June 1858.

65 *Catholic Citizen*, 10 June, 1 July 1858.

66 *New Era*, 6 April, 1 May 1858.

67 McGee to Bella Morgan, 9 February 1844, Concordia University Archives [CUA], PO30, HA256, folder 5.

68 *True Witness*, 18 June 1858.

69 Ibid.

70 *Catholic Citizen*, 15 July 1858.

71 Moylan to Morgan, n.d., LAC, Morgan Fonds, vol. 14, f. 5289; Cottrell, "Irish Catholic Political Leadership," 122; *Canadian Freeman*, 8 October 1858; McGee to Moylan, 3 September 1858, James G. Moylan Fonds, LAC, MG29-D15, vol. 1 [Moylan Fonds]; McGee to O'Donohoe, 8 November 1858, Murphy Fonds, f. 14254.

72 "Prospectus of the Canadian Freeman," enclosed in Charbonnel to Pinsonneault, 24 June 1858, Pinsonneault Papers, PAP-HF-44C-58, Diocese of London Archives; Charbonnel to Pinsonnealt, 20, 24 June 1858, and Pinsonneault to Charbonnel, 27 June 1858, Pinsonneault Papers, PAP-13HF-42C-4, 5; PAP-5LB-44-11, Diocese of London Archives. See also Bruyère to Pinsonneault, 2 July 1858, and Pinsonneault to Bruyère, 5 July 1858, Pinsonneault Papers, PAP-13HF-42C-5; PAP-5LB-44-15, Diocese of London Archives.

73 Charles Murphy to J. Quinn, 22 February 1935, McNeil Papers, ARCAT, MN AE 11.21a, 11.21c.

74 *True Witness*, 2 July 1858. See also *True Witness*, 17 April 1858.

75 *True Witness*, 2 July 1858.

76  *Globe*, 25 June 1858.

77  *True Witness*, 2 July 1858.

78  On the development of the Irish National School system, see Akenson, *Irish Education Experiment*.

79  Careless, *Brown of the Globe*, 1:266–9.

80  Thibaudeau to Brown, 1 August 1858, George Brown Fonds, LAC, MG24-B40 [Brown Fonds], f. 336.

81  McGee to Holton, n.d. [28 April 1862], Brown Fonds, f. 662; Holton to Brown, 10 May 1862, Brown Fonds, f. 664; William Scott to Ryerson, 14 January 1859, Ryerson Papers, United Church Archives. McGee subsequently denied that he had been asked to serve as a commissioner to Ireland to inquire into the National School system; see *Globe*, 24 December 1858; Canada, *Debates of the Legislative Assembly*, 1 February 1859.

82  Moore, *1867: How the Fathers Made a Deal*, 18.

83  *Canadian Freeman*, 13 August 1858.

84  *American Celt*, 16 August 1856.

85  Canada, *Debates of the Legislative Assembly*, 4 August 1858.

86  *Canadian Freeman*, 13 August 1858.

87  McGee to Charles Clark [sic], 10 December 1860, Archives of Ontario, Charles Clarke Papers, F26.


CHAPTER THREE

1  Macdonald to Vicar-General Macdonell, 20 August 1858, Archives of the Archdiocese of Kingston, Ontario, Bishop Edward John Horan Papers, DC15 C36/2.

2  *Globe*, 18 August 1858.

3  *Patriot* [Toronto], 1 September 1858.

4  Dorion to Brown, 14 September 1858, Library and Archives Canada [LAC], Brown Fonds, f. 368; McGee to Casey, 28 October 1858, Pinsonneault Papers, PAP-14HF-108L-58, Diocese of London Archives.

5  *Globe*, 17 September 1858; see also *Canadian Freeman*, 23 September 1858.

6  Brown to Luther Holton, 17 September 1858, LAC, Murphy Fonds, f. 21391.

7  *New Era*, 29 April 1858.

8  *True Witness*, 28 May 1858.

9  *Canadian Freeman*, 23 September 1858; Murphy, ed., *1825 – D'Arcy McGee – 1925*, 42–53.

10  See, for example, the letter by "Not an Irishman" in *True Witness*, 7 May 1858.

11 P. McKeon to O'Brien, 12 August 1858, William Smith O'Brien Papers, National Library of Ireland [NLI], MS 446, f. 3057; *Canadian Freeman*, 8 October 1858. On McGee's "*indiscreet* letter," see Wilson, *Thomas D'Arcy McGee*, 1:230–4.

12 *True Witness*, 28 May 1858.

13 *True Witness*, 9 July 1858, 25 March 1859.

14 *True Witness*, 4 March 1859, quoting the Toronto *Colonist*, 23 February 1859.

15 *True Witness*, 5, 19 November 1858. For Bourget's attitude to the Irish Literary and National Association, see Trigger, "Irish Politics on Parade," 181.

16 McGee to O'Donohoe, 8 November 1858, Murphy Fonds, ff. 14253–4; McGee to O'Donohoe, 10 January 1859, Murphy Fonds, ff. 14255–6.

17 McGee to Moylan, 8 November 1858, LAC, Moylan Fonds.

18 McGee to Moylan, n.d. [7 June 1860], Moylan Fonds.

19 Canada, *Debates of the Legislative Assembly*, 1 February 1859.

20 *Globe*, 8, 9 November 1858.

21 *Patriot* [Toronto], 8 September 1858.

22 *Patriot* [Toronto], 6 October 1858.

23 Ryerson, *Dr. Ryerson's Letters*, 72, 76. On the Irish Catholic hierarchy's opposition to the Irish National School system in 1858–59, see Jenkins, *Irish Nationalism*, 122–3.

24 Canada, *Debates of the Legislative Assembly*, 1 February 1859; *Globe*, 3 February 1859.

25 Canada, *Debates of the Legislative Assembly*, 1 February 1859; see also *Patriot* [Toronto], 9 February 1859 and 14 March 1860.

26 McGee, *Canadian Ballads*, 82.

27 Canada, *Debates of the Legislative Assembly*, 3, 4 February 1859; McGee, *Canadian Ballads*, 82; see also Ryerson, *Dr. Ryerson's Letters*, 48.

28 Canada, *Debates of the Legislative Assembly*, 14 March 1859.

29 Ibid., 4 February 1859.

30 *Canadian Freeman*, 6 May 1859; Canada, *Debates of the Legislative Assembly*, 28 April 1859.

31 Careless, *Brown of the Globe*, 1:291–9.

32 *Canadian Freeman*, 11 February 1859; *Globe*, 14, 15 February 1859.

33 *Globe*, 16 March, 21 May 1859.

34 *Leader* [Toronto], 30 April, 6 May 1859; *True Witness*, 6 May 1859; *Globe*, 5 May 1859.

35 *Globe*, 18 March 1859. See also McGee to O'Donohoe, 9 March 1859, Murphy Fonds, f. 14291.

36 For Devlin's earlier relationship with McGee, see Wilson, *Thomas D'Arcy McGee*, 1:311–12, 355. For his role in McGee's nomination in 1857, see *True Witness*, 18 December 1857.

37 Diary of George Clerk, Bibliothèque et Archives nationales du Québec [BAnQ], 14 September 1858.

38 *True Witness*, 25 March 1859; see also *True Witness*, 11 March 1859. Devlin wrote under the pseudonym of "An Irish Catholic."

39 McGee to Casey, 30 April 1859, Pinsonneault Papers, PAP-14HF-108L-59, Diocese of London Archives.

40 For McGee's speech against Ferguson's bill, see Canada, *Debates of the Legislative Assembly*, 31 March 1859; for his presentation of petitions to Parliament, see ibid., 1 May 1862; for Catholic-Protestant tensions in St Thomas, see *Globe*, 20 April 1859, and *True Witness*, 22 April 1859.

41 *Globe*, 25 March 1859; "McGee's Speech against Divorce," LAC, O'Gorman Fonds, folder 5.

42 *Globe*, 5 May 1859.

43 O'Brien to his daughter [probably Lucy Josephine], 16 May 1859, O'Brien Papers, NLI, MS 8653 (33). For later correspondence between McGee and O'Brien, see *True Witness*, 11 November 1859, and McGee to O'Brien, 18 November 1859, O'Brien Papers, NLI, MS 446, f. 3124.

44 *Globe*, 21 May 1859.

45 McGee to Brown, n.d. [7 June 1859], Brown Fonds, ff. 488–9.

46 McGee, "Four Letters to a Friend," Letter One, 4, O'Gorman Fonds, folder 10; see also Moir, "The Problem of Double Minority," 53–67.

47 McGee, "Four Letters to a Friend," Letter Four, 2, O'Gorman Fonds, folder 10.

48 McGee, "Four Letters to a Friend," Letter Four, 4–11, O'Gorman Fonds, folder 10.

49 McGee to Moylan, n.d. [10 June 1859], Moylan Fonds.

50 *True Witness*, 18 February, 6 May 1859. See also *Globe*, 25 March, 18 April, 25 June 1859.

51 *True Witness*, 20 May, 3 June 1859.

52 *True Witness*, 24 June, 1, 8, 15, and 29 July, 12 August 1859.

53 *Globe*, 23 August 1859. Bourget had issued an earlier endorsement of Clerk's position; see *True Witness*, 25 February 1859.

54 Pinsonneault to Bruyère, 26 August 1859, Pinsonneault Papers, PAP-5LB-4L-55, and Pinsonneault to Frank Smith [unsent], 24 August 1859, Pinsonneault Papers, PAP-5LB-4W-53, Diocese of London Archives. See also

Pinsonneault to Bruyère, 11 September 1859, Pinsonneault Papers, PAP-5LB-4L-62, Diocese of London Archives.

55 Monahan, "A Politico-Religious Incident," 45.

56 McGee to O'Donohoe, 15 September 1859, John O'Donohoe Fonds, LAC, MG27-1E12 [O'Donohoe Fonds]; O'Donohoe to Charbonnel, 24 September 1859, Charbonnel Papers, Archives of the RC Archdiocese of Toronto [ARCAT].

57 *Canadian Freeman*, 26 August 1859.

58 McGee to Charbonnel, 10 August 1859, Charbonnel Papers, ARCAT.

59 Bruyère to Pinsonneault, 15 September 1859, Pinsonneault Papers, PAP-13HF-42C-59, Diocese of London Archives. ("My letters before being sent to the press were carefully read by his Lordship [Charbonnel] who gave it as his opinion that they contained wholesome truths"); *Globe*, 27 August 1859.

60 *Globe*, 27 August 1859.

61 *Canadian Freeman*, 5 August 1859.

62 Bruyère to Pinsonneault, 15 September 1859, Pinsonneault Papers, PAP-13HF-42C-59, Diocese of London Archives.

63 The specific example is from a meeting in Logan Township on 25 August 1859, as reported in *Canadian Freeman*, 2 September 1859; for other meetings, see *Canadian Freeman*, passim, August–September 1859.

64 *True Witness*, 19 August 1859.

65 Bruyère to Pinsonneault, 15 September 1859, Pinsonneault Papers, PAP-13HF-42C-59, Diocese of London Archives; McGee to Moylan, n.d. [September 1859], Moylan Fonds.

66 McGee to Brown, 20 September 1859, Brown Fonds, f. 439.

67 *Globe*, 29 September 1859.

68 McGee to Moylan, n.d. [September 1859], Moylan Fonds.

69 Bruyère to Pinsonneault, 15 September 1859, Pinsonneault Papers, PAP-13HF-42C-59, Diocese of London Archives. See also *Globe*, 27 August 1859.

70 Canada, *Debates of the Legislative Assembly*, 28 April 1859; *Globe*, 29 April 1859.

71 McGee to O'Donohoe, 21 September 1859, Murphy Fonds, f. 14259.

72 McGee to O'Donohoe, 15 September 1859, O'Donohoe Fonds ("nothing would give me greater pleasure than to see every clergyman in Toronto, at least, at the coming Banquet"); McGee to O'Donohoe and Moylan, n.d. [September 1859], O'Donohoe Fonds ("I am really sorry you asked the clergy – if you have asked them – to the Banquet"); McGee to Brown, Montreal, 20 September 1859, Brown Fonds, ff. 439–40.

73 Brown to Holton, 11 October 1859, CUA, PO30, HA253, folder 13.

74  *Globe*, 23 August 1859.

75  Careless, *Brown of the Globe*, 1:310.

76  McGee to Brown, 20 September 1859, Brown Fonds, ff. 439–40.

77  Holton to Brown, 14 October 1859, Brown Fonds, ff. 447–50.

78  Holton to Brown, 28 October 1859, Brown Fonds, ff. 460–2; *Globe*, 31 October 1859.

79  McGee to Brown, 4 November 1859, Brown Fonds, ff. 463–5.

80  *Globe*, 10, 11 November 1859; Careless, *Brown of the Globe*, 1:314–22.

## CHAPTER FOUR

1  For McGee's comments about the Conservatives and separate schools, see "Four Letters to a Friend," Letter Four, 4, Library and Archives Canada [LAC], O'Gorman Fonds, folder 10.

2  Contract between Thomas D'Arcy McGee and Edward Carter, 30 June 1858, LAC, Morgan Fonds, vol. 14, ff. 5249–50; Slattery, *Assassination of D'Arcy McGee*, 124–5. For McGee's earlier plans to attend law school, see McGee to Bella Morgan, 9 February 1844, Concordia University Archives [CUA], PO30, HA256, folder 5; McGee to Bella Morgan, 2 March 1844, CUA, PO30, HA256, folder 6, and McGee to Bella and Charles Morgan, 13 August 1845, CUA, PO30, HA256, folder 7.

3  McGee to O'Donohoe, 10 January 1859, LAC, Murphy Fonds, ff. 14255–6.

4  McGee, *Sebastian; or, The Roman Martyr*. The play was based on Canon Frederick Oakley's dramatic adaptation of Cardinal Nicholas Wiseman's *Fabiola: Or, the Church of the Catacombs*.

5  McGee to Moylan, n.d. [May 1860], LAC, Moylan Fonds.

6  Anna J. Sadlier to Henry Morgan, 7 June 1902, Morgan Fonds, vol. 14, ff. 5306–8; Moylan to Morgan, 17 August 1901, Morgan Fonds, vol. 14, ff. 5296–7. McGee's poems to Mary include "The Parting" (Sadlier, ed., *Poems of Thomas D'Arcy McGee*, 413–14), "To Mary in Ireland" (417–19); "Live for Love" (420–1); "The Exile" (421–3); "To Mary's Angel" (423–4); "I Love Thee, Mary!" (425–6); "Memento Mori" (426–7); "Memories" (427–8); "Home Thoughts" (428), "An Invitation to the Country" (429–30); and "Mary's Heart" (440–1). All but the last poem, it should be added, were written after the rising of 1848, after McGee had escaped to the United States and before Mary joined him in August 1849.

7  Resolution of the Bradford Loyal Orange Lodge, quoted in *Canadian Freeman*, 3 February 1860.

8  *Globe*, 18 January 1860.

9 Quoted in the *Canadian Freeman*, 27 January 1860.

10 *Globe*, 18, 19 January 1860.

11 *Canadian Freeman*, 3 February 1860.

12 *Canadian Freeman*, 2 March 1860; *Globe*, 18 January 1860.

13 Moylan to Morgan, n.d., Morgan Fonds, vol. 14, f. 5293. See also *Canadian Freeman*, 19 September 1861.

14 *Canadian Freeman*, 27 January 1860.

15 Canada, *Debates of the Legislative Assembly*, 8 March 1860.

16 Ibid.

17 *True Witness*, 16 March 1860.

18 McGee to Moylan, 14 March 1860, Moylan Fonds.

19 *The Phoenix*, 24 March 1860, in "Reports by Sub-Inspector Thomas Doyle from USA, with newspaper extracts, 1859–61," National Archives of Ireland [NAI], Fenian Police Reports, 1857–83, box 1.

20 McGee to Moylan, 26 [March] 1860, Moylan Fonds.

21 Careless, *Brown of the Globe*, 2:15–21; Morton, *Critical Years*, 80–1.

22 McGee, *Speeches and Addresses*, 161, 164, 165–6.

23 Ibid., 164, 169–70, 174.

24 Ibid., 175–6.

25 *American Celt*, 25 October 1856; McGee, *Popular History of Ireland*, 1.

26 McGee, *Speeches and Addresses*, 176.

27 Cited in *Canadian Freeman*, 11 May 1860.

28 *Globe*, 9 May 1860.

29 *Globe*, 17 March 1860; Walker, *Catholic Education and Politics*, 251; Reale, "Was the Separate School Act of 1863 a Finality?" 6–7.

30 McGee to Moylan, Easter Monday [9 April 1860], Moylan Fonds.

31 *Canadian Freeman*, 20 April 1860.

32 *Canadian Freeman*, 25 May 1860.

33 *Globe*, 19 May 1860.

34 Stortz, "John Joseph Lynch," 1–6, 120–1. See also Humphreys, "Lynch, John Joseph," in *Dictionary of Canadian Biography online*, http://www.biographi.ca.

35 McGee to O'Donohoe, 5 [June] 1860, Murphy Fonds, ff. 14260–1.

36 Ibid., f. 14260.

37 McGee to Moylan, n.d. [7 June 1860], Moylan Fonds.

38 McGee to O'Donohoe, 5 [June] 1860, Murphy Fonds, f. 14260.

39 McGee to Lynch, 9 June 1860, Lynch Papers, Archives of the RC Archdiocese of Toronto [ARCAT].

40 Farrell, *Rituals and Riots*, 4, 157; Bryan, *Orange Parades*, 38–9.

41 This account is based on Radforth, *Royal Spectacle*, 164–205. See also Radforth, "Orangemen and the Crown," 69–88.

42 Quoted in Radforth, *Royal Spectacle*, 188.

43 Ibid., 192.

44 Canada, *Debates of the Legislative Assembly*, 29 February 1860. In his otherwise excellent account of the royal tour, Radforth mistakenly assumed that McGee composed the legislative assembly's address to the Prince of Wales; the error arose from a mistranslation of a report in the ultramontane newspaper *L'Ordre, Union Catholique*. Cf. Radforth, *Royal Spectacle*, 71, with *L'Ordre, Union Catholique*, 18 July 1860.

45 See, for example, *Patriot* [Toronto], 14 March 1860.

46 *Globe*, 21 August 1860; *Irish People*, 15 July 1865. In the event, the speech was given by J. Curtis Clark, on behalf of the workmen of the Grand Trunk Railway; see *Montreal Gazette*, 28 August 1860.

47 McGee to Moylan, n.d. [5 September 1860], Moylan Fonds; *Canadian Freeman*, 20 September 1860.

48 McGee to Moylan, n.d. [5 September 1860], Moylan Fonds; McGee to Moylan, n.d. [11 September 1860], Moylan Fonds.

49 McGee to Moylan, n.d. [11 September 1860], Moylan Fonds; McGee to Moylan, n.d., "P.S. (political)," Moylan Fonds.

50 Radforth, *Royal Spectacle*, 202–3.

51 *Globe*, 12 September 1860.

52 *Globe*, 14 September 1860. In reply to such criticisms, which had in fact been voiced privately by Macdonald himself, Newcastle argued that the banners of the Catholic Church were "emblematic of a faith," while those of the Orangemen were "of a rancorous party." Quoted in Radforth, *Royal Spectacle*, 177.

53 *Globe*, 23 August 1860.

54 *Globe*, 20 September 1860. There is no doubting the sincerity of Brown's remarks; see Brown to Holton, 27 September 1860, CUA, PO30, HA253, folder 13.

55 McGee to Brown, 1 October 1860, LAC, Brown Fonds, ff. 541–3.

56 McGee to Moylan, n.d. [7 June 1860], Moylan Fonds.

57 *Canadian Freeman*, 30 August, 27 September 1860.

58 *Canadian Freeman*, 8 November 1860.

59 McGee to Moylan, 8 November 1860, Moylan Fonds; on his "paroxysm of feeling," see McGee to Moylan, 30 November 1860, Moylan Fonds.

60 McGee to O'Donohoe, 9 November 1860, Murphy Fonds, ff. 14263–4. John Crawford was a prominent Toronto Protestant Conservative; John Elms-

ley was a Toronto Conservative who had converted to Catholicism in 1833. See Cottrell, "Irish Catholic Political Leadership," 127–8, for Crawford; see Nicolson, "John Elmsley," 47–66.

61 McGee to Moylan, 8 November 1860, Moylan Fonds.
62 McGee to Moylan, 30 November 1860, Moylan Fonds.
63 See, for example, *La Minerve*, 21 February 1861, and *Canadian Freeman*, 14 March 1861.
64 *American Celt*, 26 March 1853; Wilson, *Thomas D'Arcy McGee*, 1:311.
65 *Canadian Freeman*, 6 April 1860, quoted in *True Witness*, 25 May 1860.
66 *True Witness*, 25 May 1860.
67 McGee to Moylan, n.d. [7 June 1860], Moylan Fonds.
68 *Boston Pilot*, 19 April 1845.
69 *Montreal Herald*, 6 March 1861.
70 Ibid.
71 *True Witness*, 8 March 1861.
72 *True Witness*, 29 March 1861.
73 *Canadian Freeman*, 21 March 1861.
74 *Montreal Herald*, 6 March 1861.
75 *True Witness*, 29 March 1861.
76 Diary of George Clerk, BAnQ, 12 January, 12 April 1861.

## CHAPTER FIVE

1 McGee, "American Relations and Canadian Duties," 10 May 1862, in *Speeches and Addresses*, 34. Among the vast literature on the American Civil War, see Potter, *The Impending Crisis*, and Foner, ed., *Politics and Ideology*.
2 McGee, "Canada's Interest in the American Civil War," 26 September 1861, in *Speeches and Addresses*, 22. The best treatment of Canadian responses to the Civil War is Winks, *Canada and the United States*.
3 Wise and Brown, *Canada Views the United States*, 82.
4 Ibid., 82–97.
5 For McGee's criticisms of the United States, see Wilson, *Thomas D'Arcy McGee*, 1:299–300, 321–4, 336–41.
6 McGee, "The Border Counties of Lower Canada: Their Relations with the United States," 17 July 1861, in *Speeches and Addresses*, 10.
7 McGee, "Canada's Interest in the American Civil War," *Speeches and Addresses*, 13.
8 McGee, "Border Counties of Lower Canada," *Speeches and Addresses*, 11.

9 McGee, "Canada's Interest in the American Civil War," *Speeches and Addresses*, 17–18, 27; "Border Counties of Lower Canada," *Speeches and Addresses*, 11.

10 For a fuller explication of McGee's views on slavery, see Wilson, *Thomas D'Arcy McGee*, 1:88–9, 106, 108, 277–8, 314–16, 320.

11 McGee, "Along the Line!" *Canadian Ballads*, 48.

12 See, for example, Virgo, *Selected Verse of Thomas D'Arcy McGee*, xvi; Gwyn, *John A.*, 217.

13 *American Celt*, 1 March 1851; Collison, *Shadrach Minkins*. See also Wilson, *Thomas D'Arcy McGee*, 1:277.

14 McGee, "The Land We Live In," 22 December 1860, in *Speeches and Addresses*, 4. Anderson was not extradited to the United States; for his story, see Teatero, *John Anderson*.

15 *Globe*, 26 December 1860.

16 McGee, "Canada's Interest in the American Civil War," 25–6. The Dred Scott decision (1857) effectively prevented Congress from excluding slavery in the new western territories.

17 McGee, "Canada's Interest in the American Civil War," *Speeches and Addresses*, 21.

18 Ibid., 15.

19 Ibid., 23–4.

20 Canada, *Debates of the Legislative Assembly*, 17 April 1861; McGee, "Constitutional Difficulties between Upper and Lower Canada," 17 April 1861, *Speeches and Addresses*, 185–94.

21 Canada, *Debates of the Legislative Assembly*, 2 April 1861.

22 McGee, "Representation by Population," 28 March 1861, *Speeches and Addresses*, 179, 181.

23 Canada, *Debates of the Legislative Assembly*, 2 April 1861.

24 *Canadian Freeman*, 23 May 1861.

25 Walker, *Catholic Education and Politics*, 255; Reale, "Was the Separate School Act of 1863 a Finality?" 14.

26 McGee to Moylan, n.d., Montreal, Saturday [June 1861], Library and Archives Canada [LAC], Moylan Fonds; Diary of George Clerk, Bibliothèque et Archives nationales du Québec [BAnQ], 26, 28 June 1861; *True Witness*, 28 June 1861.

27 McGee to Daniel MaCarow, *Globe*, 29 June 1861.

28 McGee to O'Donohoe, n.d. [25 June or 2 July 1861], LAC, Murphy Fonds, f. 14277.

29 McGee to O'Donohoe, Tuesday, n.d. [May or June 1861], LAC, O'Donohoe Fonds.

30 McGee to O'Donohoe, 5 June 1861, Murphy Fonds, ff. 14267–9.

31 *Globe*, 20, 25, and 26 June 1861.

32 *Globe*, 29 June 1861.

33 McGee to O'Donohoe, n.d. [25 June or 2 July 1861], Murphy Fonds, f. 14277.

34 *Globe*, 13 July 1861.

35 Slattery, *Assassination of D'Arcy McGee*, 87, 151.

36 McGee to O'Donohoe, 1 August 1861, Murphy Fonds; McGee to O'Donohoe, n.d. [31 August 1861], Murphy Fonds, ff. 14287–8.

37 *Canadian Freeman*, 3 October 1861.

38 *Canadian Freeman*, 19 September 1861.

39 *Canadian Freeman*, 26 September 1861.

40 McGee to O'Donohoe, n.d. [31 August 1861], Murphy Fonds, f. 14287; McGee to O'Donohoe, n.d. [21 or 28 September 1861], Murphy Fonds, f. 14286. The circular was printed in the Toronto *Mirror* on 13 September 1861 and reprinted in the *Globe*, 21 September 1861.

41 McGee to O'Donohoe, n.d. [21 or 28 September 1861], Murphy Fonds, f. 14286.

42 *Canadian Freeman*, 19 September 1861.

43 *Canadian Freeman*, 19, 26 September 1861; *Leader* [Toronto], 25 September 1861. Moylan believed that McGee himself was behind the legal action; see Moylan to Pinsonneault, 19 October 1861, Pinsonneault Papers, PAP-14HF-110L-61, Diocese of London Archives.

44 McGee to O'Donohoe, n.d. [21 or 28 September 1861], Murphy Fonds, ff. 14285–6.

45 McGee to Moylan, 8 November 1858, Moylan Fonds; McGee to O'Donohoe, 8 November 1858, Murphy Fonds, ff. 14253–4.

46 Winks, *Canada and the United States*, 4–5, 23–4, 26–9, 48. See also 223–8, where Winks argues that the New York *Herald* editorials were not the "basic causes" for growing anti-Northern sentiment. The basic causes, in his view, were "latent anti-Americanism, nationalism as expressed in the growing Canadian desire to take advantage of the Civil War for expansion to the west and to confederate for defense and for nationhood, and a narrow continentalism as expressed in a desire to avoid a British oriented war," along with "an inchoate sense of geopolitics" which "made it evident that a Southern victory might re-establish the North American balance of power" (228).

47  Winks, *Canada and the United States*, 68–104.

48  *Montreal Herald*, 21 December 1861.

49  *Montreal Herald*, 25 December 1861.

50  Ibid.; *True Witness*, 27 December 1861. See also McGee's account of the meeting, *Montreal Gazette*, 17 August 1867.

51  The relevant clauses can be found in *Montreal Gazette*, 17 August 1867.

52  Timothy Daniel Sullivan to McGee, 18 February 1862, Concordia University Archives [CUA], PO30, HA253, folder 5.

53  *Montreal Herald*, 28 December 1861.

54  Winks, *Canada and the United States*, 98.

55  Ibid., 117–18.

56  McGee, "Canadian Defences," 27 March 1862, *Speeches and Addresses*, 199–205.

57  McGee, "American Relations and Canadian Duties," 10 May 1862, *Speeches and Addresses*, 35.

58  Ibid., 35–7.

59  McGee, "Emigration and Colonisation," 25 April 1862, *Speeches and Addresses*, 231.

60  Ibid., 228.

61  Canada, *Debates of the Legislative Assembly*, 20 March 1861.

62  "Report of the Committee on Emigration," *Globe*, 20 April 1861; McGee, "Emigration and Colonisation," 25 April 1862, *Speeches and Addresses*, 215, 220–3.

63  McGee, "Emigration and Colonisation," 25 April 1862, *Speeches and Addresses*, 212. In adopting this perspective, McGee anticipated by well over a century the arguments of immigration historians such as Donald Harman Akenson; see Akenson, *The Irish Diaspora*, 228–32.

64  McGee, "Emigration and Colonisation," 25 April 1862, *Speeches and Addresses*, 231.

65  Walker, *Catholic Education and Politics*, 264–5; Reale, "Was the Separate School Act of 1863 a Finality?" 18–19. Among other things, Ryerson and Lynch agreed that separate school supporters in different school sections could pool their resources, that separate schools could be formed in incorporated villages, and that separate school ratepayers would not need to give annual notice of their intentions.

66  Scott wanted to ensure that "Catholic Separate Schools should be entitled to their fair share of the portion of the Clergy Reserve moneys allotted to the Common Schools"; his bill would also have given priests the power of taxation, allowed separate schools to have their own holidays, and enabled

separate school trustees to regulate the curricula. See Canada, *Debates of the Legislative Assembly*, 28 April 1862. For the provisions of the bill, see Hodgins, *Documentary History*, 17:199–202. This was still not enough to satisfy James Moylan, who insisted that the superintendent of separate schools should be a Catholic appointed by the bishops, and that Catholics should have their own university, normal schools, and grammar schools. See *Canadian Freeman*, 1 May 1862, and Walker, *Catholic Education and Politics*, 266–70. For Ryerson's objections to Scott's bill, see Toronto *Leader*, 30 April 1862.

67 Canada, *Debates of the Legislative Assembly*, 1 May 1862. The previous month, Robinson had been appointed president of the Executive Council and consequently had to run again for Toronto West, where he was challenged by John George Bowes. During the election campaign, Robinson's Orange supporters argued that their candidate would stand firm against separate schools. "What loyal Orangeman can hesitate in preferring him [Robinson] to *Nunnery Bowes*, to *St Michael's College Bowes*, to *Separate Schools Bowes*?" asked an Orange handbill. Two weeks after his re-election, Robinson supported further discussion of Scott's bill – although prudently he was absent from the House when the bill finally came up for its third reading. See *Globe*, 19 April 1862; "Catholic electors!" [April 1862]; Brode, "John Beverley Robinson."

68 Canada, *Debates of the Legislative Assembly*, 1 May 1862. See also *Globe*, 9 June 1862, for a classic statement of the "thin end of the wedge" argument against separate schools.

69 Canada, *Debates of the Legislative Assembly*, 1 May 1862.

70 Ibid.

71 McGee to Holton, 2 May 1862, LAC, Brown Fonds, ff. 661–2.

72 Holton to Brown, 5 May 1862, Brown Fonds, ff. 659–60.

73 Holton to Brown, 10 May 1862, Brown Fonds, ff. 663–5.

74 *Globe*, 9 May 1862.

75 *Canadian Freeman*, 8 May 1862; *True Witness*, 9 May 1862.

76 The vote in favour was 93–19; see Canada, *Journals of Legislative Assembly*, vol. 20, 146–7.

77 Reale, "Was the Separate School Act of 1863 a Finality?" 24–8.

78 *Canadian Freeman*, 5 June 1862; *True Witness*, 6 June 1862.

79 McGee to Holton, 2 May 1862, Brown Fonds, ff. 661–2. See also *Canadian Freeman*, 19 March 1863.

80 Hodgins to Ryerson, 6 June 1862, in Hodgins, *Documentary History*, 17:217.

81 Winks, *Canada and the United States*, 111–15.

82  Ibid., 116. See also Creighton, *Macdonald*, 332–3; Gwyn, *John A.*, 262–9.

83  *Globe*, 22 May 1862.

84  Montreal *Transcript*, in Canada, *Debates of the Legislative Assembly*, 7 June 1862. For McGee's critique of Galt's budget, see *Debates of the Legislative Assembly*, 16 May 1862.

85  See, for example, *Globe*, 23 May 1862.

## CHAPTER SIX

1   *Canadian Freeman*, 16 October 1862.

2   *Montreal Transcript*, in Canada, *Debates of the Legislative Assembly*, 7 June 1862.

3   Quoted in Hodgins, *John Sandfield Macdonald*, 59.

4   *Montreal Transcript*, in Canada, *Debates of the Legislative Assembly*, 7 June 1862.

5   *Montreal Gazette*, 7, 10 June 1862.

6   James Taylor to McGee, 25 June 1862; McGee to James Taylor, 6 July 1862, James Wickes Taylor Papers, MS 20187, State Historical Society of North Dakota.

7   *Montreal Transcript*, in Canada, *Debates of the Legislative Assembly*, 7 June 1862.

8   McGee to Mary Ann Sadlier, 9 June 1862, LAC, Sadlier Fonds.

9   McGee, "Report on the Origins of Public Departments," February 1863, Executive Council Office of the Province of Canada Fonds, LAC, RG 1 E7, vol. 59; Curtis, *Politics of Population*, 237–8.

10  McGee to O'Donohoe, 31 July 1862, LAC, Murphy Fonds, ff. 14272–3.

11  McGee to T.D. O'Sullivan, 15 August 1862, National Library of Ireland [NLI], Young Ireland Miscellaneous Letters, MS 10,517.

12  Quoted in Martin, *Britain and the Origins of Canadian Confederation*, 111–12, 114.

13  Whitelaw, *Maritimes and Canada*, 179–80.

14  Hodgins, *John Sandfield Macdonald*, 59–60.

15  McGee, *Speeches and Addresses*, n.p.

16  Whitelaw, *Maritimes and Canada*, 164–5. The convention met between 10 and 13 September 1862.

17  *Globe*, 26 September 1862.

18  *Globe*, 18 September 1862; see also *Globe*, 12, 16, 19, and 29 September 1862.

19  *Globe*, 15 February 1862.

20  McGee to Sandfield Macdonald, 2 October 1862, Sandfield Macdonald Fonds, LAC, MG24-B30 [Sandfield Macdonald Fonds], f. 1007.

21  *Courier de St. Hyacinthe*, quoted in *Globe*, 28 September 1862.

22 For McGee's speech, see "The Moral Taught by Four Revolutions," 8 January 1863, LAC, O'Gorman Fonds, folder 5, and *Globe*, 29 January 1863; for his defence, see "Letter to Dorion," 14 January 1863, in O'Gorman Fonds, folder 5.

23 McGee to Sandfield Macdonald, 2 October 1862, Sandfield Macdonald Fonds, f. 1009.

24 Ibid., f. 1008.

25 *Globe*, 20 September 1862.

26 *Canadian Freeman*, 16 October 1862.

27 Hodgins, *John Sandfield Macdonald*, 61.

28 Martin, *Britain and the Origins of Canadian Confederation*, 17–18, 41–2. See also McGee, "Intercolonial Railway Diplomacy," *Speeches and Addresses*, 232–40.

29 *Canadian Freeman*, 5 March 1863.

30 McGee to Lynch, 9 March 1863, Archives of the RC Archdiocese of Toronto [ARCAT].

31 *Canadian Freeman*, 19, 26 March 1863.

32 Canada, *Debates of the Legislative Assembly*, 12 March 1863. See also *Canadian Freeman*, 26 March 1863.

33 *Globe*, 14 March 1863; Walker, *Catholic Education and Politics*, 282–3.

34 Hodgins, *John Sandfield Macdonald*, 65–6.

35 Mood, "Orange Order in Canadian Politics," 92.

36 *Patriot* [Toronto], 25 March 1863; see also *Globe*, 6 April 1863.

37 Walker, *Catholic Education and Politics*, 224; Mood, "Orange Order in Canadian Politics," 164.

38 *Peterborough Review*, 20 March 1863; John Joseph McGee to John J. O'Gorman, 26 March and 7 April 1925, O'Gorman Fonds, folder 1.

39 *Irish Canadian*, 25 March, 1 April 1863.

40 Cottrell, "Irish Catholic Political Leadership in Toronto," 140; "To the Right Reverend Dr. Lynch, Bishop of Toronto," ARCAT, LAE 0617 [erroneously dated 1867].

41 *Globe*, 18 March 1862.

42 *Irish Canadian*, 7 January 1863. On Michael Power, see McGowan, *Michael Power*.

43 *Irish Canadian*, 18 March 1863.

44 *Irish Canadian*, 25 March, 17 June, 21 October 1863, 17 February 1864.

45 *Montreal Herald*, 27, 28 September 1882; McGee, "Account of Attempts," *Montreal Gazette*, 20 August 1867.

46 *Montreal Transcript*, 20 May 1863.

47 *Irish Canadian*, 27 May 1863.

48 *Hastings Chronicle*, 4 June, 29 October 1862.

49 *Hastings Chronicle*, 26 November, 10 December 1862; *Canadian Freeman*, 6 November 1862.

50 *Hastings Chronicle*, 10 December 1862.

51 For a particularly good example, see Father Richard Beausang's public letter to McGee in *Irish Canadian*, 12 October 1866.

52 Canada, *Debates of the Legislative Assembly*, 23 February 1863.

53 *Canadian Freeman*, 26 February, 12 March, 9 April, 21 and 28 May 1863; *True Witness*, 16 January, 20 February 1863.

54 *Irish Canadian*, 28 June 1865, 21 September, 12 October 1866; see also *Irish Canadian*, 26 April, 23 August 1865.

55 *Montreal Herald*, 24 July 1867.

56 *Globe*, 6 May 1863.

57 Burns, "D'Arcy McGee and the New Nationality," 53–4; Slattery, *Assassination of D'Arcy McGee*, 186.

58 Hodgins, *John Sandfield Macdonald*, 67–8; Slattery, *Assassination of D'Arcy McGee*, 186–7; Careless, *Brown of the Globe*, 2:93–5.

59 McGee to Sicotte, 12 May 1863, Sandfield Macdonald Fonds, ff. 1021–2.

60 McGee to O'Donohoe , 16 May 1863, Murphy Fonds, f. 14275.

61 McGee to T.D. O'Sullivan, 15 August 1862, NLI, Young Ireland Miscellaneous Letters, MS 10,517; Brown to Anne Brown, 2 March 1864, LAC, Brown Fonds, ff. 867–70.

62 McGee to O'Donohoe, 16 May 1863, Murphy Fonds, ff. 14275–6.

63 *Globe*, 4 May 1863; *Canadian Freeman*, 11 June 1863.

## CHAPTER SEVEN

1 *Montreal Gazette*, 24 August 1863.

2 Canada, *Debates of the Legislative Assembly*, 24 August 1863.

3 Gerry Tulchinsky and Brian J. Young, "Sir John Young," *Dictionary of Canadian Biography online*, http://www.biographi.ca; *Montreal Herald*, 5, 7 September 1867.

4 Wilson, *Thomas D'Arcy McGee*, 1:101; see above, 25.

5 *Canadian Freeman*, 11 June 1863.

6 McGee to O'Donohoe, 16 May 1863, LAC, Murphy Fonds, ff. 14275–6.

7 *Canadian Freeman*, 11 June 1863.

8 *Globe*, 27 June 1863; see also Hodgins, *John Sandfield Macdonald*, 68–9.

9   *Montreal Gazette*, 3 July 1863.

10   McGee to Daniel MaCarow, 12 June 1863, in *Patriot* [Toronto], 1 July 1863; see also *New Era*, 19 January and 16 February 1858.

11   *Montreal Gazette*, 3 July 1863; *Morning Freeman* [Saint John], 30 July 1863.

12   *Morning Freeman* [Saint John], 11 August 1863.

13   *Acadian Recorder*, 4 July 1863; *New Brunswick Reporter*, 31 July 1863.

14   *Patriot* [Toronto], 1 July 1863.

15   *Patriot* [Toronto], 6 May 1863.

16   *Patriot* [Toronto], 1 July 1863.

17   See Wilson, *Thomas D'Arcy McGee*, 1:171–4.

18   On his visit in 1856, see *Acadian Recorder*, 26 July 1856; for accounts of his lectures in 1859, see *Nova Scotian*, 29 August 1859, *British Colonist* [Halifax], 25 August 1859, *Morning Freeman* [Saint John], 16, 18, 20, 27 August and 1 September 1859; *New Brunswick Reporter*, 2 September 1859; *Saint John Daily News*, 17, 19, and 22 August 1859.

19   On the Carlingford–Saint John connection, see Murphy, *Together in Exile*, i–vi and passim.

20   *Acadian Recorder*, 27 August 1859; *British Colonist* [Halifax], 25 August 1859.

21   *Morning Freeman* [Saint John], 28 July 1863; *Acadian Recorder*, 25 July 1863.

22   *Saint John Daily News*, 31 July 1863.

23   *Morning Chronicle* [Halifax], 23 July 1863; *Acadian Recorder*, 25 July 1863; *Saint John Daily News*, 29 July 1863; *Morning Freeman* [Saint John], 30 July 1863.

24   *Morning Freeman* [Saint John], 28 July 1863.

25   *Prince Edward Island Vindicator*, 28 August 1863; *Morning Freeman* [Saint John], 13 August 1863. The same questions have been asked by historian Ged Martin; see his *Britain and the Origins of Canadian Confederation*, 27–79.

26   *Saint John Daily News*, 3 August 1863; see also *Acadian Recorder*, 25 July 1863; *British Colonist* [Halifax], 23 July 1863; *New Brunswick Reporter*, 31 July 1863; *Saint John Daily News*, 21 August 1863.

27   *Acadian Recorder*, 25 July 1863; *Prince Edward Island Examiner*, 3 August 1863.

28   *Montreal Gazette*, 31 July, 7 August 1863.

29   *Globe*, 5 August 1863.

30   *Globe*, 8 August 1863. See also Clerk to Horan, Montreal, 14 August 1863, Archives of the Archdiocese of Kingston, Ontario, Horan Papers, D12 C33/11. Upon reading McGee's speech, Clerk mistakenly believed that McGee was keeping his political options open by supporting Reform demands for representation by population.

31 See above, 35, 45, and *New Era*, 19 September 1857.

32 Canada, *Debates of the Legislative Assembly*, 25 August 1863; *Canadian Freeman*, 11 June 1863, 18 February 1864.

33 Mary McGee to Thomas Devine, 20 August 1863, Concordia University Archives [CUA], PO30, HA254, folder 7.

34 Canada, *Debates of the Legislative Assembly*, 17 August 1863.

35 Ibid., 20 August 1863; *Montreal Gazette*, 22 August 1863.

36 Canada, *Debates of the Legislative Assembly*, 20 August 1863.

37 *Montreal Gazette*, 11 August 1863.

38 Canada, *Debates of the Legislative Assembly*, 20 August, 10 September 1863. For an example of his earlier comments on American "excitement," see *American Celt*, 12 May 1855.

39 Canada, *Debates of the Legislative Assembly*, 20 August 1863.

40 Ibid.

41 *Canadian Freeman*, 27 August 1863.

42 *Globe*, 28 August 1863.

43 *Globe*, 13 October 1863.

44 John Lowe to Henry Morgan, 26 July 1898, LAC, Morgan Fonds, vol. 14, ff. 5274–9.

45 *Montreal Gazette*, 1 September 1863.

46 *Montreal Gazette*, 12 September 1863.

47 Canada, *Debates of the Legislative Assembly*, 2 October 1863; McGee, "Intercolonial Railway Diplomacy" in *Speeches and Addresses*, 232–40. For McGee's earlier parliamentary speeches on the Intercolonial, see *Debates of the Legislative Assembly*, 1 and 23 September 1863.

48 Canada, *Debates of the Legislative Assembly*, 2 October 1863.

49 Ibid.

50 Ibid.

51 *Boston Pilot*, 21 October 1848; *Nation* [New York], 11 November 1848.

52 O'Hanly, "Letter to the Hon. Thomas D'Arcy McGee," 28 October 1863, J.L.P. O'Hanley [sic] Fonds [O'Hanly Fonds], LAC, MG29-B11, folder 7.

53 McGee to Daniel MaCarow, *Globe*, 29 June 1861; see above, 123–4.

54 Quoted in *Nova Scotian*, 7 September 1863.

55 *Irish Canadian*, 23 September 1863.

56 *Irish Canadian*, 11, 18 November 1863; see also *Irish People*, 28 November 1863.

57 For a general account of the attitudes of North American Catholic bishops to Fenianism, see Rafferty, *The Church, the State, and the Fenian Threat*, 52–82.

58 McGee, "Account of the Attempts to Establish Fenianism in Montreal," *Montreal Gazette*, 17 August 1867; St Patrick's Society Minute Book, CUA, PO26, 1.

59 *Peterborough Review*, 27 November 1863, 11 March 1864. See also McGee, "Account of the Attempts to Establish Fenianism in Montreal," *Montreal Gazette*, 17 August 1867.

60 Canada, *Debates of the Legislative Assembly*, 10 September 1863.

61 *Montreal Gazette*, 31 July 1863.

62 McGee to John A. Macdonald, 15 December 1863, LAC, Murphy Fonds, ff. 14212–14; McGee to Macdonald, n.d. [November 1863], LAC, Macdonald Fonds, vol. 231, ff. 99981–4.

63 *Canadian Freeman*, 24 December 1863.

64 *Canadian Freeman*, 18 February 1864.

65 McGee to Mary Ann Sadlier, 8 January 1864, LAC, Sadlier Fonds.

66 *British American* [Kingston], 30 January 1864.

67 McGee to Macdonald, n.d. [4 January 1864], Macdonald Fonds, vol. 231, ff. 99985–6; McGee to Macdonald, 9 January 1864, Macdonald Fonds, vol. 231, ff. 99988–90.

68 See above, 59, 124.

69 *Canadian Freeman*, 11 February 1864; see also *Globe*, 23 January, 6 February 1864.

70 See, for example, *Irish Canadian*, 8 July 1863 ("one of the most truthful, readable and useful works that has come under our notice in this colony"); *Canadian Freeman*, 14 May 1868 ("absolutely the most meritorious work of the kind in existence"); and *British American Magazine*, 2:84–8 ("its style, language and method is that of a fascinating romance, which one closes with a feeling of regret that a pleasant and most instructive recreation, rather than study, has come to an end"). At McGee's funeral, Father O'Farrell described it as the greatest of all his books, which was "confessedly the best that has been yet written, and more wonderful has been written upon a foreign soil, with such scanty material as he could here procure" (*Canadian Freeman*, 16 April 1868).

71 Generally, but not entirely; see the brief discussion in Boyce, *Nationalism in Ireland*, 249.

72 Sullivan, *Story of Ireland*, 5–6; *Canadian Freeman*, 12 May 1864.

73 *Boston Pilot*, 11 January 1845; *American Celt*, 28 May 1853.

74 McGee, *Memoir of the Life and Conquests of Art Mac Murrough*; *History of the Attempts to Establish the Protestant Reformation in Ireland*; *Irish Writers of the*

*Seventeenth Century*; *Historical Sketches of O'Connell and His Friends*; *History of the Irish Settlers in North America*.

75 See, for example, his "Popular Fallacies about Irish History," *Nation* [Dublin], 9 January 1847, and his role in creating the myth about grain exports from Ireland during the famine, in McGee, *History of the Irish Settlers*, 135–6, 140.

76 See above, 58, 95; *New Era*, 11 February 1858, 15 April 1858; *Canadian Freeman*, 3 December 1863.

77 *Canadian Freeman*, 3 December 1863.

78 McGee, *Popular History of Ireland*, iii–iv.

79 Ibid., 48.

80 Ibid., 37.

81 Ibid., 34–5, 41.

82 Ibid., 163, 174–5, 749.

83 *Irish World*, 2 February 1878.

84 McGee, *Popular History of Ireland*, 675–6, 726.

85 Ibid., 708, 720.

86 Ibid., 500.

87 Ibid., 497.

88 Ibid., 501–2, 696, 716–17.

89 Ibid., 500, 502–3, 717.

90 See Wilson, *Thomas D'Arcy McGee*, 1:52–3, 369.

91 In 1646, Sir John Temple wrote that 300,000 Protestants were massacred; shortly afterwards, John Milton doubled the estimate. See Barnard, "1641: A Bibliographical Essay," 175–6, and Canny, "What Really Happened in 1641?" 34–5. Moody, "Irish History and Irish Mythology," 73–4, argues that the figure of 4,000 is much closer to the mark.

92 For divisions among historians about the role of sectarianism in 1798, see Whelan, "Reinterpreting the 1798 Rebellion in County Wexford," 9–36; Whelan, *Tree of Liberty*, 99–130; Donnelly, "Sectarianism in 1798," 15–37; Dunne, *Rebellions*; and the exchange between Whelan and Dunne in *Irish Times*, 6, 18 March 2004.

93 McGee, *Popular History of Ireland*, 580.

94 Ibid., 156.

95 Ibid., 571, 604.

96 Ibid., 641, 643, 683.

97 Ibid., 498, 537, 679–80, 746. On the relationship between Burke's thought and William Pitt's conception of the Act of Union, see Bew, *Ireland: Politics of Enmity*, 51–7.

98 McGee, *Popular History of Ireland*, 803–4.

99 The journalist recalled the conversation in the *Irishman* [Dublin], 25 April 1868.

## CHAPTER EIGHT

1 Comerford, *The Fenians in Context*, 122–8. See also Ramón, *A Provisional Dictator*, 166–71.

2 D'Arcy, *The Fenian Movement in the United States*, 21–98; Neidhardt, *Fenianism in North America*, 9–15.

3 The best treatment of Canadian Fenianism is Toner, "The Rise of Irish Nationalism in Canada"; see also Toner, "'The Green Ghost': Canada's Fenians and the Raids," 27–47.

4 Martin, "The Idea of British North American Union 1854–1864," *Journal of Irish and Scottish Studies* 1, no. 2 (2008): 309–33.

5 McGee, "Speech on Motion for an Address to Her Majesty in Favour of Confederation," *Speeches and Addresses*, 265.

6 Careless, *Brown of the Globe*, 2:100–1.

7 Canada, *Debates of the Legislative Assembly*, 24 February 1864.

8 Careless, *Brown of the Globe*, 2:118. See also Diary of George Clerk, Bibliothèque et Archives nationales du Québec [BANQ], 26 February 1864.

9 Canada, *Debates of the Legislative Assembly*, 18 March 1864.

10 Ibid., 21 March 1864.

11 On Taché, see Curtis, *Politics of Population*, 238–49, 285–6, 290–3, 315–16.

12 McGee to Samuel Ferguson, 5 May 1864, Thomas Fisher Rare Books Library, University of Toronto, MSS General 4.086.

13 Canada, *Debates of the Legislative Assembly*, 19 May 1864.

14 Careless, *Brown of the Globe*, 2:127.

15 Ibid., 2:127–9; Creighton, *Road to Confederation*, 50–1.

16 Careless, *Brown of the Globe*, 2:131–3; Creighton, *Road to Confederation*, 53.

17 Martin, *Britain and the Origins of Canadian Confederation*, 51.

18 Ibid., 52–3.

19 Careless, *Brown of the Globe*, 2:132.

20 McGee to Brown, 22 June 1864, Library and Archives Canada [LAC], Brown Fonds, ff. 957–8.

21 Careless, *Brown of the Globe*, 2:138–40.

22 For the best general analysis of British attitudes towards Confederation, see Martin, *Britain and the Origins of Canadian Confederation*.

23 Canada, *Debates of the Legislative Assembly*, 10 March 1864.

24 McGee to Tilley, 9 May 1864, Tilley Fonds, University of New Brunswick Archives, MGH 10a.

25 Fleming to Morgan, 15 April 1895, LAC, Morgan Fonds, vol. 14, ff. 5245–7; *Montreal Gazette*, 20 July 1864. On McGee's deliberately deceptive comments about the origins and nature of the visit, see *Nova Scotian*, 22 August 1864, and McGee, "Prospects of the Union," *Speeches and Addresses*, 97.

26 See, for example, *Head Quarters* [Fredericton], 17 August 1864; *Morning Freeman* [Saint John], 9 August 1864; *Morning Chronicle* [Halifax], 12 August 1864.

27 *Morning Freeman* [Saint John], 23 August 1864.

28 *Head Quarters* [Fredericton], 10 August 1864; *British Colonist* [Halifax], 18 August 1864; *New Brunswick Reporter*, 12 August 1864; McGee, "Prospects of the Union," *Speeches and Address*, 98.

29 McGee, "Some Objections to a Confederation of the Provinces Considered," *Speeches and Addresses*, 101–5.

30 *Saint John Daily News*, 10 August 1864; *New Brunswick Reporter*, 12 August 1864; *British Colonist* [Halifax], 18 August 1864; *Nova Scotian*, 22 August 1864.

31 *British Colonist* [Halifax], 23 August 1864.

32 See, for example, *Acadian Recorder*, 13 and 20 August 1864; *Head Quarters* [Fredericton], 24 August 1864; *Morning Chronicle* [Halifax], 1 September 1864.

33 *Morning Freeman* [Saint John], 23, 25 August 1864; Baker, *Timothy Warren Anglin*, 57–61.

34 Quoted in Slattery, *Assassination of D'Arcy McGee*, 233.

35 On the possible reasons for the change in Brown's position, see Careless, *Brown of the Globe*, 2:168. According to Careless, Brown now believed that with representation by population and a strong central government, Upper Canada would have the largest number of federal seats and become the preponderant power in British North America.

36 McGee, "Some Objections to a Confederation of the Provinces Considered," *Speeches and Addresses*, 102.

37 McGee, *Notes on Federal Governments, Past and Present*, 51–3; see also the commentary in *Montreal Gazette*, 14 January 1865.

38 The proposed division of powers was outlined in the *Morning Chronicle* [Halifax], 10 September 1864, and *Montreal Gazette*, 26 September 1864.

39 Creighton, *Road to Confederation*, 117–19; Waite, *Life and Times of Confederation*, 75–7; Careless, *Brown of the Globe*, 2:154–5.

40 See, for example, Moore, *1867: How the Fathers Made a Deal*, 57–9; Waite, *Life and Times of Confederation*, 77–9; Creighton, *Road to Confederation*, 122–5.

41 *Head Quarters* [Fredericton], 14 September 1864; Careless, *Brown of the Globe*, 2:155.

42 Brown, quoted in Careless, *Brown of the Globe*, 2:156.

43 *Morning Chronicle* [Halifax], 13 September 1864.

44 For McGee's other interventions, on the structure of provincial governments and on concurrent federal-provincial responsibility for agriculture and immigration, see Minutes of the Quebec Conference, LAC, Macdonald Fonds, vol. 46, ff. 17966, 17974.

45 Minutes of the Quebec Conference, Macdonald Fonds, vol. 46, f. 18010.

46 For the proceedings of the Quebec Conference, see Creighton, *Road to Confederation*, 132–86; Waite, *Life and Times of Confederation*, 86–103; Whitelaw, *The Maritimes and Canada before Confederation*, 232–62. The best recent analysis is Moore, *1867: How the Fathers Made a Deal*, 95–132.

47 See, for example, Mercy Ann Coles, "Reminiscences of Canada in 1864," LAC, Mercy Ann Coles Fonds, MG24-B66.

48 McGee, "The Cause of the Quebec Conference," *Speeches and Addresses*, 109–10.

49 Waite, *Life and Times of Confederation*, 31–2; Careless, *Brown of the Globe*, 2:181.

50 Monck, *My Canadian Leaves*, 211.

51 Creighton, *Road to Confederation*, 184–5; Gwyn, *John A.*, 338.

52 *Globe*, 29 December 1864; *Canadian Freeman*, 5 January 1865.

53 See, for example, Rae, *Three Questions*, 207.

54 McGee, "Speech on Motion for an Address to Her Majesty in Favour of Confederation," *Speeches and Addresses*, 267. For an excellent thematic treatment of these fundamental questions, see Ajzenstat et al., *Canada's Founding Debates*.

55 McGee, "Speech on Motion," 269–76.

56 Ibid., 277–8.

57 Ibid., 278.

58 Ibid., 279–80. Connolly's letter was originally published in the *Morning Chronicle* [Halifax] and was reprinted in the *Montreal Gazette*, 26 January 1865.

59 McGee, "Speech on Motion," 281; *Nation* [New York], 8 June 1850.

60 McGee, "Speech on Motion," 281–2.

61 Ibid., 282–5. See also Moore, *1867: How the Fathers Made a Deal*, for the contrast between the inclusion of opposition members in constitution making

during the 1860s and their exclusion from the constitutional initiatives of the 1990s.

62 McGee, "Speech on Motion," 288–91.

63 Ibid., 291–2.

64 Ibid., 301.

65 Walker, *Catholic Education and Politics*, 294; McGee, "Speech on Motion," 303.

66 Walker, *Catholic Education and Politics*, 294, 299.

67 McGee, "Speech on Motion," 303; Walker, *Catholic Education and Politics*, 290–307.

68 McGee, "Speech on Motion," 304–7.

69 Ibid., 307.

70 Ibid., 307–8.

71 Waite, *Life and Times of Confederation*, 161–228.

72 Ibid., 229–46.

73 *Montreal Gazette*, 7 March 1865.

74 Careless, *Brown of the Globe*, 2:190.

75 Waite, *Life and Times of Confederation*, 246–53.

76 Careless, *Brown of the Globe*, 2:190–3.

## CHAPTER NINE

1 Stacey, "Fenianism and the Rise of National Feeling in Canada at the Time of Confederation," 238–61; Stacey, "A Fenian Interlude: The Story of Michael Murphy," 133–54; Creighton, *Road to Confederation*, 304; O'Driscoll and Reynolds, eds., *The Untold Story: The Irish in Canada*, xv.

2 The *Fenian Brotherhood Circular of the Corresponding Society for the Period Commencing 10th Sept. and Ending 28th October 1865* (New York, 1865) shows that $365.10 was raised in Montreal and $500 was raised in Toronto. Assuming the usual subscription rate of one dollar a month, and allowing for non-payments, the combined figure of one thousand seems a reasonable estimate.

3 Wilson, "The Fenians in Montreal," 109–33.

4 "List of the Irish People, up to July 14th [1865]," National Archives of Ireland [NAI], Fenian Briefs, 1865–69, carton 5, envelope 18, Business Papers.

5 See, for example, Toner, "Rise of Irish Nationalism," 39–171. See also Sheppard, "'God Save the Green': Fenianism and Fellowship in Victorian Toronto," 129–44.

6  *Globe*, 6 May 1868.

7  On the activities of Peter Mahon, see McMicken to Macdonald, 4 March 1868, Library and Archives Canada [LAC], Macdonald Fonds, vol. 240, f. 106497; McMicken to Macdonald, 16 March 1868, Macdonald Fonds, vol. 240, ff. 106553–5; *Guelph Evening Mercury*, 7, 18 May 1868; Mahon to Mc-Lagan and Innes, 24 May 1868, Department of Justice Fonds, LAC, RG13A-2, vol. 20; Mahon to Lord Monck, 9 June 1868, LAC, RG13A-2, vol. 20, folder 585. On ethnoreligious tensions around Adjala, see Smyth and Houston, *The Sash Canada Wore*, 31.

8  Toner, "'The Green Ghost': Canada's Fenians and the Raids," 46.

9  Toner, "The Fanatic Heart of the North," in Wilson, ed., *Irish Nationalism in Canada*, 34–51.

10  *Montreal Herald*, 28 September 1882.

11  *Irish Canadian*, 23 March 1864.

12  *Montreal Gazette*, 19 March 1864.

13  *Montreal Gazette*, 23 March 1864.

14  *Canadian Freeman*, 14 April 1864.

15  *Irish Canadian*, 30 March 1864.

16  *Irish Canadian*, 13 April 1864.

17  Canada, *Debates of the Legislative Assembly*, 6 May 1864; *Irish Canadian*, 11 May 1864.

18  *Irish Canadian*, 27 April 1864; see also *Irish Canadian*, 30 March 1864.

19  Toner, "'The Green Ghost,'" 27–47; for Fenian membership within the Hibernian Benevolent Society, see P.C. Burton [Patrick Nolan] to McMicken, 31 December 1865, Macdonald Fonds, vol. 236, ff. 103110–13.

20  *Irish Canadian*, 20, 27 April 1864; *Canadian Freeman*, 14 April 1864.

21  McGee Testimonial, 9 April 1864, Concordia University Archives [CUA], PO30, HA253, folder 1; *Montreal Gazette*, 28 April 1864. One of the subscribers, Owen Devlin (Bernard's brother), was later named by McGee as a founder of Fenianism in Montreal; see McGee, "Account of the Attempts to Establish Fenianism in Montreal," *Montreal Gazette*, 17, 20 August 1867.

22  *Montreal Gazette*, 11, 12 April 1864.

23  *Montreal Gazette*, 21 March 1864; *Globe*, 13 May 1868.

24  St Patrick's Society Minute Book, CUA, PO26, 2 May, 6 June 1864; see also *Canadian Freeman*, 14 April 1864.

25  St Patrick's Society Minute Book, CUA, PO26, 1 August, 5 September, 3 October 1864; see also *Montreal Herald*, 27, 28 September 1882; St Patrick's Society Roll Book, CUA, PO26, 11.

26 St Patrick's Society Minute Book, CUA, PO26, 7 November 1864, 6 February 1865.

27 St Patrick's Society Minute Book, CUA, PO26, 23 December 1864, 16 January 1865. For Linehan's arguments in favour of "total separation," see *Irish Canadian*, 15 June 1864.

28 St Patrick's Society Minute Book, CUA, PO26, 10 and 17 April, 1 May, 5 June 1865.

29 Clarke, *Piety and Nationalism*, 185–7.

30 *Globe*, 8, 19, 23, 24, and 26 November, 7 December 1864; Clarke, *Piety and Nationalism*, 188–9.

31 *Globe*, 6 December 1864.

32 — to McMicken, 28 December 1864, Macdonald Fonds, vol. 234, f. 100831; *Globe*, 20 December 1864.

33 *Globe*, 26 December 1864.

34 *Globe*, 4 January 1865.

35 *Globe*, 7 January 1865.

36 McGee, "The Irish in Canada: The Importation of Fenianism," *Speeches and Addresses*, 144.

37 Ibid., 145.

38 Ibid.

39 *Irish Canadian*, 8, 15 February 1865.

40 *Irish Canadian*, 22, 29 March 1865; *Montreal Gazette*, 21 March 1865. Most accounts of this speech note with irony that McDermott was actually an informer; see, for example, D'Arcy, *The Fenian Movement in the United States*, 41, and Clarke, *Piety and Nationalism*, 190. But although this was certainly the case during the 1880s, it is by no means clear that McDermott was supplying information to the British government in 1865.

41 *Montreal Gazette*, 21 March 1865.

42 *Montreal Gazette*, 3 March 1865; *Irish Canadian*, 5 April 1865. The letter was signed "J.M."; none of the other leading identifiable Fenians in Montreal had these initials. For John McGrath's role in the movement, see F.B. McNamee to Mr. Christian, 26 March 1866, New York Public Library, Thomas Sweeny Papers.

43 *Montreal Gazette*, 21 April 1865.

44 McGee to Mrs. Samuel Ferguson, 24 May 1865, Thomas Fisher Rare Book Library, University of Toronto, MSS General 4.086. See also McGee to Samuel Ferguson, 5 May 1864, ibid.

45 *Dublin Evening Mail*, 16 May 1865.

46  *American Celt*, 14 April, 5 May 1855.

47  *Montreal Gazette*, 26 July 1865.

48  *Canadian Freeman*, 13 August 1858; Canada, *Debates of the Legislative Assembly*, 24 February 1864.

49  *Dublin Evening Mail*, 16 May 1865.

50  McGee confirmed that he gave the written text of the speech to the *Dublin Evening Mail* in the *Montreal Gazette*, 20 August 1867. For an account of the speech that he actually gave and the remark about McGee's insertions, see *The People* [Wexford], 20 May 1865; it is, of course, possible that the insertions were made by an editor of the *Dublin Evening Mail*. For the comment about his cowardice, see the *Irish American*, 10 June 1865.

51  *Nation* [Dublin], 20 May 1865.

52  Meagher to Charles Gavan Duffy, 17 January 1853, Charles Gavan Duffy Papers, National Library of Ireland [NLI], MS. 5757, f. 387; Doheny to William Smith O'Brien, 20 August 1858, William Smith O'Brien Papers, NLI, MS. 446, f. 3058; O'Gorman to Smith O'Brien, 1 January 1859, William Smith O'Brien Papers, NLI, MS. 446, f. 3082; Mitchel to his sister, 5 March 1849, NLI, Hickey Collection, MS. 3226.

53  McGee to James Moylan, 27 October 1865, LAC, Moylan Fonds, vol. 1.

54  *Times*, 19 May 1865.

55  *Irishman* [Dublin], 3 June 1865.

56  *Nation* [Dublin], 20 May 1865.

57  Quoted in the *People* [Wexford], 27 May 1865.

58  *Dublin Evening Mail*, 16 May 1865.

59  Matthias D. Phelan to the Editor of the *Irish People*, 14 June 1865, NAI, Fenian Briefs, carton 2, envelope 3, f. 121.

60  "Wolf Dog" to the Editor of the *Irish People*, 12 September 1865, NAI, Fenian Briefs, carton 2, envelope 3, f. 166.

61  *Irish People*, 20, 27 May 1865.

62  *Irish People*, 15 July 1865; *Irishman* [Dublin], 29 July 1865.

63  *Irishman* [Dublin], 29 July 1865.

64  Ibid.; *Dundalk Democrat*, quoted in the *Irish People*, 3 June 1865.

65  *Dundalk Democrat*, quoted in the *Irish People*, 3 June 1865.

66  *People* [Wexford], 27 May 1865; *Irish People*, 24 June 1865.

67  *Dundalk Democrat*, quoted in the *Irish People*, 3 June 1865.

68  *Irishman* [Dublin], 29 July 1865; *Irish People*, 15 July 1865. "Dogan" was a derogatory term for Irish Catholics – a Canadian equivalent to the Protestant Irish use of the word "teague."

69 *People* [Wexford], 27 May 1865; for Lynch's article, see the *People* [Wexford] 14 May 1864.

70 *Irishman* [Dublin], 25 April 1868.

## CHAPTER TEN

1 Quoted in Martin, *Britain and the Origins of Canadian Confederation*, 250.

2 Ibid., 252–8.

3 Creighton, *Road to Confederation*, 278–82; Careless, *Brown of the Globe*, 2:195–8.

4 McGee to Mrs. Ferguson, 24 May 1865, Thomas Fisher Rare Book Library, University of Toronto, MSS General 4.086.

5 Careless, *Brown of the Globe*, 2:198.

6 *Canadian Freeman*, 31 August 1865.

7 *Irish People*, 27 May 1865.

8 *Irish People*, 3 June 1865.

9 *Kilkenny Journal*, 31 May, 3 June 1865.

10 *Montreal Gazette*, 8 July 1865.

11 St Patrick's Society Minute Book, Concordia University Archives [CUA], PO26, 5 June 1865; Clerk to Horan, 22 May 1865, Archives of the Archdiocese of Kingston, Ontario, Horan Papers, D12 C33/17. The plans did not materialize.

12 "Ophelia" to the Editor of the *Irish People*, 8 June 1865, National Archives of Ireland [NAI], Fenian Briefs, carton 2, envelope 4; fragment of letter in ibid., carton 3, envelope 8. A comparison of the handwriting of the letter fragment with Conroy's signature in the St Patrick's Society Roll Book yielded inconclusive results.

13 See, for example, the statements of Patrick Brennan, William O'Brien, and Thomas McCready in *Montreal Herald*, 27 June 1865; see also *Montreal Gazette*, 28 June, 7 July 1865.

14 *Montreal Herald*, 26 June 1865; *Canadian Freeman*, 23 April 1868; Charles Carroll Tevis to Frederick Bruce, 7 January 1867, NAI, Fenian A Files, A250.

15 *Irish Canadian*, 28 June 1865. For more attacks, see 12 July 1865.

16 For Feely's earlier relationship with McGee, see McGee to Moylan, n.d. [5 June 1860], Library and Archives Canada [LAC], Moylan Fonds; McGee to Brown, 1 October 1860, LAC, Brown Fonds, f. 543; *Canadian Freeman*, 4 October 1860.

17 *Irish People*, 15 July 1865.

Feely to the Editor of the *Irish People*, n.d. [July 1865], NAI, Fenian Briefs, carton 2, envelope 4.

19 Campbell, *Fenian Fire*, 154; Toner, "Rise of Irish Canadian Nationalism," 47.

20 *Montreal Gazette*, 18 July 1865.

21 *Montreal Gazette*, 26 July 1865.

22 O'Mahony to Mitchel, quoted in D'Arcy, *The Fenian Movement in the United States*, 83.

23 Quoted in ibid., 84. See also Bernard Doran Killian to Mitchel, 4 December 1865, Meloney-Mitchel Papers, Columbia University Rare Book and Manuscript Library: "At Washington, also, everything portends an advance in our relations. For reasons which will suggest themselves, I can say no more on this topic."

24 O'Mahony to Mitchel, 10 November 1865, quoted in D'Arcy, *The Fenian Movement in the United States*, 84.

25 Memorandum from Thomas Sweeny to William Roberts, 1865, New York Public Library, Sweeny Papers.

26 Toner, "'The Green Ghost': Canada's Fenians and the Raids," 33.

27 Receipt, 16 November 1865, Sweeny Papers.

28 Killian to Mitchel, 4 December 1865, Meloney-Mitchel Papers; Memorandum from Sweeny to Roberts [1865], Sweeny Papers; unsigned and undated Memorandum [1865], Sweeny Papers; George Dunn to Sweeny, 13 March 1866, Sweeny Papers.

29 Michel to Edward Cardwell, 6 November 1865, The National Archives [TNA], FO.5/1335, ff. 226–7.

30 John A. Macdonald and Hector Langevin, "Discharge of the Frontier Police Force," 26 July 1865, and McMicken to William McDougall, 4 August 1865, LAC, RG13-A2, vol. 13, f. 711.

31 *Nation* [Dublin], 8 April 1848; Reports of informant "CD," 14, 15 April 1848, Trinity College Dublin, MS 2040, ff. 17, 22; Report of informant "AB," 21 June 1848, Trinity College Dublin, MS 2037, f. 12.

32 McGee to Macdonald, 2 November 1865, LAC, Macdonald Fonds, vol. 56, ff. 22349–50. See also McGee to Macdonald, 16 October 1865, Macdonald Fonds, vol. 56, f. 22314, when he urged Macdonald to send a spy to the Fenian congress in Philadelphia.

33 See, for example, Archibald, *Life and Letters*, 169–70.

34 O'Hanly, untitled memoir, "Status of Irish Catholics," LAC, O'Hanly Fonds, folder 6.

35 McMicken to Macdonald, 3 November 1865, Macdonald Fonds, vol. 236, ff. 102940–7.

36  *Irish Canadian*, 15 November 1865.

37  *Globe*, 6 November 1865.

38  St Patrick's Society Minute Book, CUA, PO26, 6, 15 November 1865; *Montreal Gazette*, 13 November 1865.

39  *Montreal Gazette*, 22 August 1867.

40  *Montreal Gazette*, 16 November 1865; *Canadian Freeman*, 23 November 1865.

41  These were McGee's own words. For Moylan's criticism, see *Canadian Freeman*, 3 August 1865.

42  *Montreal Gazette*, 16 November 1865; *Canadian Freeman*, 23 November 1865.

43  J.J. Sullivan to McGee, 23 November 1865, LAC, Thomas D'Arcy McGee Fonds, MG27-1E9. See also "The McGee Banquet," *Irish Canadian*, 6 December 1865.

44  *Montreal Gazette*, 20 November 1865.

45  Lynch to Connolly, 1 February 1866, Lynch Papers, Archives of the RC Archdiocese of Toronto [ARCAT], L AE 0209; Connolly to Lynch, 12 March 1866, ARCAT, L AE 0614; "To the Imperial Parliament of Great Brittain," n.d., ARCAT, L AE 0206.

46  McGee to Lynch, 19 February 1866, Lynch Papers, ARCAT, L AF 0306; McGee to Lynch, 5 March 1866, Lynch Papers, ARCAT, L AF 0307.

47  Lynch to The O'Donohoe, 28 February 1866, Lynch Papers, ARCAT, L AE 0612; see also Lynch to Paul Cullen, 24 March 1866, Lynch Papers, ARCAT, L AE 0213; Comerford, *Fenians in Context*, 63–4.

48  *Canadian Freeman*, 31 August 1865.

49  Ibid.

50  *Morning Freeman* [Saint John], 11 July 1865.

51  Waite, *Life and Times of Confederation*, 247.

52  Ibid., 253.

53  Creighton, *Road to Confederation*, 307–8.

54  *Globe*, 25 September 1865.

55  Baker, *Timothy Warren Anglin*, 88.

56  *Globe*, 22 September 1865.

57  McGee to Galt, n.d. [September 1865], LAC, Alexander Galt Fonds, MG27-1D8, vol. 3 [Galt Fonds], ff. 930–3; McGee to Galt, Galt Fonds, 22 September 1865, vol. 3, f. 1042; McGee to Galt, Galt Fonds, 23 September 1865, vol. 3, f. 1043.

58  *Montreal Gazette*, 25 September 1865. There had been similar divisions in New Brunswick the previous year over the cost of hosting the Canadian visitors, but the anti-confederate press in Canada had not picked up on them. See *Head Quarters* [Fredericton], 3 August 1864.

59 Galt to McGee, Galt Fonds, 23 September 1865, vol. 3, f. 1044.

60 *Montreal Gazette*, 16 November 1865.

61 Connolly to Lynch, 12 March 1866, Lynch Papers, ARCAT, L AE 0614; Baker, *Timothy Warren Anglin*, 78; Baker, "Squelching the Disloyal, Fenian-Sympathizing Brood," 141–58.

62 Quoted in Baker, "Squelching the Disloyal, Fenian-Sympathizing Brood," 147.

63 Creighton, *Road to Confederation*, 319.

64 *Morning Freeman* [Saint John], 12 December 1865.

65 *Religious Intelligencer*, quoted in *Head Quarters* [Fredericton], 15 November 1865; *Reporter* [Fredericton], 3 November 1865.

66 *Montreal Gazette*, 16 November 1865.

67 *Montreal Gazette*, 9 December 1865. McGee made this point in a speech in the town of St John's, Canada East. It is sometimes mistakenly assumed that McGee was in St John's Newfoundland; see, for example, Slattery, *Assassination of D'Arcy McGee*, 310–11.

68 *Montreal Gazette*, 9 December 1865.

69 Baker, *Timothy Warren Anglin*, 93–5.

70 Quoted in Baker, *Timothy Warren Anglin*, 98.

71 Careless, *Brown of the Globe*, 2:208–10.

72 Ibid., 2:213–17.

73 Creighton, *Road to Confederation*, 339–40.

74 Diary of George Clerk, BAnQ, 31 December 1865.

## CHAPTER ELEVEN

1 O'Mahony to —, 9 December [1865], Meloney-Mitchel Papers, Columbia University Rare Book and Manuscript Library. See also B. Doran Killian's Defence, 1 January 1866, National Archives of Ireland [NAI], Fenian Briefs, carton 4, envelope 16, Miscellaneous Papers.

2 One can trace this right back to the United Irish movement; see, for example, Arthur O'Connor to William Tennent, n.d. [1801], Tennent Papers, Public Record Office of Northern Ireland, D 1748/A/1238/1. The same pattern appeared during the 1850s, when Michael Doheny of the Emmet Monument Society accused his rival in the Irish Emigrant Aid Society, John McClenahan, of being a British spy; see *Citizen* [New York], 15 December 1855.

3 *Irish Canadian*, 27 December 1865.

4 *Irish Canadian*, 7, 14 February 1866; *Montreal Gazette*, 16 February 1866; Burton [Patrick Nolan] to McMicken, 8 March 1866, Library and Archives Canada [LAC], Macdonald Fonds, vol. 237, ff. 103303–4.

5 McNamee to Mr. Christian, 26 March 1866, New York Public Library, Sweeny Papers.

6 Bruce to Clarendon, 8 January 1866, NAI, Fenian A Files, A87. Interestingly, Bruce's assessment of American attitudes matches that of McGee during his Wexford speech.

7 *Canadian Freeman*, 11 January 1866; Lynch to Horan, 12 February 1866, Archives of the Archdiocese of Kingston, Ontario, Horan Papers, D15 C329/11.

8 *Irish Canadian*, 6, 27 December 1865. Devany had accused McNamee of being a government spy; according to one source, McNamee put Devany's head through a window. The *Irish Canadian*'s Montreal correspondent wrote that this was "rather a novel way of testing Fenianism on the brain" and hoped that Devany would profit from this "pugilistic lesson." See also *Montreal Gazette*, 2 January 1866.

9 *Irish Canadian*, 24, 31 January 1866; see also Diary of George Clerk, Bibliothèque et Archives nationales du Québec [BAnQ], 18 January 1866.

10 *Canadian Freeman*, 1 February 1866; *Irish Canadian*, 31 January 1866.

11 "D. Thomas" to J.S. Wood, 9 February 1866, NAI, Fenian A Files, A98. "D. Thomas" was Thomas Doyle, an inspector with the Dublin Metropolitan Police, who had been sent to the United States to spy on the Fenian Brotherhood.

12 *Irish American*, 3 February 1866; D'Arcy, *The Fenian Movement in the United States*, 111–12, 114.

13 McMicken to Macdonald, 5 March 1866, Macdonald Fonds, vol. 237, ff. 103296–9.

14 D'Arcy, *The Fenian Movement in the United States*, 114–15.

15 Killian to Mitchel, 3 March 1866, Meloney-Mitchel Papers, Columbia University Rare Book and Manuscript Library.

16 D'Arcy, *The Fenian Movement in the United States*, 124–5.

17 Archibald to Clarendon, 6 March 1866, NAI, Fenian A Files, A112.

18 Burton [Patrick Nolan] to McMicken, 27 January 1866, Macdonald Fonds, vol. 237, f. 103200; Burton to McMicken, 3 February 1866, Macdonald Fonds, vol. 237, f. 103221; on Fort Erie, see McMicken to Macdonald, 6 February 1866, Macdonald Fonds, vol. 237, ff. 103239–40; for Port Huron, see Allen and Caldwell to McMicken, 4 February 1866, Macdonald Fonds, vol. 237, ff. 103223–5.

19 Ermatinger to Macdonald, 3 March 1866, Macdonald Fonds, vol. 237, ff. 103277–8; Elon Tupper to McMicken, 4 March 1866, Macdonald Fonds, vol. 237, ff. 103286–7; McMicken to Macdonald, 5 March 1866, Macdonald Fonds, vol. 237, ff. 103296–9; McMicken to Macdonald, Windsor [8 March 1866; misdated 8 February 1866], Macdonald Fonds, vol. 237, ff. 103242–3.

20 Diary of George Clerk, BAnQ, 8, 9, and 11 March 1866; *Canadian Freeman*, 15 March 1866; *Montreal Gazette*, 20 March 1866.

21 Neidhardt, *Fenianism in North America*, 37–8; *Montreal Gazette*, 9 March 1866.

22 McGee, "The Irish Position in British and in Republican North America," *Montreal Gazette*, 6 March 1866.

23 See, for example, Doyle, "The Irish as Urban Pioneers," 36–61, and Brown, *Irish-American Nationalism*.

24 Darroch and Ornstein, "Ethnicity and Occupational Structure in Canada," 305–33; see also Wilson, ed., *Irish Nationalism in Canada*, 3–4.

25 See, for example, Toner, "Rise of Irish Nationalism in Canada," and Toner, "Fanatic Heart of the North," in Wilson, ed., *Irish Nationalism in Canada*, 34–51.

26 For the information that there were 650 Fenians in the Hibernian Benevolent Society, see Nolan to McMicken, 31 December 1865, Macdonald Fonds, vol. 236, ff. 103110–13. The chief constable of Toronto, William Prince, reckoned that the actual number was closer to 174; see Prince to McGee, 19 March 1866, City of Toronto Archives, Letter Books of the Chief Constable, Fonds 38, series 90, file 1. I thank Peter Vronsky for this reference.

27 McGee to Brown, n.d. [7 March 1866], LAC, Brown Fonds, ff. 1428–32.

28 McGee to Lynch, 7 March 1866, Lynch Papers, ARCAT, L AF 0308; McGee to Brown, n.d. [7 March 1866], Brown Fonds, ff. 1428–32.

29 McGee to Lynch, 14 March 1866, Lynch Papers, ARCAT, L AF 0309.

30 "Circular to the Clergy of the Diocese of Toronto," 9 March 1866, Lynch Papers, ARCAT, L AE 0212; Lynch, "To the Reverend Clergy of the City of Toronto," 15 March 1866, newspaper clipping, ARCAT, Lynch Papers, L AE 0615.

31 McMicken to Macdonald, 18 March 1866, Macdonald Fonds, vol. 237, ff. 103398–403; *Irish Canadian*, 21 March 1866.

32 Compare the accounts in *Montreal Gazette*, 19 March 1866, and *Irish Canadian*, 4 April 1866.

33 *Irish Canadian*, 21 March 1866.

34 McNamee to Mr. Christian, 26, 28 March 1866, Sweeny Papers.

35 *Irish Canadian*, 4 April 1866.

36  Mansfield to Mr. Christian, 9 April 1868, Sweeny Papers.

37  *Montreal Herald*, 27, 28, and 29 September 1882.

38  *American Celt*, 19 August, 18 November 1854.

39  *Canadian Freeman*, 1 February 1866.

40  *Globe*, 3 March 1866; McGee to Brown, n.d. [7 March 1866], Brown Fonds, ff. 1428–32; *Montreal Gazette*, 6 March 1866.

41  D'Arcy, *The Fenian Movement in the United States*, 135–6.

42  Bruce to James Hope, 17 March 1866, NAI, Fenian A Files, A126.

43  "K" to Cullen, as reported in Dwight to MacDougall, 12 April 1866, Macdonald Fonds, vol. 57, f. 22950; Dwight to MacDougall, 4 April 1866, Macdonald Fonds, vol. 57, f. 22886; William Prince to Macdonald, 7 April 1866, Macdonald Fonds, vol. 57, ff. 22954–61; *Globe*, 11, 12 April 1866. For Moriarty's role in the rising of 1867, see Ó Lúing, "Aspects of the Fenian Rising in Kerry."

44  Dallison, *Turning Back the Fenians*, 73–93.

45  "D. Thomas" to J.S. Wood, 5 May 1866, NAI, Fenian A Files, A141; Jenkins, *Fenians and Anglo-American Relations*, 137–9; D'Arcy, *The Fenian Movement in the United States*, 136–9.

46  McGee to Brown, n.d. [7 March 1866], Brown Fonds, ff. 1428–32.

47  It will be recalled that in 1862 Mitchell had spoken with McGee at a Reform Party rally in Niagara Falls, where both men argued that an Intercolonial Railway would promote the commercial and political unity of British North America; see above, 146. The two men also worked together at the Charlottetown Conference, although there is no record of their discussions.

48  *Montreal Gazette*, 19 April 1866. Three months earlier, Killian had somewhat prematurely congratulated the Fenians in Canada for using peaceful means to "destroy Confederation," and looked forward to the establishment of independent republics in British North America; see *Montreal Gazette*, 11 January 1866.

49  *Montreal Gazette*, 20 April 1866. On the Fenians in Saint John, see Edward Kelly to Charles Carroll Tevis, 9 April 1866, Sweeny Papers.

50  Waite, *Life and Times of Confederation*, 273–6; Baker, *Timothy Warren Anglin*, 114–15; Davis, "The Fenian Raid on New Brunswick," 332–4.

51  *Morning Freeman* [Saint John], 21 April 1866; Canada, House of Commons, *Debates*, 14 November 1867, 77.

52  Archibald to Clarendon, 17 April 1866, quoted in D'Arcy, *The Fenian Movement in the United States*, 141; *Irish American*, 24 February, 21 April 1866.

53 Archibald to Clarendon, 8 May 1866, NAI, Fenian A Files, A143.

54 *Morning News* [Saint John], 8 June 1866.

55 *Morning Freeman* [Saint John], 12 June 1866.

56 Neidhardt, *Fenianism in North America*, 49.

57 This and all subsequent quotations from the letter are from the *Nation* [Dublin], 9 June 1866.

58 *Irishman* [Dublin], 25 April 1868.

59 *Dublin Evening Mail*, 16 May 1865. In its review of McGee's speech, the *Times* took the argument still further: "We think we can trace in the present state of Ireland the effects of Irish Transatlantic opinion upon Irish native opinion … The Irish in Ireland are unhappy because their countrymen in America are perpetually telling them of the happiness they enjoy and contrasting it with their real or imaginary sufferings." See the *Times*, 19 May 1865.

60 *Nation* [Dublin], 9 June 1866.

61 D'Arcy, *The Fenian Movement in the United States*, 144–5; Neidhardt, *Fenianism in North America*, 55–6.

62 Richard Slattery, Receipt, 3 May 1866; Richard Slattery to Sweeny, 9 May 1866; A.L. Morrison to Sweeny, 13 May 1866, Sweeny Papers.

63 See, for example, Nightingale to McMicken, 27 April 1866, Macdonald Fonds, vol. 237, ff. 103618–19; McMicken to Macdonald, 30 April 1866, Macdonald Fonds, vol. 237, ff. 103628–30; Hemans to McMicken, 9 May 1866, Macdonald Fonds, vol. 237, ff. 103683–5; Clarke to McMicken, 18 May 1866, Macdonald Fonds, vol. 237, ff. 103755–7.

64 McMicken to Macdonald, 17 May 1866, Macdonald Fonds, vol. 237, ff. 103745–7.

65 McGee to Wodehouse, 25 May 1866, Kimberley Papers, Bodleian Library, Oxford University.

CHAPTER TWELVE

1 Diary of George Clerk, Bibliothèque et Archives nationales du Québec [BAnQ], 1 June 1866.

2 "To the People of British America," *Irish American*, 9 June 1866.

3 Senior, *Last Invasion of Canada*, 59–89; Vronsky, "Combat, Memory, and Remembrance," 78–270.

4 Neidhardt, *Fenianism in North America*, 59–84; D'Arcy, *The Fenian Movement in the United States*, 159–64.

5  *Nation* [Dublin], 9, 16 June 1866; see also *Irishman* [Dublin], 23 June 1866.

6  Archibald to Clarendon, 5 June 1866, National Archives of Ireland [NAI], Fenian A Files, A157.

7  O'Neill quoted in *Nashville Press and Times*, 13 July 1866, in "Newscuttings Relative to Fenianism," Larcom Papers, National Library of Ireland [NLI], MS 7679. See also *Irish American*, 16 June 1866; *Nation* [Dublin], 30 June 1866.

8  *Irish American*, 23 June 1866.

9  *Canadian Freeman*, 7 June 1866.

10  Compare his views in *Nation* [Dublin], 8 April 1848, with those in *Montreal Gazette*, 22 August 1867.

11  *Canadian Freeman*, 7, 14, 28 June 1866.

12  *Canadian Freeman*, 5 July 1866; *Nation* [Dublin], 18 August 1866; Diary of George Clerk, BAnQ, 30 June 1866.

13  Lynch to Archbishop Walsh, 27 May 1887, Walsh Papers, Dublin Diocesan Archives.

14  Crown Law Department of Upper Canada Circular [1866], Library and Archives Canada [LAC], RG130-A2, vol. 15, file 667.

15  *Canadian Freeman*, 12 July, 20 September 1866.

16  *Canadian Freeman*, 12 July 1866.

17  Blake Brown, "Fenian State Trials," 38.

18  McGee to Wodehouse, 11 June 1866, Kimberley Papers, Bodleian Library, Oxford University.

19  Bruce to Clarendon, 18 June 1866, NAI, Fenian A Files, A165; Bruce to Stanley, 10 November 1866, NAI, Fenian A Files, A214; see also Jenkins, *Fenians and Anglo-American Relations*, 160–74. Lord Stanley succeeded Lord Clarendon as foreign secretary on 28 June 1866 when the Earl of Derby's Conservative government came to power.

20  Canada, *Debates of the Legislative Assembly*, 22 June 1866; *Globe*, 23 June 1866; Brown to Anne Brown, 23 June 1866, LAC, Brown Fonds, f. 1452. See also McGee to A.M. Sullivan, 25 June 1866, LAC, Murphy Fonds, ff. 14220–3.

21  McGee, "Letter to Father Hendricken," in *Montreal Gazette*, 23 June 1866.

22  Blake Brown, "Fenian State Trials," 63.

23  *Montreal Gazette*, 22 August 1867.

24  See, for example, *Canadian Freeman*, 15 November 1866.

25  McGee to Moylan, 30 October 1866, LAC, Moylan Fonds. McGee's source was John Baptist Purcell, the archbishop of Cincinnati, where McMahon served in the priesthood.

26  Blake Brown, "Fenian State Trials," 54–5.

27 *Montreal Gazette*, 22 August 1867.

28 "Report from Fenian Head Quarters," 9 November 1866, NAI, Fenian A Files, A213.

29 Blake Brown, "Fenian State Trials," 57.

30 *Montreal Gazette*, 30 November 1866.

31 *Irish Canadian*, 24 May 1866; *Montreal Gazette*, 22 August 1867.

32 *Irish American*, 30 June 1866.

33 *Globe*, 23 November 1866.

34 *Canadian Freeman*, 13 December 1866.

35 *Globe*, 30 November 1866.

36 For Brown's views, see *Globe*, 3, 11, 17, 19, 24 December 1866, 10 January 1867; for McGee's position, see *Canadian Freeman*, 13, 20 December 1866. On the false name and address of "An Englishman," see *Globe*, 15 January 1867. The possibility that Linehan was the author is inferred from the comments in Holton to Brown, 19 January 1867, Brown Fonds, ff. 1532–3, and "An Englishman's" remarks in the *Globe*, 30 November 1866.

37 McGee to Moylan, 28 August 1866, Moylan Fonds; see also Careless, *Brown of the Globe*, 2:226–37.

38 McGee to Moylan, 28 August 1866, Moylan Fonds.

39 *Canadian Freeman*, 13 September 1866.

40 *Globe*, 11 September 1866.

41 *Globe*, 4 August 1866. McGee had already explained his position on the "finality" of the Scott act during the debate on Confederation in February 1865; see above, 215.

42 *Canadian Freeman*, 20 September 1866.

43 McGee to Moylan, 28 August 1866, Moylan Fonds.

44 Moylan to Henry Morgan, n.d. [c. 1895], Murphy Fonds, ff. 14323–4.

45 McGee to Galt, 24 August 1866, LAC, Galt Fonds, ff. 1134–7.

46 *Globe*, 17, 22 August 1866.

47 *Irish Canadian*, 23 November 1866; *Globe*, 30 November 1866.

48 *Globe*, 27 September 1866.

49 See also *Montreal Gazette*, 22 November 1866, where this explanation is dismissed as "gratuitous nonsense without an atom of foundation."

50 Murphy, note, Murphy Fonds, f. 14324.

51 See the excellent discussion in Slattery, *Assassination of D'Arcy McGee*, 354–7.

52 Thibaudeau to Brown, 1 August 1858, Brown Fonds. See above, 64.

53 "A Canadian Catholic," in *Nation* [Dublin], 18 August 1866.

54 Cottrell, "Irish Catholic Political Leadership in Toronto," 261.

55  Slattery, *Assassination of D'Arcy McGee*, 346.

56  See, for example, McMicken to Macdonald, 2 August 1866, LAC, Macdonald Fonds, vol. 238, f. 104462.

57  Brown to Anne Brown, 25 July 1866, Brown Fonds, ff. 1489–90; McGee to James Sadlier, 7 August 1866, LAC, Sadlier Fonds. Along with the dangers of a Fenian invasion, Brown also mentioned the cholera outbreak in New York as a reason for leaving Canada sooner rather than later.

58  Jenkins, *Fenians and Anglo-American Relations*, 142–214.

59  "D. Thomas" to J.S. Wood, 31 July 1866, NAI, Fenian A Files, A174.

60  *Daily News*, 18 August 1866, in "Newscuttings Relative to Fenianism," NLI, Larcom Papers, MS 7679.

61  *Irishman* [Dublin], 18 August 1866. This was also an implicit riposte to McGee's comment during this Wexford speech that "there is no more national sympathy for Ireland, as Ireland, in the United States, than for Japan, and far less than exists for Russia." See *Dublin Evening Mail*, 16 May 1865.

62  *Canadian Freeman*, 12 July 1866.

63  McGee, Draft Report of the "Committee of Council to the Governor General on the Fenian Conspiracy," n.d. [July–August 1866], Macdonald Fonds, vol. 184, ff. 76916–22.

64  *Irish American*, 28 July 1866.

65  D'Arcy, *The Fenian Movement in the United States*, 200, 211–12.

66  *Irish Canadian*, 7 September 1866.

67  *Montreal Gazette*, 1, 3, 4 September 1866; St Patrick's Society Minute Book, 3 September, 1 October 1866, CUA, PO26.

68  *Montreal Gazette*, 6, 12 September 1866.

69  St Patrick's Society Minute Book, 8 October 1866, CUA, PO26.

70  Ibid., 1 October 1866.

71  *Irish American*, 29 September 1866; see also *Irish Canadian*, 21 September 1866.

72  *Montreal Gazette*, 31 October 1866.

73  St Patrick's Society Minute Book, 5 November 1866, CUA, PO26; McGee to Richard McShane, 3 December 1866, Murphy Fonds, f. 14300.

74  St Patrick's Society Minute Book, 3 December 1866, CUA, PO26.

75  Campbell to Macdonald, 28 November 1866, Macdonald Fonds, vol. 194, ff. 80717–19.

76  McGee to Macdonald, 19 December 1866, Macdonald Fonds, vol. 231, f. 99995.

77  Slattery, *Assassination of D'Arcy McGee*, 357.

78  *Canadian Freeman*, 17 January 1867.

## CHAPTER THIRTEEN

1   [Robert Anderson], "Fenianism, Historical Sketch," n.d. [1867], National Archives of Ireland [NAI], Fenian Police Reports, 1857–83, box 4.

2   Despatch from Edward Archibald, 30 November 1866, NAI, Fenian Police Reports, 1857–83; Archibald's report was based on information supplied by "Informant M," the codename for Millen. See Campbell, *Fenian Fire*, 53–74.

3   Kelly to — [Halpin?], 12 March 1867, New York Public Library, O'Donovan Rossa Papers, Maloney Collection of Irish Historical Papers, box 4, folder 60.

4   Jenkins, *The Fenian Problem*, 78–82.

5   *Mirror*, 11 June 1858; *Irish Canadian*, 7 September 1866; Toner, "The Fanatic Heart of the North," in Wilson, ed., *Irish Nationalism in Canada*, 39–40.

6   Takagami, "Fenian Rising in Dublin," 340–62.

7   Dublin Special Commission, April 1867, NAI, Fenian Briefs, box 9, no. 6(a), ff. 4, 58, 161–2.

8   County of Dublin, "Alphabetical List of Cases connected with the Fenian Conspiracy," NAI, Fenian Arrests and Discharges, 1866–69.

9   McGee to D'Israeli [sic], February, 1867, Library and Archives Canada [LAC], Murphy Fonds, ff. 14303–4.

10  "The Irish Land Question," in *The Edinburgh Review, or Critical Journal* [London], January 1870, 131:262–3.

11  "The Irish Land Question," *Edinburgh Review* 131:257–60.

12  Jenkins, *The Fenian Problem*, 68, 76.

13  Canada, House of Commons, *Debates*, 14 November 1867, 72.

14  As outlined in Wilson, *Thomas D'Arcy McGee*, 1:121–7.

15  Slattery, *Assassination of D'Arcy McGee*, 364; for McGee's views, see above, 243.

16  McGee to Macdonald, 9 April 1867, Murphy Fonds, f. 14305; "Hon. Mr. McGee to his Constituents," 1 May 1867, in *Canadian Freeman*, 30 May 1867.

17  "Hon. Mr. McGee to his Constituents," 1 May 1867, in *Canadian Freeman*, 30 May 1867.

18  Hustak, *Saint Patrick's of Montreal*, 50–3; *Montreal Gazette*, 3 December 1866; Bourget, "Pastoral Letter," in *The Case of St. Patrick's Congregation*, 11–13.

19  McGee's rejection of the "victim" stereotype reaches right back to the mid-1840s; see, for example, *Nation* [Dublin], 9 January 1847. For McGee's comments about Bourget's nativism, see above, 87.

20  *Case of St. Patrick's Congregation*, 19, 25.

21  Ibid., 31.

22  McGee to Mary Ann Sadlier, 17 March 1867, LAC, Sadlier Fonds.

23  *Canadian Freeman*, 25 April 1867.

24  McGee to Mary Ann Sadlier, 26 May 1867, Sadlier Fonds.

25  McGee to Horan, 30 May 1867, Archives of the Archdiocese of Kingston, Ontario, Horan Papers, DC16 C22/3.

26  Hustak, *Saint Patrick's of Montreal*, 57–8; "Notes and Drafts," LAC, O'Gorman Fonds, folder 11.

27  Heaman, *Inglorious Arts of Peace*, 177–81, 300.

28  McGee to Macdonald, 9 April 1867, Murphy Fonds, f. 14305.

29  McGee to Mary Ann Sadlier, 26 May 1867, Sadlier Fonds.

30  For rumours that he was going to be excluded from the cabinet, see Macdonald to Sydney Bellingham, 30 May 1867, LAC, Macdonald Fonds, vol. 513, f. 550.

31  McGee to Mary Ann Sadlier, 26 May 1867, Sadlier Fonds.

32  McGee to Macdonald, 9 April 1867, Murphy Fonds, f. 14305.

33  For an excellent discussion of the cabinet negotiations, see Slattery, *Assassination of D'Arcy McGee*, 384–91.

34  Cottrell, "Irish Catholic Political Leadership in Toronto," 237–8.

35  Macdonald to Horan, 3 July 1867, Archives of the Archdiocese of Kingston, Ontario, Horan Papers, DC15 C37/12; Macdonald to Moylan, 4 July 1867, Macdonald Fonds, vol. 513, ff. 659–62.

36  Macdonald to Lynch, 3 July 1867, Macdonald Fonds, vol. 513, ff. 637–8.

37  Macdonald to Horan, 3 July 1867, Archives of the Archdiocese of Kingston, Ontario, Horan Papers, DC15 C37/12; Macdonald to Lynch, 3 July 1867, Macdonald Fonds, vol. 513, ff. 637–40.

38  Lynch to Horan, 8 July 1867, Archives of the Archdiocese of Kingston, Ontario, Horan Papers, DC15 C29/15; *Canadian Freeman*, 4 July 1867; McGee to Macdonald, 11 July 1867, Macdonald Fonds, vol. 231, ff. 100003–6.

39  *Canadian Freeman*, 4 July 1867; *Leader* [Toronto], 9 July 1867.

40  Cottrell, "Irish Catholic Political Leadership in Toronto," 249; see also Macdonald to Moylan, 12 July 1867, Moylan Fonds.

41  *Canadian Freeman*, 30 May, 4 July 1867.

42  McGee to Macdonald, n.d., Murphy Fonds, f. 14226; McGee to Horan, 22 July 1867, Archives of the Archdiocese of Kingston, Ontario, Horan Papers, DC16 C22/4.

43  McGee to Horan, 30 May 1867, Archives of the Archdiocese of Kingston, Ontario, Horan Papers, DC16 C22/3.

44 McGee to Macdonald, 11 July 1867, Macdonald Fonds, vol. 231, f. 100006; McGee to Macdonald, 13 July 1867, Murphy Fonds, f. 14224.

45 McGee to Horan, n.d. [8 August 1867], Archives of the Archdiocese of Kingston, Ontario, Horan Papers, DC16 C22/6; McGee to Horan, 12 August 1867, Archives of the Archdiocese of Kingston, Ontario, Horan Papers, DC16 C22/5; McGee to Macdonald, n.d. [12 August 1867], Murphy Fonds, f. 14230.

46 Clerk to Horan, 26 June 1865, Archives of the Archdiocese of Kingston, Ontario, Horan Papers, D12 C33/20.

47 McGee to Macdonald, n.d. [13 July 1867], Murphy Fonds, ff. 14224–5.

48 McGee to Macdonald, n.d., Murphy Fonds, f. 14226; Macdonald to Sandfield Macdonald, 24 August 1867, LAC, Sandfield Macdonald Fonds, ff. 1179–82.

49 McGee to Macdonald, n.d. Murphy Fonds, f. 14228.

50 Macdonald to J.L. O'Connor, 14 August 1867, Macdonald Fonds, vol. 513, f. 880.

51 McGee to Horan, 30 May 1867, Archives of the Archdiocese of Kingston, Ontario, Horan Papers, DC16 C22/3. For similar sentiments, see McGee to James Sadlier, 7 August 1866, Sadlier Fonds; McGee to Macdonald, 9 April 1867, Murphy Fonds, f. 14305.

52 McGee to Macdonald, n.d. [13 July 1867], Murphy Fonds, ff. 14224–5.

53 *Montreal Gazette*, 15 December 1857.

54 *Montreal Gazette*, 8 August 1867.

55 On McNamee, Linehan, and Lyons, see *Montreal Gazette*, 22 August 1867; on Henry Murphy, see *Globe*, 17 April, 29 May 1868, and Archibald to Stanley, 9 April 1868, The National Archives [TNA], FO.5/1343, ff. 339–40.

56 For examples of Devlin's public declarations of loyalty, see *Montreal Herald*, 12, 24 July 1867.

57 *Montreal Herald*, 12 July 1867.

58 *New York Daily Tribune*, 25 August 1848.

59 For evidence that McNamee and Lyons supported the Senate wing, see McNamee to Christian, 26 March 1866, New York Public Library, Sweeny Papers; for Henry Murphy's connection with the Senate wing, see Archibald to Stanley, 9 April 1868, TNA, FO.5/1343, f. 340.

60 McGee to Macdonald, 11 July 1867, Macdonald Fonds, vol. 231, ff. 100003, 100006.

61 *Montreal Herald*, 18 July 1867.

62 J.M. Carroll to —, 12 July 1867, Macdonald Fonds, vol. 238, ff. 104290–1. According to McGee, in October 1866 Carroll and McNamee had met an

American Fenian emissary who was on a reconnaissance mission in Canada; see McGee, "Account of the Attempts to Establish Fenianism in Montreal," *Montreal Gazette*, 22 August 1867. In January 1867, the Fenian Daniel Lyons had proposed Carroll for membership in the St Patrick's Society; see St Patrick's Society Minute Book, 7 January 1867, Concordia University Archives [CUA], PO26.

63 Holton to Brown, 20 July 1867, LAC, Brown Fonds, f. 1617.

64 *Montreal Herald*, 12 July 1867.

65 See, for example, McGee to Horan, 22 July 1867, Archives of the Archdiocese of Kingston, Ontario, Horan Papers, DC16 C22/4.

66 *Montreal Gazette*, 1, 5 August 1867.

67 *Montreal Herald*, 3 August 1867; *Montreal Gazette*, 3 August 1867; Diary of George Clerk, Bibliothèque et Archives nationales du Québec [BAnQ], 6 August 1867.

68 *Montreal Gazette*, 7 August 1867.

69 *Montreal Gazette*, 5 August 1867. I have changed the newspaper report of McGee's speech from the third person to the first person.

70 *Montreal Gazette*, 10 August 1867.

71 *Irish Canadian*, 23 September 1868. One of Whelan's co-workers, Joseph Faulkner, testified that Whelan was "politically opposed" to McGee and took time off work during the election campaign; although Faulkner did not know "in what capacity he [Whelan] was employed" during the campaign, there is little doubt that he was working for Devlin. See testimony of Joseph Faulkner, in Judge William Buell Richards's trial notes, CUA, PO30, HA260, folder 1.

72 This is based on the testimony of Alec Turner, who lodged at Whelan's house in the summer of 1867. See Judge William Buell Richards's trial notes, CUA, PO30, HA260, folder 2, and Turner's testimony in the Police Magistrate's Inquiry, cited in *Irish Canadian*, 22 April 1868. Turner's testimony was corroborated in general terms by Joseph Faulkner and by James Inglis (who was also a lodger at Whelan's house); see *Trial of Patrick James Whelan*, 31–2. It should be noted that Whelan denied that Murphy was with him that night; see *Irish Canadian*, 29 April 1868.

73 Wright to Macdonald, 10 April 1868, Macdonald Fonds, vol. 341, ff. 155926–30.

74 *Montreal Herald*, 7 August 1867.

75 Holton to Brown, 20 July 1867, Brown Fonds, f. 1617.

76 Similar arguments would be used against the anti-IRA politician Conor Cruise O'Brien during the 1970s: Why, his enemies asked, was he going on

about Irish republican paramilitary violence instead of looking after practical matters such as the state of Ireland's telephone system? See O'Brien, *Memoir*, 359.

77 *Montreal Herald*, 9 August 1867.

78 McGee to Horan, 22 July 1867, Archives of the Archdiocese of Kingston, Ontario, Horan Papers, DC16 C22/4. On the state of his health in Paris, see *Canadian Freeman*, 9 May 1867.

79 McGee to Macdonald, n.d. [12 August 1867], Murphy Fonds, f. 14230.

80 McGee to Macdonald, n.d. [12 August 1867], Murphy Fonds, f. 14231; McGee requested Macdonald to get the "Fenian informations" from Charles Drinkwater at the post office, which must have meant that he was asking for intercepted letters.

81 McGee, "Account of the Attempts to Establish Fenianism in Montreal," in *Montreal Gazette*, 17, 20, 22 August 1867.

82 *Globe*, 15 November 1867.

83 McGee, "Account of the Attempts," in *Montreal Gazette*, 17, 20, 22 August 1867.

84 Ibid., 17 August 1867.

85 Ibid., 20 August 1867.

86 Ibid.

87 Ibid., 22 August 1867.

88 Ibid., 17 August 1867.

89 Ibid., 22 August 1867.

90 Slattery, *Assassination of D'Arcy McGee*, 414.

91 *Montreal Herald*, 19 August 1867.

92 *Montreal Herald*, 22 August 1867.

93 *Montreal Gazette*, 23 August 1867.

94 *Montreal Herald*, 24, 26 August 1867.

95 McNamee to Christian, 24, 26 March 1866, Sweeny Papers; see above, 266.

96 *Montreal Herald*, 27, 28 September 1882.

97 St Patrick's Society Minute Book, 16 January 1865, CUA, PO26; for Linehan's arguments in favour of "total separation," see *Irish Canadian*, 15 June 1864.

98 Wilson, "Fenians in Montreal," 115–22.

99 "McGee Testimonial," 9 April 1864, CUA, PO30, HA253, folder 1; St Patrick's Society Minute Book, 6 April 1864, CUA, PO30; *Montreal Herald*, 24 August 1867.

100 *Montreal Herald*, 24 August 1867.

101  Ibid.

102  Wright to Macdonald, 10 April 1868, Macdonald Fonds, vol. 341, ff. 155927–8; *Montreal Herald*, 19 September 1867.

103  *Montreal Herald*, 21, 22 August 1867.

104  *Montreal Gazette*, 30 January 1868.

105  *Globe*, 17 April, 29 May 1868; Archibald to Stanley, 9 April 1868, TNA, FO.5/1343, ff. 339–40.

106  *Montreal Herald*, 30 August 1867.

107  *Montreal Herald*, 5 September 1867.

108  *Montreal Gazette*, 3, 5 September 1867.

109  *Montreal Herald*, 3 September 1867.

110  *Montreal Herald*, 7 September 1867.

111  Ibid.

112  Ibid.

113  *Montreal Herald*, 9 September 1867.

114  Treadwell to McGee, 7 September 1867, Thomas Kairns Fonds, LAC, MG24-C6.

115  *Montreal Herald*, 5 September 1867.

## CHAPTER FOURTEEN

1  *Montreal Gazette*, 11 September, 2 October 1867.

2  *Irish Canadian*, 16 September 1868; see also *Globe*, 17 April 1868, *Guelph Evening Mercury*, 17 April 1868.

3  *Montreal Gazette*, 2 October 1867.

4  *Montreal Gazette*, 3 October 1867.

5  McGee to Macdonald, 18 October 1867, Library and Archives Canada [LAC], Murphy Fonds, ff. 14232–3.

6  *Montreal Gazette*, 5 November 1867 [delivered 4 November 1867]; see also McGee, "The Mental Outfit of the New Dominion," in Murphy, ed., *1825 – D'Arcy McGee – 1925*, 1–21.

7  *Montreal Gazette*, 26 November 1867.

8  Canada, House of Commons, *Debates*, 14 November 1867, 66–76.

9  *Globe*, 15 November 1867. McGee's remarks about the suspension of habeas corpus did not appear in the official version of the speech or in the "carefully corrected report" in the *Montreal Gazette*; see Canada, House of Commons, *Debates*, 66–76, and *Montreal Gazette*, 24 December 1867.

10  *Ottawa Times*, 16 December 1867.

11 Canada, House of Commons, *Debates*, 29 November 1867, 158.

12 *Montreal Herald*, 13 September 1867; Archibald to Stanley, 1 October 1867, National Archives of Ireland [NAI], Fenian A Files, A291.

13 Anonymous letter, enclosed in Archibald to Stanley, 1 October 1867, NAI, Fenian A Files, A291.

14 Canada, House of Commons, *Debates*, 29 November 1867, 158; see also *Morning Freeman* [Saint John], 29 November 1867.

15 Canada, House of Commons, *Debates*, 14 November 1867, 77; see also St Patrick's Society Minute Book, 2 December 1867, Concordia University Archives [CUA], PO26, and *Morning Freeman* [Saint John], 12 November 1867.

16 O'Hanly, "To the Hon. Thomas D'Arcy McGee, M.P.," November 1867, LAC, O'Hanly Fonds, folder 7, no. 46. Bowes was John Bowes, a prominent Irish nationalist in Ottawa.

17 Rose, *Manchester Martyrs*, 16–51; Jenkins, *The Fenian Problem*, 104–8.

18 Jenkins, *The Fenian Problem*, 118–46; Rose, *Manchester Martyrs*, 52–64, 95–111; T.D., A.M., and D.B. Sullivan, *Speeches from the Dock*.

19 Rose, *Manchester Martyrs*, 65–83, 112–22; Owens, "Constructing the Martyrs," 18–36; Owen McGee, "God Save Ireland," 39–42; Davis, *Irish Issues in New Zealand Politics*, 13–15.

20 Canada, House of Commons, *Debates*, 21 November 1867, 108.

21 *Montreal Gazette*, 21 November 1867.

22 *Irish Canadian*, 1, 8, 15, and 22 January 1868.

23 Christian Norman file, January 1868, LAC, RG13A-2, vol. 18, file 62, 1868.

24 *Ottawa Times*, 16 December 1867.

25 Canada, House of Commons, *Debates*, 18 December 1867, 310.

26 *Irish Canadian*, 1 January 1868.

27 *Irish Canadian*, 15 January 1868.

28 Minutes of the St Patrick's Society, 7, 27 January 1868, CUA, PO26; *Montreal Gazette*, 30 January 1868; *Irish Canadian*, 5 February 1868.

29 John McLaughlin to Charles Coursol, 28 December 1867, LAC, RG13A-2, vol. 17, file 36, 1868.

30 Coursol to Macdonald and Cartier, 28 December 1867, LAC, RG13A-2, vol. 17, file 36, 1868; see also Macdonald to Coursol, 14 January 1868, and Coursol to Macdonald, 3 February 1868, LAC, RG13A-2, vol. 17, file 36, 1868.

31 *Trial of Patrick J. Whelan*, 34, 46–7, 49; see also William Buell Richards, "Trial Notes," CUA, PO30, HA260, folder 5.

32 Testimony of John Joseph McGee, in William Buell Richards, "Trial Notes," CUA, PO30, HA260, folder 9; *Trial of Patrick J. Whelan*, 26, 34; testi-

mony of John Joseph McGee and Police Officer Benjamin Halbrook, Police Magistrate's Inquiry, in *Globe*, 17 April 1868; *Irish Canadian*, 16 September 1868.

33 McGee to Macdonald, 11 January 1868, LAC, Macdonald Fonds, vol. 59. f. 23938.

34 McGee to Macdonald, 25 February 1868, Murphy Fonds, vol. 48, ff. 21583–4.

35 *Montreal Gazette*, 13 November 1867.

36 *Irish Canadian*, 8 January 1868.

37 McGee to Meehan, 8 February 1868, CUA, PO30, HA261, folder 21.

38 McGee to Macdonald, 3 February 1868, Murphy Fonds, f. 14234.

39 For examples of speaking engagements that McGee had to turn down, see *Montreal Gazette*, 1, 27 November and 2 December 1867, 9, 29 January 1868; McGee to William Kerr, 1 February 1868, published in *Globe and Mail*, 10 July 1954, p. 13.

40 McGee to Macdonald, 15 February 1868, Murphy Fonds, f. 14242.

41 McGee to Macdonald, 3 February 1868, Murphy Fonds, ff. 14236–7.

42 McGee to Macdonald, 11 February 1868, Murphy Fonds, vol. 48, f. 21581.

43 McGee to Sadlier, n.d. [c. 5 March 1868], LAC, Sadlier Fonds.

44 McGee to Macdonald, 11 February 1868, Murphy Fonds, vol. 48, f. 21581.

45 McGee to Tupper, 6 April 1868, Murphy Fonds, ff. 14314–15; see also his poem "St. Patrick's Dream" in *Montreal Gazette*, 17 March 1868.

46 Draft History of Fenianism, in National Library of Ireland [NLI], Larcom Papers, MS 7517, "Fenianism"; Archibald to Stanley, 1 February 1868, NAI, Fenian A Files, A316; Report to Colonial Office, 26 February 1868, The National Archives [TNA], FO.5/1343, f. 142.

47 James Rooney (pseud.) to Francis Lousada, 4 February 1868, TNA, FO.5/1343, f. 101; Lousada to [Stanley], 6 February 1868, TNA, FO.5/1343, f. 103. Rooney's identity remains a mystery.

48 Lousada to Stanley, 3 March 1868, TNA, FO.5/1343, ff. 167–9; see also Rooney to Lousada, 4 February 1868, TNA, FO.5/1343, f. 101.

49 Diary of James Rooney, 5 March 1868, TNA, FO.5/1343, f. 194.

50 Rooney to Lousada, 4 February 1868, TNA, FO.5/1343, f. 101.

51 Diary of James Rooney, 5, 14 March 1868, TNA, FO.5/1343, ff. 194–5, 231–2; see also Lousada to Stanley, 16 March 1868, TNA, FO.5/1343, ff. 228–9.

52 Coursol to Macdonald, 17 February 1868, Macdonald Fonds, vol. 240, ff. 106458–9; McLoughlin to Coursol, 18 March 1868, Macdonald Fonds, vol. 240, f. 106572.

53 A. Sewell to Ermatinger, and Ermatinger to Macdonald, 13 March 1868, Macdonald Fonds, vol. 240, ff. 106549–50.

54 *Irish Canadian*, 25 March 1868.

55 Rooney to Lousada, 24 March 1868, TNA, FO.5/1343, f. 278; Lousada to Stanley, 26 March 1868, ibid., f. 276; Ermatinger to Macdonald, 26 March 1868, Macdonald Fonds, vol. 240, f. 106619; McMicken to Macdonald, 30 March 1868, Macdonald Fonds, vol. 240, f. 106653.

56 *Ottawa Times*, 18 March 1868; see also McGee to the Earl of Mayo, 4 April 1868, Murphy Fonds, f. 21586, and Wilson, *Thomas D'Arcy McGee*, 1:4–5.

57 McGee to Meehan, 6 April 1868, CUA, PO30, HA261, folder 7.

58 "Requiem Aeternam," in Sadlier, ed., *Poems of Thomas D'Arcy McGee*, 467–9.

59 *Canadian Freeman*, 23 April 1868; Wilson, *Thomas D'Arcy McGee*, 1:7–8.

60 *Montreal Gazette*, 17 March 1868.

61 McGee to Peggy McGee, n.d. [3 April 1868], CUA, PO30, HA254, folder 17.

62 McGee to Tupper, 6 April 1868, Murphy Fonds, ff. 14314–15.

63 Canada, House of Commons, *Debates*, 6 April 1868, 468.

64 *Canadian Freeman*, 17 September 1868; *Trial of Patrick J. Whelan*, 20–2; Testimony of Edward Stow [sic], in William Buell Richards, "Trial Notes," CUA, PO30, HA260, folder 7.

65 Canada, House of Commons, *Debates*, 6 April 1868, 468.

66 McGee to Macdonald, 15 February 1868, Macdonald Fonds, vol. 231, f. 100008; see also Wilson, "Orange Influences of the Right Kind," in Wilson, *Orange Order in Canada*, 89–108.

67 See also McGee, "Our New Nation and the Old Empire," in *Montreal Gazette*, 29 February 1868.

68 Canada, House of Commons, *Debates*, 6 April 1868, 469–71.

## CHAPTER FIFTEEN

1 *Globe*, 21 April 1868.

2 *Canadian Freeman*, 9 April 1868; J.L.P. O'Hanly, untitled memoir, n.d., "Status of Irish Catholics," Library and Archives Canada [LAC], O'Hanly Fonds, vol. 17, folder 6.

3 *Trial of Patrick J. Whelan*, 29; *Canadian Freeman*, 17 September 1868.

4 *Globe*, 10 April 1868; William Buell Richards, "Trial Notes," Concordia University Archives [CUA], PO30, HA260, folder 1; *Trial of Patrick J. Whelan*, 29–30.

5 *Irish Canadian*, 25 March 1868.

6 *Globe*, 10 April 1868; William Buell Richards, "Trial Notes," CUA, PO30, HA260, folder 1; *Irish Canadian*, 16 September 1868; *Canadian Freeman*, 17 September 1868; *Trial of Patrick J. Whelan*, 30–1.

7 As subsequently revealed by J.L.P. O'Hanly; see O'Hanly, untitled memoir, n.d., "Status of Irish Catholics," O'Hanly Fonds, vol. 17, folder 6.

8 *Globe*, 10 April 1868. At the trial, Mrs Trotter testified that Whelan's first visit was "five or six days before the murder" and that the second visit was "perhaps two or three nights before the murder"; see *Trial of Patrick J. Whelan*, 10.

9 *Globe*, 10 April 1868. On the general issue of evidence and the suborning of soldiers, see Jenkins, *The Fenian Problem*, 55–6.

10 *Globe*, 8, 9, 10 April 1868; *Trial of Patrick J. Whelan*, 34.

11 *Globe*, 16 April 1868; E.J. O'Neill to Macdonald, 13 April 1868, LAC, Macdonald Fonds, vol. 184, ff. 76961–3; *Irish Canadian*, 22 April 1868; *Trial of Patrick J. Whelan*, 33.

12 *Globe*, 10 April 1868.

13 Archibald to Stanley, 9 April 1868, The National Archives [TNA], FO.5/1343, ff. 339–40; among other things, Archibald described Murphy as "one of the principal Fenians in Montreal." On Doody, see *Globe*, 18 April 1868.

14 On Callahan, see St Patrick's Society Minute Book, 7 November 1864, CUA, PO26; McGee, "Account of the Attempts," *Montreal Gazette*, 22 August 1867; Information and Complaint of William Donohoe of the City of Montreal Police against "Felix Callaghan at present of the City of Ottawa, Printer," 17 April 1868, Macdonald Fonds, vol. 184, f. 76972; *Canadian Freeman*, 23 April 1868. On Curran, see *Globe*, 18 April 1868; *Canadian Freeman*, 23 April 1868. For McNamee's plot, see above, 266.

15 Macdonald to David Morrison, 11 April 1868, Macdonald Fonds, vol. 514, ff. 644–5.

16 [Robert Anderson], "Fenianism, Historical Sketch," National Archives of Ireland [NAI], Fenian Police Reports, 1857–83, box 4; Archibald, "Despatch," 30 November 1866, ibid.; Kennerk, "Fenianism and Assassination."

17 *Irish Canadian*, 22 April 1868; McMicken to Macdonald, 14 April 1868, Macdonald Fonds, vol. 240, ff. 106735–7; "Abstract of information in letters dated from Chicago, Il. on 23rd & 26th April 1868," TNA, FO.5/1343, f. 405.

18 O'Neill to Macdonald, 13 April 1868, Macdonald Fonds, vol. 184, ff. 76961–3.

19 Macdonald to Sandfield Macdonald, 4 May 1868, Macdonald Fonds, vol. 514, ff. 702–3.

20 As Michael Starrs subsequently explained to his grandson; see Slattery, *"They Got to Find Mee Guilty Yet,"* 399.

21 *Globe*, 4, 6 May 1866; Warrants of Commitment, LAC, RG13A-2. vol. 20, file 584. On Fenianism in and around Guelph, see McMicken to Macdonald, 4 March 1868, Macdonald Fonds, vol. 240, f. 106497; McMicken to Macdonald, 16 March 1868, Macdonald Fonds, vol. 240, ff. 106553–5; McMicken to Macdonald, 14 April 1868, Macdonald Fonds, vol. 240, ff. 106735–7; O'Reilly to Macdonald, 27 July 1868, LAC, RG13A-2, vol. 20, file 585; *Guelph Evening Mercury*, 6, 7 May 1868.

22 *Globe*, 17 April 1868.

23 Despite testimony at the inquiry that the shot had been fired on the Thursday before the murder, the police report indicated that the incident actually occurred on the Wednesday. Contrast *Globe*, 17 April 1868, with *Canadian Freeman*, 23 April 1868, and *Irish Canadian*, 15 April 1868.

24 *Trial of Patrick J. Whelan*, 33.

25 *Globe*, 18 April 1868; *Guelph Evening Mercury*, 18 April 1868; *Canadian Freeman*, 23 April 1868.

26 *Globe*, 18 April 1868.

27 *Globe*, 17 April 1868.

28 *Canadian Freeman*, 23 April 1868.

29 *Globe*, 22 April 1868; for similar descriptions of Whelan's clothing on the night of the murder, see the testimony of Francis Kirby and Eliza Tierney from the Police Magistrate's Inquiry, in *Globe*, 17 April 1868.

30 *Globe*, 23 April 1868.

31 Ibid.

32 Alexander Powell's Memorandum, in *Montreal Gazette*, 12 September 1868; *Trial of Patrick J. Whelan*, 63–4.

33 *Irish Canadian*, 23 September 1868.

34 Cochrane, ed., *The Canadian Album*, 2:478; see also Cullen's obituary in *Montreal Gazette*, 11 February 1905.

35 *Globe*, 25 April 1868. On Richard Slattery's clandestine operations within the secret service of the Fenian Brotherhood, see "Receipt," 3 May 1866, New York Public Library, Sweeny Papers, and Slattery to Sweeny, 9 May 1866, Sweeny Papers.

36 *Globe*, 25 April 1868.

37 Ibid. The *Irish Canadian*, in contrast, believed that the whole conversation had been invented by the authorities to nail Whelan. "We give the follow-

ing as one of the latest batches," it prefaced its report of the conversation, "a word of which, from beginning to end, we do not believe" (*Irish Canadian*, 29 April 1868).

38 *Ottawa Citizen*, 29 May 1868.

39 See above, 298, and "Lists of Warrants issued, arrests, discharges, 1868," NAI, Fenian Arrests and Discharges, 1866–69.

40 Wade to Macdonald, 23 December 1868, Macdonald Fonds, vol. 341, f. 156222.

41 *Trial of Patrick J. Whelan*, 37–8; *Canadian Freeman*, 17 September 1868.

42 *Trial of Patrick J. Whelan*, 37; Slattery, "*They Got to Find Mee Guilty Yet*," 376.

43 *Trial of Patrick J. Whelan*, 37–8. On the myth of McGee's cowardice see Wilson, *Thomas D'Arcy McGee*, 1:257.

44 Archibald to Stanley, 9 April 1868, TNA, FO.5/1343, f. 342.

45 Rooney to Lousada, 7 May 1868, TNA, FO.5/1343, f. 377.

46 Patrick James Whelan, the Irish American journalist, is mentioned in the *Globe*, 20 October 1865.

47 See above, 108.

48 *Trial of Patrick J. Whelan*, 66–7.

49 Swainson, "John Hillyard Cameron," *Dictionary of Canadian Biography online*, http://www.biographi.ca.

50 *Guelph Evening Mercury*, 14 May 1868.

51 The phrase (and the argument) can be found in O'Hanly to John Hearn, 4 May 1868, O'Hanly Fonds, vol. 1.

52 *Irish Canadian*, 16 September 1868.

53 *Globe*, 8 September 1868.

54 Matthew Barlow, "Fear and Loathing in Saint Sylvestre: The Corrigan Murder Case, 1855–58," 67, 85.

55 *Globe*, 11 September 1868.

56 O'Reilly to Macdonald, 10 February 1869, Macdonald Fonds, vol. 184, ff. 77023–4.

57 The story was recounted by Charles Murphy to Isabel Skelton; see Murphy to Mrs O.D. Skelton, 2 May 1934, LAC, Murphy Fonds, vol. 27, ff. 11591–2.

58 *Trial of Patrick J. Whelan*, 13–15.

59 Ibid., 17–18, 23–6.

60 *Irish Canadian*, 23 September 1868; *Trial of Patrick J. Whelan*, 82.

61 *Globe*, 11 September 1868.

62 *Trial of Patrick J. Whelan*, 82.

63  *Irish Canadian*, 16 September 1868; *Trial of Patrick J. Whelan*, 6.

64  *Trial of Patrick J. Whelan*, 46–50.

65  Ibid., 46.

66  Francis Ritchie to McMicken, 21 September 1868, Macdonald Fonds, vol. 241, ff. 107529–31.

67  *Trial of Patrick J. Whelan*, 47.

68  *Irish Canadian*, 23 September 1868; *Trial of Patrick J. Whelan*, 48–9.

69  *Irish Canadian*, 23 September 1868; *Trial of Patrick J. Whelan*, 71.

70  *Irish Canadian*, 16 September 1868; *Trial of Patrick J. Whelan*, 34.

71  *Globe*, 10 September 1868.

72  *Irish Canadian*, 16 September 1868; *Trial of Patrick J. Whelan*, 35.

73  *Irish Canadian*, 29 April 1868.

74  The witnesses were William Goulden, Susan Wheatley, John White, William White, James Kinsella, Patrick Eagleson; *Trial of Patrick J. Whelan*, 45, 50–4.

75  *Guelph Evening Mercury*, 8 April 1868.

76  *Trial of Patrick J. Whelan*, 45, 50–4.

77  Ibid., 34.

78  Ibid., 71–2.

79  Ibid., 34–6.

80  *Irish Canadian*, 23 September 1868.

81  Ibid.; *Trial of Patrick J. Whelan*, 36.

82  *Trial of Patrick J. Whelan*, 32.

83  Ibid., 70.

84  *Irish Canadian*, 16 September 1868; *Trial of Patrick J. Whelan*, 20–1.

85  *Irish Canadian*, 16 September 1868.

86  *Globe*, 28 May 1868.

87  *Irish Canadian*, 16 September 1868; *Trial of Patrick J. Whelan*, 10, 29, 33.

88  *Trial of Patrick J. Whelan*, 28.

89  *Irish Canadian*, 16 September 1868.

90  *Irish Canadian*, 23 September 1868; *Trial of Patrick J. Whelan*, 69–70.

91  *Trial of Patrick J. Whelan*, 40.

92  *Irish Canadian*, 16 September 1868; *Trial of Patrick J. Whelan*, 40–1.

93  *Trial of Patrick J. Whelan*, 41.

94  *Irish Canadian*, 23 September 1868.

95  As reported in *Montreal Gazette*, 9 September 1868.

96  *Irish Canadian*, 16 September 1868; *Trial of Patrick J. Whelan*, 30–1.

97  *Irish Canadian*, 23 September 1868; *Trial of Patrick J. Whelan*, 44–5.

98  *Trial of Patrick J. Whelan*, 45–6.

CHAPTER SIXTEEN

1  *Trial of Patrick J. Whelan*, 67.
2  Ibid., 69–70.
3  Ibid., 70–2.
4  Ibid., 73–6.
5  Ibid., 76–7.
6  Ibid., 77.
7  Ibid., 77–8.
8  *Globe*, 15 September 1868; *Montreal Gazette*, 15 September 1868.
9  *Trial of Patrick J. Whelan*, 78–9.
10  Ibid., 79–80.
11  Ibid., 80–1.
12  Ibid., 81–2.
13  Ibid., 78, 83.
14  *Globe*, 15 September 1868.
15  *Montreal Gazette*, 11 September 1868.
16  *Trial of Patrick J. Whelan*, 83.
17  *Globe*, 15 September 1868.
18  *Mail and Empire* [Toronto], 7 April 1934.
19  *Trial of Patrick J. Whelan*, 85.
20  Whelan to Macdonald, 14 September 1868, Library and Archives Canada [LAC], Macdonald Fonds, vol. 184, ff. 76993–6.
21  *Trial of Patrick J. Whelan*, 86.
22  Ibid., 87.
23  Ibid., 88.
24  Ibid. Whelan never wavered from this position. The day before his execution, he received a letter from Mary McGee, forgiving him for killing her husband. Such forgiveness was unnecessary, he replied, since he had not committed the crime; *Globe*, 11 February 1869.
25  As in, for example, the notorious Birmingham Six case after the IRA's bombing of two pubs in the city centre in 1974.
26  *Globe*, 16 September 1868.
27  Slattery, *"They Got to Find Mee Guilty Yet,"* 331–4.
28  Lucas, "The Assassination of D'Arcy McGee," 7–9.
29  Slattery, "A Plot Denied: The Murder of D'Arcy McGee," *Ottawa Journal*, 22 June 1974. See also "The Mystery of the McGee Murder Bullet," 9, and Slattery, "McGee's Murder: Did This Gun Fire That Bullet?" *Montreal Gazette*, 3 November 1973.

30 Slattery, *"They Got to Find Mee Guilty Yet,"* 335–6.

31 See, for example, *Trial of Patrick J. Whelan*, 31; *Irish Canadian*, 16 September 1868.

32 Lucas, personal communication, 27 June 2010.

33 Slattery, *"They Got to Find Mee Guilty Yet,"* 216.

34 *Globe*, 8 September 1868; Slattery, *"They Got to Find Mee Guilty Yet,"* 58–61; Wilson, "Was Patrick James Whelan a Fenian and Did He Assassinate Thomas D'Arcy McGee?" 77–8.

35 O'Hanly, "Status of Irish Catholics," LAC, O'Hanly Fonds, vol. 17, folder 6.

36 For the *Irish Canadian*'s coverage of the appeal process, see 25 November, 23 December 1868, 13, 27 January and 17 February 1869. In the *Irish Canadian*, 13 January 1869, there was a sarcastic comment about Judge Richards ("no greater ornament, or a more impartial judge, occupies the Canadian Bench"), but no reference to any conflict of interest.

37 Statement of Patrick James Whelan, 9 February 1869, Macdonald Fonds, vol. 184, f. 77013; Macdonald to O'Reilly, 12 February 1869, Macdonald Fonds, vol. 515, ff. 551–2.

38 Slattery, *"They Got to Find Mee Guilty Yet,"* 320.

39 *Irish Canadian*, 22 April 1868. A similar story was in circulation twenty-five years later. In 1893 the *Montreal Gazette* reported that Whelan decided to "make a clean breast of it" the day before his execution, and told a leading figure in the city that "I could save my own neck and put the rope round the necks of five others, if I wished to turn stag. If I did so, there is no place on earth where I would be safe, so I'll die game. My pistol shot McGee, but my hand did not pull the trigger that fired the shot" (*Montreal Gazette*, 7 April 1893).

40 Interestingly, the one hard fact from his speech that can be checked catches Whelan in a lie. As part of his effort to distance himself from Fenianism, he said that he was born in Edinburgh. In fact, he was born in Ireland; see his marriage certificate, 13 February 1867, St Patrick's Basilica, Montreal.

41 Macdonald to O'Reilly, 12 February 1869, Macdonald Fonds, vol. 515, ff. 551–2.

42 *Trial of Patrick J. Whelan*, 22.

43 *Globe*, 17 April 1869.

44 Warrant of Commitment for James Kinsella, 17 April 1868, "Papers re. parties charged with Fenianism in Ottawa," LAC, RG13A-2, vol. 20, file 510, 1868.

45 *Trial of Patrick J. Whelan*, 52–3.

46 Michael Kinsella to Macdonald, 27 April 1868, Macdonald Fonds, vol. 59, ff. 24057–60.

47 *Globe*, 20 April 1869.

48 *Canadian Freeman*, 17 September 1868.

49 R.E. Gosnell, draft article on McGee, 1925, in LAC, Murphy Fonds, ff. 17964–5; Wade to Macdonald, 1 March 1869, Macdonald Fonds, vol. 342, ff. 156344–7; Alexander Campbell to Macdonald, 4 September 1882, Macdonald Fonds, vol. 196, ff. 82037–42.

## CHAPTER SEVENTEEN

1 *Globe*, 9 April 1868; Daly to Macdonald, 7 April 1868, LAC, Macdonald Fonds, vol. 184, f. 76933.

2 *Canadian Freeman*, 16 April 1868.

3 For a brief account of the funeral procession, see Goheen, "Symbols in the Streets: Parades in Victorian Urban Canada," 237–43.

4 Diary of George Clerk, Bibliothèque et Archives nationales du Québec [BAnQ], 13 April 1868.

5 *Canadian Freeman*, 16 April 1868.

6 *Halifax Evening Reporter*, 25 April 1868. A week later, Connolly wrote to Archbishop Paul Cullen in Dublin describing McGee as "our O'Connell"; see Connolly to Cullen, 1 May 1868, Cullen Papers, Diocesan Archives of Dublin, file 111, 334/8/11/12.

7 *Canadian Freeman*, 16 April 1868.

8 Minutes of the St Patrick's Society, 8 April 1868, Concordia University Archives [CUA], P026. For McGee's expulsion from the society and McNamee's comments, see above, 331.

9 *Irish Canadian*, 8 April 1868.

10 *Irish Canadian*, 15 April 1868. See also *Irish Canadian*, 30 March 1864, 28 June and 22 November 1865, 30 May 1866, and above, 283.

11 H.C. Moore to Cartier, 20 April 1868, Macdonald Fonds, vol. 59, f. 24039; Moore to Cartier, 28 April 1868, Macdonald Fonds, vol. 59, ff. 24061–4; W. Lambert to McMicken, 7 May 1868, Macdonald Fonds, vol. 240, ff. 106830–1; Rev. E.P. Roche to Bishop Horan, Archives of the Archdiocese of Kingston, Ontario, Horan Papers, DC18 C18/19; MacNeil Clarke to Macdonald, 8 April 1868, Macdonald Fonds, vol. 184, f. 76978; Statement of John Clare, 16 April 1868, Macdonald Fonds, vol. 184, f. 76970. See also Nora Daly, "Sketches of Our Ancestors: The Thomas Daly Family," private manuscript, 1968, 2–3, and Wilson, *Thomas D'Arcy McGee*, 1:9–10.

12 *Canadian Freeman*, 14 May 1868.

13 Mary McGee to Bella Morgan, 1 June 1868, CUA, PO30, HA256, folder 17; Sadlier, ed., *Poems of Thomas D'Arcy McGee*.

14 McGee to Sadlier, Ottawa, 7 August 1866, LAC, Sadlier Fonds.

15 Mary McGee to Bella Morgan, 26 April 1869, CUA, PO30, HA256, folder 18.

16 Euphrasia McGee Quinn to Morgan, 7 October 1902, LAC, Morgan Fonds, vol. 14, ff. 5299–300.

17 Newsclipping, CUA, PO30, HA254, folder 5.

18 Berger, *Sense of Power*, 49–52.

19 Foster, *Canada First: or, Our New Nationality*, 31–6. See also McGee, "Speech on Motion for an Address to Her Majesty in Favour of Confederation," *Speeches and Addresses*, 304, and [Morgan], "'Canada First.' Address of the Canadian National Association to the People of Canada," in Morgan, ed., *Canadian Parliamentary Companion*, 576.

20 Mair, "In Memory of Thomas D'Arcy McGee," 11 April 1868, in Morgan Fonds, vol. 40, unnumbered; the poem was published in *Dreamlands and Other Poems*, 67–71.

21 *New Era*, 22 October, 8 December 1857.

22 Haliburton, "The Men of the North and Their Place in History," *Montreal Gazette*, 1 April 1869; Berger, *Sense of Power*, 128–33.

23 McGee to Morgan, 18 March [year unknown], Morgan Fonds, vol. 47, unnumbered.

24 See especially Morgan Fonds, vol. 14, ff. 5244–304. For a discussion of the early biographies of McGee, see Wilson, *Thomas D'Arcy McGee*, 1:35–43.

25 *Daily News*, 14 April 1868.

26 Berger, *Sense of Power*, 58–9, 73.

27 Dawson "Sermon at the Requiem of the Hon. Thomas D'Arcy," 8; see also *Montreal Gazette*, 10 April 1869.

28 *Catholic Weekly Review*, 9 April 1892.

29 *Catholic Weekly Review*, 8 February 1890.

30 *Catholic Register*, 4 October 1894.

31 *Catholic Register*, 11, 25 October 1894.

32 *Montreal Gazette*, 7 April 1893; G.B. VanBlaricom, "The Biggest News Scoop in Canada," *Maclean's*, 3 July 1908, 88.

33 Murphy, "The Location of the McGee Statue," LAC, Murphy Fonds, ff. 20257–64.

34 *Saturday Night*, 17 May 1913; *Globe*, 6, 14 February 1923; John Joseph McGee to Murphy, 18 September 1922, Murphy Fonds, ff. 20865–6; Murphy to

John Joseph McGee, 21 October 1922, Murphy Fonds, ff. 20870–1; Thomas D'Arcy McGee [nephew] to Murphy, 10 November 1922, Murphy Fonds, f. 20872; Thomas D'Arcy McGee [nephew] to Mackenzie King, 10 November 1922, Murphy Fonds, f. 20873; Murphy, "Location of the McGee Statue," Murphy Fonds, f. 20261.

35 Murphy to the Rev. R. Graham, 9 April 1925, Murphy Fonds, f. 17814.

36 Murphy to President [William Thomas] Cosgrave, 30 January 1925, Murphy Fonds, f. 19337; see also ff. 19419, 19476.

37 R.M. Meredith to Murphy, 6 February 1925, Murphy Fonds, f. 17774; see also Sir William Mulock to Murphy, 14 February 1925, Murphy Fonds, f. 19651.

38 J.B. Maclean to Murphy, 20 April 1925, Murphy Fonds, ff. 17880–1; see also Maclean to Murphy, 20 January 1925, Murphy Fonds, f. 19492.

39 Murphy to Mackenzie King, 15 March 1925, Murphy Fonds, f. 18295.

40 *Montreal Gazette*, 15 April 1925.

41 Murphy to O.D. Skelton, 16 February 1925, Murphy Fonds, f. 19520; *Ottawa Citizen*, 15 April 1925.

42 "Centennial Celebration," in Murphy, ed., *1825 – D'Arcy McGee – 1925*, 298.

43 Ibid., 332.

44 Harvey, *Thomas D'Arcy McGee*; Brady, *Thomas D'Arcy McGee;* Skelton, *Life of Thomas D'Arcy McGee*.

45 Bennett to Murphy, 9 April 1925, Murphy Fonds, ff. 19711–13.

46 See, for example, *Ottawa Citizen*, 14, 15, 16 April 1925, and *Montreal Gazette*, 14, 15, 16 April 1925.

47 Murphy to Alexander MacGregor, 25 February 1927, Murphy Fonds, f. 7330; Murphy to Emmet J. Mullally, 14 February 1935, Murphy Fonds, ff. 9409–10.

48 McEvoy, "Canadian Catholic Press Reaction to the Irish Crisis," in Wilson, ed., *Irish Nationalism in Canada*, 121–39; *Catholic Record*, 18 September 1920.

49 Jolivet, "Entre nationalisme irlandais et canadien-français," *Canadian Historical Review* 92 (March 2011): 43–68; see also McLaughlin, "Irish Canadians and the Struggle for Irish Independence."

50 W.P. Burns, quoted in McLaughlin, "Irish Canadians and the Struggle for Irish Independence," 218.

51 *New Freeman*, 21 August 1920, quoted in McLaughlin, "Irish Canadians and the Struggle for Irish Independence," 217.

52 *Sentinel*, 17 August 1920.

53 *Sentinel*, 1 April 1920.

54 Adamson to Murphy, 20 April 1925, Murphy Fonds, ff. 19749–51.

55 Barrett to Murphy, 22 April 1925, Murphy Fonds, ff. 19765–6.

56 *Sentinel*, 7 April 1925.

57 Murphy to F.J. Jackman, 30 December 1929, Murphy Fonds, ff. 5503–4.

58 Murphy to Adamson, 12 November 1926, Murphy Fonds, ff. 39–40; Barrett to Murphy, 23 March 1927, Murphy Fonds, f. 445.

59 Murphy to Bishop Fallon, 8 March 1927; *Montreal Gazette*, 24 May 1927.

60 Jackman to Murphy, 20 December 1928, Murphy Fonds, f. 5499; Murphy to Jackman, 30 December 1929, Murphy Fonds, ff. 5503–4.

61 *Irish Times*, 15 April 1925.

62 Personal communication, 30 October 2009.

63 Griffin, *An Irish Evolution*, 3–33.

64 Murphy to T.P. O'Connor, 8 November 1913, Murphy Fonds, ff. 9872–3.

65 After partition, the idea that McGee's Canadian career could inspire "the people of the Twenty-six and the Six Counties in Ireland to live together in federal equality and common patriotism" was occasionally voiced, but few were listening. See, for example, *Irish Times*, 6 October 1950.

66 Quoted in McEvoy, "Diefenbaker in Ireland," 14.

67 Sadlier, ed., *Poems of Thomas D'Arcy McGee*, 159, with the opening lines: "Am I remember'd in Erin – ? / I charge you, speak me true – / Has my name a sound, a meaning / In the scenes my boyhood knew?"

68 O'Brien made this comment during a conference on "Canada and the Celtic Consciousness," organized by the Celtic Studies Program at the University of Toronto in March 1978.

69 Murphy to Fallon, 13 December 1913, Murphy Fonds, f. 3593.

# Bibliography

## MANUSCRIPT SOURCES

Archives of the Archdiocese of Kingston, Ontario
    Bishop Edward John Horan Papers
Archives of Ontario
    Charles Clarke Papers
Archives of the Roman Catholic Archdiocese of Toronto
    Bishop Charbonnel Papers
    Archbishop Lynch Papers
    Archbishop McNeil Papers
Bibliothèque et Archives nationales du Québec
    George Clerk Fonds, P701 S2 SS1 D20
City of Toronto Archives
    Letter Books of the Chief Constable, Fonds 38, series 90, file 1
Columbia University Rare Book and Manuscript Library
    Meloney-Mitchel Papers
Concordia University Archives
    St Patrick's Society of Montreal Collection, P026
    Thomas D'Arcy McGee Collection, P030 .
Diocese of London [Ontario] Archives
    Bishop Adolphe Pinsonneault Papers
Dublin Diocesan Archives
    Archbishop Paul Cullen Papers
    Archbishop William Walsh Papers
Library and Archives Canada
    George Brown Fonds, MG24-B40
    Brown Chamberlin Fonds, MG24-B19

    Mercy Ann Coles Fonds, MG24-B66

    Alexander Tilloch Galt Fonds, MG27-ID8

    Thomas Kairns Fonds, MG24-C6

    John A. Macdonald Fonds, MG26-A

    John Sandfield Macdonald Fonds, MG24-B30

    Thomas D'Arcy McGee Fonds, MG27-IE9

    Henry Morgan Fonds, MG29-D61

    James G. Moylan Fonds, MG29-D15

    Charles Murphy Fonds, MG27-IIIB8

    John O'Donohoe Fonds, MG27-IE12

    J.J. O'Gorman Fonds, MG30-D20

    J.L.P. O'Hanley [sic] Fonds, MG29-BII

    James Sadlier Fonds, MG24-C16

    Department of Justice Fonds, RG13A-2, vols. 13–20

    Executive Council Office of the Province of Canada Fonds, RG I E7, vol.
    59 (formerly vol. 59A)

National Archives of Ireland

    Fenian A Files, 1866–67

    Fenian Arrests and Discharges, 1866–69

    Fenian Briefs, 1865–69

    Fenian Police Reports, 1857–83

The National Archives [United Kingdom]

Foreign Office, General Correspondence, Fenian Brotherhood, vol. 2, 1865
    (Oct–Dec), 5/1335

Foreign Office, General Correspondence, Fenian Brotherhood, vol. 10, 1868
    (Feb–June), 5/1343

National Library of Ireland

    Charles Gavan Duffy Papers, MS 5757

    Hickey Collection, MS 3226

    Thomas Larcom Papers, MS 7679

    William Smith O'Brien Papers, MSS 446, 8653

    Young Ireland Miscellaneous Letters, MS 10,517

New York Public Library

    Jeremiah O'Donovan Rossa Papers, in the Maloney Collection of Irish
    Historical Papers

    Thomas Sweeney [sic] Papers

Oxford University, Balliol College

    David Urquhart Papers, I/J6

Oxford University, Bodleian Library
 Clarendon Papers, box 53
 Kimberley Papers
Public Record Office of Northern Ireland
 Tennent Papers, D1748
State Historical Society of North Dakota
 James Wickes Taylor Papers, MS 20187
Thomas Fisher Rare Book Library, University of Toronto
 McGee to Samuel Ferguson, 5 May 1864, MSS General 4.086
Trinity College Dublin
 Reports of Informants, MSS 2037, 2040
United Church Archives, Toronto
 Egerton Ryerson Papers
University of New Brunswick Archives
 Samuel Leonard Tilley Fonds, MGH 10a
Nora Daly, "Sketches of Our Ancestors: The Thomas Daly Family," private
 manuscript, 1968

## NEWSPAPERS

*Acadian Recorder,* 1856–63
*American Celt* [Boston, Buffalo, New York], 1850–56
*Boston Pilot,* 1845–48
*British American* [Kingston], 1864
*British American Magazine,* 1864
*British Colonist* [Halifax], 1859–63
*Brockville Recorder,* 1858
*Canadian Freeman* [Toronto], 1858–70
*Catholic Citizen* [Toronto], 1858
*Catholic Record,* 1920
*Catholic Register,* 1894–95
*Catholic Weekly Review,* 1890, 1897
*Citizen* [New York], 1855
*Daily News* [Quebec], 1868
*Dublin Evening Mail,* 1865
*Edinburgh Review,* 1870
*Globe* [Toronto], 1850–70, 1923
*Globe and Mail* [Toronto], 1954

*Guelph Evening Mercury*, 1868

*Halifax Evening Reporter*, 1868

*Hastings Chronicle*, 1862

*Head Quarters* [Fredericton]

*Irish American*, 1865–66

*Irish Canadian* [Toronto], 1863–70

*Irishman* [Dublin], 1849–68

*Irish People* [Dublin], 1863–65

*Irish Times*, 1925, 1950, 2004

*Irish World* [New York], 1878

*Leader* [Toronto], 1858–67

*Mail and Empire* [Toronto], 1934

*La Minerve* [Montreal], 1861

*Mirror* [Toronto], 1858

*Montreal Daily Transcript*, 1857

*Montreal Gazette*, 1857–70, 1893, 1905, 1925, 1927, 1973

*Montreal Herald*, 1861–82

*Montreal Pilot*, 1857–58

*Montreal Transcript*, 1863

*Morning Chronicle* [Halifax], 1863

*Morning Freeman* [Saint John], 1859–67

*Nation* [Dublin], 1845–66

*Nation* [New York], 1848–50

*New Brunswick Reporter*, 1859–63

*New Era* [Montreal], 1857–58

*New York Daily Tribune*, 1848

*Nova Scotian*, 1859–63

*L'Ordre, Union Catholique* [Montreal], 1860

*Ottawa Citizen*, 1863–68, 1925

*Ottawa Journal*, 1974

*Ottawa Times*, 1867–68

*Patriot* [Toronto], 1857–64

*The People* [Wexford], 1865

*Peterborough Review*, 1863–64

*Prince Edward Island Examiner*, 1863

*Prince Edward Island Vindicator*, 1863

*Quebec Morning Chronicle*, 1865

*Saint John Daily News*, 1859–63

*Saint John Morning News,* 1863–66

*Saturday Night,* 1913, 1927

*Sentinel,* 1925 [no date, chapter 17, no. 52]

*Times* [London], 1865

*True Witness* [Montreal], 1857–68

*Wexford Independent,* 1842


PRINTED SOURCES


Ajzenstat, Janet, et al., eds. *Canada's Founding Debates.* Toronto: Stoddart 1999

Akenson, Donald Harman. *The Irish Education Experiment: The National System of Education in the Nineteenth Century.* London: Routledge and Kegan Paul 1970

– *The Irish in Ontario: A Study in Rural History.* Montreal & Kingston: McGill-Queen's University Press 1984

– *The Orangeman: The Life and Times of Ogle Gowan.* Toronto: J. Lorimer 1986

– *The Irish Diaspora: A Primer.* Port Credit: P.D. Meany 1993

Archibald, Sir Edward Mortimer. *Life and Letters of Sir Edward Mortimer Archibald K.C.M.G., C.B.* Toronto: Morang 1924

Baker, William M. "Squelching the Disloyal, Fenian-Sympathizing Brood: T.W. Anglin and Confederation in New Brunswick, 1865–6." *Canadian Historical Review* 55, no. 2 (1974): 141–58

– *Timothy Warren Anglin, 1822–96: Irish Catholic Canadian.* Toronto: University of Toronto Press 1977

Barlow, Matthew. "Fear and Loathing in Saint Sylvestre: The Corrigan Murder Case, 1855–58." MA dissertation, Simon Fraser University 1988

Barnard, Toby. "1641: A Bibliographical Essay" In *Ulster 1641: Aspects of the Rising,* edited by Brian Mac Cuarta, 173–86. Belfast: Institute of Irish Studies, Queen's University Belfast, 1993

Begg, Paul. *Jack the Ripper: The Definitive History.* London: Longman 2003

Berger, Carl. *The Sense of Power: Studies in the Ideas of Canadian Imperialism, 1867–1914.* Toronto: University of Toronto Press 1970

Bew, Paul. *Ireland: The Politics of Enmity, 1789–2006.* Oxford: Oxford University Press 2007

Boyce, D.G. *Nationalism in Ireland.* 2nd edn. London, New York: Routledge 1991

Brady, Alexander. *Thomas D'Arcy McGee.* Toronto: Macmillan 1925

Brode, Patrick. "John Beverley Robinson." In *Dictionary of Canadian Biography online*, http://www.biographi.ca

Brown, Blake. "'Stars and Shamrocks Will Be Sown': The Fenian State Trials, 1866–67." In *Canadian State Trials*. Vol. 3: *Political Trials and Security Measures, 1840–1914*, edited by Barry Wright and Susan Binnie, 35–84. Toronto: University of Toronto Press 2009

Brown, Thomas. *Irish-American Nationalism, 1870–1890*. Philadelphia: Lippincott 1966

Bryan, Dominic. *Orange Parades: The Politics of Ritual, Tradition, and Control*. London: Pluto Press 2000

Burns, Robin B. "D'Arcy McGee and the New Nationality." MA dissertation, Carleton University 1966

Campbell, Christy. *Fenian Fire: The British Government Plot to Assassinate Queen Victoria*. London: HarperCollins 2002

Canada. Department of Agriculture. *Censuses of Canada, 1665 to 1871. Statistics of Canada*, vol. 4. Ottawa: I.B. Taylor 1876

Canada. House of Commons. *Debates. First Session–First Parliament*. Ottawa 1867

Canada, Province of. Legislative Assembly. *Debates, 1858–1866*

– Legislative Assembly. *Journals, 1858–1866*

Canny, Nicholas. "What Really Happened in 1641?" In *Ireland: From Independence to Occupation, 1641–1660*, edited by Jane H. Ohlmeyer, 24–42. Cambridge: Cambridge University Press 1995

Careless, J.M.S. *Brown of the Globe*. Vol. 1: *The Voice of Upper Canada, 1818–1859*. Toronto: Macmillan 1959

– *Brown of the Globe*. Vol. 2: *Statesman of Confederation, 1860–1880*. Toronto: Macmillan 1963

– *The Union of the Canadas: The Growth of Canadian Institutions 1841–1857*. Toronto: McClelland & Stewart 1967; rpt. 1979

*The Case of St Patrick's Congregation: As to the Erection of the New Canonical Parish of St Patrick's, Montreal*. [Montreal?: s.n.] 1866

Clarke, Brian. *Piety and Nationalism: Lay Voluntary Associations and the Creation of an Irish-Catholic Community in Toronto, 1850–1895*. Montreal & Kingston: McGill-Queen's University Press 1993

Cochrane, William, editor. *The Canadian Album: Men of Canada; or Success by example, in religion, patriotism, business, law, medicine, education and agriculture: containing portraits of some of Canada's chief business men, statesmen, farmers, men of the learned professions, and others, also, an authentic sketch of their lives.* Brantford, ON: Bradley, Garretson 1891–1896

Collison, Gary. *Shadrach Minkins: From Fugitive Slave to Citizen.* Cambridge, MA: Harvard University Press 1993

Comerford, R.V. *The Fenians in Context.* Dublin: Wolfhound Press 1998

Cottrell, Michael. "Irish Catholic Political Leadership in Toronto, 1855–1882: A Study of Ethnic Politics." PH D dissertation, University of Saskatchewan 1988

– "St. Patrick's Day Parades in Nineteenth-Century Toronto: A Study of Immigrant Adjustment and Elite Control." *Histoire sociale/Social History* 25 (May 1992): 57–73

Creighton, Donald Grant. *John A. Macdonald.* Vol. 1. Toronto: Macmillan 1952–55

– *Road to Confederation: The Emergence of Canada, 1863–1867.* Toronto: Macmillan 1966

Curtis, Bruce. *The Politics of Population: State Formation, Statistics, and the Census of Canada, 1840–1875.* Toronto: University of Toronto Press 2001

Cuthbertson, Brian. *The Old Attorney General: A Biography of Richard John Uniacke.* Halifax: Nimbus 1980

Dallison, Robert L. *Turning Back the Fenians: New Brunswick's Last Colonial Campaign.* Fredericton: Goose Lane Editions 2006

D'Arcy, William. *The Fenian Movement in the United States, 1858–1886.* 1947; rpt. New York: Russell and Russell 1971

Darroch, A. Gordon, and Michael D. Ornstein. "Ethnicity and Occupational Structure in Canada in 1871: The Vertical Mosaic in Historical Perspective." *Canadian Historical Review* 61, no. 3 (1980): 305–33

Davis, Harold A. "The Fenian Raid on New Brunswick." In *Canadian Historical Review* 36, no. 4 (1955): 316–44

Davis, Richard P. *Irish Issues in New Zealand Politics, 1868–1922.* Dunedin: University of Otago Press 1974

Dawson, Aeneas. "Sermon at the Requiem of the Hon. Thos. D'Arcy McGee." n.p. [1868]

Denieffe, Joseph. *A Personal Narrative of the Irish Revolution Brotherhood.* New York: Gael Publishing Co. 1906

Doheny, Michael. *The Felon's Track* [1848]; rpt., Dublin: M.H. Gill 1918.

Donnelly, James S., Jr. "Sectarianism in 1798 and in Catholic Nationalist Memory." In *Rebellion and Remembrance in Modern Ireland*, edited by L.M. Geary, 16–37. Dublin: Four Courts Press 2000

– *The Great Irish Potato Famine*. Phoenix Mill, Gloucestershire: Sutton Publishing 2001

Doyle, David Noel. "The Irish as Urban Pioneers in the United States, 1850–1870." *Journal of American Ethnic History* 10 (Fall 1990/Winter 1991): 36–61

Duffy, Charles Gavan. *Four Years of Irish History, 1845–49: A Sequel to Young Ireland*. London: Cassell, Petter, Galpin 1883

– *Young Ireland: A Fragment of Irish History, 1840–45*. Vol. 2. London: T. Fisher Unwin 1896

Dunne, Tom. *Rebellions: Memoir, Memory, and 1798*. Dublin: Lilliput Press 2004

Durham, John George Lambton. *Lord Durham's Report: An Abridgement of Report on the Affairs of British North America*, edited by Gerald M. Craig. Ottawa: Carleton University Press 1982

Evans, Stewart P., and Paul Gainey. *The Lodger: The Arrest and Escape of Jack the Ripper*. London: Century 1995

Farrell, Sean. *Rituals and Riots: Sectarian Violence and Political Culture in Ulster, 1784–1886*. Lexington: University Press of Kentucky 2000

*The Fenian Brotherhood Circular of the Corresponding Society for the Period Commencing 10th Sept. and Ending 28th October 1865*. New York 1865

Foner, Eric, ed. *Politics and Ideology in the Age of the Civil War*. New York: Oxford University Press 1980

Foster, William. *Canada First; or, Our New Nationality; An Address*. Toronto: Adams, Stevenson 1871

Goheen, Peter G. "Symbols in the Streets: Parades in Victorian Urban Canada." *Urban History Review* 18 (Feb. 1990): 237–43

Gray, Peter. *Famine, Land, and Politics: British Government and Irish Society, 1843–1850*. Dublin: Irish Academic Press 1999

Griffin, Watson. *An Irish Evolution*. Toronto: Ontario Place c.1912

Gwyn, Richard. *John A. The Man Who Made Us: The Life and Times of John A. Macdonald*. Vol. 1: *1815–1867*. Toronto: Random House Canada 2007

Haines, Robin F. *Charles Trevelyan and the Great Irish Famine*. Dublin: Four Courts Press 2004

Haliburton, Thomas Chandler. *An Address on the Present Condition, Resources and Prospects of British North America: Delivered by Special Request at the City Hall, Glasgow, on the 25th of March, 1857*. Montreal: J. Lovell 1857

Hamilton, Pierce [Peter] Stevens. *Observations Upon a Union of the Colonies of British North America*. Halifax: English and Blackader 1855

Harvey, Daniel Cobb. *Thomas D'Arcy McGee, the Prophet of Canadian Nationality, being an account of how Thomas D'Arcy McGee, by precept and example, strove manfully to convert the abstract idea of Canadian nationality into a compelling sentiment of tolerance and goodwill among sects and races, of faith, hope, charity and neighborliness among individuals.* Winnipeg: University of Manitoba 1923

Heaman, E.A. *The Inglorious Arts of Peace: Exhibitions in Canadian Society during the Nineteenth Century.* Toronto: University of Toronto Press 1999

Hodgins, Bruce W. *John Sandfield Macdonald, 1812–1872.* Toronto: University of Toronto Press 1971

Hodgins, J. George. *Documentary history of education in Upper Canada, from the passing of the Constitutional Act of 1791 to the close of the Reverend Doctor Ryerson's administration of the education department in 1876: forming an appendix to the annual report of the minister of education.* Vol. 17: *1861–1863.* Toronto: L.K. Cameron 1907

Holmgren, Michele J. "Native Muses and National Poetry: Nineteenth-Century Irish Canadian Poets." PH D dissertation, University of Western Ontario 1997

Houston, Cecil J., and William J. Smyth. *The Sash Canada Wore: A Historical Geography of the Orange Order in Canada.* Toronto: University of Toronto Press 1980

– *Irish Emigration and Canadian Settlement: Patterns, Links, & Letters.* Toronto: University of Toronto Press 1990

Hughes, John. "Reflections and Suggestions in Regard to What is Called the Catholic Press." In *The Metropolitan* 4 (Dec. 1856): 652–61

Humphreys, Charles W. "Lynch, John Joseph." In *Dictionary of Canadian Biography online,* http://www.biographi.ca

Hustak, Alan. *Saint Patrick's of Montreal: The Biography of a Basilica.* Montreal: Véhicule Press 1998

"The Irish Land Question," *The Edinburgh Review, or Critical Journal, for January and April, 1870* (New York: Leonard Scott Publishing Company, 1870), vol. 131: 135–6

Jenkins, Brian. *Fenians and Anglo-American Relations during Reconstruction.* Ithaca, NY: Cornell University Press 1969

– *Irish Nationalism and the British State: From Repeal to Revolutionary Nationalism.* Montreal & Kingston: McGill-Queen's University Press 2006

– *The Fenian Problem: Insurgency and Terrorism in a Liberal State, 1858–1874.* Montreal & Kingston: McGill-Queen's University Press 2008

Jolivet, Simon. "Entre nationalisme irlandais et canadien-français: les intrigues québécoises de la Self Determination for Ireland League of Canada and Newfoundland." *Canadian Historical Review* 92, no. 1 (2011): 43–68.

Keep, George Rex Crowley. "The Irish Migration to Montreal, 1847–67." MA dissertation, McGill University 1948

Kennerk, "Fenianism and Assassination." Unpublished paper, presented at "The Black Hand of Republicanism: Fenianism in Modern Ireland" conference, held at Queen's University Belfast, 2008

Kerr, Donal A. *"A Nation of Beggars"? Priests, People, and Politics in Famine Ireland, 1846–52.* Oxford: Clarendon Press 1994

Kinealy, Christine. *This Great Calamity: The Irish Famine, 1845–52.* Dublin: Gill and Macmillan 1994

Loughlin, James. "Parades and Politics: Liberal Governments and the Orange Order, 1880–1886." In *The Irish Parading Tradition: Following the Drum,* edited by T.G. Fraser, 9–26. New York: St Martin's Press 2000

Lucas, Douglas. "The Assassination of D'Arcy McGee," Ontario Centre of Forensic Sciences, Thomas D'Arcy McGee file. Obtained under the Freedom of Information Act

McCulloch, Michael. "'Dr. Tumblety, the Indian Herb Doctor': Politics, Professionalism and Abortion in Mid-Nineteenth-Century Montreal." *Canadian Bulletin of Medical History/Bulletin canadien d'histoire de la médecine* 10 (1993): 49–66

McEvoy, Frederick J. "Canadian Catholic Press Reaction to the Irish Crisis, 1916–1921." In *Irish Nationalism in Canada,* edited by David A. Wilson, 121–39. Montreal & Kingston: McGill-Queen's University Press 2009

– "Diefenbaker in Ireland." Unpublished paper, presented at the Canadian Association of Irish Studies conference held in Halifax, Nova Scotia, 2010

McGee, Owen. "'God Save Ireland': Manchester-Martyr Demonstrations in Dublin, 1867–1916." *Éire-Ireland* (Fall–Winter 2001): 39–66

McGee, Thomas D'Arcy. *Historical Sketches of O'Connell and His Friends.* Boston: Donahoe & Rohan 1845

– *The Irish Writers of the Seventeenth Century.* Dublin: James Duffy 1846

– *Memoir of the Life and Conquests of Art Mac Murrough, King of Leinster, from A.D. 1377 to A.D. 1417: With Some Notices of the Leinster Wars of the 14th Century.* Dublin: James Duffy 1847

– *Memoir of Charles Gavan Duffy, Esq., as a Student, Journalist, and Organizer.* Dublin: W. Hogan 1849

– *History of the Attempts to Establish the Protestant Reformation in Ireland and the Successful Resistance of That People. (Time: 1540–1830).* 2nd edn. Boston: P. Donahoe 1853

– *A History of the Irish Settlers in North America, from the Earliest Period to the Census of 1850.* 1851; 6th edn., Boston: P. Donahoe 1855

– *Canadian Ballads, and Occasional Verses.* Montreal: Lovell 1858

– *Sebastian, or, The Roman Martyr: A Drama, Founded on Cardinal Wiseman's Celebrated Tale of Fabiola.* New York: D. & J. Sadlier 1861

– *Popular History of Ireland: From the Earliest Period to the Emancipation of the Catholics.* Montreal: D. & J. Sadlier 1863

– *Notes on Federal Governments, Past and Present, with an appendix, containing the Federal Constitution of the New Zealand Colonies.* Montreal: Dawson 1865

– *Speeches and Addresses Chiefly on the Subject of British-American Union.* London: Chapman and Hall 1865

McGowan, Mark G. "Irish Catholics." In *Encyclopedia of Canada's Peoples*, edited by Paul Robert Magosci, 1–30. Toronto: University of Toronto Press 1999

– *Michael Power: The Struggle to Build the Catholic Church on the Canadian Frontier.* Montreal & Kingston: McGill-Queen's University Press 2005

McLaughlin, Robert. "Irish Canadians and the Struggle for Irish Independence, 1912–1925: A Study of Ethnic Identity and Cultural Heritage." PH D dissertation, University of Maine 2004

Mair, Charles. *Dreamland and Other Poems.* Montreal: Dawson Brothers 1868

Martin, Ged. *Britain and the Origins of Canadian Confederation, 1837–1867.* Vancouver: University of British Columbia Press 1995

– "The Idea of British North American Union 1854–1864." *Journal of Irish and Scottish Studies* 1, no. 2 (2008): 309–33

Moir, John S. "The Problem of Double Minority: Some Reflections on the Development of the English-speaking Catholic Church in Canada in the Nineteenth Century." *Histoire sociale/Social History* 4 (April 1971): 53–67

Monahan, Arthur P. "A Politico-Religious Incident in the Career of Thomas D'Arcy McGee." In Canadian Catholic Historical Association *Report* 24 (1957): 39–51

Monck, Frances E.O. *My Canadian Leaves: An Account of a Visit to Canada in 1864–65.* London: R. Bentley 1891

Mood, W. James S. "The Orange Order in Canadian Politics, 1841–1867." MA dissertation, University of Toronto 1950

Moody, T.W. "Irish History and Irish Mythology." In *Interpreting Irish History: The Debate on Historical Revisionism*, edited by Ciaran Brady, 71–86. Dublin: Irish Academic Press 1994

Moore, Christopher. *1867: How the Fathers Made a Deal*. Toronto: McClelland & Stewart 1997

Morgan, Henry J. "'Canada First.' Address of the Canadian National Association to the People of Canada." In *The Canadian Parliamentary Companion*, edited by Henry J. Morgan, 573–85. Montreal: n.p. 1874

Morris, Alexander. *Nova Britannia, or, British North America, Its Extent and Future: A Lecture*. Montreal: J. Lovell 1858

Morton, W.L. *Critical Years: The Union of British North America, 1857–1872*. Toronto: McClelland & Stewart 1964

Murphy, Charles, ed. *1825 – D'Arcy McGee – 1925; A Collection of Speeches and Addresses, Together with a Complete Report of the Centennial Celebration of the Birth of the Honourable Thomas D'Arcy McGee at Ottawa, April 13th, 1925*. Toronto: Macmillan 1937

Murphy, Peter. *Together in Exile*. Saint John: Lingley Printing Co. 1990

"The Mystery of the McGee Murder Bullet," Ontario Centre of Forensic Sciences, Thomas D'Arcy McGee file. Obtained under the Freedom of Information Act

Neidhardt, W.S. *Fenianism in North America*. University Park: Pennsylvania State University Press 1975

Nicolson, Murray W. "John Elmsley and the Rise of Irish Catholic Social Action in Victorian Toronto." Canadian Catholic Historical Association, *Historical Studies* 51 (1984): 47–66

O'Brien, Conor Cruise. *Memoir: My Life and Themes*. Dublin: Poolbeg Press 1999

O'Driscoll, Robert, and Lorna Reynolds, eds. *The Untold Story: The Irish in Canada*. Toronto: Celtic Arts of Canada 1988

Ó Gráda, Cormac. *Black '47 and Beyond: The Great Irish Famine in History, Economy, and Memory*. Princeton: Princeton University Press 1999

Ó Lúing, Seán. "Aspects of the Fenian Rising in Kerry, 1867." In *Journal of the Kerry Archeological and Historical Society* 3 (1970): 131–53

Owens, G. "Constructing the Martyrs: The Manchester Executions and the National Imagination". In *Images, Icons and the Irish Nationalist Imagination*, edited by L.W. McBride, 24–8. Dublin: Four Courts Press 1999

Phelan, Josephine. *The Ardent Exile: The Life and Times of Thos. D'Arcy McGee*. Toronto: Macmillan 1951

Potter, David M. *The Impending Crisis, 1848–1861.* New York: Harper & Row 1976

Rabinovitch, Victor. "The Golden-Tongued Martyr." In *Literary Review of Canada* 16, no. 4 (2008): 23–4

Radforth, Ian. *Royal Spectacle: The 1860 Visit of the Prince of Wales to Canada and the United States.* Toronto: University of Toronto Press 2004

– "Orangemen and the Crown." In *The Orange Order in Canada*, edited by David A. Wilson. Dublin: Four Courts Press 2007

Rae, Bob. *Three Questions: Prosperity and the Public Good.* Toronto: Viking 1998

Rafferty, Oliver P. *The Church, the State, and the Fenian Threat, 1861–1875.* New York: St Martin's Press 1999

Ramón, Marta. *A Provisional Dictator: James Stephens and the Fenian Movement.* Dublin: University College Dublin Press 2007

Reale, Paul. "Was the Separate School Act of 1863 a Finality?" MA research paper, University of Toronto 2003

Rose, Paul. *The Manchester Martyrs: The Story of a Fenian Tragedy.* London: Lawrence & Wishart 1970

Ryerson, Egerton. *Dr. Ryerson's Letters in Reply to the Attacks of the Hon. George Brown, M.P.P., "Editor-in-Chief" and Proprietor of the "Globe."* Edited with Notes and an Appendix. Toronto: Lovell and Gibson 1859

Sadlier, Mary Ann, ed. *The Poems of Thomas D'Arcy McGee.* New York: D. & J. Sadlier 1869

Senior, Hereward. *The Last Invasion of Canada: The Fenian Raids, 1866–1870.* Toronto and Oxford: Dundurn Press in collaboration with the Canadian War Museum, Canadian Museum of Civilization 1991

Sewell, Jonathan, and John Beverley Robinson. *Plan for a General Legislative Union of all the British Provinces of North America.* London: W. Clowes 1824

Sheppard, George. "'God Save the Green': Fenianism and Fellowship in Victorian Ontario." *Histoire sociale/Social History* 20 (May 1987): 129–44

Simpson-Hayes, Kate. "D'Arcy McGee as I Saw Him," *Saturday Night*, 25 June 1927, 3

Skelton, Isabel. *The Life of Thomas D'Arcy McGee.* Gardenvale, QC: Garden City Press 1925

Slattery, T.P. *The Assassination of Thomas D'Arcy McGee.* Toronto: Doubleday Canada 1968

– *"They Got to Find Mee Guilty Yet."* Toronto: Doubleday 1972

Stacey, C.P. "Fenianism and the Rise of National Feeling in Canada at the Time of Confederation." *Canadian Historical Review* 12, no. 3 (1931): 238–61

– "A Fenian Interlude: The Story of Michael Murphy." *Canadian Historical Review* 15, no. 2 (1934): 133–54

Stevenson, Garth. *Parallel Paths: The Development of Nationalism in Ireland and Quebec*. Montreal & Kingston: McGill-Queen's University Press 2006

Stewart, A.T.Q. *The Shape of Irish History*. Belfast: Blackstaff 2001

Stortz, Gerald J. "John Joseph Lynch, Archbishop of Toronto: A Bibliographical Study of Religious, Political and Social Commitment." PH D dissertation, University of Guelph 1980

Sullivan, A.M. *The Story of Ireland*. 1867; rpt., Dublin: Gill 1898

Sullivan, T.D., A.M., and D.B. *Speeches from the Dock*. Revd. edn., Dublin: Gill and Macmillan 1968

Swainson, Donald. "John Hillyard Cameron." In *Dictionary of Canadian Biography online*, http://www.biographi.ca

Takagami, Shin-chi. "The Fenian Rising in Dublin, March 1867." In *Irish Historical Studies* 29 (May 1995): 340–62

Taylor, Cliona. "A Fatal Affray in Toronto: The Murder of Matthew Sheedy and the St. Patrick's Day Riots of 1858." M A research paper, University of Toronto 2005

Taylor, Fennings. *Thomas D'Arcy McGee: Sketch of His Life and Death*. Montreal: Lovell 1868

Teatero, William. *John Anderson, Fugitive Slave*. [Kingston, ON]: Treasure Island Books 1986

Tone, Theobald Wolfe, "Autobiography, 7 August – 8 September 1796." In *The Writings of Theobald Wolfe Tone*, vol. 2, edited by T.W. Moody, R.B. McDowell, and C.J. Woods, 260–306. Oxford: Clarendon Press 1998

Toner, Peter M. "The Rise of Irish Nationalism in Canada, 1858–1884." PH D dissertation, University College Galway 1974

– "'The Green Ghost': Canada's Fenians and the Raids." *Eire-Ireland* 16 (Winter 1981): 27–47

– "The Fanatic Heart of the North." In *Irish Nationalism in Canada*, edited by David A. Wilson, 34–51. Montreal & Kingston: McGill-Queen's Press 2009

*Trial of Patrick James Whelan for the Murder of the Hon. Thos. D'Arcy McGee*. Ottawa: Desbarats 1868

Trigger, Rosalyn. "Irish Politics on Parade: The Clergy, National Societies, and St Patrick's Day Processions in Nineteenth-century Montreal and Toronto." *Histoire sociale/Social History* 37 (Nov. 2004): 159–99

Tulchinsky, Gerry, and Brian J. Young. "Sir John Young". In *Dictionary of Canadian Biography online,* http://www.biographi.ca

Tumblety, Francis. "Be Wise Before It Is Too Late." Handbill. Montreal 1857

– *Narrative of Dr. Tumblety: How he was Kidnapped during the American War, his Incarceration and Discharge.* New York: Russells' American Steam Printing House 1872

– *A Sketch of an Eventful Career.* Brooklyn: Eagle Book and Job Printing Department 1889

VanBlaricom, G.B. "The Biggest News Scoop in Canada." *Maclean's,* 3 July 1908, 88–90

Virgo, Seán. *Selected Verse of Thomas D'Arcy McGee.* Toronto: Exile Editions 2000

Vronsky, Peter. "Combat, Memory, and Remembrance in Confederation Era Canada: The Hidden History of the Battle of Ridgeway, June 2, 1866." PH D dissertation, University of Toronto, 2010

Waite, Peter B. *The Life and Times of Confederation, 1864–67: Politics, Newspapers, and the Union of British North American.* 2nd edn. Toronto: University of Toronto Press 1962

Walker, Franklin A. *Catholic Education and Politics in Upper Canada: A Study in the Documentation Relative to the Origin of Catholic Elementary Schools in the Ontario School System.* Toronto: J.M. Dent & Sons 1955

Whelan, Kevin. *The Tree of Liberty: Radicalism, Catholicism and the Construction of Irish Identity, 1760–1830.* Cork: Cork University Press 1996

– "Reinterpreting the 1798 Rebellion in County Wexford." In *The Mighty Wave: The 1798 Rebellion in Wexford,* edited by Dáire Keogh and Nicholas Furlong, 9–36. Dublin: Four Courts Press 1996

Whitelaw, William Menzies. *The Maritimes and Canada before Confederation.* Toronto: Oxford University Press 1934

Wilson, David A. "The Fenians in Montreal, 1862–68: Invasion, Intrigue, and Assasination." *Eire-Ireland* 38 (Fall–Winter 2003): 109–33

– "'Orange Influences of the Right Kind': Thomas D'Arcy McGee, the Orange Order and the New Nationality." In *The Orange Order in Canada,* edited by David A. Wilson, 89–108. Dublin: Four Courts Press 2007

– *Thomas D'Arcy McGee.* Vol. 1: *Passion, Reason, and Politics, 1825–57.* Montreal & Kingston: McGill-Queen's University Press 2008

– "Was Patrick James Whelan a Fenian and Did He Assassinate Thomas D'Arcy McGee?" In *Irish Nationalism in Canada,* edited by David A. Wilson, 52–82. Montreal & Kingston: McGill-Queen's University Press 2009

– ed. *Irish Nationalism in Canada*. Montreal & Kingston: McGill-Queen's Press 2009

Winks, Robin W. *Canada and the United States: The Civil War Years*. 1960; revd. edn., Montreal: Harvest House 1971

Wiseman, Nicholas. *Fabiola: or, The Church of the Catacombs*. London: Burns & Oates 1854

Wise, S.F., and Robert Craig Brown. *Canada Views the United States: Nineteenth Century Political Attitudes*. Toronto: Macmillan 1967

Woodham-Smith, Cecil. *The Great Hunger: Ireland 1845–1849*. 1962; rpt., Toronto: Penguin Books 1991

# Index

203–5, 206, 215; and Felix Prior case, 293–4, 331; and Fenianism, 7, 103, 153–4, 181–2, 194–5, 196–7, 212, 219, 221, 223–5, 230–1, 235–6, 238, 241, 247, 252–4, 262–5, 273–7, 279–80, 281–5, 290–2, 298–300, 314, 316–20, 326, 330, 385, 393, 397, 404; "Four Letters to a Friend," 81–2; and Francis Bernard McNamee, 267, 316, 318–19, 331, 383, 385–6; and Francis Tumblety, 30–1; and French Canada, 18, 26–9, 32, 34–5, 58, 67, 70, 75, 81, 84, 87, 99, 104–5, 112, 122, 131–2, 142–3, 145–6, 157, 161, 166, 173–4, 182, 207, 213–15, 279–80, 301–2, 305, 320, 400; funeral, 384–7, 432n70; on the future of Canada, 22–4, 31, 34, 40, 43, 66, 68, 100–1, 145, 173, 185, 208, 213–14, 243, 303, 325, 337, 390, 397, 404; on the future of Ireland, 336; and General Tom Sweeny, 250, 274; and George Brown, 57–68, 70–3, 75–6, 81–3, 87–9, 91, 105, 109–11, 126–7, 136, 173, 229, 284–6, 290, 301, 305, 421n54; and George-Étienne Cartier, 10, 46–7, 103–4, 110–11, 122–3, 166, 177–8, 198–9, 243, 267, 304–5, 335, 384, 397; and George Clerk, 48, 50, 58, 82–7, 111–14, 123, 137, 204, 259, 278, 307, 385, 430n30; and the *Globe*, 175–6, 268, 284–6; and the Grand Trunk Railway, 165, 308, 321; and the Great Famine, 6, 12, 17, 23–4, 65, 78, 183, 196, 236–7, 274, 301–2; and the Hibernian Benevolent Society, 76, 91; illness, 209, 315, 324, 331–4; and immigration to Canada, 38, 104, 132–3, 139–43, 151, 159, 161, 166, 199, 234, 241; as independent candidate, 45–8, 160–2, 165; and indigenous peoples, 27; and Intercolonial Convention, 144, 170; and informers, 198, 225, 235, 251, 267, 280, 315–18, 320, 323, 330, 383; and Intercolonial

Railway, 144–7, 151, 161, 165–6, 170–2, 177, 202–4, 208; and *Irish American*, 246, 283–4; and *Irish Canadian*, 154–5, 224–7; and the Irish Catholic Convention (1867), 305–6; and Irish National School system, 63–4, 71–2, 84, 148, 416n23; and the Irish, 273, 275; and the *Irish People*, 239, 245–8; and Irish Protestant Benevolent Society, 296, 335; and James Moylan, 61, 69–70, 78, 82–3, 85, 96, 98, 101, 104–5, 107, 110–12, 114, 123, 125–8, 137, 148, 150, 175, 225, 238, 253, 280, 286, 288, 290, 306, 348–9, 387; and John A. Macdonald, 10, 50, 65–7, 123, 151, 162, 173, 177, 182–4, 198–200, 204–5, 226, 234, 240, 243, 251, 267, 280–1, 285–90, 295, 300–1, 304–8, 316, 324, 326, 332–3, 335, 338, 384, 456n80; and John O'Donohoe, 56, 59, 84, 94, 102, 111, 124–5, 127, 161, 166; and John O'Hanly, 179–80, 327–8; and John O'Mahony, 224–5, 235, 248, 268; and Know-Nothing movement, 34, 83, 87, 118, 175; legal studies, 93–4; and Leonard Tilley, 170, 202, 384; and Liberal-Conservative Party, 11–12, 45, 49, 56–60, 65–6, 70–1, 74, 76, 81–2, 91, 97, 108, 124, 134–5, 141, 150–1, 162, 177–9, 198, 296; and literature, 25–8, 39, 170, 324–5, 334, 336; and Loyal Irish Society of Canada, 125–6; and Luther Holton, 46–8, 67, 135–6, 159–60, 165–6, 174, 177, 199–200, 312, 315; and Manchester Martyrs, 330–1; and Mary Ann Sadlier, 9, 28, 182, 187, 304, 333, 388; Memorial Camp for Boys, 401; memory, 390–405; and Militia Bill (1862), 138–9; as minister of agriculture, immigration and statistics, 13, 198, 233, 304; and minority rights, 10–11, 14–15, 31, 39, 46, 70, 122, 148–9, 194, 207, 209–10,